The Adventures
of Amos 'n' Andy

The Adventures of Amos 'n' Andy

A Social History of an American Phenomenon

MELVIN PATRICK ELY

THE FREE PRESS
A Division of Macmillan, Inc.
NEW YORK

Maxwell Macmillan Canada
TORONTO

Maxwell Macmillan International
NEW YORK   OXFORD   SINGAPORE   SYDNEY

The Free Press
A Division of Macmillan, Inc.
866 Third Avenue, New York, N.Y. 10022

Maxwell Macmillan Canada, Inc.
1200 Eglinton Avenue East
Suite 200
Don Mills, Ontario M3C 3N1

Macmillan, Inc. is part of the Maxwell Communication Group of Companies.

Printed in the United States of America

printing number
1   2   3   4   5   6   7   8   9   10

Library of Congress Cataloging-in-Publication Data

Ely, Melvin Patrick.
    The adventures of Amos 'n' Andy : a social history of an American phenomenon / Melvin Patrick Ely.
        p.   cm.
    Includes bibliographical references and index.
    ISBN 0-02-909502-6
    1. Amos 'n' Andy (Radio program)   2. Amos 'n' Andy (Television program   3. Afro-Americans in television broadcasting.
4. Broadcasting—Social aspects—United States.   5. United States—Race relations.   6. United States—Social conditions.   7. United States—Popular culture.   I. Title.
PN1991.77.A6E49   1991
791.44'72—dc20   91-7837
                                                                         CIP

To the memory of my father,
CLARENCE PATRICK ELY
(1910–1980)

Contents

Acknowledgments

It would be difficult to imagine a more uniformly pleasant and helpful set of associations than those that enabled me to write this book.

I am deeply grateful for the confidence in me that several institutions expressed through their abundant material and intellectual support. The Carter G. Woodson Institute for Afro-American and African Studies at the University of Virginia granted me a postdoctoral fellowship that allowed me to work for a year in my beautiful native state among talented, gracious colleagues. I thank Armstead L. Robinson, William E. Jackson, and Gail Shirley; the Ford Foundation, which supported the Woodson Institute's graduate and postdoctoral fellowship program; Joseph Kett; and Paul M. Gaston, who was particularly kind during my year at the University of Virginia. I received equally generous financial and moral support for this project from the Danforth Foundation, where Warren Bryan Martin, Lillie Rose Marquis, and John Ervin were especially solicitous; and from the Graduate School and Department of History at Princeton University.

The unbounded hospitality of my friends Miriam and Sidney Rochlin, Naomi Rochlin Roosevelt, and Benjamin and Sharon Roosevelt allowed me to do much of my basic research in Los Angeles in the most pleasant of conditions.

No researcher could ever launch a project, much less complete one successfully, without the aid of the experts who run libraries and archives. The staff on whom I made by far the most demands was that of the Department of Special Collections, Doheny Library, University of Southern California. I thank Robert Knutson, Lindy Narver—and above all, Ned Comstock, who took responsibility for my welfare and selflessly helped me create this book.

Several highly knowledgeable people at the University of California, Los Angeles, generously shared their expertise, particularly Eleanore Tanin, Ron Staley, Beverly Robinson, and the staff of the Theater Arts Library. I also appreciate the timely help of Jeffrey

Rankin and Flora Ito of UCLA; and the assistance of the Margaret Herrick Library of the Academy of Motion Picture Arts and Sciences and the Louis B. Mayer Library of the American Film Institute, both in Los Angeles.

One of the real pleasures in this project has been my introduction to radio's golden age through some of the medium's talented, warm-hearted veterans. My special thanks go to those connected with Pacific Pioneer Broadcasters, Inc., of Hollywood, who eagerly offered me leads and put me in touch with their former colleagues in broadcasting. Art Gilmore deserves special mention, as does Bob Jensen, whose help was especially valuable. Ron Wolf of PPB was a cordial host during my visits to the association's archives. Another source of important information in Hollywood was Mark Lipson of Hal Roach Studios, who located files on the *Amos 'n' Andy* television series from the 1950s and allowed me to borrow them. The eagerness of all these men and women to help piece together the history of America's entertainment media should stand as an example to an industry that has done far too little to preserve its own past.

Many talented people on the East Coast, too, have left their mark on this book. Mary Ann Jensen of the Theater Collection at Firestone Library, Princeton University, got me started in the right direction, assisted me along the way, and saved me much wasted time; her colleague, Michelle McIntyre, was likewise ever ready to help, as were the staff of the Music Collection, Afro-American Studies Collection, and Interlibrary Services office at Firestone. I am grateful to Marianne Roos, Jacqueline Goggin, and Charles J. Kelly of the Manuscript Division, Library of Congress, who offered their advice during my research there.

Several archivists and librarians at Yale University have graciously helped with my research: Patricia Willis and Nancy LeRoy of the Yale Collection of American Literature, Beinecke Rare Book and Manuscript Library; Richard Warren Jr. and Barbara Migurska of the Historical Sound Recordings Collection in Sterling Memorial Library; and Susan E. Crockford-Peters and her colleagues in Cross Campus Library. I also thank the staff in other departments of Sterling Library; at the New York Public Library's Schomburg Center for Research in Black Culture, and in the same library's Performing Arts Research Center at Lincoln Center; at Alderman Library of the University of Virginia, the Richmond Public Library, Boatwright Library of the University of Richmond, and the Virginia State Library. I am grateful to the National Association for the Advancement of Colored

People and to the National Urban League for allowing me to examine their papers in the Manuscript Division of the Library of Congress. In Richmond, Teresa Roane of the Valentine Museum, Corrine Hudgins of the Museum of the Confederacy, and Gwen Wells of Richmond Newspapers, Inc., kindly helped me locate illustrations.

I owe an extraordinary debt to Richard Correll, who gave me unsupervised and unrestricted access to his father's personal mementos, and who has shown perfect respect for the historian's right to draw his or her own conclusions. The American public's access to its own history and to that of its public figures would be enhanced if all private custodians of the historical record shared Mr. Correll's open, generous attitude. Alyce Correll and Jane Gosden also gave their help with no strings attached.

Almost everyone whom I interviewed received me with warmth and devoted much time, energy, and good will to answering my endless questions. I hope these people will not think me ungrateful if, rather than give all their names here, I refer the reader to the list in the Word About Sources at the end of this book. I assure all who shared their memories with me that I regard that list as a roll of honor. Several people whom I interviewed have already been mentioned in other connections. Certain others did me kindnesses even beyond submitting to my interrogations. These include Alvin Childress, Jester Hairston and Mrs. Hairston, and Bob Greenberg.

Two of the foremost historians of American media, Thomas Cripps and Erik Barnouw, epitomized the kind of generosity that younger scholars hope to find in senior ones; each drew on his vast knowledge and wide circle of acquaintances to open up new avenues of inquiry to me. Charles Hardy, producer of "Goin' North," a masterly radio documentary series on the Great Migration to Philadelphia, shared both his expertise and recordings of blackface comedy dialogues. Andrew Buni lent me rare photographs of Robert Vann. John Denis Mercier's interest in my work has been avid and constant over a period of some years; the daily mail frequently brought some new tidbit from Professor Mercier, whose own work on popular images of blacks deserves a wide readership. I also appreciate the help of Marianne Cooley, a scholar of Black English, and that of my student Kenneth Obel.

A number of others have shared their ideas, skills, and knowledge. These include John W. Blassingame, Gerald David Jaynes, David Montgomery, Norman Hodges, Jacqueline Swain, Claude M. Monteiro, Charles McDowell Jr., Barry Friend, and Majel Stein. Edward Caffarella helped me at several critical points. Roberta D. Gross-man solved problems that had stumped a dozen other people, and Harry A. Miskimin assiduously looked out for my welfare. Elizabeth R. Varon, a talented young historian, brought a fresh and meticulous eye to the manuscript near the end of its evolution.

I owe many debts to people at Princeton University in addition to those named above. Diane Price's heroic efforts and sympathetic attitude deserve special mention. I offer heartfelt thanks also to William G. Bowen, the late Cyril E. Black, Arno J. Mayer, Stanley Stein, Richard D. Challener, Leona Halvorsen, Charlotte Skillman, and Alice Lustig.

Albert J. Raboteau commented astutely on my work; getting to know him was a much-valued *lagniappe* of this project. James M. McPherson has long personified high standards in historical research and writing. He believed in the potential of this project from the first moment we discussed it, when some others were skeptical. His encouragement made my work easier; his suggestions made it better.

Henry N. Drewry, my friend, teacher, and fellow Southerner, has offered a unique personal and intellectual example during the nearly two decades I have known him. He is first and foremost a teacher—as I am, in part because of his influence. Teaching with him remains a highlight of my career, and his candid sharing of his life's experiences helped equip me to write this book.

My debt to Nancy Weiss Malkiel is just as profound. During our first association in 1972 and 1973, she proved to be the consummate intellectual mentor—tough-minded but never domineering. Although her energy seems boundless, I have occasionally worried in the succeeding years that she was devoting more of it to me than she ought. She has been my adviser, career counselor, advocate, and stalwart, patient friend. To have got here without her is inconceivable.

In bringing this book before the public, I have had the good fortune to work with three people of integrity and vision who love ideas and the written word. I thank my publisher, Erwin Glikes, for his active interest in my work. Joyce Seltzer's faith in this project matched my own; her devoted and insightful work as my editor drew out of me the book that lurked within. My literary agent, Richard Balkin, with his rare and endearing preference for doing rather than promising, made all this happen and became my friend. I hasten to add my thanks to Edith Lewis and the staff of The Free Press for their cordiality and efficiency.

An old friend and several members of my family have contributed to my work. The seed of this book was planted during a conversation with Michael Troy Robinson. That seed germinated during, and because of, a talk with my brother Gordon; on several occasions since then, he has helped me find the fortitude to carry the endeavor through.

I profited from the intellectual example of Amotz Zahavi and Arthur Aryeh Goren without their realizing it. As though this were not enough, Artie Goren also introduced me to his niece, who became my wife; that simple act of his greatly improved the quality both of this book and of my life. Amotz Zahavi and Avishag Kadman-Zahavi, my wife's parents, have supported me and my work in a hundred ways. I thank them for their faith in me and for their friendship.

My mother, Vivien Ely Kilborn, gave me life and education. She provided the latter not only in the usual ways, but above all by rearing me to respect people of all faiths and colors. That ethic did much to shape my life and my career. My mother's vivid reminiscences of the 1920s and 1930s helped me understand and describe the period, and she took care of me during one long, hot summer of editing.

My wife, Naama Zahavi-Ely, has done all those myriad things for which spouses are typically thanked in prefaces to books. But her role has far transcended emotional and practical support, important as these are. A historian and thinker of uncommon perceptiveness, with a command of English style that most educated native speakers might envy, Naama has made many vital contributions to this book; there are sections in which every page bears her mark.

I take special joy in expressing my love and thanks to my son, Oren, and my daughter, Kinneret; their arrival complicated the latter stages of this project in the most delightful way imaginable.

Finally, I thank my father, who, at great sacrifice, enabled me to do what I thought important. He did justice, loved mercy, and walked humbly with his God; his life helped me believe that the South, and human beings in general, are redeemable. His integrity set a standard for me, and his memory sustained me. Accordingly, this book is a memorial to him.

Richmond
Thanksgiving 1990

1

White Men, Black Voices

By ten o'clock on a snowy January evening in 1926, it had already been dark for hours. Thousands of families in the American Midwest sat at home listening to their radio receiving sets and enjoying the warmth of fireplaces, woodstoves, or radiators. The appeal of radio was strongest during these long, cold evenings of midwinter, especially in areas like the Great Lakes region and the Plains. The freezing weather ended the farmer's workday early during that season and tended to concentrate the city-dweller's after-supper recreation in the home.

Radio was still new and unsure of itself. Broadcasting networks did not yet exist. Six hundred local stations throughout the United States haphazardly filled the ether—as "the air" was often called in those days—with performances borrowed from vaudeville and concert stages and from lecture halls. Still, the disembodied sounds of live performances issuing from a piece of furniture in one's living room remained a source of wonder, as did the knowledge that thousands of others might be sharing the experience at any given moment.

The midwestern listeners who had tuned in Chicago station WGN as they warmed their feet on Tuesday evening, January 12, heard a ten-minute dialogue whose Deep South setting contrasted sharply with the wintry scenes outside their windows: two black men named Sam and Henry talked as a mule conveyed them toward Birmingham,

Alabama. The radio audience knew the pair were black, because they spoke in what anyone reared on minstrel shows, blackface vaudeville comedy, or Uncle Remus stories—as most Americans had been—instantly recognized as "Negro dialect."

Having worked for years as farm laborers, Sam and Henry now rode to the railroad station to set out for a new life in WGN's home city—a life that listeners could follow six nights a week as a radio serial. As the dialogue began, an impatient Sam exclaimed, "I hope dey got faster mules dan dis up in Chicago."[1] Thus *Sam 'n' Henry* focused right away on the most dramatic development in Afro-American life between the two World Wars: the Great Migration of rural southern blacks to big cities, largely in the North. And from Sam and Henry's very first steps along the path to a new career that Henry was sure would make them millionaires, it was clear to WGN's audience that these two naive country fellows would find life in Chicago as strange as Alabama dirt farming would be to a bank clerk in the Second City or a Polish-American factory worker in Cleveland.

The dialogue between Sam and Henry prompted each listener to supplement the sounds on the radio with rich visual images of his or her own creation. The broadcast used few if any sound effects, and at most a brief narrative introduction; it included a few lines from Sam's ladyfriend Liza, a ticket salesman at the depot in Alabama, and the train's conductor. Beyond this, Sam and Henry's voices were the only sounds heard. Yet the listener could almost see the two men approaching the station with their plodding mule, arriving among the crowd of friends gathered to see them off, buying the tickets, bidding farewell to the well-wishers, boarding the train, and settling down for the long ride northward.

The maiden broadcast of the series outlined the contrasting personalities of the two black emigrants. Henry's booming voice conveyed bravado and bossiness—a know-it-all swagger made tolerable mainly by the listener's certainty that some rude surprises awaited Henry in Chicago. Sam's quieter, reedier speech and more hesitant manner emphasized his earnestness and insecurity, his sentimental nature, and his tendency to defer to his friend. Two actors had written the dialogue and now supplied the voices. This pair bore little resemblance to the figures that populated their listeners' fantasies—for the two men sitting before the microphone in a small room in Chicago were white.

Charles Correll, thirty-five, was short, stocky, muscular. His full head of slicked-back brown hair framed a slightly plump face, often

graced by a friendly, impish smile. He played the part of the domineering Henry in a suitably imperious basso. Freeman Gosden, who
played Sam in a high-pitched, gravelly, sometimes plaintive voice,
stood half a head taller than Correll; he was slimmer and almost a
decade younger than his partner. Gosden's close-cropped, curly,
blond-brown hair was already receding, lengthening his thinnish, ovu-
lar face. Though he shared with Correll a bantering, wisecracking
sense of humor, Gosden's demeanor suggested an energy, an intensity, a certain sharp edge, almost as surely as Correll's betokened a
relaxed, benign temperament.

For a man who now portrayed a black character on the radio,
Correll had known few Afro-Americans as he grew up in Peoria, Illinois. Gosden, by contrast, had been born and reared in the center of
Richmond, Virginia, an area with a large black population. He retained something of the distinctive southern accent of whites from the
Tidewater and Piedmont regions of his native state, and he felt well
qualified to portray Sam Smith and other black characters. Both partners drew on years of experience in blackface comedy as itinerant
directors of amateur minstrel shows.

Since scientific audience ratings did not exist in 1926, no one
knew how many people in the cities and towns of the Midwest and
beyond, and on those farms that had electricity and radio sets, tuned
in the debut of *Sam 'n' Henry*—or how many of those who did would
listen again. The management of station WGN could only advertise
the series and wait for listeners to react to it.

····•◉•····

The heat of a summer Saturday was already building in the
crowded streets of Chicago's black South Side. The mid-August sun
that morning in 1931 promised classic weather for a day in the park.
As early as seven o'clock, children had begun assembling at points in
this and two other Afro-American neighborhoods to be taken to the
second annual picnic organized by Chicago's weekly black newspaper, the *Defender*. At ten o'clock, a parade of motorcycle policemen,
floats, Boy Scouts, and local notables in touring cars set forth from
35th Street traveling southward on South Parkway. The wail of sirens
from the police cycles and from an ambulance supplied by a local
undertaker provided a raucous counterpoint to the music of a drum-
and-bugle corps and a twenty-five-piece band.[2]

Most of the day's festivities were to take place around the duck
pond at 52nd Street in Washington Park. Nearby, city workers had
built a large bandstand. By about eleven o'clock, thousands of people

had congregated there. (The *Defender* afterward claimed attendance of 35,000; at the other extreme, *Time* magazine, with characteristic superciliousness, referred to the gathering as "a crowd of 6,000 pickaninnies."[3]) From the bandstand, Duke Ellington's orchestra played several numbers to enthusiastic applause, as did Lucius "Lucky" Millinder's ten-piece band.

But the stars of the show—the men whose agreement to "head the long list of hosts" had merited an eight-column, front-page headline in the *Defender* a week earlier—were yet to be introduced. At a cue from the master of ceremonies, Ellington's Cotton Club Band began to play a tune from the 1915 motion picture *The Birth of a Nation*. The black audience burst into applause; like most other Americans, the picnickers recognized "The Perfect Song" not from D. W. Griffith's movie glorifying the Ku Klux Klan, but rather from a nightly radio show which used that melody as its theme, and whose stars were the *Defender*'s guests of honor.

Freeman Gosden and Charles Correll stood, then climbed up onto chairs. Until that moment, few in the crowd had recognized the two among the other well-dressed men of both races who were gathered on the bandstand. Now the audience cheered the two stars of *Amos 'n' Andy*, who smiled, waved, and attempted to speak through megaphones. As the applause washed over them, the isolation and uncertainty Gosden and Correll had felt on the frigid night of their first broadcast as Sam 'n' Henry in 1926 must have seemed like a memory from another life.

The pair had built the continuing story of their southern black émigrés into a regional hit before moving in 1928 to another Chicago radio station, where they redubbed their central characters Amos and Andy. Gosden and Correll wrote all the scripts themselves and furnished voices for the members of Amos and Andy's fraternal lodge, the Mystic Knights of the Sea, and for a whole array of other characters. Several dozen radio stations around the United States picked up the *Amos 'n' Andy* show, and when the series joined the National Broadcasting Company (NBC) in 1929, it quickly evoked a national mania. Sales of radio sets soared during the months after *Amos 'n' Andy*'s debut, and the show became a powerful locomotive pulling all of commercial radio along behind it.[4]

Freeman Gosden and Charles Correll were now earning the remarkable sum of $100,000 a year from their radio contract and up to $7,500 per week when they made personal appearance tours.[5] The nightly adventures of Amos, Andy, and the Kingfish—the wily leader of their fraternal order—were piped into restaurants and hotel lobbies, and into movie theaters between shows, to prevent a drastic loss of clientele. The show gave birth to a daily *Amos 'n' Andy* comic strip, a candy bar, toys, greeting cards, and phonograph records, as well as two books and a film. Expressions used by Gosden and Correll's characters—"check and double-check," "holy mackerel," "I'se regusted," and others—had become commonplace in colloquial American English and even infiltrated literature and political discourse; Huey P. Long, the flamboyant political boss of Louisiana and contender for the presidency, gleefully adopted the title "Kingfish" from the radio series.

The warm reception given Gosden and Correll at the *Defender*'s picnic in Chicago was the most dramatic of many signs that the two men's portrayal of Afro-Americans in the big city had a large following among blacks themselves. Some Afro-Americans, however, had bitterly criticized the humor of *Amos 'n' Andy* as demeaning to their people. The title characters' ignorance of city life and of book-learning libeled the modern Afro-American, these critics said. So, they added, did Andy's pretentiousness, his ineptitude as a businessman, and the crookedness of most of the pair's lodge brothers. Even as the *Defender* was organizing its parade and picnic, another popular black weekly newspaper, the Pittsburgh *Courier*, was conducting a relentless campaign to ban Gosden and Correll's show from the air. Yet *Amos 'n' Andy*'s detractors had sparked not only the crusade against racial stereotyping that they desired, but also a heated debate within the black community; the young newspaperman Roy Wilkins—later head of the National Association for the Advancement of Colored People (NAACP)—was only one of many who saw no harm and much good in *Amos 'n' Andy*, and who were ready to say so in public.

Facing the friendly black crowd that sunny Saturday in Washington Park, Correll and Gosden behaved like men who felt vindicated. The band struck up "Hail, Hail, The Gang's All Here," and the two stars waved their megaphones in time to the chorus. Correll, wrote a *Defender* reporter, was in such good spirits that he "jumped down from his chair and danced a jig." As he and Gosden moved toward their car to leave the park a bit later, a crowd of black children and adults accompanied them. The two men drove off to further applause from residents of the very same Afro-American community to which the fictional Sam and Henry had migrated five and a half years earlier.

·····➤●◄·····

One Thursday evening in late June 1951, many of the 750 delegates to the annual convention of the NAACP sat in the Atlanta
Municipal Auditorium watching *Amos 'n' Andy* on television. The
program they saw from eight-thirty to nine o'clock focused on the
Kingfish of the Mystic Knights of the Sea lodge, but other characters
familiar to fans of the radio series—including Amos, Andy, and the
Kingfish's wife Sapphire—also appeared prominently on the show.

The broadcast the delegates watched was a curious blend of future
and past. A pioneer TV situation comedy, *Amos 'n' Andy* was the only
series in the new but already popular medium to have an entirely
black cast. On the other hand, the Columbia Broadcasting System
(CBS), which now owned the series, had worked hard with Gosden
and Correll to produce a faithful adaptation of the still-popular radio
show. The writers of the TV version were the same men whom
Gosden and Correll had hired to take over the writing of their radio
scripts a decade earlier. The principal members of the new black cast
had been chosen largely for their ability to play the roles as Gosden
and Correll had, all the way down to vocal pitch and inflection. A
number of the actors playing supporting roles and minor parts in the
TV series were veterans of the radio show who brought their long-
established characterizations from the old medium to the new.

The counterpoint of tradition and change, so evident in the *Amos
'n' Andy* TV series, pervaded the situation of black Americans in 1951.
The New Deal and the industrial boom of the Second World War had
accelerated the Great Migration to northern cities. These changes,
and America's confrontation with Nazi racism, had shaken old ideas
and old ways, whetting the appetite of blacks for further change.
Pressure for reform had begun to bear fruit. Afro-Americans in 1941
had demanded and got a federal executive order forbidding racial
discrimination in hiring by defense industries. A Supreme Court decision in 1944 voided the whites-only Democratic primary, one of the
devices southern states had used to exclude the minority race from
political life. The growth of the black vote in northern cities had
spurred the national Democratic party to adopt a strong civil rights
plank in its 1948 platform. By the time of the forty-second national
convention of the NAACP in Atlanta, blacks were watching with
interest and excitement as the armed services abandoned racial segregation under an executive order issued by President Harry Truman
in 1948, and as several school-desegregation suits slowly moved toward resolution in the United States Supreme Court.

At the same time, the activists of the NAACP knew how much

remained to be done. Jim Crow segregation lived on in the South, where Afro-Americans still had almost no voice in the governments that ruled them. No civil rights bill had passed the Congress, and black poverty remained acute in all regions. But on the evening of June 28, some of the delegates in the Municipal Auditorium were thinking less about voting rights or school desegregation than about Amos, Andy, and the Kingfish.

By a coincidence the network quickly came to regret, CBS had scheduled the television premiere of *Amos 'n' Andy* for the same week the NAACP was to meet. The NAACP's leader, Walter White, urged delegates to watch the show Thursday evening on a television set installed in the auditorium;[6] many were disappointed, and some downright appalled, at what they saw. After the broadcast, the convention unanimously passed a resolution condemning *Amos 'n' Andy* and *Beulah*, a one-year-old network TV comedy whose characters included a black maid and several of her friends. Such programs, the NAACP declared, "depict the Negro and other minority groups in a stereotyped and derogatory manner" and thus "definitely tend to strengthen the conclusion among uninformed or prejudiced people that Negroes and other minorities are inferior, lazy, dumb and dishonest." The NAACP called on its branches to press television stations and sponsors to cancel the offending series—if necessary, by boycotting the sponsors' products.[7]

Afro-Americans in the country at large, however, were divided in their reactions to the television treatment of *Amos 'n' Andy*. Some observers found the black "man in the street" quicker to criticize the TV show than he had been to complain about its radio parent; but the *Journal and Guide*, a black weekly newspaper based in Norfolk, Virginia, surveyed sixteen viewers and discovered that eleven enjoyed the new incarnation of *Amos 'n' Andy*. Several other black papers and an organization of Afro-American performers in New York attacked the NAACP's position.[8] One black critic even faulted the new series with its all-black cast for failing to match the quality of the old radio show—or of the *Amos 'n' Andy* movie of 1930 in which Gosden and Correll had performed in blackface makeup.[9] Ironically, Roy Wilkins, who had defended *Amos 'n' Andy* in 1930, now helped lead the NAACP's fight against the show, while the show-business columnist of the once-indignant Pittsburgh *Courier* found the premiere of the TV series "well-paced, funny more often than not, directed and produced with taste."[10]

Despite months of protests and hurt feelings, the CBS network eventually renewed *Amos 'n' Andy* for a second season. Meanwhile, the time came for the black Chicago *Defender* to stage its annual parade and picnic for the Afro-American children of Chicago. The event had been born during *Amos 'n' Andy*'s infancy as a network radio series and had welcomed Freeman Gosden and Charles Correll as its guests of honor in 1931. Now, two decades later, the sponsors of the new TV series brought the show's three principal cast members from Los Angeles to Chicago to ride in the very same parade. Alvin Childress, a veteran stage actor and director who now played the role of Amos, met his wife and daughter, who had traveled from New York City to join him for the big day. Childress and his two fellow black actors believed that *Amos 'n' Andy* was bringing them to an undreamt-of pinnacle of fame and earning power. After arriving in Chicago, however, the three men learned that they would not be allowed to participate in the parade after all. They and their show had become too controversial.

Determined not to let the occasion go entirely to waste, Alvin Childress took his family from their hotel room down to the street to see the parade. Childress, excluded and unrecognized, watched the floats, the cars, the marchers, and the musicians moving southward along the broad boulevard toward Washington Park, where a generation earlier two white veterans of blackface minstrel shows had been the South Side's men of the hour.[11]

••• ◼◉◼ •••

The *Amos 'n' Andy* television series attracted a sizable audience and won an Emmy nomination in 1952. But commercial sponsors became harder to find, at least partly because of the racial controversy surrounding the show. CBS finally canceled *Amos 'n' Andy* after its second season, but then syndicated it to scores of local stations across the United States and even sold it to several foreign countries. The popular show thus remained on the small screen until the mid-1960s, serving up the characterizations of the early '50s to a whole new generation even as America's racial landscape changed radically.

Television had long since supplanted radio as the main source of entertainment in American homes, and the radio version of *Amos 'n' Andy* petered out along with the medium it had done so much to create a generation earlier. In the mid-1950s, Correll and Gosden's long-lived series adopted a new, watered-down format consisting mainly of recorded popular music with snatches of Amos 'n' Andy patter between numbers. After thirty-five years together on the air, Gosden and Correll made their last broadcast on November 25, 1960.

"Radio is being taken over by the disc jockeys and newscasts and there's no room for us any more," Correll explained.[12]

What Correll did not mention was that he and Gosden by 1960 were the last of a dying breed: white men who played blacks. Their trade was already nearly a century old when the team broke into radio in the mid-1920s; generations of whites had donned blackface makeup to entertain each other with song, dance, and comedy. The wonder is not that America in the 1960s had no place for Gosden and Correll, but rather that, during thirty-five years of profound social change, a radio and television series with roots in nineteenth-century minstrel shows had given Americans their most popular, pervasive, sustained picture of what purported to be black life and personality. *Amos 'n' Andy*'s popularity crossed boundaries of region, social standing, age, ethnic origin, and even race. Roy Wilkins and Walter White of the NAACP had a point when they asserted that a large part of what millions of white Americans "knew" about blacks had been learned from *Amos 'n' Andy*.

What did these white fans "learn"? Racial stereotypes inherited from minstrel shows and blackface vaudeville acts often reared their heads in the five-thousand-plus *Amos 'n' Andy* broadcasts Americans heard or saw over the years. It was this caricaturing that so incensed the Pittsburgh *Courier* in 1931 and the NAACP two decades later. By the 1980s, the final verdict seemed to be in: a sweeping array of opinion-makers—black and white, scholarly and popular, ranging from a top official of Rev. Jerry Falwell's right-wing Moral Majority, through TV talk-show host Phil Donahue, to the NAACP (now under new leadership)—consigned *Amos 'n' Andy* to the trash bin of racist stereotyping without a second thought.[13] For many, the show had become the ultimate metaphor of whites' casual contempt for blacks, its very name a synonym for mindless prejudice.

Yet if Gosden and Correll's work was nothing more than a heap of racist clichés, it is hard to explain their show's unique popularity and influence among both black and white—especially when America's airwaves and movie screens abounded with other traditional depictions of blacks. The team gave the world the lazy, pretentious dolt Andy—but also a succession of intelligent, accomplished minor characters. The Kingfish fleeced his lodge brothers relentlessly and traded insults with his domineering wife Sapphire. But earnest, honest Amos worked his way through the Great Depression and married the bright and dignified Ruby Taylor. Amos and Ruby's marriage was a model of mutual respect and devotion, a foil—especially in the show's early years—for the Kingfish's stereotyped marital woes. A fresh look at *Amos 'n' Andy* turns up more than just an electronic rehash of the hoary show business traditions its white creators had grown up with. While the radio and TV scripts overflow with survivals of classic American blackface comedy, they also contain modifications of that legacy and even departures from it.

The time has come to explore *Amos 'n' Andy*'s racial images against the background of the period that produced them. Simply to write off *Amos 'n' Andy* as unacceptable by the standards of the late twentieth century—which in many ways it is—all too conveniently ignores the important questions that the show's history raises. So does the accurate but unenlightening observation that most people of an earlier time—including many Afro-Americans—considered Gosden and Correll's series harmless and good-natured. The responses of Americans white and black to *Amos 'n' Andy* demand a closer look. Did reactions vary from group to group, person to person, decade to decade? How did the show's racial images and the public's attitudes influence one another?

For many black Americans, *Amos 'n' Andy* was no mere curiosity on the margins of popular culture—it raised critical and often emotional issues among the race it claimed to portray. This debate within Afro-America, spanning a quarter-century and more, can tell us something about the way blacks saw themselves and their condition in a society dominated by whites. The same disputes, in which the battle-lines shifted and individuals sometimes switched sides, show how complex the path to modern black consciousness and protest could be.

Some whites replied publicly to black criticism of *Amos 'n' Andy*; those responses—some obtuse or hostile, others thoughtful and sympathetic—help fill in our picture of white Americans' values from the 1920s to the eve of the mass movement for civil rights. And when *Amos 'n' Andy*'s parent networks reacted—or failed to react—to black complaints, they revealed a great deal about the way the American broadcasting industry operates and, in effect, decided how radio and TV would depict Afro-Americans for years to come.

The tale of *Amos 'n' Andy*, then, is not a simple one. Indeed, its vitality lies largely in the complexity and the surprises of the plot. It would be presumptuous to claim that the history of this one radio comedy team offers a panoramic view of American racial attitudes in the first half of the twentieth century. Yet the *Amos 'n' Andy* story can serve as a small but clear window which, like all windows, reveals more and more as one draws nearer to it.

2

···——◉——···

Boyhood Dreams and
Racial Myths

Charles Correll lived and died believing in the American dream. For him, hard work, talent, and a healthy dose of good luck had made the dream come true. Though not an arrogant man, Correll saw his life as "a story of going from nothing to something." In the later years of that long life, he contemplated his past from the luxurious mansion that he had built just off Sunset Boulevard in the Holmby Hills section, overlooking the Los Angeles basin. Surrounded by three acres of land, which he had adorned upon his arrival in 1938 with transplanted, forty-foot-high palm trees and a man-made stream with footbridge and waterfall, Correll recalled with fondness and some wonder his boyhood as a brickmason's son in Peoria.[1]

The Corrells had lived simply but comfortably in a substantial, two-story brick house. Charles's family, which eventually included a sister and two younger brothers, considered itself of Scotch-Irish background. Charles's paternal grandmother and her parents had come from the Deep South, and had even been imprisoned for a time by Union forces in Chattanooga during the Civil War. The Corrells were paroled in 1864 on the condition that they remain at least a hundred miles north of the Ohio River for the duration of the war. Charles's grandmother married an Irish immigrant and settled in Illinois,[2] where her grandson Charles was born a quarter-century later, in February 1890.

Charles's grandmother did not forget her southern origins; her own mother was said by the family to have been a first cousin of Confederate President Jefferson Davis.[3] Yet the Corrells were no die-hard devotees of the South's Lost Cause. They lived out their lives in the North; Charles himself neither spoke with any trace of a southern accent nor became particularly adept at imitating one.

Peoria served both as an industrial city and as the commercial center for the surrounding farming region. The second-largest city in Illinois, it was no one-horse town. Still, with some 56,000 inhabitants at the turn of the century, Peoria was a remote second to Chicago.[4] Charles Correll grew up in a largely working-class neighborhood whose residents, in his words, represented "all sorts of nationalities." Years later, he remembered the boys who grew up with him there as having been "pretty rugged."[5] About one in ten Peorians was black, and this Afro-American community, exactly half a century afterward, would produce its own star of American comedy—Richard Pryor. Charles's circle of boyhood acquaintances, however, seems to have included few if any blacks.[6]

Even the publicity for *Amos 'n' Andy* in 1929–1930—which trumpeted every conceivable qualification Correll and Gosden had for impersonating Afro-Americans—stated that Correll had learned what he knew of black speech and character from his experience with other whites in blackface minstrel shows and from Virginian Freeman Gosden. Throughout the *Amos 'n' Andy* years, he deferred to Gosden's judgment as to how black speech should be rendered,[7] and Correll never approached his partner's skill as a mimic. Even so, Charles did not lack exposure to what whites sometimes referred to with a giggle as "negrology." His elementary education in that field came mostly from two "classrooms": Peoria's Opera House and Main Street Theater, where blackface acts were a staple, and where a fascinated Charles spent countless hours.[8]

While attending high school, Correll won what seemed to him a dream job—as an usher at the Main Street vaudeville theater. Though earning only two dollars a week, he got what he wanted most, the chance to see every production that came to the hall. Watching the same bill a number of times never bored Charles; he virtually memorized the lines in all the acts of each show during its one-week run, and he envied the performers their colorful way of life.

Yet Correll's enchantment with show business scarcely figured in his and his parents' practical thoughts about his own career. He lacked the family background that made college a matter of course—and the income that might have made it a reasonable option. So Charles spent his teen years learning several trades that might offer the respectability and security his father had achieved as a skilled craftsman and construction foreman. In high school, the boy enrolled in what was known as the commercial course, studying typing, shorthand, bookkeeping, and "manual training."

Charles did well in his high school studies, particularly in the stenographic skills, which many males learned in those days. (That training later enabled Correll to take down the daily *Amos 'n' Andy* dialogues as rapidly as he and Gosden composed them; with no stenographer present, the two men could free-associate in "black" dialect without feeling self-conscious.) Despite his success in school, Correll and his family assumed he would follow his father, with whom he was always close, into the bricklaying trade.

During these same years, though, Correll was developing one of the talents that would lead him into show business and eventually into partnership with Freeman Gosden. Like countless children of middle-class and would-be middle-class parents, Charles got a dose of "culture" in the form of piano lessons. The experiment did not last long—ten months, shortly before Correll began high school. Nonetheless, Charles was no stereotypical freckle-faced lad seated at the piano under a stern maternal gaze, forlornly grinding out scales against the taunting counterpoint of a sandlot baseball game just outside. Charles, who had a measure of musical talent and enjoyed playing, rose early in the morning and practiced before school. His brief formal training began a lifelong attachment to the instrument and a growing facility at playing by ear. Correll's peers and teachers recognized his musical ability; he led the school orchestra for two years and accompanied a mandolin duo at his high school commencement. His mother, who sang and played guitar, encouraged him all the while by precept and example.[9] Still, Correll did not seriously consider trying to make a living as a musician.

After Charles finished high school in 1907, he spent a year as a stenographer. He then joined his father, who had been hired to supervise the building of a dining hall at the Southern Illinois Penitentiary. Here Charles began learning his father's trade. The young man was deeply impressed by his conversations with the prison's inmates. These veterans of a harsh penal system admonished Charles to avoid getting into trouble at all costs, even if confronted by the ultimate provocation to a man of that era—an insult or transgression against his mother, sister, or wife. Charles came to know the convicts as human beings whom he considered "unfortunate" rather than evil.

Correll's three months at the "pen" bolstered his belief in the profound importance of hard work and self-control: society set certain clear standards of conduct, and even a momentary, unthinking violation could ruin a man's life. At the same time, Correll's encounters with the convicts reinforced his inclination to accept people who differed from himself, and especially those to whom he felt life had dealt a poor hand. His later wealth and popularity would not weaken his feeling for all the "young fellows . . . who may think they will never get anywhere"—for whom all "hope . . . to become any kind of success is lost."[10]

This combination of social conservatism and easygoing tolerance of others would make itself felt in *Amos 'n' Andy*. Correll would relate to black actors in the series with an unforced friendliness devoid of condescension.[11] The same traits in Correll's personality would also make possible his harmonious thirty-five-year collaboration with Freeman Gosden. For the Virginian combined a similar conservative bent with a nervous energy and a tendency to dominate the production of the series that could quickly have led to clashes with a partner less flexible than Correll.

···—◉◐—···

Freeman Gosden was born almost a decade later than Charles Correll, in May 1899, on the eve of a new century. Like Correll, he was close to his family, but he lost both of his parents, a brother, and a sister by the time he was eighteen and thus found himself without the sort of anchor in his home town that Correll retained for many years. Gosden grew up in a southern city where blacks were an integral part of the daily scene. For that reason, and because Gosden was the creative powerhouse of the *Amos 'n' Andy* team, it was primarily he who determined how the show's black characters would be portrayed.

The Gosden family claimed English descent. Freeman's father, Walter W. Gosden Sr., had fought for the Confederacy in the Civil War. The elder Gosden worked in local banks from the end of the conflict until ill health forced him to retire some months before his death in 1911. Walter Gosden was a bright, well-read man, and a stable one: he served as a bookkeeper in a single firm for the last quarter-century of his life. He was already in his mid-fifties and his wife Emma—daughter of a Richmond physician—nearly forty when Freeman was born. Freeman's three brothers and his sister were much

older than he. The Gosdens, though far from poor, had limited means
even while Freeman's father was still alive. The family moved frequently, renting rather than owning most if not all the residences they
lived in over the years; Freeman and the other Gosden boys went to
work full-time while still in their mid-teens.[12]

The backdrop for Freeman's earliest childhood memories was a
pleasant area called Gamble's Hill, overlooking the James River, near
a small park where the neighborhood's many children played and its
black nursemaids pushed baby carriages and supervised white
toddlers.[13] After several moves, the Gosdens ended up a few blocks
from Jackson Ward, the area that contained much of Richmond's
black population, as well as many of the schools, churches, and businesses around which Afro-American life in the city largely revolved.
In all their wanderings, Gosden's family remained a few minutes'
walk from the center of Richmond. Also within walking distance were
the drug store where Freeman worked as a boy and the YMCA, where
he could amuse himself at no cost. And on nearby Broad Street stood
the Bijou Theater, where his mother often took him on Saturday
afternoons. More inclined to dream than Charlie Correll was, a cap-
tivated Gosden—as he recalled years later—"never wanted to do anything but act in those shows."[14]

Yet another of young Freeman's neighborhood haunts was the
pleasant, grassy square surrounding the Virginia state capitol, which
had housed the Congress of the Confederate States. The atmosphere
of Gosden's Richmond was deeply affected by the city's Confederate
past. Many Richmonders of the early twentieth century, like Gosden's own father, had lived through the Civil War—an unforgettable
four years of excitement and turmoil, and ultimately of privation,
fear, and despair as Union armies beset and finally conquered the
southern capital. By the decade of Freeman Gosden's birth, however,
the more painful memories of the war and its aftermath had faded,
and the conflict took on a new, highly romanticized shape in Richmond's collective consciousness.

In 1890, tens of thousands attended elaborate ceremonies in Richmond to unveil a heroic equestrian statue of Robert E. Lee atop a
massive marble pedestal. Three years later, Confederate President
Jefferson Davis's body was brought from its original burial place in
New Orleans to the city of Davis's wartime travail, where it lay in
state in the Virginia capitol before being ceremoniously reinterred
before a throng of 20,000.[15] Historical markers sprang up at Civil War
sites around the city, and commemorative projects of all kinds

abounded; Richmond had become the capital of the cult of the Lost Cause.

Freeman Gosden's generation, more than any other before or since, was reared on this romantic southern mythology in its full-blown form. One still saw parades of Confederate veterans in uniform; many of these men lived in a complex of buildings set aside for them on six square blocks at the city's western outskirts. Richmond's Sunday newspaper regularly ran "Our Confederate Column," which published at great length readers' reminiscences of the War Between the States. About the time Gosden turned eight years old, stately memorials to Jefferson Davis and General J. E. B. Stuart joined the Lee statue on Monument Avenue, a handsome new boulevard that was becoming an outdoor pantheon of the Confederate legend. The dedication of the Davis and Stuart monuments served as focal points for the largest Confederate reunion ever. Some 18,000 southern veterans celebrated with adoring citizens of Richmond for an entire week.[16]

These events and this atmosphere in his home city made a lasting impression on young Freeman. The boy took pride in his father's wartime service under Colonel John Singleton Mosby—a dashing Confederate partisan leader known as the Gray Ghost, who led guerrilla raids against the Yankees in northern Virginia. The Civil War, indeed, was the defining episode of Walter Gosden's life. "Served Under Colonel Mosby," read the headline above the prominent obituary of the "Gallant Confederate Soldier" in 1911. Years later, during *Amos 'n' Andy*'s heyday, a newspaper columnist compiled a lavish, widely published six-part biography of the show's two creators. His interviews with Gosden yielded a story that devoted hundreds of words and four large pictures to Walter Gosden's Civil War adventures. In 1933, Freeman Gosden took time out from the Richmond stop on a furiously busy personal appearance tour for a ceremony commemorating his father's years with Mosby. He was given the sword his father had carried during the Civil War and two bayonets the elder Gosden was said to have captured.[17]

At some point in his adult life, Freeman Gosden became a genuine Civil War buff, reading with particular relish about the exploits of the Gray Ghost. On his office wall hung a photograph of Mosby with Walter Gosden and other rangers, and for his home he framed another portrait of the colonel and a statement in which John S. Mosby himself, in the elegant hand of a nineteenth-century gentleman, testified to the "gallant" service of W. W. Gosden under his command. Freeman spoke of the Mosby connection widely and proudly enough that, according to his widow, the producer of a movie about Mosby once considered casting Gosden in the role of his own father.[18]

The rise of the cult of the Lost Cause before and during Gosden's boyhood was accompanied by dramatic changes in relations between white and black Southerners. In 1890, some forty percent of Richmond's 80,000 inhabitants were black. Illiteracy was still widespread among these black citizens, many of whom had once been slaves; the great majority of those in the city's work force were unskilled laborers.[19] Still, Richmond had more skilled Afro-American craftsmen and more businesses owned by blacks than many other southern towns and cities did. Two of the earliest black-owned banks in the United States and one of the South's first black newspapers, the Richmond *Planet*, were founded in the city during the several decades after Reconstruction.

Segregation of public facilities by race was far from rare in Virginia and elsewhere in the South before the 1890s, and whites had already used physical intimidation, fraud, economic pressure, and suffrage restrictions to dilute the modest political influence blacks had won after the Civil War. But once conservative white leaders had displaced Reconstruction governments in the various southern states during the 1870s, their racism could sometimes take a paternalistic form. Some of them even liked to think of themselves as benefactors of an inferior race which needed their help and protection. This the conservatives offered within certain narrow limits.

Blacks, the conservatives believed, should be politically subordinate to whites and socially separate from them. Yet until about 1890, the conservatives did not attempt to deprive all black men of the vote. Neither, after the end of Reconstruction, did they generally see a need to use physical terror to intimidate blacks. They did not at first impose an all-encompassing, legally codified system of racially segregated public accommodations. They tended to accept the idea that a bit of schooling—especially vocational training—could help blacks contribute to the South's economic development. Under the conservative regime in Virginia, Afro-Americans served on Richmond's Common Council and Board of Aldermen up to 1896. As late as the beginning of 1898, the year before Freeman Gosden was born, Virginia had as its governor a conservative, Charles T. O'Ferrall, who fought against lynching and considered himself friendly to the race in the paternalistic tradition.[20]

But more extreme racial attitudes were rapidly gaining ground. The notion that blacks would degenerate into savagery if not held in check by whites—an idea once useful in justifying slavery—had sunk its roots into the popular mind well before the Civil War and had never died out. Then, after the war, influential writers had begun to misapply Charles Darwin's theory of natural selection to the realm of human society. Some races, they said, were naturally inferior— doomed to degenerate into crime and depravity as they moved down the path to extinction. Such beliefs accelerated white repression of blacks, which was already intensifying because of economic and political developments in the South.[21]

The policies of the South's conservative leaders favored financial and industrial interests and large landholders. Farmers and others with economic grievances challenged the conservatives in various elections after Reconstruction ended—most prominently through Virginia's Readjuster party in the years around 1880, and through the Populist party revolt that boiled over in many states a dozen years later. Some of the politicians who fought the conservatives were black, and the Populists often sought the support of black voters, as the Readjusters had done before them. The besieged conservatives responded by manipulating and falsifying the black vote—and, at the same time, by condemning their challengers as traitors to the white race. In defeat, some Populists blamed their failure on the black vote and its fraudulent exploitation,[22] an attitude that made it harder to defeat subsequent efforts by conservatives to eliminate black voting altogether.

In some places—most strikingly, in South Carolina—demagogic politicians appealing to the small-farmer vote got in the first racist blows. They attacked the conservative paternalists for their alleged friendship with the blacks, and they lashed out at blacks for supposedly voting conservative. When the conservatives saw their power threatened, they often responded by trumpeting their undying dedication to white supremacy.

In all southern states, by the turn of the century, a decade or more of political Negro-baiting and white terrorism had done much to poison the racial atmosphere, and conservatives moved to eliminate blacks and troublesome whites from political life once and for all. No more Afro-Americans were elected to Richmond's governing bodies after 1896, and the new Virginia constitution of 1902 finished the job by disfranchising the state's black citizens. Even the local Republican party, once the political home of most blacks, now went "lily-white," excluding Afro-Americans from participation.[23] During these same years, just before Freeman Gosden's birth and during his boyhood, southern lawmakers extended the system of racial segregation into virtually every area of life. Growing agitation in the press and elsewhere led the Virginia legislature early in the new century to pass laws requiring segregation on trains and streetcars. Strict separation of the races now prevailed in other public facilities as well.

The southern popular literature of Freeman Gosden's childhood reflected both the paternalistic form of racism and the rise of a cruder sort of bigotry. Thomas Nelson Page, a nationally famous author of novels and stories who grew up and spent the first half of his life in and near Richmond, idealized the plantation life of the antebellum and Civil War years; he portrayed blacks with affection—but only in the role of faithful, submissive slaves or aged, deferential freedmen. By 1904, a nonfiction work by Page revealed a shift in his tone through its very title—*The Negro: The Southerner's Problem*. Novelist Thomas Dixon of North Carolina, meanwhile, wrote admiringly of hooded white vigilantes who, during Reconstruction, forcibly rid their southern community of stereotypical scheming carpetbaggers and bestial blacks. Dixon's novel, *The Clansman*, became a popular play and provided the basis for the inflammatory movie, *The Birth of a Nation*, ten years later. Whatever the differences between Page and Dixon, both men's writings, along with most of the "scientific" racist treatises of the era, led to a common conclusion: the inherent shortcomings of blacks as a race required that they be kept under the firm control of whites.

The new racial regime was largely in place by the end of Freeman Gosden's early childhood. Just as significant, the spirit among whites that had demanded that new order was still very much alive; it even led during Freeman's adolescence to a city ordinance forbidding blacks to live in certain areas of Richmond. Later generations of whites might conveniently assume that the all-encompassing Jim Crow system had always existed and was therefore immutable. The generation of Gosden's parents had molded the system with its own hands.

At the same time, the black adults living in Richmond when Freeman was growing up had vivid memories of better times. They had witnessed the white South's relentless assault on their status as citizens and as human beings, and they still resisted on occasion. As late as 1904, when Freeman turned five, the editor of the black Richmond *Planet*—though he had generally moderated his paper's crusading tone—led his community in a lengthy boycott of Richmond's segregated streetcars. In the end, the cars remained segregated in Richmond as in other southern cities where boycotts took place.[24] Just the same, if the Afro-American community Gosden knew as a boy was defeated and oppressed, black Richmond was not altogether silent or supine.

Nor, as trying as life became for Afro-Americans, was the regime in Richmond quite so ruthless, or blacks so utterly helpless, as in many other parts of the South. Lynching of blacks, a shockingly frequent practice during these years, was less common in large cities and never came into fashion in Richmond. Murderous pogroms of whites against defenseless blacks, like those that exploded in Atlanta and in Wilmington, North Carolina, did not occur in Freeman's home city. And the Afro-American community in Gosden's Richmond possessed many autonomous institutions—for example, the *Planet*, fraternal and mutual-benefit societies, the black-owned banks and other businesses—that had great symbolic and practical value.

Even so, the new racial order was a system of social control that aimed to reassert as much of the discipline of slavery itself as was possible in post-Emancipation America.[25] By contrast, the rites of the Confederacy that Freeman Gosden knew so well were not aggressively racist, and leaders of the cult now professed their contentment that slavery had ended. But most Afro-Americans could muster little nostalgia for a cause whose most basic element had been the desire to keep them or their parents in bondage; indeed, the Confederate cult celebrated the mythical "faithful slave" and urged the blacks of the New South to take him as a model.[26] Flowering as it did in the very period when blacks were being strictly segregated from whites and disparaged as innately inferior, the Confederate cult may have appealed all the more strongly to many whites precisely because blacks were largely absent[27] from the ranks of its votaries. The myth of the Lost Cause was closely linked with other myths that *were* explicitly racist—of Reconstruction as a period when ignorant, corrupt black men had joined white carpetbaggers and scalawags to misgovern the decent white people of the South, and of the white conservatives' recapture of power as a "redemption" from those abominations. And however innocent some of the impulses underlying the cult of the Lost Cause may have been, its ceremonies and its totems—especially the Confederate monuments—served, among their other functions, as oblique but highly visible symbols of white hegemony.

Compared with the era's direct, blatant assaults on the black community, white Richmond's celebrations of the Civil War cult during Gosden's formative years seemed constructive and genteel. After all, the city's middle and upper classes liked to think of their home as the black novelist Robert Deane Pharr, a native of Richmond, later described it—as "a town of the cavalier, not the cracker."[28] The brand of southern racism Freeman Gosden grew up with in Richmond did at times have a polite veneer. But the racial system it produced was a profoundly confining and often mean-spirited one.

···—●◉●—···

Environment deeply affects attitudes, but it does not dictate them absolutely; and a child's world revolves not around social conditions at large, but rather around specific persons and intimate events. Some of Freeman Gosden's early experiences challenged him dramatically; his childhood, adolescence, and young manhood were fraught with tragedy and radical change. His older brother Willie sank into chronic depression and became addicted to morphine. When Freeman was almost three, Willie took his own life in the family's house with an overdose of that drug on his nineteenth birthday. Then, when Freeman was twelve, the father he so admired died after an illness of six months.[29]

During the six years following Mr. Gosden's death, the family moved three times within a single middle-class area of Richmond's West End. They lived frugally on the salary of Freeman's elder brother, eventually supplemented by young Freeman's own pay as a clerk for a shoe manufacturer, the earnings of a brother-in-law who moved in with the family, and the money his mother made by taking in boarders. Then, late in the summer of 1917, while Freeman was serving in the Navy, his mother and sister were killed only half a mile from their home—thrown from a touring car when it was struck from the side by another auto at an intersection. Such crashes were still rare in that era of slow speeds and relatively few cars, and the accident shocked the city. The memory of it remained deeply painful to Gosden for the rest of his days.[30]

By age eighteen, the most basic certainties in Freeman Gosden's life—the emotional moorings provided by his family—had crumbled one by one until almost nothing was left. Gosden could have sought the stability denied him in his family life by wrapping himself in the comfortable conventions of middle-class Richmond. Or else, he could set out on a brand new course in the hope of kinder days to come.

Freeman had already taken a big step toward a different, challenging sort of life by joining the Navy when the United States entered World War I. The Navy put him through a course for radio technicians at Harvard University. Gosden served in that specialty both at sea and on land while stationed at Virginia Beach. He was prone to seasickness and found little charm in military life, but he did see something of the Northeast, and he developed a lasting interest in the new technology of radio.[31]

After the war, Gosden stayed in Virginia for a short time. But then, in 1919 or 1920, he chose a path that introduced him to a much wider variety of experiences than most Richmonders ever encountered. He got a job as an itinerant director of amateur minstrel shows for the Joe Bren Company, a Chicago-based concern which helped civic clubs stage their annual fund-raising productions, and which already employed Charles Correll.[32] Gosden now spent most of each year on the road in various regions of the United States, seeing new places whose customs, racial and otherwise, might differ from those he had known as a boy. He eventually took a position in the Bren organization's home office in Chicago, the city where he and Correll went onto create *Sam 'n' Henry*. Richmond still held sad memories for Gosden, and he visited his former home only three times after the early 1920s.[33]

The heartaches of Freeman's youth, and his family's modest means, affected more than Gosden's career; they influenced his adult personality and behavior. Although he lived in luxury after becoming a star, he would always worry about money and speak of his years in Richmond—with sincerity, if not with perfect accuracy—as a period of near-poverty.[34] To ward off adversity, Gosden sought as much as possible to control his environment; by insisting that every detail of his artistic and business affairs meet his exacting standards, he could create some of the certainty and stability that his early life had so conspicuously lacked. He was sure he knew exactly how *Amos 'n' Andy* should sound and was noted for running the show as a "tight ship." This trait irritated many of Gosden's associates, but the success and the durability of *Amos 'n' Andy* owed much to it.

The weekly shows at Richmond's Bijou Theater did not only add a dash of color to young Freeman Gosden's simple day-to-day existence. Those performances, and Freeman's fantasies about starring in them, freed him, however briefly, from the emotional burdens of life in the unfortunate Gosden household. For decades to come, Gosden would often recall two high points of his childhood in Richmond. Both memories came from the period of his father's illness and death, and both were of shows Freeman took part in: he appeared as a volunteer in a performance by the famous magician Howard Thurston, and competed in a diving contest in Annette Kellerman's pool when the shapely, swimming "water nymph" brought her "tank show" to town.[35]

Just as Freeman's dreams of a career in show business helped to ease the pain of his early life, so the pursuit of those dreams offered the mature Gosden a way to leave the ruins of his traumatic early years behind. And moving on, he found outlets for his talents that his home city could never have provided.

···━●━···

One other kind of intimate experience in childhood notably affected Freeman Gosden's portrayal of black characters in *Amos 'n' Andy*—his interactions with real Afro-Americans. Unlike many other white Southerners of his generation, Gosden did not claim to have acquired deep knowledge of Afro-American ways on the lap of a black "mammy." Although some early press biographies of Gosden and Correll did state in passing that Freeman's mother reared him with the help of a "mammy," Gosden himself rarely if ever mentioned any such woman in later years.[36] The one Afro-American who did clearly influence young Freeman was a childhood friend named Garrett Brown. Gosden sometimes spoke of Brown in later years, attributing one specific *Amos 'n' Andy* character, and traits of several others, to Brown's example.[37]

When Gosden was growing up, whites frequently amused themselves by applying supposedly humorous nicknames, individually and generically, to blacks. Someone in Richmond dubbed Garrett Brown "Snowball," and the name stuck.[38] Black youngsters in Richmond often worked at odd jobs for white families, but the Gosdens apparently took this particular boy into their home to live. Freeman later told a reporter that Brown arrived when both boys were five; on another occasion, he said that Garrett remained in the Gosden home until age sixteen.[39] That Brown made a lasting impression on Gosden is not surprising, for the racial code permitted a degree of intimacy across racial lines among children. Ann Webb, a relative of Gosden's who lived with the family for a time, later recalled that Freeman and Garrett carried on extemporaneous, skit-like dialogues and performed two-man, minstrel-style shows for Freeman's ailing father.[40]

In a newspaper article she wrote at the height of the *Amos 'n' Andy* craze, Ann Webb portrayed young Brown as the family jester. She referred to his speech as "jargon" (albeit "the most inimitable and original I have ever heard"); she quoted him, for example, as stammering over the word "inferential" before mispronouncing it as "in-fernerenshal." In many ways, Webb's "Snowball" fits the cherished stereotype of the "lovable" black male—comical, deferential, and therefore unthreatening.

At the same time, though, Webb found Garrett to be like Free-man in some striking ways: outgoing, observant of people and events around him, and gifted at mimicry. She also credited him with having "an almost uncanny shrewdness for one of his years," "a crude phi-losophy of his own," and a "really astonishing"—if apparently not infallible—faculty for "grappling with unfamiliar and multi-syllabled words." "Crude philosophy" was a commodity that condescending whites of that era often imputed to blacks, and Webb's attitudes, though not malevolent, drew heavily on the racial orthodoxy of her society. But it is precisely her biased racial assumptions that make Webb's high estimate of Garrett Brown's talents so convincing.

The other main source of information about Brown is the portrayal in *Amos 'n' Andy* of a character named Sylvester. Although he was only a secondary figure in the series, Sylvester loomed large in some of the best-known episodes of the show's first year, and Gosden said he modeled the character on his own boyhood friend.

The Sylvester of *Amos 'n' Andy*, unlike the "Snowball" whom Ann Webb described, is neither obviously self-assured, nor assertive, nor especially talkative. No joker, Sylvester is the picture of earnestness and industry. He values nothing so much as the friendship of Amos—another prudent, conscientious, and ingenuous character who Gosden said was partly based on Garrett Brown. Patient, unostentatious, speaking in an untutored dialect, and held in disdain at first by the blowhard Andy, Sylvester turns out to be bright and talented. He finds Amos and Andy their first job in Chicago, puts their ancient and hopelessly rundown taxicab into working order, earns the first profits from that vehicle after Amos and Andy fail to make any, and foils a burglary. In short, although Sylvester's gentleness made it easy for conservative white listeners to accept him, he is more than a mere caricature. Just beneath his apparent naiveté lie a survivor's instinct and host of virtues; beyond his seeming vulnerability, an understated belief in himself.

It is impossible to reconcile completely the "Snowball" recalled by Ann Webb—witty, irrepressible, a bit saucy even when talking to whites—with Gosden's own creation, the unfailingly serious-minded Sylvester, who is deferential, and at times obsequious, even toward fellow blacks of his own social milieu. Yet several observations help the real Garrett Brown and his influence on Freeman Gosden's attitudes to emerge from among the contradictions.

Gosden surely excluded Brown's lively sense of humor from the makeup of Sylvester for the same reason that no important figures in *Amos 'n' Andy* were jokesters: the humor of the series flowed from personality, situation, and language itself rather than from self-conscious jests by its characters. At the same time, Ann Webb probably described Garrett Brown as more of a joker than he really was. This, after all, was the face many whites of the time thought they saw—and wanted to see—when they looked at Afro-Americans, especially black children. Then too, Brown himself may have concluded at an early age that maintaining a jocular demeanor around most whites offered the best promise of staying out of trouble.

But Freeman Gosden perceived even more complexity in the black boy's character than Ann Webb did, and viewed him as something more than a lovable source of merriment. The crucial points of agreement between Gosden's Sylvester and Ann Webb's "Snowball" round out the picture of Brown that young Freeman saw. Sylvester is utterly guileless, Webb's "Snowball" partly though not entirely so. Both figures are friendly and decent, and both have considerable native intelligence. These traits, then, along with the sense of humor that the radio Sylvester had to do without for reasons of dramatic technique, were probably the outstanding characteristics of Freeman Gosden's friend, Garrett Brown.

Growing up in the times he did, and knowing Brown as well as he did, Gosden, as much as any southern writer before or since, was exposed to the bizarre combination of repulsion and intimacy that characterized relations between whites and blacks in the South. He was bright and open enough to see something beyond the racist stereotypes; yet both he and Charles Correll were products of a turn-of-the-century America in which the axioms of white supremacy were more widely and heartily accepted than they had been since the days of slavery. Neither man showed any early inclination to challenge those assumptions, and both would come before the radio microphone steeped in the racial images that Americans had long imbibed from plantation literature and minstrel shows. Those images, indeed, were the very wares that Gosden and Correll carried with them when they took to the road as traveling minstrel-show directors after the First World War.

3

-•-•◉•-•-

Jefferson Snowball, Traveling
Minstrel

Shortly before May Day 1917, Freeman Gosden and a group of his friends traveled from Richmond fifty miles north to Fredericksburg. The young men had formed a minstrel company, and Freeman was about to make his debut as a paid performer. The group was appearing at the end of the annual convention of the United Daughters of the Confederacy (UDC) for Virginia's fourth district.[1] The UDC was holding its meeting at a place rich in associations with the war for southern independence. Here, halfway between the two Civil War capitals, some of the conflicts' bloodiest battles had been fought: Fredericksburg, Chancellorsville, the Wilderness, Spotsylvania Court House.

During their half-week in Fredericksburg, the ladies of the UDC tapped three currents that merged in the cult of the Confederacy. The first of these, of course, was reverence for the sacrifices of the men who had fought to preserve the old regime. Beneath portraits of Generals Robert E. Lee and Stonewall Jackson, hung against a backdrop of Confederate flags, the convention heard reports on campaigns to build monuments to the Confederate dead, and on the UDC's relief work for "needy Confederate women" who survived southern soldiers.

Between the banners of the militant South, however, the UDC had hung the flag of the United States, framing a portrait of President Woodrow Wilson. The combined flags of two once hostile peoples symbolized the second historical current that animated the UDC and the rest of the white South: the reconciliation of the two sections. Wilson, a son of Virginia and the first Southerner to occupy the White House since 1869, was now leading a united nation into an idealistic martial crusade in Europe. The president of the Virginia UDC painted a stirring picture of a World War fought by "sons and grandsons of Confederate veterans side by side with their northern brother, knowing never a difference—one as much as the other 'our boys.' "

The gathering of the UDC drank deeply of a third stream that fed the cult of the Confederacy: the image of the Afro-American as a figure to be loved and laughed at—indeed, loved precisely insofar as he seemed laughable, sentimental, and unthreatening. Here, Freeman Gosden and his minstrel companions entered the picture.

The comic-nostalgic burnt-cork stage Negro still held a prominent place on the vaudeville stage, and in the amateur entertainments of Fredericksburg as of countless other places. When a local one-room school ended its yearly session at the time of the UDC meeting, its pupils greeted the summer vacation with a program that included a rendition of the "Darky song, 'Suwanee River.' "[2] The UDC convention's own entertainment program offered a number from antebellum minstrelsy: a young woman, "dressed as a Southern Mammy," sang "Dixie." And as the UDC gathering ended, the ladies of the organization's Spotsylvania chapter sponsored the Richmond troupe's minstrel show. With almost poetic aptness, the proceeds from the performance would go toward the erection of a local monument to the fallen of the Confederacy. Local stores sold fifty-cent tickets for the production throughout the week of the convention. Meanwhile, the ladies promoted the show in a newspaper advertisement and in handbills sporting pictures of Gosden's colleagues in standard, liver-lipped blackface makeup and outlandish apparel.[3]

Enough spectators braved a pounding rain on Friday evening to fill Fredericksburg's Opera House theater. Some slogged through muddy country roads from their homes in neighboring counties; a few hardy souls arrived in horse-drawn vehicles. The "fine, good-natured gathering" of white Virginians knew that the performers were only semiprofessionals, and the audience watched the show with an indulgent eye,[4] never guessing that two of the young men on the stage would later become nationally known. One, the interlocutor or master of ceremonies, was a young accountant named Coleman Andrews. He would go on to reform the Internal Revenue Service under President Dwight D. Eisenhower; he would also become a founder of the John Birch Society and a leader of segregationist presidential candidate George Wallace's campaign in 1968.[5]

With Andrews as their straight man, several of the troupe's comedians—known in minstrelsy as "endmen" because they sat at each end of the chorus—drew laughter with their blackface repartee. The show's singing minstrel quartet won an enthusiastic reception, as did a duo that included the other future luminary in the troupe, Freeman Gosden. He and his partner performed songs and "eccentric dances," some of which were descended from steps that early white minstrels claimed to have learned from blacks. Freeman's capers made him his first dollar as an entertainer. And a dollar is just about what he earned; Coleman Andrews later recalled that his own share of the evening's take had been $1.58.[6]

The show ended, and several hundred white Virginians filed out of the Opera House into the soggy spring night feeling that they had been well entertained while supporting a worthy project. The United Daughters of the Confederacy of district four departed with two days' worth of memories and patriotic inspiration. The UDC ladies of Spotsylvania Court House took with them a tidy sum for the building of a Confederate memorial at their village. And Freeman Gosden returned to Richmond a professional blackface *artiste*, tucking away as a souvenir one of the handbills for the performance that had just ended.

··· ➡◉◀ ···

With his minstrel friends, young Gosden had fallen heir to a tradition nearly a century old. By 1830, white performers had begun darkening their faces and imitating—with much artistic license—the songs, dances, and dialect of Afro-Americans. They traveled about the country, appearing solo in circuses or during intermissions between the several plays included on a typical dramatic bill in those days.[7] Gosden's endman descended from two essential characters—often known as Jim Crow and Zip Coon—that the minstrel pioneers created.

Jim Crow was supposed to epitomize the plantation slave. A Jim Crow character might boast with humorous extravagance of his strength and skill, but he was physically grotesque, sporting a distorted version of African features, disheveled clothing, and a perpetual grin. Early minstrels portrayed Jim Crow as a blissfully ignorant, emotionally childlike, fun-loving creature endowed with an innate musical and rhythmic sense. The character's bizarre postures and loose-limbed movements were forerunners of Freeman Gosden's "eccentric dances."[8]

Zip Coon, whom minstrels represented as an urban, northern character, dressed in ostentatious finery and affected a graceful carriage; he boasted of his wide-ranging knowledge and of his magnetism among the fair sex. The "joke" lay largely in Zip Coon's pretensions, for despite his haughtiness he had much in common with the crude Jim Crow: ignorance, musicality, a love of the sensual, and an outlandish appearance including grossly caricatured Negroid features. The fictional Zip Coon confirmed the prejudices of white audiences in northern cities, where minstrelsy won its greatest popularity; his manifest inferiority reassured those who resented and feared the black man as an economic competitor.[9]

The habit of applying the epithets "Jim Crow" and "coon" to real blacks, well established by Freeman Gosden and Charles Correll's day, showed how readily many white Americans identified their darker countrymen with the minstrels' comical, exotic stereotypes. Although the essence of Zip Coon and Jim Crow still thrived on the stages of Gosden and Correll's early years, the format of the minstrel show and its place in American entertainment had changed over the decades. The early, solo performers had first combined into duos and trios. Then, in New York City in 1843, the four Virginia Minstrels made a great hit in the first show to feature minstrelsy only; the form quickly became America's most popular type of entertainment.

Ever larger companies soon developed a format that included three standard parts, and whose main features survived in the minstrel shows that *Amos 'n' Andy*'s creators performed in and directed. The first act offered a minstrel chorus, whose comic endmen bounced much of their humor off the interlocutor. Jokes, eccentric dances, and humorous ditties alternated with serious romantic and sentimental songs sung by one or more soloists. Then came the second part of the production, an "olio" or mini-variety show consisting of non-blackface novelty acts and a "stump speech" on some topic of current interest; a blackface comedian delivered the speech, using abundant malapropisms and exaggerated gestures. The show concluded with a one-act blackface farce relying heavily on slapstick humor.

After the Civil War, minstrel companies began to tour extensively rather than remain in their home cities; their shows evolved into baroque spectaculars. The famous Haverly's United Mastodon Minstrels, for example, included forty performers by 1879 and featured "magnificent scene[s]" set in Turkish palaces and other locales far removed from the antebellum plantation. Even before the Civil War, romantic minstrel balladeers had begun to sing sentimental songs that had little or no connection with the supposed peculiarities of black culture and were not delivered in "Negro" dialect. In these numbers, blackface became a stage convention with little connection to race. Burnt cork finally lost even that status in some of the biggest troupes, which eliminated most of their "Negro" characterizations in the 1880s.[10]

Yet important elements of blackface minstrelsy outlived the baroque period and the demise of most great minstrel companies by the 1890s. Many former minstrels moved on to vaudeville—the variety shows on which Correll and Gosden were raised, and which presented touring acts to audiences in nearly every corner of the United States. Some vaudevillians still wore burnt cork for the specific purpose of caricaturing Afro-Americans. But others carried on the traditions of the romantic minstrel balladeers, and of comic minstrels who, though "blacked up," had performed in the supposed dialect of "ethnic" whites. On the vaudeville stage, performers in this second category became what one show business journalist called "blackface entertainers" but "not Negro impersonators."[11] Some performers, meanwhile, drew on both these blackface styles—the "Negro" and the non-"Negro"—obscuring the boundary between them.

Still other vaudevillians adapted forms developed by the minstrels, but performed them without burnt cork. One of Freeman Gosden's specialties as an amateur minstrel—the long, rambling, almost monologic "explanation" or rejoinder, full of zany tangents and non sequiturs—owed a great deal to the antebellum minstrel shows' stump speech. Joe Cook, a vaudeville star whose monologues influenced Freeman's style, did his act without blackface makeup. Gosden, however, must have rendered his version of the routine in burnt cork, if only because he had to be blacked up for his other role as an endman.[12]

Freeman Gosden, though heavily influenced by these varied minstrel traditions, was no narrow sectarian. Though shy with strangers in everyday encounters, young Freeman somehow always felt free and comfortable before an audience. Among his boyhood friends, he tried his hand at clog and tap dancing, impersonations of Charlie Chaplin and other stars, ventriloquism, and singing. He went on to perform in amateur shows in Richmond and in the Navy.[13] As a teenager, Gosden graduated from the minstrel dialogues that he and his black friend Garrett Brown had performed for Freeman's father to the local minstrel company that took him to Fredericksburg. Among Freeman's partners was a boy whose older brother belonged to the Al G. Field minstrels, one of the few surviving professional troupes. The brother secured secondhand costumes, perhaps castoffs from the Field group, for the Richmond boys, who then played one-night engagements for modest fees.[14] By the time Gosden felt ready to strike out on his own a couple of years after the war, he was well prepared for life in small-time show business—with or without blackface makeup.

···—●●—···

Charles Correll's background as a performer resembled Gosden's in many ways, not least of which was a long and intimate acquaintance with blackface and with other traditions in entertainment and popular literature that had been evolving since before the Civil War. While growing up in Peoria, Correll entered local dance contests and talent shows. He also played in a type of stage production that, like minstrelsy, had indelibly influenced white Americans' racial perceptions: the young Correll acted in amateur stagings of *Uncle Tom's Cabin*, "chas[ing] the hounds across the ice."[15] Those who have read Harriet Beecher Stowe's famous novel about slavery will have trouble recalling that scene in the book—for it does not exist. This discrepancy and many others in the productions of *Uncle Tom* that the young Correll saw and appeared in reveal much about the ways American writers and actors portrayed blacks up to the time of Correll's adolescence.

Most American literature and drama before the Civil War had either presented blacks as bumpkins, primitives, and buffoons or ignored the Afro-American altogether. In *Uncle Tom's Cabin*, published in 1852, Stowe departed dramatically from that tradition by creating a wide variety of important black characters: where Uncle Tom never wavers in his Christian love for the master who sells him down the river, for example, Eliza's husband George escapes from slavery and defends his freedom by force of arms. Some of Stowe's creations drew on stereotypes but were too complex to fit them entirely: though Tom's fellow Kentucky slave Black Sam behaves like a sycophant, he astutely calculates his actions so as to improve his situation. Like other liberal writers of her own era and afterward, Stowe did ascribe gentleness and resignation to a full-blooded black character (Tom) while making her defiant figures (George and Eliza) those with substantial white ancestry.[16] Yet her novel still presented a powerful challenge to the unflattering images of blacks that prevailed at the time.

The *Uncle Tom's Cabin* that Charles Correll acted in was—literally—a different story. The original novel's fantastic success outside the slaveholding South had spawned a number of plays; *Uncle Tom* became the most frequently performed story on American stages and remained so for decades. Most versions, however, diluted Stowe's egalitarian, abolitionist message. Some of the earlier dramatizations even turned the story into an apologia for southern society, while blackface minstrels, unwilling to see the Union break up over the issue of slavery, deprecated Stowe's *Uncle Tom* by adding parodies of the novel to their shows.[17]

After the Civil War, popular blackface "Tom shows" almost invariably stressed melodramatic or comic aspects of the now-mutated story. "Tommers" even added music and novelties of various kinds. Uncle Tom might perform buck-and-wing dances; the angelic white character, little Eva, often became the star of the show.[18] "Tommers" toned down or eliminated the novel's profound social and moral message for some audiences, while hamming it up and trivializing it for others. It was not enough for the fugitive slave Eliza to jump with her child across a fissure in the ice of the Ohio River just a few steps ahead of her pursuers, as she had done in the novel. Now—as in the productions young Charles Correll played in—the slave-catchers had a pack of bloodhounds, which chased Eliza across teetering floes. By Gosden and Correll's day, *Uncle Tom* had become a comedy-adventure story whose remaining antislavery content could be made innocuous enough to appear on stages in the Jim Crow South. Charles's experience in stilted productions of *Uncle Tom's Cabin* offered him, at best, a brief and imperfect glimpse of a few relatively serious black characters, precariously afloat on the ocean of stereotypes that flooded both the stage and the printed page during his childhood.

True, some popular writers during the years preceding Charles Correll's debut as an amateur "Tommer" had followed Stowe's example, treating black characters sympathetically and the problem of race seriously. The liberal white Southerner George Washington Cable published stories and novels in the 1870s and early '80s, while the "carpetbagger" Albion W. Tourgee's novels of Reconstruction went through several editions beginning in 1879. Mark Twain's trenchant *Huckleberry Finn* (1884) and *Pudd'nhead Wilson* (1894) reached many readers, and the black author Charles W. Chesnutt made his mark around the turn of the century.[19] Nevertheless, Gosden and Correll's childhood years found minstrel-style images and the faithful "dark-eys" of Thomas Nelson Page and his heirs sitting securely at the top of the heap.

Plantation stereotypes flourished even in the work of black writers, a few of whom were widely read by whites as Correll and Gosden grew up. During the years around 1900, as Correll approached adolescence, most black poets either ignored Afro-American themes altogether, or they wrote in "dialect," often presenting a comical-sentimental picture of their simpler brethren. Daniel Webster Davis of Richmond expressed anguish at racist cruelty and the disfranchisement of his people, but he also wrote poems that seemed to satirize the idea of education for blacks and to romanticize slavery. Paul Laurence Dunbar, the foremost Afro-American literary figure of the period, treated blacks with affection, captured aspects of their folk life, and occasionally addressed the real problems facing them with a unique eloquence. Yet he often portrayed life on the old plantation in a nostalgic, romantic light. In the early years of the new century, black novelists like James Weldon Johnson and W. E. B. Du Bois, along with some white liberal authors in both North and South, tried to present a different picture of blacks and of American race relations. Those writers, however, reached much smaller audiences than did the traditionalists whom they meant to challenge.[20]

For popularity and sheer influence on the attitudes of the public, the minstrels had had few rivals for much of the nineteenth century. Though most of the professional minstrel companies had died out by the time Correll and Gosden were born, a few groups managed to survive the challenge of musical comedy, vaudeville, and burlesque. These continued to tour through the years when Correll and Gosden haunted the theaters of their respective home towns, and a couple of them lasted until the late 1920s. Meanwhile, minstrelsy won a new lease on life as a mainstay of American amateur theatricals; publishers would still be selling how-to booklets and scripts for minstrel-style shows as late as the 1950s.[21]

Ironically, professional Afro-American minstrels had done much to keep the blackface tradition alive after their white counterparts largely abandoned it in the post-Civil War years. In fact, the white minstrels had moved away from plantation themes and from the universal wearing of blackface makeup partly because of competition from all-black minstrel companies, which advertised themselves as the genuine article in "Ethiopian" entertainment. Having begun to appear in the latter 1850s, black companies—most of them owned by whites—

flourished for some years beginning in the '70s. They reintroduced plantation motifs to the minstrel stage, and they infused their shows with elements of authentic Afro-American culture—most notably, the spiritual. While their shows included dollops of nostalgia for the plantation, the black performers pined more for their long-gone friends and family than for Ol' Massa. Like the earliest white minstrels, they occasionally lamented slavery's tribulations. And sometimes they sang joyfully of the Emancipation, or offered glimpses of small, Br'er Rabbit-style triumphs of weak over strong.[22]

Yet at best, the black minstrels challenged racism only by nuance. "Subversive" subtexts in their material, to the extent there were any, had to be kept almost imperceptibly subtle whenever whites were listening. By and large, then, the black acts reinforced white Americans' belief in what the poet and critic Sterling A. Brown later damned as the "eternal triangle" of "the Negro and possum and watermelon."[23] Billy Kersands, perhaps the best-known of the Afro-American minstrels, made a trademark of his huge, usually grinning mouth—a feature that was supposed to typify the "coon," and which minstrels accentuated by leaving a wide border of unblacked skin or light greasepaint around their lips. (Placing an entire cup and saucer or a number of billiard balls into his mouth was part of Kersands's act.) Black minstrels even took to using burnt cork; in effect, this prevented the blacks' varied complexions from suggesting that one "coon" was any different from another.

The Afro-American performers whose work the young Charles Correll and Freeman Gosden knew best were successors to the black minstrels. Many, in fact, had begun their own careers on the minstrel stage. They appeared on the white-dominated vaudeville circuits and in all-black musical comedies. The musicals had evolved during the 1890s and reached the peak of their popularity shortly after the turn of the century. Bert Williams and George Walker—who collaborated on the musicals *Sons of Ham* and *In Dahomey*—were among the most distinguished of a generation of gifted black performers active while Correll and Gosden were growing up.

Popular prejudice and the entertainment business that responded to it confined these stars, too, to comic roles that owed much to the tradition of minstrelsy; they still wore burnt cork, for example. The best of them—like Bert Williams, who became a pillar of the Ziegfeld Follies in the World War I era—could evoke universal human emotions in song and sketch. On occasion, they might even obliquely twit American racism.[24] And they could be sure that if they did not portray their race with some measure of integrity, then white men would do so with none at all. But the result was that, in order to compete with white blackface comics, Williams and Walker felt compelled during Charles Correll's most impressionable years to bill themselves explicitly—as other black acts did implicitly—as "Two Real Coons."

While young Correll soaked up all these show-business images of blacks and continued his amateur pursuits on the stage, he concentrated on the practical business of earning a living. Having finished high school and begun to learn bricklaying on the penitentiary job, he followed his father and several other relatives into the construction business in Peoria. After a few years, Correll moved to Rock Island in northwestern Illinois, where, from about 1912 until 1918, he worked first as a brickmason and then as a stenographer.[25]

In the area around Rock Island, Moline, and Davenport (just across the Mississippi in Iowa), Correll earned his first regular income as a performer. During slack periods in the construction business, he accompanied silent movies on the piano in a local theater. He also joined a vocal group called the Metropolitan Minstrels Quartet as piano accompanist. The singing quartet had been a standard feature of the minstrel show for nearly the entire history of the genre. Like the quartets of the old-time troupes, the Metropolitans wore blackface, but they performed mainly a kind of material commonly found in the amateur minstrelsy of their own day: light and sentimental songs in Standard English, rendered in barbershop harmony. The typical repertoire of such groups might also include an occasional comical number about black characters or a few traditional minstrel songs relying on some measure of stage dialect. Pianist Correll eventually took the place of one of the singers in the Metropolitan Quartet.[26]

Later, Correll sang and played in a trio, which he formed with one of the former Metropolitans and another young man. The group sometimes earned as much as forty to fifty dollars for an evening's work. In the same years, Correll appeared in local amateur shows, many of which included segments borrowed from minstrelsy. Correll served as endman, singer, and dancer, much as Gosden was doing in Richmond at the time, and he directed several student minstrel shows at a local high school.[27]

In the fall of 1917—six months after Freeman Gosden appeared in the UDC's minstrel benefit at Fredericksburg—Correll took part in an amateur minstrel-style show staged by the Davenport Elks Club and directed by a professional coach from the Joe Bren theatrical

company of Chicago. Correll sang a solo, performed in the quartet—
probably in blackface—and may well have served as an endman. His
performance apparently convinced the director to recommend him for
a job directing similar amateur shows for the Bren organization,
though the young man could not immediately leave his position as a
wartime worker at the Rock Island Arsenal. When the World War
ended in 1918, Correll hit the road as a Bren coach—a road that would
soon lead him to partnership with Freeman Gosden. By catching the
Bren Company's eye, he had reached what he later called "the turning point in my life, as I had then gotten into something I really
wanted to do."[28]

The Bren organization's show season ran from September until
June. Bren usually kept two crews in the field, each consisting of
three or four directors and coaches. A given crew rehearsed and staged
shows in three, four, or even five towns a month, typically presenting
two or three performances on successive evenings in each place. Although a Bren coach might come to town a couple of weeks before
opening night to begin preparing for the show, the director himself
often had only one week to turn a cast of local amateurs into a passably entertaining company of performers.[29]

The Bren Company's clients were civic and fraternal organizations: Elks, Shriners, American Legionnaires, Kiwanis. Each club
that sponsored a production also furnished most of the stars-for-a-
weekend who appeared in it. Joe Bren and his employees would write
a show and then present it with minor variations in one town after
another throughout a particular year. The first act featured the songs
and comedy of a company of minstrels. The second and final portion
of the show usually comprised one or two comic skits with songs, as
well as a variety of comedy acts, individual song and dance numbers,
and perhaps a "mind-reading" segment or other novelty.[30]

Correll and his fellow Bren directors worked hard. They parceled
out the costumes, props, scripts, and music that their company supplied, collecting and shipping everything on after each engagement.
They had to see that the company got its full share of the ticket
receipts. They "schooled [their amateur charges] in the art of
makeup"—particularly the use of burnt cork or its equivalent for the
blackface performers. They did the blocking for the shows. They
rehearsed the actors, singers, and dancers, as well as the orchestra,
which also consisted of local people; Correll often led the musicians
from the piano as he played. Beyond all this, the Bren coaches themselves appeared in many of the shows they directed. Their own acts—

which the Bren men had already performed many times—at least did not need to be practiced, and they ensured that each show would contain a few polished moments, no matter how inexperienced the local talent.[31]

Correll and his colleagues also had to promote their shows by winning free coverage of casting and rehearsals in each town's newspapers. It took no prompting by local reporters to draw expansive commentary from the Bren men on the sterling quality of the scripts and the cornucopia of talent they had found in the community. Likewise, Bren's functionaries took care to cultivate the groups that sponsored the shows, on whose good will a repeat engagement for the next year depended. Freeman Gosden, hired by Bren about two years after Correll, could not "say too much about the wonderful executive ability" of the local chairwoman of a Bren show he directed in Alabama in 1922—and he just happened to say it to a local newspaper writer.[32]

Other methods of publicizing shows required just as little money as did judicious flattery of the natives, but demanded more energy and audacity. In at least one town, Correll, Gosden, and a colleague stopped traffic at an intersection by performing clownlike antics in the street and "dash[ing] hither and yon" in front of cars—which, fortunately for them, traveled slowly in those days. The men gave away candy at another crossing, and finally played leapfrog and ring-around-the-rosy in the lobbies of a hotel and a theater. They succeeded in winning the attention of passersby and of the town's newspaper. As another lure, Correll and his fellows often mounted a minstrel parade, in which performers marched through town to the theater shortly before the first evening's show.[33]

Correll and other Bren directors had one further function, which greatly influenced the company's fortunes. On rare occasions, one of the coaches would spot a man in a local show who demonstrated both real talent as a performer and the potential to lead others. The Bren company hired several such men, including Charles Correll and Freeman Gosden, on the recommendation of its directors. Bren trained a new employee in whirlwind fashion by assigning him to a seasoned man for a few days and then sending him out on the road to guide shows himself.

Although some newspaper stories in later years reported that Correll himself discovered Gosden, this was a bit of apocrypha. In reality, the Bren Company's Chicago headquarters ordered Gosden—recently recruited by another director—to serve a week's apprenticeship around the first of September, 1920, with a Bren veteran who was rehearsing a show in Durham, North Carolina. Gosden's assigned mentor was Charles Correll; the two men had never met. Told by an inattentive desk clerk at Correll's hotel in Durham that no Charles Correll was registered there, a nervous Gosden spent the next couple of days seeking his trainer-to-be elsewhere in the city and worrying that his new career would end before it even started. When he heard that the local Elks were rehearsing an amateur show, Gosden went to the site and, to his great relief, found a man at the piano directing the practice who turned out to be Correll. The pair worked together for several days before Gosden went on to Elizabeth City, where he successfully directed a show himself.[34]

By one later account, Gosden filled in as a blackface endman and sang a solo as early as the second night's performance in Durham. When he rejoined Correll in Charlotte—the next stop after Durham and Elizabeth City—the two men teamed up in an act that featured Correll's piano playing, Gosden's dancing, and some comic dialogue. Eventually, Gosden began playing the ukulele in the two men's joint appearances. For the rest of that season and beyond, Correll and Gosden worked together often both in the wings and onstage, with Gosden typically serving also as Correll's advance man.[35]

Correll and Gosden blacked up regularly in the months and years that followed. Correll served when needed as a blackface endman or singer. Gosden, too, often sang and joked in the role of minstrel endman, and he performed his long-time specialty, the monologue— a standard feature of the Bren show's second act. Probably done in blackface, the monologue must have drawn on both the traditional minstrel stump speech and the Joe Cook-style filibusters of Gosden's early days on the Richmond stage: Gosden "put out a rapid fire line of pitter-patter" which, in at least one North Carolina city, "brought wave on wave of applause and appreciation."[36]

In several striking ways, the productions that Correll and Gosden directed resembled the big baroque minstrel shows of the latter nineteenth century. Both traded heavily on elaborate scenery and the ornate garb of their players, and both included numerous performers who did not wear blackface. During Gosden's first season on the road, for instance, the Bren Company set the first act of its show at the winter home of a fictional wealthy family in Palm Beach, Florida. This provided an excuse to use a beautiful set and to dress the "proprietor" of the estate and a chorus of his well-heeled "guests"—all white, of course—in fancy costumes. It also permitted the show to open, before the minstrels themselves came onstage, with a couple of

songs that showed off the women of the cast, whom tradition excluded from the minstrel chorus itself. The "host" then introduced
the entertainment he had secured for his guests—a minstrel troupe of
sixteen to twenty men dressed in flashy red, blue, and green silk suits
with lace trim. Only the comics—the endmen—wore burnt cork.[37]

Correll and Gosden's amateur minstrels performed the traditional
comic repartee between interlocutor and endmen—a rapid alternation
of straight, set-up lines and punch lines. In addition, both blackface
and unblacked members of the minstrel company sang solos. Since
the early days of minstrelsy, burnt-cork artists had rendered both
sentimental and comic songs, and they continued to do so in Gosden
and Correll's shows. The Bren Company's blackfaced protégés, however, had a narrower musical repertoire than the romantic balladeers
of pre-Civil War minstrelsy, who, although blacked up, had sung
serious, sentimental songs in formal clothing and with relatively dignified bearing.

Even those classical balladeers had not broadened the white public's conception of Afro-Americans. Nineteenth-century audiences
came to see the burnt-cork makeup of the balladeer—unlike that of
the endman—as a superficial artifact that did not necessarily link the
singer with the black race of the real world. Blackface balladeers sang
freely of their love for pale, blonde-tressed damsels—sentiments that
no white audience would have accepted from an actor it understood as
actually portraying a black man. Women characters, played by men,
appeared in some shows of the nineteenth century as objects of the
balladeers' affections, but the minstrels had to endow them with
graceful carriage and semi-Caucasian features such as a "yellow" skin
tone before white audiences would accept them as fitting objects of
romantic love. Female characters in other segments of the minstrel
show, known as "funny ol' gals," were just as heavily caricatured as
the male comedians were, and their role was to evoke laughter
through low-comedy antics. It was speech and mannerisms, then, not
burnt cork alone, that determined whether people saw performers as
genuinely, racially black: the comic stereotypes had become the very
definition of "real" blackness.[38]

Minstrels had largely resolved the paradox of the "de-racialized"
balladeer by the time Correll and Gosden came on the scene. In the
Joe Bren shows, performers with white faces were available to sing
obviously "white" songs like "That Old Irish Mother of Mine." So,
while a blacked-up endman could briefly abandon his comic capers to
render "a song of tender sentiment," his few serious songs usually

contained "black" themes or nuances.[39] White listeners now became much less likely to de-racialize the blacked-up singer than they had been in the era when, in all-blackface shows, he had sung of *his* old Irish mother.

This racial division of labor among tear-jerking balladeers could cut two ways. On the one hand, a blackface performer singing of his dear black "mammy," possibly with traces of identifiably "Negro" stage dialect, might suggest something that the essentially raceless, all-purpose burnt-cork balladeer had not: that real Afro-Americans felt universal human emotions. On the other hand, by turning burnt cork into a consistent token of actual racial identity, minstrels like Gosden and Correll made the rest of the package—the massive lips, pop-eyes, extravagant gestures, and ludicrous pretensions of the blackfaced endmen—seem more real, too, and more typical of even the most tenderhearted black man.

In a broader sense, though, the Bren minstrels were following one of the oldest traditions in minstrelsy: portraying Afro-Americans partly as sentimental figures, yet limiting the scope of those sentiments and their prominence in the show. During the first decade of the full-fledged minstrel show, performers had occasionally depicted the sadness or even the resentment of the slave sold away from his family or subjected to other cruelties of bondage. But then, during the 1850s, when agitation over slavery threatened to destroy the Union, minstrels muted or reversed that theme.[40] The slave in Stephen Foster's "My Old Kentucky Home," for example, circumspectly expresses his woe at being sold down the river to the Deep South; he yearns not for freedom, however, but rather for the life he has known with his former master. "Longin' for the old plantation" remained a crucial part of the minstrel character's emotional makeup down to the time of Gosden, Correll, and Joe Bren.

One blackface figure who particularly loved Ol' Massa and was cherished by him in return had become the most popular of minstrel characters after the Civil War and remained a favorite for decades afterward. This was the Old Uncle, the kindly, aged slave, full of affection for his family, "his" white folks, and humankind in general.[41] He was lovable but one-dimensional—Mrs. Stowe's Uncle Tom, minus Tom's moral profundity and his experience of suffering at the hands of whites. Stephen Foster's Old Black Joe might wait for death to take him "to a better land"—but to hear the minstrels tell it, life on earth had been pretty rosy for him, too, at least as long as Ol' Massa still lived. Popular writers helped to keep the Old Uncle very much alive well into Gosden and Correll's young manhood. Joel Chandler Harris's Uncle Remus—whose fables at least had authentic roots in Afro-American folk traditions—epitomizes the type, as do the "good" old slaves and former slaves of Thomas Nelson Page. No wonder, then, that audiences came to Correll and Gosden's minstrel shows in the early 1920s expecting a dose of sentimentality from blackface characters—or that Joe Bren's endmen-soloists offered that quota of "tender sentiment" from behind makeup that grotesquely caricatured Negroid physiognomy. The comical yet lovable stage Negro—an emotional creature with lots of heart if little in the head—had been the safest, most reassuring of fictional black male figures for three quarters of a century.

Tender sentiment, however, always took a back seat to comedy in the blackface performances that Correll and Gosden directed. Endmen in a Joe Bren production rendered at most only a couple of serious songs amid a barrage of humor, much of it racial, which continued after the minstrel chorus itself had left the stage.

The second act of a typical production presented two scenes of "tabloid musical comedy." The cast of characters always included at least one black figure. His name was invariably a joke based on his race, and his role usually a lowly one. Jazz Johnson was "the colored porter" in a hotel, while Indellible (*sic*) held the same job in a railroad station. Blackface redcaps carried luggage in some scenes, and a figure called Sambo waited tables. While the dialogue of the white characters in these skits was comical, too, the black figure in the Bren shows, with his grotesque blackface makeup, his stage dialect, and his stereotyped behavior, was clearly meant to be what one small-town reviewer in Ohio called him: the "principal funmaker" of the sketches.[42]

One fictional blackface character who appeared in some of Joe Bren's musical comedies proved more versatile than Sambo or Indellible. His name—Jefferson Snowball—must have reminded Freeman Gosden of his black boyhood pal back in Richmond, who had also been called Snowball. The Bren shows of 1920 to 1922—Correll and Gosden's first two years as co-workers—portrayed this Snowball as a sort of world traveler who turned up in locales far removed from both the plantation and the "Darktowns" of America's cities. In one of his more mundane incarnations, he assisted a floorwalker in a department store scene. But Snowball also appeared in a comic burlesque of a bullfight set in Spain and starred in another segment as a black aviator in the South Pacific.[43]

To some in the audience, these sketches about Jefferson Snowball the flier may have suggested a possibility that whites in those days rarely considered—that a black man could practice a highly skilled profession. But even Snowball's role as an aviator abounded with hoary racial stereotypes. He was still billed as a "blackface comedian" and provided "the bulk of the humor of the performance." When played by a skillful person, as in one Texas town, Jefferson Snowball could keep the audience in "an almost continuous uproar."[44]

Speaking in "black" stage dialect laden with malapropisms, Snowball at times resembled the classical minstrel stump speaker, whose pretentious, maladroit commentary on politics and current affairs had parodied the self-importance and the fads of the "better" class of whites. But the anti-elitist, satirical sting of the stump speech—its ability to make the yammerings of the white upper crust sound ridiculous—had depended on its being delivered by an ignorant, fatuous blackface character, who claimed a high level of "edjumkation" even as he twisted the English language almost beyond recognition.[45] In the Joe Bren shows, Jefferson Snowball's ludicrous pronouncements on politics and world affairs—for example, his discussion of the League of Nations, which he called the "leakin' nations"[46]—may likewise have packed a satirical punch that went beyond race. But they also conveyed a clear racial message: that blacks lacked the intelligence to comprehend "white folks' business."

Joe Bren's writers designed the aviator sketch, like Snowball's other scenes, to be "a scream of an act," as a Georgia critic called it in his review of a production that Correll and Gosden directed together. The script had the globetrotting Jefferson Snowball land on a Pacific island whose king never smiled. Snowball promised that, if the king would return with him to the United States, he would make the monarch laugh or else pay all the expenses of the trip. A subsequent scene portrayed Snowball's adventures after returning to America.[47] Although surviving descriptions of these skits are short on detail, Snowball's task of provoking the king to laughter must have furnished an ample excuse for comic capers of the traditional sort.

Jefferson Snowball's island scene was not the only one of its kind that Correll and Gosden directed for Bren. The 1920 show, for instance, had portrayed "the Isle of Gazook," complete with a royal court, a chorus of "natives," a musical number called "Jungoland," and a "burlesque love scene."[48] Bren's employees undoubtedly peopled both these islands with blackface characters who resembled the African and island "natives" of the era's comic strips: jet-black figures with huge, pendulous white lips and bug-eyes, who typically carried spears, tended toward cannibalism, and spoke—if at all—with "Me Tarzan"-style, pseudo-pidgin syntax.

Joe Bren's amateur minstrels, then, drew on traditions from various eras. The basic blackface characterizations and the stump speech dated from the antebellum period; popular songs and the funnies had made heavy use of "native" stereotypes at least since America's emergence as a ruler of darker peoples overseas in the latter 1890s. Joe Bren, and his employees Correll and Gosden, wrapped these elements in the elaborate sets, large casts, and sumptuous costumes of the grand, showy minstrel troupes of the 1870s and '80s. And they added yet another mainstay of minstrelsy's post-Reconstruction baroque age: burlesques of serious drama.

Although the high baroque tradition did not dictate that such burlesques be performed in blackface, Correll and Gosden's clients seem to have played at least some of them—like the love scene on the isle of Gazook—in burnt cork. During Gosden's first season with Bren, for example, the show's "travesty on grand opera"—a standard part of the second act—included a "sextet from *Lucia* in ragtime."[49] Ragtime scenes were a blackface specialty in Bren's productions; ragtime music had been created mainly by Afro-Americans, and the public still associated it with blacks. The humor of an opera parody in burnt cork surely revolved—like Jefferson Snowball's latter-day stump speeches—around black stage dialect and the supposed absurdity of any attempt by blacks to embrace "white" learning and culture.

The shows of Freeman Gosden's first season on the road offered another ragtime burlesque in blackface. In one Ohio town, Gosden himself played the lead role in that scene. He and the sketch—called "If They'll Only Play My Wedding March in Ragtime"—aroused such mirth that the local paper described the action in detail. Gosden, as a black preacher, conducted a wedding in which the "dusky bride" was played, in old-time minstrel fashion, by a man in burnt cork. The groom—a standard-issue "coon" who became hopelessly confused when called upon to function in the white man's realm—showed up for the ceremony with a dog license rather than a marriage license. "Preacher" Gosden nevertheless proceeded with the rite, explaining, "That's all right, he'll lead a dog's life anyhow" as a married man.[50] Few scenes could better illustrate so many of the essential fixtures of blackface, minstrel-style comedy and the attitudes that underlay it: the ignorance and ineffectuality of the male "darkey" character; the "funny ol' gal" brand of cross-racial transvestism; and yet another mainstay of classical minstrelsy—comic barbs aimed at wives, mothers-in-law, married life in general, and sometimes at the entire female sex.[51]

Correll and Gosden's amateur shows based their appeal on a couple of elements besides sentimental and comical songs, blackface humor, flashy costumes, and colorful sets. Musical comedies, revues, burlesque, and vaudeville had supplanted minstrelsy in part by bringing pretty women to the stage, and the Bren shows did the same. The Bren men and their clients recruited a "beauty chorus" of young women from each community's respected bourgeoisie—"young . . . matrons[,] debutantes, sub-debs," or the nearest local equivalent. Having assembled a wholesome "bevy" of the town's "most popular and attractive young ladies," the showmen could run advertisements promising "Girls! Girls! Girls! Girls!," yet still avoid any taint of the "girlie" show. The occasional blackface female roles, as in the ragtime wedding scene, were played by men, for laughs. The real, white women in the show were meant to be "Bewildering, Bewitching, Capricious, Captivating."[52]

The Bren shows also featured caricatures of ethnic groups other than blacks. The comic Irishman and German (or "Dutchman") had been prominent in nineteenth-century minstrel shows; vaudeville added Jewish, Italian, and Chinese comic types. The railroad scenes in which Gosden and Correll directed Indellible the porter and Sambo the waiter also included a railway passenger whom the program listed as "Count D'Kackyack, of Hebrew origin."[53] Needless to say, he would not have been so identified if the script had not exaggerated his supposed ethnic traits to draw laughs. A few years later, two of Correll and Gosden's fellow Bren directors would create a radio series around another ethnic specialty, the "Dutch act." The pair, known as "Herr Louie and the Weasel,"[54] very likely had both performed and directed others in "Dutch" routines for the Bren shows.

Still, there was a quantum difference between the treatment of blacks and of "ethnic" whites, both in vaudeville and in the Bren productions. The more firmly a given white group established itself in America, the less tolerant of ethnic slights its members became—and performers toned down their material accordingly. Gosden, Correll, Joe Bren, and their colleagues wrote scripts knowing that their amateur performers, and their audiences as well, often included German-Americans, Irish-Americans, and members of other immigrant nationalities. For example, at least one man with a Jewish surname, presumably a member of the sponsoring Kiwanis Club in West Virginia, appeared in the show whose cast of fictional characters featured the "Hebrew" count.[55] Bren's depictions of figures like the count thus had to be innocuous by the standards of the time.

The "coon," meanwhile, remained the most heavily caricatured of all the ethnic types. The public's appetite for "darkey" comedy had reached a new peak during the 1890s and early 1900s with the vogue of "coon songs" and "coon jokes." Ditties with titles like "He's Just a Little Nigger, But He's Mine, All Mine" and "Hottest Coon in Dixie" gave new life to the most belittling minstrel-show portrayals of blacks. Sometimes adding a dose of malice to the ridicule of old, "coon" material placed more emphasis than ever on physical caricature and on the supposed proclivity of black men to gamble and fight with razors.[56]

"Coon" songs and humor entered countless American homes through sheet music, songbooks, and joke books during the years when Gosden and Correll were growing up; such material furnished a smirking facade for the increasingly malevolent racism of the time. The Bren shows may have avoided the very crudest of these stereotypes. But because the sponsors, performers, and audiences for the shows were all white, Bren's writers did not need to apply the kind of brake in portraying Afro-Americans that they did when writing a Jewish or "Dutch" role.

The Bren men made the most of their freedom in depicting blacks. Bren understood, and Gosden and Correll quickly learned, that blackface comedy was the most potent of the many attractions in their shows. Newspaper publicity for the performances trumpeted "coal-black comedians"; the typical advertisement for Correll and Gosden's minstrel revues sported a drawing of a blackface character with huge, grotesque white lips and eyes. One version of the ad pictured such a character in an eccentrically cut tuxedo alongside a noncaricatured white man in top hat and tails.[57] Old Zip Coon—his hopeless pretensions and obvious inferiority to the white man nearly a century old now—was alive and starring in the Joe Bren shows.

The blackface components of the Bren productions held a special appeal that even the few surviving professional minstrel troupes lacked. Correll, Gosden, and the other Bren directors found that their shows went over best when, in Correll's words, they could "get the mayor, a few lawyers, maybe a college professor" into the minstrel company they put together in each town—if possible, in the role of endmen.[58] Gleeful newspaper accounts of Bren productions show

how thoroughly audiences enjoyed the once-a-year opportunity to see the local elite as blackface comics. One luminary in a North Carolina city "out-darkied any darkey you ever heard of, whether of flesh or fable." A doctor in West Virginia won applause by "turning himself loose without restraint" in Bren shows and proving that he "possessed in a wonderful degree the talent to assume the exaggerated and glorified characteristics of the shuffling, singing Senegambian."[59]

By subjecting themselves to the laughter of their fellow townspeople, these amateur endmen suggested that they were "regular folks"—a distinct asset to a merchant or a politician. But they also tacitly claimed prestige so great and status so secure that they could play the "coon" in public without fearing any loss of face. (The modern "celebrity roast" works on a comparable premise.) These contrasting social meanings of the local notables' blackface capers both depended on one simple, widely shared assumption: that the black man was an inferior and often ridiculous figure.

Joe Bren's directors could count on finding that attitude wherever they went. Far from having to write different material for the North than for supposedly benighted southern audiences, Bren's men could present essentially the same show to spirited applause from New York state and Pennsylvania to Louisiana and Texas—in Kansas and Iowa, Minnesota and Wisconsin, South Dakota and the Canadian province of Ontario. Minstrelsy, after all, had been born in the North and enjoyed its greatest acclaim there. From 1919 to 1921, Correll's engagements in the Midwest and Northeast easily outnumbered those in southern and border states—in the first of those two show seasons, by two to one. And although small cities and towns, especially in Bren's midwestern home region, provided the bulk of the company's clientele, Correll and his colleagues also coached performances in larger cities, not all of them in the old Confederacy: Trenton, Louisville, Atlanta, Nashville, Memphis, New Orleans, and Ottawa in Canada.[60]

Gosden and Correll's years together on the road after World War I confirmed that Jefferson Snowball, like Jim Crow and Zip Coon before him, traveled very well indeed—and not only in the sense of popping up in Spain or on a Pacific isle in the Joe Bren comic sketches. In his appeal to white Americans of all climes—and in his ability not merely to reflect American society's attitudes toward its real black members, but also to rationalize and reinforce them—Jefferson Snowball could justly claim to be a national figure.

4

...➖◉➖...

Inventing Radio and
Toying with Color

On the road for Joe Bren, Freeman Gosden and Charles Correll built the foundation for their future career as radio artists. Working closely with thousands of people in a variety of cities and towns gave them a good understanding of popular tastes and sharpened their skills as performers.[1] But the job was hard and sometimes tedious, and the two men probably welcomed the chance to work mainly in Bren's Chicago office beginning about 1924. Gosden put together a small Joe Bren circus and became its director, while Correll managed the company's amateur show division. Both men still spent part of their time in the hinterland, sometimes traveling and working together.[2]

In addition to his managerial duties, Correll wrote the dialogue for one of Bren's annual amateur show scripts. Gosden may have contributed to his friend's script-writing when he was not embroiled in circus business. Correll, now single after his marriage failed to survive his itinerant years, had taken a room in Chicago's Alexandria Hotel. Employees of the Bren organization often gathered at Correll's place for sing-alongs, which the host accompanied on the piano. Gosden sang there, too, and played his ukulele. He soon began rooming with Correll, and the two men frequently sang and played informal duets.[3]

By 1925 the Bren Company was in a slump; the circus department went out of business altogether. The company meanwhile had assembled acts that included both its own veteran employees and other performers, offering their services for banquets, conventions, exhibitions, and private parties. Gosden and Correll, each playing his musical instrument, appeared as a singing duo and may have done some dancing as well. The pair found little satisfaction or promise, however, in what Correll called "writing and performing . . . for shoe conventions for 10 and 20 bucks a night." Their ambition by this time was to build a career on the vaudeville stage.[4]

Correll and Gosden also dabbled in radio. They had made their first broadcast in New Orleans while directing a Bren amateur production there during the season of 1920–1921. As a publicity stunt for the show, Correll later remembered, the men accepted an invitation to talk over an experimental transmitter—"the kind that used to go on the air if somebody would telephone to ask . . . so he could test his receiving set." Afterwards, a woman called in with the impressive news that she had heard the voices distinctly in her home a full four blocks from the transmitter.[5]

By early 1925, Correll and Gosden took to the airwaves again. Some of the performers affiliated with the Bren Company were then appearing on radio programs in the Chicago area; Gosden and Correll sang once from a small station in Joliet, Illinois, and again on the midnight program of KYW, a major Chicago station. The two friends also served among the endmen on a weekly show presented over station WLS by Bren's own minstrel company.[6]

Around the first of April, 1925, Gosden and Correll took their singing act to station WEBH, which had been on the air only a year, broadcasting from Chicago's Edgewater Beach Hotel. While continuing to work for Bren, the partners sang frequently over WEBH, generally on Friday nights, but more and more often on other evenings as well. In those early days of radio, acts often performed without pay; Gosden and Correll's only compensation came in the form of free dinners at the hotel on the evenings they sang. The new medium of radio interested them mainly as a means to make themselves better known so they could break into vaudeville.[7]

Correll and Gosden had other reasons besides their meager remuneration at WEBH for not taking radio seriously. In 1925, broadcasting was less than five years old, and some still saw it as a mere fad. In Chicago as elsewhere, ordinary people talked about radio and columnists wrote about it. But there were other, hotter topics, like the

Charleston dance and the popular controversy over whether women—
who had won the vote only five years before and were still fighting for
the right to serve on Illinois juries[8]—could "bob" their hair and still
be considered respectable. Many Americans had no idea which if any
of these various novelties reflected anything more than the general
giddiness of the 1920s.

No one denied that radio broadcasting stations had blanketed the
country with remarkable speed. By the time of Correll and Gosden's
debut on WEBH, the number was approaching six hundred, which
officials at the Department of Commerce thought to be the maximum
possible without chaotic interference among signals. Many of these
transmitters, however, were tiny operations which broadcast only a
fraction of the time. Stations closed down and new ones appeared at
a rapid, sometimes dizzying pace. The Secretary of Commerce, Herbert Hoover, took measured and sometimes ineffectual steps to keep
the airwaves from dissolving into anarchy. For his pains, the man who
as President would be damned as too passive in the face of the Great
Depression was attacked in 1925 by some in the industry as a "supreme czar" wielding "one-man control of radio."[9]

People who owned receiving sets avidly picked their way through
the radio thicket, making a sport of pulling in distant signals. Chicago
stations had made a gesture to these aficionados which, by the standards of today's broadcasting industry, seems touchingly gallant.
Banding together in a benign restraint of trade, the station owners had
agreed that Monday would be Chicago's "Silent Night." None of
them would operate then, so that Chicagoans could scan the dial for
faraway stations without interference from local transmitters.[10]

Problems of radio reception were legion, particularly during the
summer. Static and "spark"—hallmarks of the plague known as
"summer reception"—led newspapers to publish tips on "How to
Coax Your Radio in Heated Months." One entrepreneur offered an
invention called the Statichoke. He promised that his device would
eliminate "the agony of static," a malady that radio owners in 1925
found even graver than the heartbreak of psoriasis. Fortunately for
Correll and Gosden, the static often diminished by their broadcast
time of 9:30 or 11:30 P.M., enabling more people in distant parts to
hear their act. Yet even at night and in the cooler months, a newspaper columnist in Chicago reported, the chorus of snap, crackle, and
pop could make "radio life . . . unlovely" and even "vicious." Radio
listeners in the mid-1920s also suffered from fading signals and wave-
length drift—the tendency of stations to move away from their orig-

inal locations on the dial. Although the problem of drift occurred less often by 1925 than it had earlier, one writer complained at the beginning of that year that tuning was "slipping back rapidly to the guess 'em period."[11]

Given all these difficulties, the radio page found in most major newspapers devoted much attention to technical developments and attempts to regulate the broadcasting industry. In 1925, coverage of the content of shows and of radio stars—of whom there were still very few—was just beginning to come into its own. Articles on the newly invented light current tube or about a trader in the Arctic who picked up a station transmitting from Springfield, Massachusetts, got prominent play. And editors still assumed they could catch the reader's eye with riveting headlines proclaiming, "Expert Tells How Potentiometer Acts" and "British Plan New Radio Bill." A new folk art arose in the land aiming to improve radio reception, but its nostrums were not foolproof. Some listeners discovered that their bedsprings—while still inside the bed—made a good antenna, but a radio columnist for the Chicago *Daily News* warned his readers that lying on the bed during a broadcast could ruin everything by changing the length of the "aerial."[12]

With all its problems, though, radio had begun to prove itself. The national political conventions of 1924 and the presidential inauguration of Calvin Coolidge in 1925 had been the first ever broadcast; a chain of nearly twenty stations had carried them throughout the country.[13] Radio stations had demonstrated that they could cover football, baseball, and other sports live from the scene. By the mid-1920s, some of those involved in the medium even expected a new form of radio—called television—to appear within a few years. Many already saw in radio the potential for reaching and influencing large audiences. The Ku Klux Klan in the summer of 1925 announced its desire to set up a chain of KKK stations—possibly based in New Jersey, Indiana, Texas, and several southern states—if the Commerce Department made any new bands available.[14]

Still, American radio in 1925 lacked something essential—something that even clear, reliable reception could not have provided. Radio programs, as critic Wilson Wetherbee put it in the Chicago *Tribune*, had consistently failed to show that "certain 'flair' which would . . . establish them as a kind of entertainment entirely different from that which might be found in the theater or concert hall. . . . [T]he radio technique," he complained, "has yet to be discovered." What radio needed, Wetherbee thought, were "new ideas," along with some means of weaving the varied components of a given broadcast into an organic continuity that would be unique to the infant medium.[15]

Correll and Gosden offered nothing of the kind. During some seven months on WEBH, they generally shared a bill with other musical acts to which they had no connection. Their songs and their delivery were no different from what listeners could find in the vaudeville theater or on any number of other radio shows; male harmony duos were a dime a dozen at the time. The pair did manage to parlay their performances on WEBH into a bit of publicity here and there. Their picture occasionally appeared in the local press, and a publishing company sold sheet music of some of the songs they broadcast— sentimental or lighthearted fare with titles like "Head Over Heels in Love" and "I'm Knee Deep in Daisies." Each of these scores for piano and ukulele sported a photograph of the men posing rakishly in formal dress with the tools of their musical trade; the song sheets identified the duo as "exclusive artists" of WEBH.[16]

Gosden and Correll found these small successes a modest return at best on their investment of time and effort over the airwaves. They would have preferred, at a minimum, that their "exclusive" relationship with WEBH embrace the notion of a (nonedible) salary. After some five months on the air, the two concluded that their hopes for a career in vaudeville lay in a direct assault upon the ramparts of the "real" show world. While still working for Joe Bren and singing on WEBH, they wrote a musical comedy revue and submitted it to bandleader Paul Ash, who was then appearing at the McVickers Theater in Chicago's Loop. Ash bought the show and asked Gosden and Correll to appear in it.[17]

This was a real coup: one Chicago movie columnist reported that a hundred or more amateurs wrote Ash every week "just dying" to try out for his shows. Ash, a bushy-haired German-American, led a large, "semi-symphonic" jazz orchestra; his band became popular in both New York and Chicago in the mid- to late 1920s, and he employed the young Benny Goodman and Glenn Miller. Staging a new musical revue each week at the McVickers, Ash had won a big following in 1925, especially among women, a thousand of whom were said to have formed a club pledged to attend all of his productions.[18]

The show that Correll and Gosden wrote for Ash was a brief one. The maestro performed four or five times a day; because he shared the bill with a movie, each of his appearances ran no longer than about twenty minutes. (This combination of film and live show had already become common by 1925, although most people did not yet recognize it as a step in the decline of vaudeville and stage revues in favor of motion pictures.) With a cast of two or even three dozen people, Ash typically presented several solo and duo acts and a "musical comedy" segment.[19]

Gosden and Correll's revue, called *Red Hot*, offered music in blues, Charleston, and jazz styles, a solo "dancing dynamo," an organist, a "harmonica blue blower," and "Harmony Syncopation" by Correll and Gosden, who as usual sang to the accompaniment of their own instruments. The pair also performed a segment called "A Night with the Mind Reader," inspired by a mind-reading stunt they had often done in the Joe Bren shows. Gosden and Correll's song was a popular fox-trot number called "The Kinky Kid's Parade." In a comical-sentimental vein, the song's lyric evoked the antics of a group of black children—the "kinky kids" of the title.[20]

Audiences seemed to agree with poet and author Carl Sandburg—who at the time was writing an entertainment column for a Chicago newspaper—when he called *Red Hot* "a snappy dancing, singing, mirth making show." Gosden and Correll's revue went over so well during its week-long run that another bandleader associated with Ash used the show to kick off his own heavily promoted run at the Pantheon Theater on Chicago's North Side.[21] Delighted with their success, Gosden and Correll wrote another show, working largely in their dressing room between performances of *Red Hot*. *Paul Ash in Hollywood* opened for a week's run at the McVickers in early October 1925, less than a month after the premiere of their earlier show. The two men's new script combined "a jazz satire on the doings of the sheiks and shebas of filmland" with a local touch—a "Chicago Travesty" called "A Night in Crook County Jail."[22]

Even though Ash's advertising did not mention them by name, Gosden and Correll hoped that his shows would begin a new chapter in their career. The partners accepted offers to broadcast on a radio program in Columbus, Ohio, and to perform for two weeks in St. Louis. They resigned from the Bren organization, quit WEBH, and prepared for further appearances on the stages of movie theaters in Chicago.[23]

The two men sought leads from a booking agent who worked for a theater chain. Sometime in the fall of 1925, the agent learned that WGN, the Chicago *Tribune*'s radio station, was looking for a harmony duo. Henry Selinger, music and program director of the station and himself a radio performer billed for a time as "the Phantom Violin," had failed to sign a team with a big name. Probably after listening to Gosden and Correll on WEBH and seeing them in *Red Hot*, Selinger offered to hire them as "staff artists" at a weekly salary of $100 or $125 each. This was no quantum jump in their income; still, the position at WGN looked much better to the pair than their old job at WEBH or their prospects had they stayed with Joe Bren. For their pay, Gosden and Correll performed a variety of tasks: preparing and presenting their own act as they had on WEBH, writing, announcing, and, in Correll's words, doing "everything but sweeping up the studio."[24]

Gosden and Correll's boyhood stage performances, and then their livelihood with the Bren Company, had depended largely on a type of entertainment—minstrelsy—that purported to imitate blacks. In 1925, the two men had got their first big break with Paul Ash, whose shows catered to white people's infatuation with jazz and other musical forms created by Afro-Americans. The pair's success on the McVickers stage had owed something to a song about "kinky kids." And now, at WGN, the perennial appetite of the white public for comical and sentimental portrayals of blacks changed Gosden and Correll's lives forever.

At first, the two men's performances on WGN resembled those of the previous half-year at WEBH. The pair worked hard, performing in one-hour blocks twice each evening, five days a week. Billed as "harmony kings" and later as "the two song birds," they presented hits of the day, sometimes with humorous lyrics written by Gosden. And just before Christmas of 1925, the men began recording songs for the Victor Talking Machine Company.[25]

Partly because they had so much air time to fill, Gosden and Correll added "happy banter and jesting" between their musical numbers. The pair rendered some of this material in "black" stage dialect, which came naturally after years of experience in the genre. Likewise, one of the two songs Correll and Gosden recorded in their first session for Victor was the same "Kinky Kids' Parade" that they had sung in Paul Ash's *Red Hot*. Victor did not release the record; at about the same time, the company was producing versions of the number by both the Duncan Sisters and bandleader Paul Whiteman—well-known artists who would sell better than Correll and Gosden. Nevertheless, the two men sang "The Kinky Kids" on WGN from time to time, adding some blackface "patter."[26]

Meanwhile, Ben McCanna, a *Tribune* executive with authority over the radio station, was searching for what columnist Wilson Wetherbee had called for earlier in 1925, and what no one had yet provided: a new kind of program that would make the most of radio's assets. Soon after Correll and Gosden arrived at WGN, McCanna had an idea. As a newspaperman, he knew how faithfully readers followed the comic strips. A serial "radio theater," with a regular cast of characters offering "bits of drama and musically pictured incident," might win the kind of audience that never missed the daily adventures of Little Orphan Annie and Moon Mullins. McCanna and Selinger asked Correll and Gosden to develop a radio series based on the comic-strip family known as *The Gumps*.[27]

Gosden and Correll proposed instead a comedy about a couple of black characters. Gosden felt that he knew Afro-Americans, and the two men's entire career up to the mid-'20s had prepared them for nothing if not to play comical black roles. The countless depictions of blacks that they had seen, read, and acted over the years had taught the pair what seemed to them an axiom. It would last them a lifetime. "We chose black characters," Gosden said a half-century later, "because blackface could tell funnier stories than whiteface comics."[28]

When Gosden and Correll broadcast the adventures of their "two Negro characters from Birmingham" beginning on January 12, 1926, they conveyed their story without benefit of the "musically pictured incident" that Ben McCanna had suggested. Indeed, almost the only sounds in *Sam 'n' Henry* were the voices of Correll and Gosden reading the dialogue they had written themselves. Six nights a week, at 10:00 or 10:10, the team spoke for ten minutes. Their nightly introduction, given by the Scottish-American announcer and WGN station executive Bill Hay, consisted at most of a few sentences. For weeks, Hay never mentioned Gosden and Correll's names on the air; they feared that a flop as Sam 'n' Henry might hinder their career as a singing team.[29] Their show was unpretentious and, by later standards, downright threadbare. Just the same, *Sam 'n' Henry* offered something new: a situation comedy which told a continuing story.

Hardworking, sentimental Sam Smith and lazy, pretentious, domineering Henry Johnson took the long train ride, so familiar to many thousands of black Americans, from the Deep South to Chicago. Confused by the ways of the big city, they waited for hours on a street corner for change from a driver to whom they had paid taxi fare; he never came back. Several urban sharpers bilked the credulous newcomers. Meanwhile, they found a rooming house on Chicago's black South Side. After working on a construction site and in a meatpacking plant, the pair opened a hauling business using a rickety wagon pulled by a horse named Gram'pa. At first Sam pined for the sweetheart he had left behind in Alabama, but at the same time, he and Henry made friends. They joined a fraternity, the Jewels of the Crown, and came under the influence of that order's formidable but shifty leader, known as the Most Precious Diamond.

And to the surprise of Gosden and Correll, people listened. Many of those who tuned in got "hooked" on the story line. Station WGN quickly began to promote the addiction, chronicling fans' enthusiastic response in the pages of the *Tribune* and urging the public through billboards to "Follow the Radio Comic Strip." Only a few months into the series, Gosden and Correll missed two broadcasts; the *Tribune* said it received 2,500 calls from concerned listeners on the first evening alone. By the time *Sam 'n' Henry* was a year old, fans were writing to WGN from as far away as New York State, and Gosden and Correll had entertained a crowd of some 15,000 workers in a single appearance at a factory in the team's home town of Chicago.[30]

It must have seemed ironic to the would-be vaudeville singers that, although their musical show remained popular, their renown as "humorous colored boys" eclipsed their image as "harmony wizards" within a few months of *Sam 'n' Henry*'s premiere. In the fall of their new show's first year, and again in 1927, Sam 'n' Henry were the only act from west of the Appalachians invited to perform at the annual Radio Industries Banquet in New York, which in the latter year was carried throughout the country over some eighty stations. When their employer, the *Tribune*, proudly announced the pair's selection for the 1927 broadcast, it saw no reason to mention their real names; even the accompanying photos, where the stars wore no blackface makeup, identified the two men simply as "Sam" and "Henry"—the only names much of the public now knew them by.[31]

In exploiting Sam 'n' Henry's appeal, WGN went so far as to include them in the station's special remote broadcasts of sporting events. The pair offered their observations in stage dialect from the Jack Dempsey–Gene Tunney heavyweight boxing rematch—the famous "long count" fight of 1927—and from the Kentucky Derby and the Indianapolis 500 auto race (where they also sang) in both 1926 and 1927.[32]

Gosden and Correll meanwhile recorded several dozen songs for the Victor Company. These met a kinder fate than the unreleased "Kinky Kids' Parade" of December 1925, but here, too, Sam 'n' Henry became bigger draws than Correll and Gosden. Victor issued records of some fourteen *Sam 'n' Henry* dialogues and began to include snatches of the characters' blackface patter on Correll–Gosden musical discs. In its promotions, Victor took care to identify the singers by their fictional names in addition to—or even instead of—their real ones. Stores in cities as far from Chicago as Philadelphia, Richmond, and New Orleans advertised both the comedic and the musical records, for listeners in many parts of the United States could receive WGN at least occasionally.[33]

The *Tribune* found new ways to profit from the team's popularity. Every Sunday during much of 1927, the newspaper published the script of a current *Sam 'n' Henry* episode, written in "dialect" and accompanied by caricatures of the principal characters in action. The paper used the feature as one of the main selling points for its new Metropolitan Section—a weekly collection of humor columns, adventure narratives, and other attractions—and it syndicated the *Sam 'n' Henry* column to other newspapers. The *Tribune*—whose circulation sometimes surpassed one million—commissioned a survey of women readers; Gosden and Correll's columns turned out to be by far their favorite feature in the Metropolitan Section. Meanwhile, a publisher in Chicago produced a book containing two dozen *Sam 'n' Henry* episodes, offering it for sale in stores and even through the Montgomery Ward catalogue.[34]

A local company manufactured a Sam 'n' Henry children's toy. It consisted of a red and yellow horse-drawn wagon made of metal, on which sat miniature sponge-rubber figures of Sam and Henry. Another manufacturer introduced a five-cent Sam 'n' Henry candy bar; its wrapper lured consumers with caricatures of Sam and Henry, each alongside a characteristic phrase from the radio series. The producer of the candy bar promoted it to stores far beyond Chicago, assuring them that *Sam 'n' Henry*'s "national" renown would lead to good sales.[35]

Although their regular salary at WGN may never have exceeded $150 a week per man, Gosden and Correll's new popularity paid off in other ways. The two men organized "radio revues"—personal appearances by WGN's regular artists, with Gosden and Correll's own act as the climax. On their days off, the pair performed, often in blackface, in movie theaters, before civic organizations and private clubs, and at radio exhibitions in Illinois and neighboring states. Correll later recalled that *Sam 'n' Henry* had become "a gold mine," from which he and Gosden earned $800 and up for each outside engagement.[36]

Gosden and Correll now understood that their future lay mainly in their blackface characterizations. The pair asked WGN to let them record their *Sam 'n' Henry* episodes and lease the records to other radio stations throughout the country. WGN, jealous of its monopoly on the popular series, refused. Even though the *Tribune* owned the rights to their show and its title, Correll remembered later, "We were just young and gutsy enough to quit."[37]

In February 1928, as the contract for their second year as Sam 'n' Henry lapsed, the pair set out on a whirlwind thirty-day personal appearance tour. They performed in fifteen cities ranging from Birmingham to Louisville and from Dallas to Wichita, Kansas. They knew their show had built up a following, but, as Correll once said of the tour, "we were almost surprised out of our skins the way people stormed the box offices." At about the same time, the two men accepted an offer from their erstwhile employer's rival—station WMAQ, the outlet of the Chicago *Daily News*—to begin broadcasting a *Sam 'n' Henry*–like serial in mid-March 1928. The *Daily News* would also publish and syndicate to other newspapers a daily comic strip, drawn by a staff artist with dialogue supplied by Gosden and Correll, which would portray their radio characters' nightly adventures. The two performers agreed to perform on a separate, half-hour minstrel program each week, and they would continue recording both dialogues and songs for Victor.[38]

Gosden and Correll had to rename their radio characters, since the *Tribune* owned the rights to Sam 'n' Henry. When the partners drafted their first two scripts for WMAQ, they called their principals Jim and Charley. Not satisfied, the pair rechristened the leads Tom and Harry in the next two installments they wrote. Even then, as the new show's broadcast debut neared, the search for the "right" names continued. Gosden, Correll, and their publicists told different stories over the years about how the men made their final choice. Their mini-biography of 1929, for example, assured fans that they had "made a study of the more common names used in the South by colored people." In fact, the men based their choices simply on euphony and appropriateness to the personality of each character.[39]

"A telephone book suggested Amos," Gosden said in 1939. The men first used that name in the second script they wrote, but only for a minor character. Then the partners decided that the name Amos sounded like the figure known earlier as Sam—"sort of meek and inoffensive," as Gosden put it. Correll later recalled that the name's biblical association, too, had appealed to him and Gosden, since they wanted to portray the former Sam as "a character of virtue."[40]

The men then sought a second name beginning with the letter "A" for the domineering figure once called Henry. As Gosden told the story, "we both liked the important sound of Andrew," which they quickly shortened to Andy. To Correll, that sounded "pleasant, round and juicy"—and thus well-suited to a voluble character whom Correll's deep-voiced performance and newspaper illustrations alike portrayed as big and beefy.[41] So it was not Jim 'n' Charley or Tom 'n' Harry, but rather Amos 'n' Andy, whom listeners heard in the first broadcast of the new series on March 19, 1928.

Gosden and Correll made other superficial changes in their daily drama. Amos and Andy, new Chicagoans like Sam and Henry, now hailed from the area of Atlanta. Sam and Henry's fraternity, the Jewels of the Crown, had dubbed its officers and its lower ranks with the names of various gems. Amos and Andy's lodge called itself the Mystic Knights of the Sea and took its hierarchical appellations from the world of ichthyology. Accordingly, the leader of the lodge, known to Sam and Henry as the Most Precious Diamond, now became the Kingfish, who was assisted by the Whale, Swordfish, Mackerel, and Shad. Where the principals of Gosden and Correll's earlier series had opened a hauling business with an aged horse, Amos and Andy turned a roofless jalopy into the Fresh Air Taxi Company. These alterations were small enough to allow any fan of *Sam 'n' Henry* to transfer her loyalty to *Amos 'n' Andy* without missing a beat.

The big change came in the method of broadcasting the show. Experiments with hookups between radio stations for shared broadcasts had begun as early as 1923, and New York station WEAF had put together a chain of a dozen stations by 1925.[42] But national networks, which would dominate the broadcasting industry within a few years, were still in the formative stage. Gosden and Correll therefore created what they called a "chainless chain." They wrote *Amos 'n' Andy* and recorded the episodes on discs six weeks or more in advance. They then sent copies at no charge to radio stations that would agree to broadcast the show for a month. Thirty or forty stations that sampled the series became paying subscribers after the trial run; six nights a week, interested listeners from Boston to California could now count on hearing the adventures of Amos and Andy.[43]

Gosden and Correll forged their "chain" out of primitive technology. Since a disc in those days could only hold about five minutes of material, they had to divide each ten-minute episode in half, putting the two parts on separate records. The stations were supposed to play them on double turntables to keep the dialogues continuous. Nevertheless, the scripts from those days contain handwritten interpolations of "stalling" dialogue—for example, one character asking another for a match and the second fumbling about for one—at the halfway point of each episode. Gosden and Correll designed these interludes to cover up any gap in syndicated broadcasts between the end of the first disc of an episode and the beginning of the second.

Gosden wanted each show to be perfect, but he and Correll could not even play back a master recording until the record factory plated and stamped it. When the pair finally received the finished discs, any mistake or flaw required that they redo the entire master and then wait for it, too, to be processed. As a result, Gosden and Correll's scriptwriting and their twice-weekly recording sessions consumed much of their time.

The pair realized, too, that their makeshift chain had a limited future. They tried to imitate a real network by having stations air each episode at the same hour—7:11 P.M. Central Time—that Gosden and Correll broadcast the same installment live from WMAQ; they also required stations to return the records after that one playing. But on some of their subscriber stations, programs provided by real radio chains—those connected by wires—soon preempted Gosden and Correll's preferred time. The partners had to sacrifice their wish for a simultaneous nationwide broadcast, allowing some stations to play the show at 10:00 P.M.

Still, the chainless chain made *Amos 'n' Andy* even more famous than *Sam 'n' Henry* had been. Sixteen months after the new show's debut, the *Telegram* of New York—not a city easily impressed by new acts—could say that Amos 'n' Andy had "made national radio reputations." A continent away, another paper reported that many Californians listened to the team every night. Rand McNally published a book containing the history of the *Amos 'n' Andy* show and its creators, descriptions of the characters in the series and of Gosden and Correll's broadcasting technique, answers to fans' questions, a sample script, and numerous photographs of the two radio stars both in and out of character. Correll and Gosden themselves remained obscure figures; glowing newspaper articles about their act might still confuse one man with the other or mangle their real names in a variety of ways. But the fictional Amos 'n' Andy were fast becoming coast-to-coast celebrities.[44]

Not long before the *Telegram* declared Amos 'n' Andy stars, the formidable Pantages theater chain signed Gosden and Correll to play its houses in eight western cities. The pair, who had kept in performing trim through personal appearances in their new radio roles around Chicago, devoted May and June of 1929 to this grand tour, visiting Los Angeles, San Francisco, Fresno, San Diego, Salt Lake City, Kansas City, Memphis, and Minneapolis. Pantages promoted the team's shows in every conceivable way. Retailers in the eight cities seized the chance to cloak their products in *Amos 'n' Andy*'s aura; they hawked merchandise ranging from radios to bottled water by tying in their newspaper advertising to the duo's visit. Ads for the performances themselves, combined with such tie-ins, could fill one or even two full pages of a daily newspaper.[45] The two stars became "the central figures at civic receptions" and parades; they played to full, even record-breaking houses several times a day for one or two weeks in each city, and made radio broadcasts from local stations as well. Amos 'n' Andy proved such a "sensation" that other acts on the bill were shortened to let Gosden and Correll extend theirs.[46]

Amos 'n' Andy's triumphs caught the eye of Lord & Thomas, the prestigious advertising agency, and of the National Broadcasting Company. The agency suggested that one of its clients, Pepsodent toothpaste, sponsor the radio series on one of NBC's two national chains. Executives at NBC knew that *Amos 'n' Andy* drew large radio audiences each evening in many of the cities where the company had affiliates. Preferring to embrace rather than fight Gosden and Correll, NBC called them to its Chicago office, which it had opened only a year and a half earlier.[47]

The two performers knew they were bargaining from strength, and they got a rich deal from NBC: $100,000 a year for a fifteen-minute show six nights per week. They would also make personal appearance tours, which the network would organize and promote. NBC would provide a microphone and an engineer for them at each stop on these tours so that they could broadcast their series live every night.[48] On August 19, 1929, Amos and Andy—now residing in Harlem instead of Chicago's South Side—made their debut on the NBC Blue network. Just over four years after they first sang on the radio for a free hotel dinner, Gosden and Correll had the ear of the entire United States.

···◄◉►···

In early May of 1929, a few months before the NBC deal, Freeman Gosden and Charles Correll arrived in San Francisco for their engagement at the Pantages Theater. The two performers reached the city by ferry. As they debarked, the radio stars "were literally swept off their feet" by some of the thousands of friendly, curious citizens who awaited them. The city's mayor and chief of police met Gosden and Correll, and the pair climbed into an open touring car labeled "Fresh Air Taxi" in honor of Amos and Andy's fictional vehicle. The car joined a parade of other, similarly decorated automobiles, which had assembled to convey the two visitors from the ferry slip to San Francisco's civic center.[49]

"Many thousands" of spectators lined Market Street along Gosden and Correll's route to the civic center, a local reporter wrote. The same journalist assured his readers that the crowd included "large sprinklings of colored folk who enjoy Amos 'n' Andy." The two radio performers, he explained, "never slur or make fun of the colored race, and portray their characters in a human, appealing manner at all times."[50]

Still more thousands congregated at San Francisco's city hall, where the mayor and the police chief formally greeted Gosden and Correll and exchanged witticisms with them on the building's front steps. Gosden, in the voice of Amos, wailed that character's trademark answer to Andy's exhortations and incitements: "I ain't goin' *do* it! I ain't goin' *do* it!" The crowd broke into laughter and cheers.[51]

The next night, a packed house awaited Amos 'n' Andy's appearance at the Pantages. But at the announced curtain time, the curtain did not move. Instead, the audience heard a disembodied, five-minute Amos 'n' Andy dialogue, "broadcast" over a loudspeaker. The curtain finally opened to reveal the office of the Fresh Air Taxicab Company. As was his custom, a sleeping Andy reclined in his swivel chair. The ever-industrious Amos entered, carrying two tires, and reported the day's profit-and-loss figures: he had earned thirty-five cents, but had been forced to spend thirty-five cents on gasoline. "Den we ain't los' nothin'," a complacent Andy replied.[52]

The pair then played out a couple of their best-known routines. Andy dictated a letter to Amos, "who painfully picked out the letters on his typewriter" amid much confused discussion between the two men of how certain words should be spelled. Next Amos, though thrown off balance by his own shyness and by heavy-handed coaching from Andy on the sidelines, did his best to conduct a long-distance phone conversation with his sweetheart, Ruby Taylor.[53]

Then came the big surprise. Gosden and Correll pulled off their black, wiry-haired wigs and, with a single tug on a special drawstring, jettisoned the baggy, ill-matched clothing of Amos and Andy to reveal the formal attire they always wore for their singing performances. As the two men walked to the front of the stage, a change of lighting played on a new kind of makeup they wore, turning the blacked-up pair instantly white. The metamorphosis drew an excited buzz of surprise and then a burst of laughter and applause. Someone rolled out a piano; Correll sat down and began playing, and the duo, abandoning all traces of "black" speech, sang one of their standard songs.[54]

Now Gosden and Correll offered one more surprise. They presented another favorite *Amos 'n' Andy* bit, reverting to their usual "black" stage dialect—but without abandoning their now-white faces and formal garb. In this scene, Amos and Andy puzzled over their accounts; Andy ended the discussion by "proving" to Amos that seven times thirteen made twenty-eight. The content of the sketch was standard vaudeville stuff, but the incongruity between the men's Caucasian appearance and their "Negro" speech was extraordinary. It exactly reversed the tradition of the blacked-up romantic balladeers of minstrelsy and vaudeville who often sang like whites. Unlike those time-honored acts, whose audiences had long ago ceased to pay much conscious attention to the gratuitous burnt cork, Gosden and Correll's show created "the odd impression of seeing one act and listening to another." The public reacted with near abandon. At this and other performances in San Francisco over the next two weeks, thunderous applause brought Gosden and Correll back onstage for a curtain call. "The only way they escape[d]," a reporter wrote, was "to make a closing speech and beat it" so that the theater could show its movie feature.[55]

···—◉—···

Gosden, Correll, and their creations Amos and Andy had come a long way toward stardom even before they joined NBC; their reception in San Francisco and other cities in the late spring and early summer of 1929 proved that. They needed no new gimmicks. Why, then, did the pair alternate between "black" and white on that tour in the way they did?

Radio fans wondered what the broadcasters of *Amos 'n' Andy* looked like. The pair's quick-change performances, like the parades and "civic receptions," capitalized on that curiosity by revealing the real people behind the blackface characters.[56] Gosden and Correll may also have wanted to share—in their own, true identities—some of the acclaim that had made the names and voices of their fictional alter egos far better known than their own. Then too, the switch from blackface to white, and then to "black" dialogue with white faces, called attention to Gosden and Correll's virtuosity as impersonators, and it filled vaudeville's prescription for keeping an audience's atten-

tion: give people something unusual every so often, and avoid showing them any one thing for more than a few minutes at a time.

But Gosden and Correll's chameleonlike alternation between
black and white grew out of something deeper, too. This was their
grasp—however unarticulated and distorted—of a principle that the
black scholar and activist W. E. B. Du Bois had stated twenty-six
years earlier: that the problem of the twentieth century was the problem of the color line. The white creators of *Amos 'n' Andy* certainly did
not see race as a "problem" in anything like the way that Du Bois did.
But they instinctively recognized, and their popularity seemed to
confirm, white Americans' age-old fascination with race and with the
"exotic" Afro-American—a fascination mingled with condescension
and often with fear and disgust, but a profound one just the same.
Since World War I, that ancient national obsession had become more
volatile and fraught with uncertainty as tens of thousands of Afro-
Americans moved to northern cities and black activists pressed their
case for racial equality. On their Pantages tour in 1929, Gosden and
Correll played heavily on white America's shifting but still intense
race-consciousness. They did so by jumping back and forth across the
color line in a manner both cavalier and surreal—indeed, in a way that
caused the line, in the last moments of each show, to blur altogether.

In many ways, *Amos 'n' Andy* offered nothing new. After all, to
portray Andy as an indolent blowhard gave solid support to a stereotype at least as old as Zip Coon. So did the suggestion that he and
Amos, even when they pooled their powers, could barely manage to
write a letter and fared even worse when faced by an arithmetic
problem. Here Gosden and Correll simply joined all the other impersonators of Afro-Americans whose names crowded the annals of popular entertainment for the previous century.

But the two performers did more than just this in San Francisco. For
one thing, they presented Amos as a character who, whatever his limitations, was not only lovable—as many stage blacks had been since the
days of Stephen Foster's Old Black Joe—but also determined to improve himself through honest effort. Could Gosden and Correll perhaps transcend the stereotypes of their own act? Or would they, in the
end, go the easy and obvious route, presenting an occasional good, safe
black figure like Amos while using him and their other characters
mainly as hooks on which to hang "coon" jokes? Either way, the white
actors' unique way of toying with color on the stage left the distinct
impression that for them race was not incidental, their black stage identities no mere habit or prop. Color played a central role in their art.

5

•••━●━•••

The Great Black Migration into America's Living Room

Of all the changes that the First World War brought to American life, one was obvious at a glance: what had long been a slow, steady stream of southern blacks to northern cities swelled into a flood—a Great Migration. The war in Europe cut off the flow of immigrants coming from the Old World to work the factories of the United States—at the very time those plants were gearing up to supply the Allies in their total war against the Central Powers. The industries of the American Northeast and Midwest until then had generally used black workers either as strikebreakers or not at all; but now management had to look south for the unskilled hands it needed to operate the assembly lines.

The blandishments of labor recruiters helped to propel tens and eventually hundreds of thousands of Afro-Americans to New York, Chicago, Philadelphia, Detroit, and other cities. Exuberant reports from the pioneers of the migration reached the ears of those they had left behind, and the black exodus quickened. Chicago's black population, for example, rose from 44,000 to 109,000 during the decade ending in 1920.[1] The northern states had always been home to some of America's blacks, and the northern ghetto had begun to develop by the beginning of the twentieth century. But this new migration, which would continue for much of the next five decades, helped to create a radically new landscape—both physical and social—in the cities of the United States.

It was the blacks of the Great Migration whom *Sam 'n' Henry* and *Amos 'n' Andy* attempted to portray. Neither series wasted any time getting its two central figures out of the South—and under circumstances that resonated in many ways with the real experience of thousands of Afro-Americans. Early in the very first episode of *Sam 'n' Henry*, the two central characters arrive, packed and ready to go, at the Birmingham railroad station. Sam reads aloud to the ticket salesman an offer of employment from a construction company in Chicago, which has received Sam and Henry's names from its southern recruiter. The two friends are rolling toward the big city before the first ten-minute installment of the series ends.[2]

When their remodeled radio series made its debut in March 1928, Gosden and Correll had Amos and Andy tarry a little longer in Georgia than their precursors had done in Alabama; the new show took all of five episodes to get Amos and Andy chugging northward. Gosden and Correll used those first few days to establish the bucolic character of Amos and Andy's life in Georgia, to depict the excitement and the apprehensions of southern blacks facing the fateful journey north, and to lay the foundation for one of the major early themes of the series: the travails of the countryman newly arrived in the city.

The announcer opened the very first installment of *Amos 'n' Andy* by informing the audience that the principals "have heard good high salaried jobs are available" in Chicago. The prospect of moving there so enthralls Amos—who is milking a cow when first introduced to the listeners—that half the milk he extracts misses the bucket. The deep-voiced Andy expresses a feeling shared by many Afro-Americans in the southern countryside: "Dis job we got now aint no good. If we git up to Chicago, son, we kin make some big money."[3]

But not everything Amos and Andy have heard about the North is as appealing as the prospect of high wages. Their friend Jim, whom they meet by chance in town during the second episode, tells the pair about some friends who have migrated to Chicago. Far from getting rich, two of these have been forced to write home for money. Another man's ears have frozen as he searched for work in the cold. For Amos, a worrier by nature, such stories heighten the fear of the unknown that tempers the thirst for change.[4]

Indeed, southern blacks of the Great Migration—even young, single men like Amos and Andy[5]—seldom pulled up stakes without a care or a look back, and Gosden and Correll portrayed that truth. Sam/Amos's sorrow at leaving his friends—and especially his ladyfriend—conveyed briefly but poignantly the pain that accompanied the optimism of the Great Migration. In *Amos 'n' Andy*, homesickness reared its head early and emphatically. Its victim, naturally, was the sentimental Amos. Toward the end of the fifth episode, as their Chicago-bound train rolls across north Georgia, he muses, "Look out dere at all de farms an ev'vything—yo' know I kind-a hate to leave dis heah part o' de country." With typical bravado, Andy admonishes his partner not to get "cold feet. . . . Nuthin' gets me mo' regusted. . . ." But even Andy softens as the train pulls into Chattanooga. Amos decides to step off the train for a moment:

Andy: Whut yo' wanna do—stretch yo' legs?
Amos: No, I jus' wanna git my feet in Dixie once mo'—dat's all.
Andy: Wait a minute—I'll go wid yo'—come on, let's go.[6]

Thus the first week of Gosden and Correll's new series ended with a fond look backward, even as its characters left the South for good.

Afro-American emigrants, like people who came to the New World from Europe and Asia, did cherish fond memories of the old home. Well before World War I, southern-born blacks in northern cities formed organizations with names like the Sons and Daughters of South Carolina and the Sons of Virginia,[7] much as Jews from eastern Europe—to cite but one example—formed *landsmanshaftn* with fellow emigrants according to the towns or regions of their origin. But the Great Afro-American Migration resembled other large population shifts in a second way, too—it arose from conditions that pushed people out of their place of origin as well as from factors that attracted them to their new homes. In the case of southern blacks during and after World War I, the push was as important as the pull.

This push lay in the remorseless poverty and oppression that white racism had produced and now perpetuated. Since the latter nineteenth century, the institution of tenant farming and sharecropping, combined with frequent crop failures, had kept many Southerners in hopeless debt. That debt could place the tenants—a large portion of whom were black—firmly under the landholder's control. Lynchings, often occurring at the rate of several per month, and race riots in which whites attacked blacks, had provided dramatic punctuation to the southern campaign around the turn of the century to deprive blacks of the vote and to subject them to the humiliations of sweeping Jim Crow segregation.

This was the system that drove southern blacks to northern cities in such great numbers once the war created a place for them there. But one could listen to Gosden and Correll's broadcasts without picking up any clue of the trials of black life in the South. At the outset of *Amos 'n' Andy*, the pair are employees, not sharecroppers or tenants, of a white farmer. Their responsibilities include tasks like milking and fence-mending rather than tending tobacco plants or picking cotton all day in the hot sun. Andy eludes even these assignments—napping, with no apparent fear of being apprehended by his employer, while Amos carries them out. Andy's single remark that the farm job "ain't no good" is no indictment of southern life. The very same episode, and many later ones, make it clear that Andy has a similar opinion of *any* job that involves actual work and offers no chance to make quick millions. Even when their white boss is out of earshot, Amos and Andy utter no serious complaints about their lot.[8]

In reality, many southern whites—especially those with black tenants—resisted and sometimes prevented outright both the recruitment of blacks by northern industry and the spontaneous departure of rural Afro-Americans seeking a better life. The whole plantation system depended on the permanent presence of a large, uneducated black populace held in place by debt, by laws supporting landowners' contractual prerogatives, by police and judges who enforced these and other ordinances rigorously, and by a lack of opportunity for blacks elsewhere. The economy of the World War I years threatened the southern system by removing the last-mentioned of these props.

But Mr. Hopkins, Amos and Andy's boss, raises no objection to the pair's plans to leave. And the white ticket agent at the railroad station in the premiere of *Sam 'n' Henry* is downright cordial. The letter the two black men have received from their prospective employer in Chicago, which Sam reads to the ticket salesman, contradicts the southern racial code by addressing Sam twice with the title "Mr." Furthermore, the letter's contents make it clear that Sam and Henry have been recruited by a Yankee employment agent—one of those men whose activities in fact were so resented by many white Southerners. Yet the ticket-seller's response could hardly be more solicitous. "Well, that's fine boys—good luck to you," he says, and urges them to hurry in order to get a good seat on the train.[9] Such an exchange was not impossible in real life, but it certainly did not represent the temper of the time and place it was supposed to depict. Suggestions of hardship in the South remained exceedingly rare in Gosden and Correll's work—and always oblique: Amos explains to Andy that he cannot ask his Georgia girlfriend's mother for a loan because "dey takes all de money dey kin work fo' to keep livin'."[10]

A comedic series, of course, is not the place to look for gritty, realistic depictions of racism and poverty. Still, among purveyors of "Negro" comedy in their era, Gosden and Correll were unusually, perhaps uniquely, careful to tiptoe around the Jim Crow system and racial differences in general. E. K. Means and Octavus Roy Cohen were the most popular writers of comic stories about blacks—usually in southern settings—at the time. Both men referred to race and segregation frequently and explicitly, yet in a matter-of-fact way that implied no criticism of southern mores. Trying to cajole a black man into buying a horse, a friendly white character in an E. K. Means story says—with what Means obviously intended as paternal cordiality— "Don't make any mistake, little yeller nigger—that horse can run!" Means's blacks use similar language among themselves ("Lawda-mussy, niggers!").[11] *Sam 'n' Henry*, by contrast, mentioned its characters' race—always using the polite term "colored"—mainly in the narrator's brief introductions to episodes, and *Amos 'n' Andy* generally shied away even from this level of candor. Cohen affected the precision of a micrometer in differentiating among his black characters' skin hues, and when they travel by train, he casually but clearly states that their accommodations are segregated ("The Jim Crow car disgorged many tired passengers"[12]). Gosden and Correll never even hint that their characters are awaiting the Chicago train in the "colored" waiting room, or that the good seats the friendly ticket agent hopes they get, and to which the conductor directs them, will be in a segregated car.

Though not imposed by law, segregation by race pervaded northern life in the 1920s, and white Northerners by and large had long since ceased to feel squeamish about the South's handling of its "Negro problem." Cohen, Means, and other portrayers of southern blacks sold their stories by the dozens to the *Saturday Evening Post* and other northern-based, nationally circulated magazines. Some of the most prestigious northern houses—Alfred Knopf and Little, Brown, among others—published their books. Means, Cohen, and the rest took for granted or even endorsed the racial order as it existed in the South. But in all their conservatism and complacency, they ironically offered a kind of realism that their contemporaries Gosden and Correll did not: they gave some inkling—if a far too benign one—that race mattered in southern life.

Nevertheless, to assert, in Dorothy Parker's famous phrase, that the emotions and experiences Gosden and Correll allowed to their northward-bound southern blacks ran the gamut from A to B, gives those men too little credit. Afro-Americans' excitement at the prospect of a better income, their worry about the unknown, their wistfulness at leaving their friends and the only home they had ever known—all these found expression in the early episodes of *Amos 'n' Andy*, if only briefly in *Sam 'n' Henry*. There were major gaps even in this part of the picture; Amos and Andy never mention parents, brothers, or sisters among those they are leaving behind. Some details do not quite ring true—for instance, Amos's fond reference to his home region as "Dixie," a term little used in normal conversation by southern whites, much less by blacks. But even here, the problem lies more in nuance than in a tendency to burlesque. All in all, the radio team rendered their emigrant characters' emotions with a certain respect—as universal rather than as exotic, "Negro" impulses.

Moreover, Gosden and Correll moved on to examine social phenomena that few other white portrayers of blacks had considered: the Great Migration itself, and the new, sometimes puzzling life Afro-Southerners found at the end of the long road north. Many of the black characters of Means and other writers still dwelt in rural southern backwaters, those of Cohen in a Deep South city, Birmingham. But the focus of black fascination, dreams, creativity, and struggle in the 1920s was the urban communities, especially in the North, that the Migration now filled with black humanity and black energy. This new Afro-American society abuilding—or at least a certain version of it—was the world of *Sam 'n' Henry* and of *Amos 'n' Andy*.

From the moment their heroes board the train, Gosden and Correll, even as they gloss over the railroad's Jim Crow accommodations, introduce subtle but realistic details typical of the Migration. Like many black migrants, Sam and Henry have spent almost all their savings on their train tickets; Sam carries food along to avoid having to buy any during the long trip. The pair bring few possessions with them and must get by with makeshift luggage. Henry uses a box as a suitcase—a container whose sturdiness is questionable enough that Sam suggests tying a rope around it to avoid losing its contents.[13] Although the general tone of these scenes is droll and folksy, Gosden and Correll present the telling details without undue emphasis—in a manner designed to help establish atmosphere and character rather than to evoke laughter.

Other early scenes, however, blur or erase the line between realism and thoughtless stereotyping. In the second episode, Sam and Henry, alighting in Chicago, meekly approach a policeman to ask for directions. "Take off your hat now when you git up to de man dere," Henry admonishes, "take off your hat boy—the first thing you know you gonna git in jail right off the bat." Sam readily complies, addressing the officer hat in hand. In the following episode, the fear of arrest arises again when Sam considers removing his tight shoes in the railroad station. "Leave dem shoes on," Henry warns; "dat policeman goin' come over here and put you in de jailhouse in a few minutes."[14]

To some listeners, these scenes might suggest one of the constant worries of real southern blacks: the fear of arbitrary arrest and physical abuse at the hands of white law enforcement officers, whose actions were nearly immune from scrutiny by white prosecutors and from condemnation by all-white juries. The hapless, helpless black man standing before the stern white southern judge, in fact, had long been a staple of minstrel and vaudeville shows—which thus recognized a genuine fact of southern race relations even while making light of it. But Gosden and Correll presented their black characters' obsequiousness toward white authorities without any hint of historical or social context—their judges and policemen were consistently polite and helpful, or at least businesslike. The hat-in-hand behavior thus ended up simply ratifying the stereotype of the shuffling, cowardly black male.

Gosden and Correll portrayed some other difficulties of ghetto life in more balanced fashion. Where Sam and Henry came north with a promise of employment in hand, Gosden and Correll brought Amos and Andy to Chicago with little more than the latter's cocky certainty that employers there are desperate for workers: "Listen heah son— when we gits to Chicago, de minute we step off de train, dey is li'ble to come right up to us an' grab us."[15] Correll and Gosden denied Amos and Andy the security of a job offer mainly in order to develop the character of the overly self-assured Andy and the worry-prone Amos. But whatever their motives, the creators of the series placed their characters in a situation shared by many black Southerners who came north; the glowing reports of high-paying jobs simply waiting for takers had been exaggerated. Gosden and Correll made the point neatly in a scene in the first Chicago episode of *Amos 'n' Andy*. Expecting an eager employer to approach them in the station or on the street and offer them attractive work, Andy thinks his moment has arrived when, at the end of the episode, a man makes his way toward him and Amos. But instead of tendering them a job, the man begs for a quarter, explaining that he has been unemployed for six months. His worst fears confirmed, Amos asks, "Andy—is yo' sho' dey needs mens up heah?"[16]

Their ill-starred search for work is but one of many trials confronting Gosden and Correll's heroes. Several unscrupulous Chicagoans bilk Sam and Henry; for example, the cab driver they engage to transport them to the Loop—an "ethnic" white, judging by his accent—takes a circuitous route to run up the fare.[17] Short of money and shocked by Chicago prices, Sam and Henry, tired, hungry, and disoriented by the crowds and the unfamiliar streets, accidentally end up back at the railroad station. Similarly, Amos and Andy, traveling on foot with luggage in hand—or more accurately, in the exploited Amos's hands—conduct an exhausting search for lodgings. They end up in a small room, able to afford only beans for sustenance and wondering where subsequent meals on even that scale will come from.[18]

On another topic, however, the transplanted pair's expectations are realistic from the very beginning: in an unusual, though still discreet, burst of racial candor, Gosden and Correll have their two newcomers assume that blacks in Chicago live apart from whites. Having just arrived in the city, Henry asks a policeman, "Where is a good place for two colored boys to get a room?" When the pair report to the office of the contractor for whom they are to work, the clerk suggests in a matter-of-fact tone that they seek a room in a boarding house on South State Street, the main avenue of the city's growing black district on the South Side.[19]

With equal accuracy, Gosden and Correll made it clear through dialect and context that their heroes' landlord and their neighbors—indeed, all the people they meet in their new neighborhood—are black. But not all these people are alike. Many, apparently, are blue-collar workers; some, the listener is told, are unemployed. Other black residents of the neighborhood, however, clearly live in some comfort. Amos and Andy's new landlord, Mr. Washington, who appeared in brief but fairly frequent exchanges during the early months of the series, is far from rich—he lives with his family in his boarding house—but he makes a comfortable living. When Amos and Andy first arrive at their new home, the Washingtons have just finished eating "a great big roast beef."[20] Mr. Taylor, a black entrepreneur whose daughter Ruby becomes Amos's love interest, is wealthy. His construction company is erecting buildings on several different sites, and Amos learns that Taylor owns a clothing store and "a garage or sumpin' " as well. Mr. Taylor sends Ruby—who, like other female characters, was often referred to but never heard—to New York to attend school.[21]

The accommodations Amos and Andy find at Mr. Washington's house, though spartan, are not the least bit dingy. Rats or roaches are nowhere in evidence. Although the heroes' money problems continue, the narrative never even intimates what grave consequences poverty brings in the real world. On the contrary, Amos and Andy not only find work, but soon save enough money to open a business of their own—albeit a small, rickety, and generally unprofitable one. Just five months after the premiere, the taxicab entrepreneurs are buying camping equipment and embarking on a motoring vacation.[22] So much for the realistic picture of the trials facing black migrants that the early episodes of *Amos 'n' Andy* seemed to promise.

Mr. Taylor's wealth and status, meanwhile, present a paradox: they add both accuracy and fantasy to Gosden and Correll's picture of the ghetto economy. The radio team were not the first popular artists to portray black entrepreneurs; Octavus Roy Cohen filled his Eighteenth Street with black-owned businesses. But what Cohen found amusing was the very existence of an urban Afro-American bourgeoisie, which in his stories is capable only of a ludicrous, Zip Coon-style attempt to imitate white culture. Even the names of their enterprises are caricatured—like Exotic Hines' Artistic Photograph Gallery and Keefe Gaines' Mortuary Emporium, which promises "Embalming Neatly Done."[23] Cohen seemed to believe that peculiarities—which he implicitly defined to include both any variance from *and* any aspiration to "white" norms—exist in the black community because blacks are inherently peculiar people.

The Taylor family in *Amos 'n' Andy* were *not* peculiar. Mr. Taylor embodied a truth that Cohen's work largely ignored: that there *were* successful Afro-American businesspeople, and that they made their money by founding companies that were not merely amusing caricatures of white-owned enterprises. On the other hand, such rich Afro-Americans were even more exceptional among their own race than white millionaires were among theirs—and unlike Mr. Taylor, they tended to be as reluctant to see their daughters courted by penniless, unsophisticated fellows like Amos, fresh off the train from the Deep

South, as wealthy whites were to marry theirs off to working-class immigrants from southern or eastern Europe. All in all, then, the early *Amos 'n' Andy* tossed aside some stereotypes; but in doing so it made black Chicago's median standard of living too high and its class structure too fluid.

Still, merely by showing that there *was* differentiation by income and education in the growing black communities of the North—and indeed by portraying a northern black *community* in the first place—Gosden and Correll presented a picture not often seen by mass audiences of whites in that or earlier times. For much of the 1920s, black roles in movies—increasingly filled by real Afro-Americans, but sometimes still by blacked-up whites—fell mostly into categories established a generation or two earlier. The habit of confining blacks to minor parts as servants was so ingrained during the '20s that historian Thomas Cripps cites occasional roles as trainers of boxers or of racehorses as minor breakthroughs. To see an Afro-American in an occupation that demanded some knowledge and afforded some degree of independence from white supervision was a novelty for most moviegoers.[24]

Radio and vaudeville performers of the period rarely presented Afro-American characters in coherent settings or situations. But the innovative daily serial format of *Amos 'n' Andy* allowed the show's authors to build a fairly complex black society—and to create countless situations that traditional acts, as brief, self-contained "bits" of plotless set-up lines and punch lines, could not. The Two Black Crows, the most famous white blackface team in vaudeville during *Amos 'n' Andy*'s heyday, rarely even mentioned their surroundings, and then only as a hook on which to hang a joke. In one routine, the straight man announces that he is going down to feed the pigs. His partner suggests the straight man keep his hat on so that he, the comic, will be sure to recognize him among the swine. But there have been few if any earlier hints that the characters are even on a farm, and the Crows sustain the situation for only a couple of lines.[25] By contrast, Amos and Andy are indentifiable personalities, not merely straight man and comic. Each character has a past history of which the regular listener is aware. Both function in a particular place at a given time and react to a single, concrete, and often relatively plausible situation in the present tense. Today's episode grows out of yesterday's and leads into tomorrow's, and *Amos 'n' Andy* takes on a real-life texture that was unique in its day.[26]

Comic strips—the medium whose success inspired station WGN

to inaugurate *Sam 'n' Henry*—broke slightly more new ground in portraying Afro-Americans in the 1920s and early '30s than movies did.
Moon Mullins's black sidekick, Mushmouth, joined in many of
Moon's adventures and frequently shared the spotlight of a given
day's episode. He and Moon conversed with a freedom not often seen
between black and white adult males in American popular literature
and entertainment. The strip offered some other unusual moments:
in one episode in 1931, Moon watches from one train in consternation
as another pulls out of the station carrying a black porter and Moon's
suitcase. As Moon shouts angrily at the porter, the black man replies,
"You ah de dumb one, boss—you is on de wrong train!"[27] Still,
Mushmouth was a servant, depicted primarily as an adjunct to the
white world rather than as a member of a black community like that
in *Amos 'n' Andy*. And the artist portrayed Mushmouth with the dialect, some of the personality traits, and—as his name suggests—all
the physical features associated with the "coon" stereotype.

Other comic strips of the era offered even fewer innovations in the
portrayal of Afro-Americans. Artists who presented blacks with affection largely confined them to "safe" roles revolving around their relationships with white superiors. Rachel, the rotund black maid—really
a "mammy"—in *Gasoline Alley*, typifies this category. *The Pixeys* depicted cross-racial friendship, but in an "acceptable" form—between
two adolescent boys. Fans of the funnies most often saw blacks as non-
recurring, incidental characters falling into two main categories: bellboys, waiters, and the like; or primitive natives of desert islands and
other remote locales. Obviously, the comics did not portray blacks of
either type as members of a complex, organic black community like
those that were actually burgeoning in America's cities.[28]

Unlike the northern city of old Zip Coon and his heirs, Gosden
and Correll's Chicago was a place where blacks as a group seemed to
belong—despite the jarring adjustments they faced upon arrival from
the South and the expectation that they would live in segregated
neighborhoods.[29] It was a world in which, however inept Amos and
Andy themselves might be, black men and women could and often
did work hard, improve their lot, and—like the Taylors—even excel.
Gosden and Correll saw on the South Side at least some of the human
variety that new arrivals from the South found in cities like Chicago—
where a black bourgeoisie had arisen in the latter 1800s, and where
since around the turn of the century Afro-Americans had built an
elaborate network of black community institutions and businesses.[30]
The South Side according to *Amos 'n' Andy*—especially in the com-

munity's middle and upper strata—was more than just a ridiculously clumsy imitation of white society. Gosden and Correll from the very beginning played many of their black bourgeois characters straight, and in this they were unusual among those who wrote or performed for the mass audience.

Of course, *Amos 'n' Andy* did not concern itself primarily with well-to-do blacks. Much of the humor in *Sam 'n' Henry* and in the early *Amos 'n' Andy*[31] revolved around one of the oldest themes in comic literature, a theme that emerged naturally from Gosden and Correll's focus on the Great Migration: the attempts of the rural bumpkin to come to terms with the big city. The two principal characters, for example, are apparently accustomed to going barefoot or wearing work shoes. The two men's confused wanderings through the streets of Chicago turn country boy Sam's shoes into instruments of torture; he finds relief only by cutting off the toe end of the greater offender of the pair.[32]

If anything, Amos is even less prepared for city life than his forerunner Sam. Discussing the impending journey north, Amos proposes that he and Andy buy mules and ride them to Chicago. To suggest that the most uneducated, deprived southern black man would think he could travel from Georgia to Chicago on muleback is about as plausible as having Amos assume that, because Chicago is "out West," "ev'vybody out dere dress up like a cowboy an' day had buffalos runnin' 'round an' ev'vything."[33] To be sure, popular drama and comedy often rely on exaggeration. But a comparison of material like this with the more understated references to Sam's uncomfortable shoes and his makeshift luggage illustrates the difference between droll characterization and outlandish caricature, as well as the coexistence of both these elements in the work of Gosden and Correll.

Henry/Andy is scarcely more sophisticated than Sam/Amos. Both principal characters are exceedingly naive, but their innocence manifests itself in very different ways. Andy conceals his lack of knowledge under a cloak of loudly proclaimed omniscience and impatience with the failings he imputes to Amos. So insistently does Andy assert his infallibility that he often seems to convince even himself of his own sophistication. The wide-eyed, credulous, high-voiced Amos, mild and deferential by nature, often bows to his partner's supposed knowledge and obeys his commands, however unreasonable or peremptory.[34]

The characters' shared naiveté and their different ways of showing it bore much of the comic load in the early weeks of Gosden and Correll's two series. On their overpriced taxi ride to the Loop, for instance, Sam mistakes Lake Michigan for the Atlantic Ocean, and he marvels that "they got trains runnin' all over bridges here." A disdainful Henry confidently explains that the water is "the Great Lake," and that those elevated trains are "subways."[35] In Gosden and Correll's new series, the explanation of elevated railways that Andy offers Amos before they leave Georgia is even farther off the mark:

Andy: You is done been in buildin's down heah dat go up in de air, aint yo'?
Amos: Yeh—I done been in some o' dese heah office buildin's . . . dat has de elevators in 'em.
Andy: Well, dey tell me up in Chicago, dey go sideways.
Amos: Whut yo' mean, dey go sideways?
Andy: Dis fellow was tellin' me dat when yo' wanna go from one part of de town to de otheh part, yo' git on de elevator—it take yo' right dere.

Shortly after the pair arrive in Chicago, Andy responds with similar pompous certitude to Amos's remark that he knows someone who lives in the city: "You'll neveh find him. . . . Dey got 15 or 20 thousan' people in dis town."[36]

The main characters' wariness and amazement as they confront urban phenomena as simple as a revolving door "goin' 'round like a buzz saw"[37] reflect the genuine awe that country people of any race feel when they visit a great city for the first time. Indeed, the characters' experience in Chicago, like their earlier life in the South, is *too* universal to be believed in a series about the Great Migration. The principals in both *Sam 'n' Henry* and *Amos 'n' Andy* have various run-ins with white urbanites ranging from police to con men and criminals, but no white character commits any racial slight, and no black one mentions the color line. Strangely, Amos and Andy's blackness is an essential part of the series, yet not a factor in its storyline.

A scene from the early *Sam 'n' Henry*, depicting yet another surprise of the sort that the big city holds for rural newcomers, illustrates this basic paradox. Sam and Henry accept work at a construction site without realizing the job will require them to work on the sixteenth story of a skyscraper's skeleton. When told they will be "shot up" to their workplace in a hopper, the pair have to ask a workman, whose speech indicates he is white, what this means. "A couple more dumb bells," he replies; "where are you rubes from?" Sam and Henry soon find themselves hurtling skyward in the hopper, suspended from a cable—both of them afraid, and Sam actually wailing with fear. Arriving on the sixteenth floor, the two receive another shock when told by the foreman what their task will be. "W-w-w-what you mean—catch dem hot rivets?" asks Sam. Told to catch the rivets in a bucket, the timorous Sam suggests an alternative that may improve his chances of success—and of survival: "Mister, you ain't got no wash-tub up here, is you?"[38]

The scene capitalized on a classic comic conceit—placing characters in a situation they find utterly unfamiliar and frightening. But it also gave a distorted picture both of race relations and of supposed racial traits. By having Sam and Henry, less than a week removed from the farm, hired at the drop of a hat for a tricky job on which the safety of workers both white and black depends, Correll and Gosden glossed over the skepticism and discrimination that blacks faced in the northern cities of the 1920s. One might also doubt whether "dumb bells" and "rubes" would be the specific epithets chosen by an impatient, disdainful white workman when addressing two southern blacks.

By presenting Afro-Americans in such a setting, Gosden and Correll did depart from the plantation motifs found in traditional portrayals of black characters. But the stereotype of the cowardly, quaking Negro was at least as old as the need of whites in the antebellum South to manage their fear of slave rebellion. Popular literature and entertainment had firmly implanted that stereotype in the minds of Americans in all regions. By drawing on tradition at the same time they departed from it in some respects, Gosden and Correll created an odd hybrid with which even conservative listeners could feel comfortable.

At other times, the legacy of ancient, patently racial, plantation-style stereotyping made its way undiluted into the modern urban landscape of Correll and Gosden. Blacks' supposed fear of ghosts or "hants" and avoidance of cemeteries was a classic variant of the cliché of black cowardice and superstition. And even in their depiction of the Afro-American world of the future—the northern metropolis—the creators of *Amos 'n' Andy* found room for this old warhorse. Andy accepts a job as a night watchman, the main attraction of which is that it requires him only to sit in a chair for several hours each night. But he and Amos hurriedly depart when they discover that the company offering the job is a funeral parlor:

Andy: I ruther git a job paintin' flag poles dan I would bein' a night watchman in a undertaker's place. . . . It's mo' hants in a undertaker's place dan anyplace in de world.

Amos: I'se scared o' hants too—I ain't goin' mess 'round none of 'em. I'se still scared—I dont guess I goin' be able to go to sleep tonight.

Andy: If you wanna take dat job, you kin go back down dere an' take it but not me.

Amos: I dont want de job—I aint goin' fool 'round no morgue.

Andy: De man say all you gotta do is sit dere.

Amos: Till one o' dem hants come out o' dere an' grab me—I know—I aint goin' mess wid it.[39]

A scene in which Andy's fear of "hants" is enough to override even the slothfulness that persuaded him to take the job in the first place hardly constituted an imaginative leap in the portrayal of the "new" Afro-American.

While Amos shares Andy's fear of ghosts, Andy's aversion to toil, like his pomposity, distinguishes him utterly from his partner. The black community that *Amos 'n' Andy* gave its listeners contained a variety of personalities as well as of social and economic groups, and the contrasts began with the two title characters. In his introduction to *Amos 'n' Andy*'s premiere episode on March 19, 1928, the announcer told the radio audience that "Amos is a hard working little fellow who tries to do everything he can to help others and to make himself progress, while his friend Andy is not especially fond of hard work and often has Amos to assist him in his own duties."[40]

In fact, Andy evades work as nimbly as his real-life contemporary, the football halfback Red Grange, eluded opposing tacklers. Though seldom lifting a finger around the farm, Andy asserts expertise in all areas. "Dat's what yo' git fo' not tendin' to yo' bizness," Andy scolds his partner after the nervous Amos has squirted half the cow's milk on the ground. "If I'd been milkin' dat cow, son, I wouldn't-a wasted a drop o' milk." (As it turns out, it was Andy whom Mr. Hopkins told to milk the cow in the first place.) Before he ever leaves Georgia, Andy has considered his future life in Chicago and "got my job all picked out." His goal embodies both his laziness and his cockiness:

"I'se goin' be super-tendent of sumpin'—I goin' be kind-a foreman of de job."[41] Andy sees himself as a man of destiny; he never tires of " 'splainin' to Amos . . . dat a fellow wid my-a, re-bility could go up to Chicago dere an' clean up a fortune."[42]

Even though no employer snaps Amos and Andy up when they arrive in Chicago, Andy never considers lowering his sights in the job-hunt. He convinces his friend that, once the pair find a place to live, Amos should go out immediately to pound the streets looking for work while Andy remains in the room to receive any messenger who might bring an offer from a would-be employer. "If I staht worryin' 'bout a job fo' myself," Andy frets, "I'se li'ble to git sick from worry an' de fust thing I know I'll be in bed."[43] Indeed, the listener by now grasps that Andy's ending up supine is an ever-present possibility. When he and Amos open their taxicab business, Andy elects himself president. His function will be to "think" and make decisions; Amos will drive and maintain the cab. Inspiration, Andy finds, comes most readily when he is lying in bed at home or reclining in his swivel chair at the office with his eyes closed.

Andy's frequent failures in the big city are always a result, at least in part, of his pretensions. When Amos and Andy are drafted by the Kingfish of the Mystic Knights of the Sea fraternity to run—and finance with their own money—a daily "Tired an' Hungry Bizness Men's Lunch" at the lodge hall, Andy names himself chairman on the strength of his formidable "zecketive-billys" (executive abilities). A chagrined Andy steps down from the chairmanship after only one day, in which he has managed to lose $16.75—a tidy sum by his and Amos's standards.[44]

Never chastened for long, however, Andy generally tries to conceal his defeats by blaming others or concocting outlandish stories. After failing to get beyond Dubuque, Iowa, during a week-long vacation with Amos in their disaster-prone jalopy, Andy returns with tales of "fishin' dere in de Atlantic Ocean—an' den de fish wasn't bitin' dere so we went oveh to de Pacific ocean—dey was bitin' better dere."[45] This kind of boasting differs markedly from the hyperbole about superhuman feats that one finds in the previous century's characterizations of Paul Bunyan, Mike Fink, and occasionally even the Jim Crow of the early minstrel shows. Here, Andy's rodomontade is a deliberate deception, liberally larded with ignorance, concocted by a maladroit character—whom the audience recognizes as such—to salve his own wounded pride.

Gosden and Correll portrayed Andy as inept and pretentious rather than evil or vicious—and in this as in other ways, he resembled many earlier "coon" characters. At the same time, many of Andy's traits could easily belong to a white character. He had a way of "letting" Amos perform the "good jobs"—the ones that actually involved work—in much the same way that Mark Twain's Tom Sawyer recruited other children to whitewash the fence. Andy's imperiousness and his impatience with Amos's ignorance—which in reality hardly exceeded his own—recall the behavior of white movie comedian Oliver Hardy toward his partner, Stan Laurel. The famous comedy team of Weber and Fields offer an earlier white precedent for Amos and Andy's relationship. In the latter nineteenth and early twentieth centuries, that duo portrayed a pair of ignorant German-American buddies, Mike and Meyer. One historian's description of Fields's Meyer as an "aggressive hustler" who "bullied the mild, trusting . . . Mike"[46] could, with little alteration, have been written about Amos and Andy. That Andy had so much in common with white characters, and yet seems such a "black" stereotype, says a great deal about the variety of impressions that the humor of *Amos 'n' Andy* could convey to the radio listener.

There is a type of ethnic humor that depends entirely on a character's race or nationality: the "pickaninny" falls into the flour barrel and emerges white; the "coon" sees a ghost and turns pale with fear; a group of such "coons" engages in a watermelon-eating contest. *Amos 'n' Andy* contained little or no humor of this kind, in part because Gosden and Correll kept even innocuous references to color at a minimum. Used every day, especially in a medium with no visual dimension, explicitly racial jokes would quickly have grown stale— even apart from questions of fairness and taste.

A second kind of humor may take on a racial flavor depending on the color of the characters who present it and on the attitudes of the reader or listener. A group of children of both races, for example, gets a scare in a "haunted" house, and everyone's hair stands on end; but that of a black girl is gathered into a dozen or so little braids tied with ribbons, and these all rise like tiny flags. The comic convention of the wife or mother-in-law as a tyrannical battle-ax did not depend on race. But the old stereotype of a matriarchal black society with corpulent, domineering "mammy" types lording it over innocuous or psychologically emasculated "coons" could endow the battle-ax and her victim with specifically racial overtones when both were black.

Finally, there is a category of humor in which race seems to play no role, even if the characters involved are black: Andy hides $160 of lodge funds in the clock at the lodge hall for safekeeping, and the Kingfish—unaware of this—sells the clock.[47] Or, in a scene spanning two episodes of *Sam 'n' Henry* about halfway through the show's two-year run,[48] Sam is tidying up his and Henry's room before a visit from some of their friends; he lodges a large splinter in his foot while sweeping the wood floor barefooted. Then he fills a washtub and begins to bathe. When the guests arrive early, the wet and naked Sam hides under the bed, where he remains for an hour while the oblivious female visitors decorate the room. The only way Sam can lessen his discomfort is by drying himself off with a garment stored in a box under the bed—which turns out to be Henry's clean "Sunday shirt."

The slapstick elements of the scene—which skillfully aroused the listener's visual imagination without the use of pictures—did not depend on Sam's color for their effect. In fact, Gosden and Correll did not play the splinter for a big laugh, deftly using it instead to reinforce both physical setting (the stark, bare-floored but clean room Sam and Henry live in) and characterization (Sam as industrious but perpetually unlucky). Furthermore, both Sam's sweeping and the presence of Henry's laundered Sunday shirt subtly contradicted the racist notion that blacks are careless about cleanliness.

But a look at the rest of the scene turns up another kind of humor that is less race-neutral than it seems at first glance. Several jokes—or more accurately, a single joke repeated several times—revolve around Sam's midweek bath. "You mus' be in love wid dis heah gal Miss Ella," Henry tells him, speaking of one of the guests, "cause you don' want to never take a bath 'cept on Saturday." A few lines later, the subject arises again:

Sam: . . . Um—um, dis heah water certainly is warm and nice, yo' know it? I goin' staht takin' mo' baths,—dat's what I goin' do.
Henry: You fixin' to ketch pneumonia—yo' know dat—anybody git used to takin' a bath on Sat'day and den take one some other, dey goin' ketch a cold—dat's what dey goin' do.

In the next day's episode, the announcer reminds listeners that Sam, "desirous of looking his best" for his guests, took a bath "regardless of yesterday being Tuesday."

The joke about bathing habits—milked though it was three times in two days—was not inherently racial. The once-weekly Saturday night bath was an institution in many American families into the present century, although the joking mention of it shows that, by the time of *Sam 'n' Henry*, it had come to be associated with the rural and the unsophisticated. References to Saturday night bathing, without any racial connotations, have remained a staple of folk humor among whites—at least those middle-aged or older—up to our own time. But when the character who bathed only once a week was black, and when the stereotype of blacks as unclean was widespread in the popular mind, what did the listener hear when she tuned in these two installments of *Sam 'n' Henry*—a jest about country people, or one about black people? Many in the audience must have absorbed the joke on both levels without sorting them out consciously.

Whites in the 1920s held such an array of prejudices about Afro-Americans—the black male as both stupid, childlike, fawning "coon" and devious, bestial potential rapist, to cite the most obvious example—that it became difficult to create a black character who would not resonate with some stereotype or other. White Americans differed among themselves in their attitudes toward blacks, and a given white could feel differently toward one black or group of blacks than he did toward another. But this only blurs the line between racial and nonracial humor even further. In the end, there exists not a neat, well-defined boundary, but rather a broad realm of ambiguity whose location, dimensions, and contours—like the no-man's-land between the obscene and the nonobscene—differed in the mind of each observer. The racial message of *Sam 'n' Henry* and *Amos 'n' Andy* depended as much if not more on the receivers as on the transmitters.

Still, Gosden and Correll depicted Andy with a set of specific failings that whites for decades had commonly associated with Afro-American men. A white character could be just as inept and lazy, just as big a know-it-all as Andy. But the ridiculously maladroit aping of "white" knowledge and culture by ignorant but garrulous black characters had taken a central place in the humor of the minstrels' Zip Coon and their stump speaker, and in the popular literature that drew on minstrelsy. Correll and Gosden knew that tradition intimately from the shows they had watched as boys, and they had mastered it themselves while teaching amateur blackface artists how to render Jefferson Snowball's pronouncements on the "leakin' nations" and similar topics. White listeners who were so inclined could easily see Andy's ill-founded arrogance, like his other weaknesses, as a natural corollary of his color.

Gosden and Correll drew Amos in striking contrast to Andy, just as their "unlucky but lovable Sam" had served as a foil for "his domineering, overbearing partner, Henry."[49] This opposition be-

Freeman Gosden (left) and Charles Correll created a daily radio series in 1926 that told the continuing story of two black characters and their many friends. Playing all the roles themselves, the pair built their series—eventually called *Amos 'n' Andy*—into the greatest sensation in radio history. (*WMAQ Radio*)

BILLY BURKE MINSTRELS

BILLY BURKE, Comedian

THE QUARTETTE
Stephen Chasia
Jack Byrns
Albert Tillery
Meredith Owens

EARL PUMPHREY, Comedian   SIDNEY CLAY, Comedian

Louis O'Neil and Freeman Gosden, Singers and Eccentric Dancers
Chorus of Ten Singers and Dancers
Coleman Andrews, Interlocutor
Ellis Smith, Musical Director

CHARLEY VAUGHAN, Comedian

FREDERICKSBURG OPERA HOUSE

Friday Night,   8:30 o'clock,   **April 27th, 1917,**

BENEFIT SPOTSYLVANIA

United Daughters Confederacy Monument Fund

ADMISSION 50 CTS.

Freeman Gosden had grown up in Richmond, Virginia, during a time of deepening racial segregation. He made his show business debut in a blackface minstrel show that raised money for a Confederate war memorial. (*Cinema-Television Library and Archives of Performing Arts, University of Southern California [USC]*)

Gosden and Correll chose a novel subject for their new radio serial in 1926: the Great Migration of Afro-Americans from the impoverished rural South to northern cities during and after World War I. (The Negro in Chicago, *1922*)

Amos 'n' Andy's creators based a few of their characters on those exceptional Chicago blacks who lived in upper-middle-class neighborhoods; they soft-pedaled the desperate conditions under which four out of ten black Chicagoans lived. (The Negro in Chicago, *1922*)

Amos 'n' Andy drew on various models. Zip Coon (left), a swaggering but ignorant urban character invented by white minstrels before the Civil War, found echoes in Andy and the Kingfish; some of the show's dialogues were copied from black acts like Miller and Lyles (right). *(Harvard Theatre Collection, Harvard College Library; Performing Arts Research Center, New York Public Library)*

Despite Gosden and Correll's innovations, publicity and props for the team's *Sam 'n' Henry*, forerunner of *Amos 'n' Andy*, sometimes caricatured Afro-Americans as grotesquely as the minstrels had. *(Correll Family Collection)*

Correll and Gosden worried that a poor showing by their radio series would hurt their "real" career as a "song-and-patter" duo. *(Cinema-Television Library and Archives of Performing Arts, USC)*

By the summer of 1929, however, Gosden and Correll's personal appearances in their *Amos 'n' Andy* roles played to packed houses. Their success won them a $100,000-a-year contract with the National Broadcasting Company (NBC). *(Cinema-Television Library and Archives of Performing Arts, USC)*

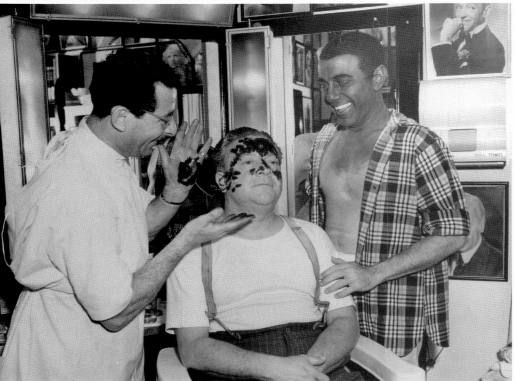

Amos 'n' Andy's creators almost never mentioned race in their broadcasts, yet they gave clear signals that color was central to their art. In photos from 1938, the team look into a "mirror," and a "blacked-up" Gosden watches Correll in the makeup chair. *(Correll Family Collection)*

W. J. Walls, a bishop of the African Methodist Episcopal Zion Church (left), launched a protest against *Amos 'n' Andy* in 1930; he complained that the radio series focused on the underside of black life. (Abbott's Monthly) The following year, Robert L. Vann used his black weekly newspaper, the Pittsburgh *Courier*, to condemn *Amos 'n' Andy* as a slander against Afro-Americans. (*Courtesy of Andrew Buni*)

Robert Vann sponsored a petition demanding that *Amos 'n' Andy* be banned from the airwaves. By the fall of 1931, Vann's *Courier* said that its readers had collected nearly 750,000 signatures. (*Cinema-Television Library and Archives of Performing Arts, USC*)

WANTED!

One Million Signers

A Nation-wide Protest Against

"Amos 'n' Andy"

WHEREAS, For more than a year, two white men, known as "Amos 'n' Andy" to the radio world, have been exploiting certain types of American Negro for purely commercial gain for themselves and their employer; and

WHEREAS, The references made to the Negro are of such character as to prove detrimental to the self respect and general advancement of the Negro in the United States and elsewhere; and

WHEREAS, Already Negro womanhood has been broadcast to the world as indulging in bigamy, lawyers as schemers and crooks and Negro Secret Orders as organizations where money is filched from its members by dishonest methods, thereby placing all these activities among Negroes in a most harmful and degrading light; and

WHEREAS, The Pittsburgh Courier has inaugurated a nation-wide protest against the further practices of these white men who are commercializing certain types of American Negroes at a reputed salary of Six Thousand Dollars per week;

THEREFORE, We, the undersigned, do most solemnly join the protest of The Pittsburgh Courier and ask that the comedians so exploiting our group be driven from the air as a menace to our self respect, our professional, fraternal and economic progress, and to that end do sign our names and addresses hereto. We authorize The Pittsburgh Courier and other like agencies to present this protest to whatever authorities may have the power to make this protest most effective and conclusive.

Name   *Address*

RESENTED BEING CALLED 'AMOS'–KILLS; GETS 3 YEARS

TRIAL CREATES BIG SENSATION; VERDICT OF JURY SURPRISES

YORK, Pa., Sept. 3—George V. Carroll, white, termed by ne daily press of this city as a "bully," will never call another Negro "Amos."

For today he lies resting in a local cemetery, while Francis Barnes, respected Negro citizen of the city, has started to serve , three-year prison sentence, following his conviction on a

COURIER SEEKS 5,000 MINISTERS TO TALK ON SELF-RESPECT

A national "Protest Day," with the support and endorsement of 5,000 ministers of all denominations, who will preach rom their pulpits on the night of Sunday, October 25, on the ubject of "Self Respect," bearing directly on the infamous nd insulting propaganda over the air as promulgated nightly y Amos 'n' Andy, and the passing of the half-way mark arked the highlights in the fight drive the couple from the air.

For over six months in 1931, the Pittsburgh *Courier* attacked *Amos 'n' Andy* in its news and editorial columns. The paper reported that a black man had killed a white for calling him "Amos," and that thousands of Afro-American clergymen had agreed to preach against the radio series on a single evening. But *Amos 'n' Andy* kept many of its black fans, and the *Courier's* protest fizzled. (*Cinema-Television Library and Archives of Performing Arts, USC*)

Amos 'n' Andy occasionally featured dignified Afro-American professional characters, but the series also included heavily stereotyped, vaudeville-style segments. In an early publicity photo, Amos and Andy labor in vain to balance the books for their one-car Fresh Air Taxicab Company. (*Correll Family Collection*)

THIS MAN is not responsible for THIS MAN
even if they do belong to the same race.

AMERICAN LOGIC

THIS MAN is responsible for all that THIS MAN
does because they belong to the same race.

Some Afro-Americans believed that *Amos 'n' Andy* taught white listeners to write all blacks off as inept, unsophisticated, and dishonest. This cartoon from 1913 expresses a common complaint: that whites lumped black achievers together with the "low elements" of the race. (The Crisis) tween the two characters meant that, in a couple of important ways, Amos contradicted the "coon" stereotype.

Amos was no mere drudge; he worked hard out of principle. Thrift, diligence, honesty, and a healthy caution gave Amos's clear desire to improve himself a flavor entirely different from Andy's grandiose, self-defeating ambition. Correll and Gosden established these facets of Amos's character from the very first episode of *Amos 'n' Andy*. Though fearing a scolding from Mr. Hopkins, Amos is sure that "we ought to tell him" about the spilled milk because "dat's de right thing to do." Here Amos begins to seem the perfect "white man's Negro" who accepts his lot in life and lives to please his boss. That stereotype was just as insidious as that of the "coon" and even more comforting to whites. But Amos makes another argument against topping off the milk bucket with water—that the deception may cost him and Andy their jobs before they are ready to leave for Chicago and a new livelihood.[50]

Amos's prudence in guarding his chance for a more promising, more independent future subtly keeps him from becoming an unalloyed Sambo, toeing the boss's line solely out of love or gratitude. And in fact, once Amos and Andy establish themselves in Chicago, there is no white boss—and few white characters of any sort—to curry favor with. That fact alone prevented "Uncle Tomming" from becoming a major theme of the series, no matter how meekly Amos might behave toward other blacks.

Amos's pragmatism—a constant contrast to Andy's unjustified confidence—again and again saved him from seeming only timid or sentimental. Bound for Chicago with no job lined up, Amos expresses some sorrow at leaving the South, but his feeling flows from something more than nostalgia for the "old plantation": "I'se jus' thinkin' dat we aint got no friends up dere. Might be a good idea to kind-a hold on to whut little money we got till we git sumpin' to do."[51] In the same way, even as Amos expresses fear—a classic trait of the "coon"—he contradicts the equally common stereotype of laziness supported by dissimulation or petty thievery. "I willin' to do anything," he proclaims after turning down a construction job on a skyscraper. "I'll sweep de streets, do anything to do an honest livin'— but dont get me way up in de air where I cant keep my feet on the ground."[52] Later, Amos works with unflagging energy to make a go of the taxi business he and Andy set up. Though some have said that Gosden and Correll "reassured white listeners that their new neighbors from the South were . . . less diligent than themselves,"[53] Amos, at least, did just the opposite: he personified the American work ethic.

Beyond his scruples and his energy, Amos showed a measure of horse sense and a healthy but not overbearing streak of pride; but both these traits vied against their opposites for control of his actions and emotions. Amos was often uncertain or even skeptical of Andy's schemes, but his tendency to defer to his headstrong partner frequently outweighed his better judgment. At other times, though, Amos's good sense prevailed—as when he prevents a crooked fortune-teller from conning an all too gullible Andy out of $500 that the pair have come by in a windfall.[54] By the second year of *Amos 'n' Andy*, in fact, Amos almost invariably refused to invest any of his hard-won savings in Andy's harebrained ventures.

Amos occasionally suffered attacks of low self-esteem that drove home the meek and weak-willed side of his character. In one early episode, Amos has cost himself and Andy a job prospect by accidentally hitting Ruby's father with a board while visiting one of Mr. Taylor's construction sites. The two have fled the scene to prevent the momentarily stunned Taylor from finding out who struck the blow. "I done messed up ev'vything—I KNOW I is," Amos wails. ". . . I neveh will have no sense. I jus' feel like I aint no good, yo' know it?"[55] Yet Amos's crises of confidence were seldom this extreme, and he could stand up to Andy if his self-respect was threatened. When Amos's new friend Sylvester offers the financially strapped pair free lodging at his mother's house, Andy wants not only to accept, but also to try to wangle free board out of his benefactors. Amos insists that they not move in with Sylvester without paying rent: "I'd ruther starve to death dan do sumpin' like dat—I aint got de heart to do it[,] dat's all."[56]

When Andy accuses him of wanting to marry Ruby Taylor in order to live on her wealthy father's charity, Amos bristles. "I'se big enough to take care o' her," he insists. "I dont want her papa to give me nuthin'. Den I would be under ob-lirations to her papa."[57] Although Amos's mispronunciation of the word "obligation" detracts from the gravity of his declaration, Gosden and Correll nevertheless present his feelings as sincere and unshakable.

The white creators of the radio series could respect Amos's strengths even when this limited their options in plotting. Gosden and Correll used a trip by Amos and Andy to an amusement park to present a slapstick fiasco: Andy gets wet on the shoot-the-chutes ride, and his new suit shrinks to hopelessly small dimensions. Yet when the pair arrive at the booth where people throw baseballs at the head of a boy in a cage, Gosden and Correll forgo the chance to exploit the situation for cheap laughs at the expense of their heroes. Invited to substitute for the human target, both Amos and Andy—true to character—refuse. Here the radio team parted company yet again from acts like the Two Black Crows, who performed a long comic dialogue about the service of one of the pair as the target in an egg-throwing carny booth.[58]

By including so much humor that was not narrowly racial, Gosden and Correll not only allowed each listener some freedom of interpretation; they also opened up more options for themselves as writers than they sacrificed. They added variety to their stories in two other, related ways as well. As with Amos, they did not allow the behavior of any single major character to become absolutely predictable; and they occasionally presented a character who, though part of the same blue-collar world as Amos and Andy, possessed both virtue and intelligence.

Gosden and Correll kept up their audience's interest—and presumably their own, too—by having Amos put his foot down from time to time. When a stranger makes crude overtures to Ruby and ignores Amos's polite request to stop, Amos decks him with one punch.[59] Likewise, Amos let Andy push him only so far; and when he pushed back, Andy's cocky facade could crumble. Having given Amos all the menial jobs in the taxi company—and dressed up each task with a grandiose title—Andy spends the bulk of one episode trying to pare down the honorifics he himself has invented for his exploited partner. "People's li'ble to think you IS somebody," Andy grouses. Finally, Amos can take no more:

Amos: I'se gittin' mad.
Andy: Whut you mean, you'se gittin' mad?
Amos: Ev'vy time I open my mouth you find fault wid me—no matteh
        what I say, it's wrong—you is always right—. . . right or
        wrong, you is right—sometimes I-I-I just has to hold myself—
        one o' dese days I goin' fo'git myself an' I goin' take my fist an'
        I'm goin' pop you right in de head.

As the day's broadcast ends, the "president" of the company backs down: "Now, wait a minute—cant you take a little joke—aint no use to git mad all de time."[60] Over the next few years, Amos rebelled again on occasion, rousting Andy out of bed or swivel chair to drive the taxi—sometimes for days at a time—before the old pattern reasserted itself.

A real person does not invariably respond to similar situations in the same way. By reflecting this simple truth, Gosden and Correll kept their major characters from becoming absolute stereotypes, racial or otherwise. And the radio team usually managed to turn the tables without taking their creations wholly out of character.

Gosden and Correll also proved themselves capable of developing a prominent black male character who combined kindness and uprightness with brains—yet who clearly did not belong to the rarefied circle of the wealthy Mr. Taylor. The best example from *Amos 'n' Andy*'s first year is Sylvester, the nineteen-year-old garage mechanic inspired by Freeman Gosden's childhood friend Garrett Brown. Gosden and Correll at first kept Sylvester's light under a bushel. But the pair deliberately used the young man's deference to "Mr. Amos" and "Mr. Andy" and his lack of formal education to deceive their audience. The listener's first impression of Sylvester as an amiable nonentity permitted Gosden and Correll to depict his eventual triumphs with that extra flourish that comes with the element of surprise.

In one early episode, Amos and Andy have bought a decrepit used car to use as a taxi, and Sylvester has volunteered to try to repair the engine at no charge. When the partners pay him a visit, they find he had dismantled the motor and laid all its parts out on the ground. He explains to the shocked Amos and Andy that his grandmother advised him "to take it to pieces first an' clean ev'vything."

> *Andy:*   Is yo' Gram'ma a mechanic?
> *Amos:*   Do yo' Gram'ma know anything about automobiles Sylvester?
> *Sylvester:* Yo' see—it sort o' runs in de fam'ly. My papa used to work in a boiler factory an' my Gram'ma used to fix his lunch fo' him ev'vy day.

"You betteh git yo' Gram'ma oveh heah to fix dis car," Andy replies with disdain. ". . . Yo' know I is de president of the comp'ny an' all dis falls on my shoulders."

Having apparently set Sylvester up to rival even Andy in ignorance, Gosden and Correll gradually drop hints that all is not as it seems:

Andy:	Where did yo' git dat stove pipe from?
Sylvester:	Dat aint no stove pipe—dat's de exhaust pipe.
Amos:	Is dat whut dat thing is?
Andy:	Whut is dese things right heah?
Sylvester:	Dat is de timin' gear.
Andy:	Oh yeh—dat's whut I thought dat was. Is dat got a clock in it?
Sylvester:	Nosir, nosir—dat aint got no clock—I'll 'splain dat to yo'.
Andy:	No, no—dat's alright—dont tell de president.

By the following episode, Andy has "fired" Sylvester from his unsalaried job and had the car towed to a garage for reassembly. Amos and Andy visit the repair shop and ask its owner—who clearly was played as a white man—about their vehicle's future. The prognosis is bleak: "If it was my car, I'd set it on fire." But the garage owner does offer one ray of hope: "We've got a new man here that we've just put to work who is an excellent mechanic. . . . He's about the only man that I know in this part of the country that can fix a job like that." A knock on the door, and in walks the man uniquely qualified for the task at hand—Sylvester. Andy must now pay him to reassemble the engine.[61]

Gosden and Correll weakened Sylvester's impact as a counterstereotype by keeping him almost cloyingly humble, even after his white boss's tribute to his unique skills. In fact, they tended to invest assertiveness and "smoothness" in characters who were shiftless or downright dishonest—or both. Charlie Johnson, a resident of the boarding house where Amos and Andy live, was one of the few characters in the series who more or less shared the pair's economic status, yet spoke without most of the dialect features found in the principal figures' speech. He is self-confident and glib but lazy—alert, but particularly to opportunities for easy money, as when his roommate Ed vainly suggests a game of poker to the inexperienced Amos and Andy. Ed, meanwhile, is the quintessential "coon." He will "sleep standing up, sitting down, laying down or running," Charlie says; "the only way you can wake him up is to fry bacon." Beyond food and slumber, Ed's interests extend to drinking, as becomes clear when Amos invites him to take a nap if he wishes:

Ed: Did you say nip or nap?
Amos: I said nap.
Charlie: Dont send his blood pressure up like that.[62]

Gosden and Correll seem to have felt that a fast-talking, street-wise character—even a ne'er-do-well like Charlie—required a more traditional counterweight such as Ed.

Comedy, of course, feeds on human foibles and has little room for paragons. But the contrast between Charlie and Sylvester, like that between Amos and Andy, shows how much Gosden and Correll conceded to a central tradition of American popular writing and entertainment portraying blacks: though they made some of their characters assertive and others virtuous, they rarely combined both these attributes in a single Afro-American male figure. (Ruby Taylor's father, an exception to this rule, actually joined in the radio dialogues only infrequently; his strength of character was conveyed mainly when other characters mentioned his accomplishments.)

Gosden and Correll had too much imagination to segregate the backbone from the heart with a mechanical consistency. The humble Sylvester, for instance, not only spoke the wordless language of concrete achievement, but also—like Amos—bristled at the imperious Andy when provoked too flagrantly.[63] Still, Amos 'n' Andy tended to link urban sophistication and self-confidence with deviousness and laziness.

One character, Jack Young, arrives in Chicago flaunting his knowledge and worldliness and trumpeting the superiority of his home city, New York—"the capit[a]l of the world." He speaks a dialect closer to Standard English and at the same time far more "hip" than that of Amos and Andy—whom he considers a "couple of R.F.D. boys." Having heard that "de old buzzard Taylor" has "plenty of bucks," Young immediately sets his sights on Ruby and secures a job as manager of her father's garage.

Unlike Zip Coon, the urbanite of early minstrelsy, Jack Young is no buffoon; he is a villain. The Kingfish of Amos and Andy's lodge receives a report that Young is a con man who has deserted his wife and child. Before long, the newcomer is plotting with two accomplices to steal $6,000 from the safe in Mr. Taylor's garage. Sylvester, following Amos's instructions to keep an eye on Young, overhears the conspirators' critical conversation; he informs Amos, who in turn goes to the police.

With two detectives, Amos and Andy wait in ambush in the darkened garage office on the night of the planned crime. Andy plays the standard, chickenhearted "coon," cowering under a desk throughout the episode. ("I wish I was home undeh de bed," he says.) But Amos, incensed at the plot against the family of his Ruby, willingly takes a gun in hand, crawls coolly through the dark room to verify the safe's location for the detectives, and plays a central part in springing the trap. With droll exaggeration, but with obvious bravery as well, Amos shouts, "Put 'em up high—stick dem hands up in de air—dont mess wid us—we got 15 men heah—we'll shoot yo' head off." Afterward, speaking with a grateful Mr. Taylor, Amos characteristically gives Sylvester all the credit for Jack Young's apprehension.[64]

Amos 'n' Andy did not imply that the big city necessarily corrupted the Afro-American character. Rather, in the Jack Young affair, Gosden and Correll suggested that city life can further harden those already disposed toward evil, but can nurture the best in others— Amos's quiet nobility and Sylvester's alertness, for example. And the truly urbane blacks, the Taylors, are not only the real "class" of *Amos 'n' Andy*—they are Young's victims. Nevertheless, it is the unsophisticated characters—and in Amos's case, the one most recently transplanted from the countryside—who thwart the designs of the evil New Yorker; and dozens of slippery city types (if less dangerous ones than Jack Young) would follow Charlie Johnson into Amos and Andy's vicinity. Such images could resonate with old prejudices about where in the American landscape blacks did and did not belong, and with racist expectations about life in the new urban ghetto—a world that many white viewers "saw" for the first time in *Amos 'n' Andy*.

Blacks did not hold a monopoly on deviousness or criminality in *Amos 'n' Andy*. When the Mystic Knights of the Sea stage a carnival to raise money, they hire an itinerant company of white men to provide the equipment and run the affair—an arrangement Correll and Gosden knew well from their own work with white clients of the Joe Bren Company in the early 1920s. Amos, Andy, and the Kingfish eventually overhear the carny manager, Honest Tom, berating his employees at length for running the carnival games too honestly, allowing one customer to win a pound of candy and another a basket of fruit. Tom ends his tirade—which he aims at other whites without realizing that blacks are listening—with another of Gosden and Correll's eerily unrealistic, nonracial epithets: "Dont let these yokels win nothing— get me?"[65] As in the very first installments of *Sam 'n' Henry*, the audience hears white scoundrels cheating blacks.

But the other side of the coin is that this white cupidity feeds on black stupidity[66]—as when the Kingfish enthusiastically signs Honest Tom's transparently exploitative contract. More important still, most confidence games in *Amos 'n' Andy* were perpetrated by black characters. The bunco schemes of the principals' fraternity brothers became a staple of the series early on; all in all, they gave a dismal impression of the influence urban life could allegedly have on black behavior.

The radio audience of the 1920s and '30s probably perceived fewer racial shadings than today's listeners might in the extravagant rituals and terminology of the radio characters' lodges—Sam and Henry's Jewels of the Crown and Amos and Andy's Mystic Knights of the Sea. Afro-American fraternal orders and mutual benefit societies did tend to take names and indulge in ceremonies that seem eccentric today. But so did white orders, as anyone knows who is acquainted with the rites of the Shriners, the Improved Order of Red Men—or, for that matter, the Ku Klux Klan. Parodies of such lore, without reference to race, have long been a mainstay of American humor.[67]

The everyday behavior of Amos and Andy's lodge brothers is another story. Most if not all of them seemed to be either natives or long-time residents of the big city. A few were professional men who, in their brief appearances in the storyline, sounded intelligent and competent. When the police mistakenly accuse Amos and Andy of a robbery, the pair hire as their lawyer a member of the Mystic Knights recommended by the Kingfish. The attorney speaks the English of a well-educated man, clearly knows his profession, and gives the impoverished pair a break on his fee.[68]

By and large, however, the lodge is a den of amiable thieves. When Amos and Andy receive a $1,500 reward for identifying the real robbers, a lodge brother no less articulate than the lawyer sells them a $500 interest in some nonexistent diamond mines in South Dakota.[69] Other Mystic Knights are neither educated nor honest; for example, the Swordfish of the lodge, an ignorant purveyor of questionable life insurance, finds easy marks in the two naive newcomers from the South.[70]

Neither individual lodge brothers nor their common treasure are immune to members' depredations. Brother Ellis, the janitor, steals the lodge hall's rug and skips town; the Kingfish complains that the theft of lodge property by the fraternity's own members is chronic. Worse still, the Kingfish finds himself compelled to put the order's Shad (treasurer) under surveillance on suspicion of embezzling lodge funds. It is the Shad's unreliability that persuades the Kingfish to put Honest Tom, the professional showman, in charge of the lodge's carnival, ignoring Amos's warnings about the pitfalls in the contract Tom proposes.[71]

For all his concern about the larceny of others, the Kingfish himself was a confidence man whose fleecing of Amos and Andy provided fodder for the radio series for years to come. In the middle of a "big meetin' " of lodge officers, the Kingfish emerges and persuades Andy to pay a "special 'cessment" of five dollars, promising to "put [him] down as one of de star fish" and write his name "in great big letters up on de roll of honor." The executive meeting turns out to be a crap game among the officers, in which the Kingfish was running short of money.[72]

The Kingfish talks Amos and Andy into opening a "loan company" with the last $500 of their reward money. True to form, he issues the first "loan" to himself. The leader is catholic in his choice of victims, however. The other loans, he explains, will go to lodge brothers; each client "signs a note dat he pays us int'rest an' we kin make dat int'rest 'cordin' to how dumb de man is." But the lodge brothers have their own ideas. When the "company" announces that money is available, they descend on the taxi office in "a wild dash," extracting all the money in "loans" that clearly are unlikely to be repaid.[73]

Scenes like these show the dark side, the danger, of Gosden and Correll's theme of country boys in the big city: its resonance with the stereotype of the ignorant southern "coon." Are Amos and Andy so easily duped simply because they are rural naifs—or because they are black and therefore supposedly stupid? Even the former answer to that question was hardly flattering to Afro-Americans; any listener who did not attribute the principal characters' gullibility to their race nonetheless heard a legion of black bandits fleecing them. Similarly, some in the audience might notice that the many black characters who bilked Amos and Andy (and each other) were far from stupid; but their cunning was not the kind of mental alertness that, in the white listener's mind, would provide a healthy counterbalance to the lead characters' ignorance.

The bunco theme was not an inherently "racial" one in the sense that, say, watermelon-stealing would have been; many humorists had exploited the interaction between white con men—like the King and the Duke in Mark Twain's *Huckleberry Finn*—and their white dupes. And scams abound in any community, regardless of race or nationality, that absorbs thousands of immigrants unfamiliar with their new environment.

But by creating the only radio series that depicted an all-black world, Gosden and Correll painted themselves into a corner. At first glance, the radio team's practice of avoiding any hint of unpleasantness between the races seems an enlightened one—and an easy policy to follow simply by using almost no white characters. But the result was that virtually all of the show's countless larcenies and deceptions were committed by blacks against other blacks. However benign Gosden and Correll's intentions may have been, and however similar in principle their black con artists to Twain's white ones, *Amos 'n' Andy*'s fans could easily see the series not only as a traditional burlesque of universal human greed, but also as a portrait of Afro-American character and communal values. That picture was no compliment to the race.

The very vividness of the Kingfish—probably the most memorable character Gosden and Correll ever created—quickly made him indispensable, and thus ensured that the theme of con man and mark would remain one of the most prominent in *Amos 'n' Andy*. More than that, the Kingfish tended to bring out other characters' more stereotypical side. One example: the Kingfish tries to draft Amos and Andy for the lodge's carnival committee so that he can assign them all the real work. When the two principals wisely resist, the Kingfish announces that the committee will lead the carnival parade in formal dress. Gosden and Correll had never made Zip Coon–style dandyism a notable feature of Amos's or Andy's behavior; but coming from the Kingfish, an appeal to their vanity works like magic. The two men jump to join the committee as soon as their leader dangles the role of latter-day darktown strutters before them.[74]

The schemes of the Kingfish and his fellow charlatans fed on the gross ignorance of their victims. That ignorance yielded other scenes which, unlike the most vital and innovative serial material in *Amos 'n' Andy*, recall the self-contained, semiabsurd, noncontextual vaudeville dialogues of acts like the Two Black Crows. In fact, it was precisely these scenes that Gosden and Correll recorded for sale on phonograph records, for fans could appreciate them without reference to any storyline.

The radio partners used a number of variations on the scene in which Andy "de-tates" a letter to Amos. In one episode, Andy formulates a complaint to a Cabinet officer about his and Amos's problems finding a job:

Andy: "Dear secketary of de interior o' Labor—"
Amos: How yo' spell "dear secketary o' de Interior o' Labor"?
Andy: D—double e—r; dear-a; s—s—s
Amos: How many s's in dat thing?
Andy: In whut thing?
Amos: In dat word you is essin'.
Andy: I aint got but one "s" down dere—I aint said but one "s."
Amos: You said s—s—s.
Andy: Dat shows yo' how dumb you is. Dat was de same "s" I was essin' oveh again.
Amos: Start at de beginnin' again—take it again.
Andy: Dear secketary o' de interior o' Labor.
Amos: I done heerd yo' say dat.
Andy: Well, put it down. It's got e's an' c's an' t's an' y's in it.
Amos: De main thing is though, how yo' gonna routine 'em.[75]

The scene—which continued for many more lines—based its humor partly on the references to "essin' " a word and "routin[in']" letters. In fact, southern speakers, both black and white, sometimes appropriate nouns bodily for use as verbs; Gosden must have known the process from his childhood. These unorthodox verbs, with their ring of authenticity in the southern ear and the novelty they presented to other listeners, lent the scene a dash of folksy charm.

Yet the dialogue also played on the stereotype of black illiteracy, and the reference to the "secketary o' de Interior o' Labor" smacked of the minstrel stump speech. Other, similar scenes in *Amos 'n' Andy* traded almost wholly on these stereotypes, with few hints of originality, grammatical or otherwise—as when Andy, using a sample in an instructional manual, "teaches" Amos how to write a business letter:

Andy: Dear sir—we beg to a-c-k-n-o-w-l-e-d-g-e—
Amos: Dat aint "acrobat," is it?
Andy: Wait a minute now—we beg to a-c-k-n—acna; o—o—acna-o; w-l-e—wheel; d-g-e—dij; acna-o-wheel-dij.

. . .

Amos: Whut does acna-o-wheel-dij mean?

. . .

Andy: Amos—de word acna-o-wheel-dij—is a combilation of lettehs stuck togetheh dat mean things dat you dont know nuthin' 'bout. You take de fust part o' dat word.
Amos: Take it where?

Andy: No, no, leave it alone—leave it alone.

Amos: I aint messin' wid it—all I ast yo' to do is to 'splain it to me—whut it mean—acna-o-wheel-dij.

Andy: How would you like to re-press somebody wid yo' re-po'tance?

Amos: I aint crazy 'bout doin' dat to nobody.

Andy: How would you like to have Ruby Taylor think dat you is got some sense?

Amos: I'd LIKE to have her think I got SOME sense.

Andy: Den de next time dat you see her, you wanna use a big word like dat—so just walk up to her—an' say—Ruby, I beg to acna-o-wheel-dij.[76]

White comics appearing *as* whites could and did perform this kind of material. But when rendered in "black" dialect, the routine could readily support the notion—fostered by American literature, entertainment, and folk bias since the days of Zip Coon—that education was wasted on the Negro. So could the equally famous scenes in which Amos and Andy attempted simple calculations. Told that train tickets to Chicago cost $26.72 apiece, the pair spend half of an early episode trying to determine the cost of *two* tickets. Andy insists—not unreasonably—that they should "mulsifly" $26.72 by two rather than "stackin' 'em up" (that is, adding). Through an elaborate process of "timesin' " and "carry[in']," however, the men arrive at a figure of $216, which they assume still must be doubled:

Amos: Well, when did we git up in dem big figures?

Andy: Dat's whut happen when yo' mulsifly.

Amos: Well, go ahead, do it. You knows whut you'se doin' dere.

Andy: Two times 216—lemme see—how much is $216.00 times two?

Amos: Well, figurin' it out in my own head heah, I figures dat dat's over $400.00.

Andy: I b'lieve you is right. Dat IS right—dat's oveh $400.00. Two times $26.72, de way I figures heah is oveh $400.00.

Amos: Dat certainly is a lot o' money fo' us to git up dere on, aint it?

Andy: Listen—I got a idea—we'll fool 'em. I'll go one day an' give $26.72—den de nex' day, don't say nuthin' to 'em an' you give $26.72 an' we'll both git dere.

Amos: Dat's a idea—boy you certainly do think of 'em.[77]

Audiences in the late 1920s found such material familiar, and not only from the work of white actors in blackface. In fact, Gosden and

Correll drew key portions of their dialogues about "routinin' " letters and "revidin' " and "mulsiflyin' " figures from the famous Afro-American comedy team of Flournoy Miller and Aubrey Lyles;[78] Miller eventually threatened to sue the white broadcasters for plagiarism. But by presenting such traditional scenes in a novel context—a radio serial that turned out to be the wave of the future—the creators of *Amos 'n' Andy* helped to ensure that the old stage bits would live on even as vaudeville was dying.

Gosden and Correll used material like the "de-tatin' " and "mul-siflyin' " scenes often, and audiences—like those on the Pantages tour of 1929—seem to have enjoyed them. But those bits fit only tenuously into the overall scheme of the radio series. This is espe-cially true of the occasional, quick doses of creaky, burlesque-style repartee ("You take de fust part o' dat word"—"Take it where?"). Like the wisecracks of Amos and Andy's fellow roomer Charlie, these seem forced and out of place—even when the context itself is as hackneyed as the "de-tatin' " scene. Perhaps some listeners saw such gags as adornments to the dialogue, like mistletoe at Christmastime. But these bits, like mistletoe in the forest, were in fact parasites; the tree that supported them was *Amos 'n' Andy*'s continuing story of recognizable people responding to situations that at least vaguely resembled those of day-to-day life. It was this—not the vaudeville-style jokes that audiences could hear from any number of other acts—that made Gosden and Correll's show the hit of the decade.

The same principle applies, if less obviously, to entire scenes like those involving dictation or arithmetic. These routines were little more than pieces of equipment in Gosden and Correll's bag of tricks. The pair could pull one of them out and rearrange its innards a bit whenever they needed to—for example, when writer's block collided with the remorseless demand for a new script every day. Such stock bits often had little to do with the show's continuing story, and they might even contradict it in some particulars. In a different episode, for instance, Amos fluently reads aloud from a letter, and Andy at least passably from a newspaper clipping;[79] yet in the "de-tatin' " scene, both struggle in vain to decipher the word "receipt."

Again, the essence of *Amos 'n' Andy* lay somewhere else, and that essence overshadowed all the bits of chicken-crossing-the-road corn and even the cleverest of the show's set pieces: beyond the laughter, the series told a story, and that story conveyed a variety of images. Andy was a conceited blowhard with little to be conceited about; Amos remained uniformly modest, sensible, and considerate. Andy shiftlessly exploited the good will of others, while his partner personified industry and responsibility. The two title characters lacked money and education, but the Taylors possessed wealth, learning, and refinement. Most of the Mystic Knights of the Sea, like their Kingfish, were freeloaders and cheats, but Sylvester and Amos incorruptibly defended honesty and decency. Amos combined clumsiness when pursuing matters of the heart with a deep capacity for love; meekness with bravery when extraordinary circumstances called for it; and submissiveness with a pride that asserted itself when a real point of principle was at stake. Andy, though dependably pretentious, was also vulnerable in his ignorance and at times sympathetic as a result. Sylvester might be deferential almost to the point of fawning, yet he was bright and competent as well.

As Gosden and Correll portrayed their Afro-American characters, then, they gave with one hand and took with the other. Even their innovations could cut two ways. Ironically, the very humanity of Gosden and Correll's characters made them seem real, and that in turn could make their overwhelming ignorance and their other stereotyped traits and behavior seem equally genuine and characteristic of Afro-Americans as a race. Still and all, if this radio team gave and took, some of what they "gave" made them virtually unique among the ancient and mighty blackface legion: the picture of a complex, northern, urban black community, and the day-in–day-out portrayal of characters whom the listener—if he or she cared to—could get to know intimately.

6

...━▶◉◀━...

The Mystic Knights and Their Ladies

Freeman Gosden and Charles Correll faced a dilemma. They could hardly depict a northern black metropolis while leaving out the half of that community who were female. Several black women leaders in the cities, including Ida Wells-Barnett and Mary Church Terrell, had won national reputations during the previous few decades. Afro-American women schoolteachers in northern black communities, though few, were highly visible, and several black female entrepreneurs—like Madame C. J. Walker, manufacturer of black hair-care products—had achieved "spectacular" successes that attracted notice even from whites.[1] The all-black musical shows that swept urban stages in the 1920s owed much of their very essence to women performers.

Afro-Americans in big northern cities knew how formidable the achievements of ordinary black women were in an age when they were five times as likely as white women to carry the burdens of both homemaking and outside employment. Older women of the race, moreover, were playing a central role in sustaining storefront churches and other institutions that helped stabilize community life in rapidly changing areas like Harlem and Chicago's South Side.[2] Although some of these developments surely escaped the notice of Gosden and

Correll, the overall importance of women in building the Afro-American community of the future was too obvious to ignore. Besides, to broadcast *Amos 'n' Andy* without women characters would deprive the radio team of countless inviting dramatic options.

Yet Gosden and Correll decided not long after Sam's ladyfriend Liza saw him off at the railroad depot in the first episode of *Sam 'n' Henry* that they were not comfortable doing women's voices. The pair's solution was simple but audacious: they would create female characters *without* voices. The radio dialogues first mentioned Ruby Taylor, Amos's future wife, only two weeks after the premiere of the series in 1928, and the action in *Amos 'n' Andy* often included women characters over the next quarter-century. But for years the program presented these through its narrative prefaces and through the male characters, who discussed the women, "conversed" with them on the telephone, and occasionally read aloud from their letters. Amazingly, Gosden and Correll managed to give each of these silent female figures a vivid personality of her own and, at times, a crucial part in the drama.

The two broadcasters made Amos above all a character of the heart, of feeling, and none of his emotions took a more important place in *Amos 'n' Andy* than his love for Ruby. Amos leaves a lady-friend behind in Georgia but remains devoted to her as he seeks his fortune in the big city. When his Mamie marries another man and sends Amos a "Dear John" letter, the news so devastates him that he takes sick and emerges from his bed only after two more episodes.[3] Yet in the following weeks, a new love discreetly develops with Ruby Taylor after a long period in which Amos—loyal to Mamie until she jilts him—has responded platonically to Ruby's obvious interest.

By the fifth month of *Amos 'n' Andy*, the indirectly conveyed but lively interaction between Amos and Ruby became a central theme of the show. In a crucial episode, Amos returns home from Ruby's house with a full heart; in many respects, his description of their evening together sets the tone in the listener's mind for the couple's later relationship.[4] "I'm in love wid Ruby I b'lieve," he tells Andy. "She's such a sweet gal—she's so cute an' nice. . . . You know," he adds, "I b'lieve she loves me too."

Andy: How come yo' b'lieve she love you?
Amos: Well, tonight, while she was playin' de piano, some kind o' song she was playin'—"I love you"—an' just de way she looked at me an' de way she was singin' it just made me think dat she did.

Andy, as usual, reacts cynically, exclaiming, "You don't b'lieve ev'vything yo' heah?" But Amos knows what he has seen and felt: "We was sittin' dere kind-a holdin' hands an' she kissed my hand."

Amos is "too happy to go to bed now. . . . I couldn't go to sleep noway. I wanna sit up heah an' think." First, though, he has more to relate:

Amos: You know Andy—we was talkin' tonight an' she held my hand
         real tight an' she looked in my eyes an' she says to me—she says
         "Amos"—an' den she say—I a-dore you.

. . .

Andy: Aint no gal goin' tell me dat an' git away wid it.
Amos: Whut do dat mean—A-dore?
Andy: Dat means she think you is a blockhead. You know a door is
         made out o' wood, dont yo'. She means dat she thinks yo' head
         is made out o' de same thing.
Amos: She didn't mean dat though 'cause right after she told me dat[,]
         she told me she was always thinkin' bout me an' she couldn't git
         me off her mind.

Amos and Ruby's developing relationship already faces the first of many perils Gosden and Correll would lay in its path: Mr. Taylor's long-standing plan to send his daughter away to school. Ruby's anxiety has led that evening, Amos tells Andy, to "sumpin' . . . dat I never will fo'git—it cert'ny was touchin'."

Andy: Whut happened?
Amos: I looked her in de eye an' Ruby was sittin' dere cryin'.
Andy: Whut she cryin' 'bout—was she crazy or sumpin?
Amos: She was cryin' 'bout me, she told me. Den I started cryin'—
Andy: Now, wait a minute—dont staht cryin' 'round heah—GIT TO
         BED!

Andy, however, cannot suppress his curiosity for long:

Andy: Did yo' kiss her goodnight when yo' left dere?

. . .

Amos: I wanted to kiss her goodnight but I didn't ast her—I didn't
         wanna make her mad or nuthin'—so we just looked at each
         other fo' 'bout a minute or two widout sayin' a word—den
         sumpin' else happened.

Andy: Whut happened now?
Amos: Den I started away an' I say—"Goodnight Ruby"—an' den—an' den—
Andy: An' den whut?
Amos: An' den Ruby say—goodnight precious—an' I got so excited dat I fell down de steps.
Andy: So precious fell down de steps. GIT TO BED!

This was no *Romeo and Juliet.* In some ways, Amos's relationship with Ruby more closely resembles the secondary love affair which—in dramas ranging from Shakespeare to American musical comedy—provides a comic counterpoint to the main plot involving the hero and heroine. It could hardly be otherwise as long as Gosden and Correll portrayed Ruby only through Amos's exchanges with Andy, or through telephone "conversations" in which Andy usually interjected comments from the sidelines. Almost any such scene was sure to include a heavy dose of comedy based mostly on Andy's displays of cynicism about women and love. Then too, Gosden and Correll portrayed Amos as shy and often tongue-tied around women, and as usual the pair turned his lack of education to comic effect.

On the other hand, the two writers always depicted Amos's love for Ruby as heartfelt, and Ruby herself as a serious, mature, refined woman; they never played her emotional, romantic side, or any other facet of her personality, for laughs. (Andy's disdainful commentary made him, not Ruby, appear laughable.) Presenting black characters sentimentally, of course, was nothing new. The tenderhearted black male of song and story had long served to reassure whites that all was well between the races—and specifically to neutralize their fear of the vengeful "bad nigger." Amos, too, was gentle and lovable, and his emotional nature—especially his tendency to weep—ran counter to the popular notion of masculinity. Yet his love was directed toward a black woman rather than an Ol' Massa. And from the first, Gosden and Correll gave Amos another, firmer side in affairs of the heart as in other spheres: when Amos's former love Mamie leaves her new husband and begs Amos to take her back, he shows pride, good sense, and dedication to Ruby by refusing to answer Mamie's letter.[5]

The prominence of Amos and Ruby's relationship over a period of years made *Amos 'n' Andy* unusual for its time. Movies of the 1920s, notes historian Thomas Cripps, had rarely acknowledged the possibility of romantic love between black characters. When the film *In Old Kentucky* gave some attention to a romance between servants played by Carolynne Snowden and Stepin Fetchit in 1927, the move was so unusual that both black actors "proudly boasted of it for the rest of their lives." Harry Pollard's *Uncle Tom's Cabin* of the same year managed only a "brief focus" on the slave couple George and Eliza—whose deep love the Stowe novel had presented with great prominence and dignity—and assigned blacked-up white actors to the roles.[6]

Even *Amos 'n' Andy*'s heavy overlay of comedy—as in Amos's tumble down the steps of Ruby's front porch—let enough believable human emotion show through to engage those in the audience who were at all disposed to see and appreciate it. Amos's exaggerated non-Standard dialect at least forced the audience to see his deepening love and respect for Ruby as emotions of a black man, unlike the romantic songs of the de-racialized minstrel balladeers of old. The broadcasters' highly romantic portrayal of Amos and Ruby quietly challenged two overlapping cultural stereotypes: the promiscuous black hedonist, and the black man who dreams—as in D. W. Griffith's *Birth of a Nation*—of possessing a white woman.

Strangely, Gosden and Correll did not mine the class difference between Amos and Ruby for as much dramatic interest as they might have. Still, by picturing Ruby as sophisticated and well-to-do, they made it clear that her love for Amos spanned a social chasm between the two. The *Amos 'n' Andy* comic strip, published and syndicated by the Chicago *Daily News* during the year and a half before the radio show moved to NBC, offered one thing that radio could not: the strip made the gap between Amos and Ruby strikingly visual. But the differences between the two characters turned out to depend only partly on their disparate social origins, for male characters in general differed dramatically from females both in the comic strip and in Gosden and Correll's own work.

The artist, Charley Mueller, drew Amos and the other principal male characters just as white cartoonists of the day usually rendered black men: as minstrel endmen minus the radiant costumes, with enormous white lips and pop-eyes, melon-shaped heads and jet-black faces. Physically, they differed from one another only in size and in their clothing; Mueller's allegiance to the standard caricature was so deep that he made their faces all of a single grotesque type. Mueller rendered the speech of the central male characters in the strip much as Gosden and Correll wrote it in their radio scripts.

Ruby presented another picture entirely. Mueller drew her as slender and pretty, with an attractive, moderately curly "bobbed" hairdo and stylish, tasteful clothing. Her dark skin—which, however, was several shades lighter than Amos's—made it clear that she was black, but her facial features differed little if at all from those of a comparable white character. (Cartoons of the period—even in Afro-American newspapers—seldom if ever portrayed beautiful women with distinctly Negroid features.) Mueller's Ruby spoke the English of a well-educated person; though an occasional contraction kept her speech from seeming stilted, the language of the two lovers contrasted markedly:

> Ruby: We've had a lot of trouble lately. The lights go out every night for five or ten minutes. Father tells me they are working on the wires. They'll be back on in a minute. . . . Let's sit over here on the sofa.
> Amos: It's over in dis corner heah some where, ain't it?[7]

But the difference in dialect paled next to the bizarre contrast in the appearance of the two. Physically—with Amos resembling an illustration for a Joe Bren minstrel-show handbill—the couple looked as though they came from different planets.

In the *Amos 'n' Andy* comic strip, Ruby was not the only woman who fared better than the principal male characters. The Widow Parker—actually a divorcee who has run through five husbands, and who plots to make Andy number six—clearly occupied a lower moral and social plane than Ruby. Moreover, if any major character in the *Amos 'n' Andy* strip was a candidate for depiction as a hefty "mammy" type, it was the widow. Yet although the cartoonist made her (plausibly) less slender than Ruby, she lacked any eccentric physical features. Mrs. Parker's speech made only a few concessions to literary "Negro" dialect—for example, "an' " rather than "and."

The artist of the *Amos 'n' Andy* strip exempted minor male characters from the extreme caricature he used in drawing the leads. Ruby's father's eyes were a bit on the large side, but otherwise his medium-dark complexion and close-cropped curly hair made him look like a normal black man. The occasional black bank officer or lawyer who appeared in the strip looked equally uneccentric and spoke Standard English. The differences among characters in the comic strip thus depended on their social class as well as their sex. But overall, the strip suggested an intimate correlation between gender, physical carriage, speech, and behavior—and the women had by far the better side of the contrast.[8]

The *Amos 'n' Andy* comic strip ran for only seventeen months; it reached a far smaller audience—and presumably made less of an impression on those it did reach—than the radio broadcasts did. But Gosden and Correll furnished the storyline,[9] which followed that of the radio show, and the two men—especially Gosden—almost surely had something to say about the physical makeup of the daily comic. The strip thus gives some indication of how the creators of the radio series envisioned their characters and tried to portray them.

Correll, Gosden, and their funny-page collaborator were by no means the first whites to present attractive black women characters to the masses: female impersonators in minstrel shows had played their roles with comeliness and grace. The minstrel soloist had to direct his romantic ballads to someone, whether she was present on the stage or merely addressed in the lyric. Since the minstrel men wore blackface, any "women" who actually appeared alongside them had to be black as well. But white standards of beauty dictated that they be light-skinned, and the nature of the songs required that these female characters embody romance rather than raw sex appeal.[10]

The romantic content of the minstrel balladeer's songs likewise set limits on the racially caricatured behavior he could indulge in while singing them. And when a graceful female character appeared alongside the balladeer, she may have reinforced those limits or even pulled the blacked-up ballad singer's portrayal of her beau a few notches higher in dignity.[11] To some extent, Ruby exerted a gravitational pull of this kind on Amos: his relationship with her led to some of the more touching and human moments in Freeman Gosden's depiction of him. But Amos, unlike the romantic balladeer of minstrelsy, approached the object of his love as a poor, shabbily dressed, ignorant, clumsy country boy. Ruby crossed the great divide of class and background to love Amos, rather than pulling him into her world and making him like her and her father. The result, as the *Amos 'n' Andy* comic strip showed so vividly, was that the polished, poised Ruby stood out much more starkly among Gosden and Correll's male characters than the minstrel "woman" had when appearing next to the balladeer.

The radio team thoroughly distinguished Ruby from another fictional black female type of more recent vintage: the woman who combined the beauty of the minstrel ladies with an emphatic sexiness. By the time of *Amos 'n' Andy*, such characters sometimes appeared in comic fiction and in illustrated advertisements for all-black stage revues and nightclub acts. As in the *Amos 'n' Andy* comic strip, the gap between the sexes in such pictures could be striking—for example, a young, shapely black woman in a revealing hotel maid's costume dancing with a monkeylike black bellhop.[12] Yet as sharply as Ruby Taylor contrasted with her own male partner, she was no vamp, any more than she was a stylized minstrel belle; *Amos 'n' Andy* presented Ruby as a physically appealing woman, but a dignified, conservative one.

Given the racism in traditional American entertainment and in American society at large, one might wonder why Gosden and Correll felt so free to make of Ruby what they did. By creating an all-black fictional world, the two white men gained a large measure of flexibility in portraying the adventures of its inhabitants. True, when all the characters in a story were black, all their foibles, too, were by definition those of blacks. But with whites essentially absent from the landscape, many of the constraints imposed by American racial etiquette could be loosened as well.

Gosden and Correll could portray Andy as a domineering type—as long as those he lorded it over, like Amos and Sylvester, were also black. They could make Mr. Taylor rich, well-educated, and socially polished, for the community that accorded him status and respect consisted of other blacks. Sylvester could not only excel as a mechanic but also be recognized as preeminent in his field by his fictional white boss; Sylvester appeared in the mythical integrated garage for only five seconds at the very end of one episode, uttering just six words. In the next day's installment, the action shifted back to Amos and Andy's South Side neighborhood. Real white mechanics in the listening audience who did not care to work alongside blacks did not have to face the idea long enough, or explicitly enough, to upset their digestion. Even the meek Amos could take gun in hand and threaten to shoot a criminal's head off—for the criminal, too, was black.

Likewise, the creators of *Amos 'n' Andy* could present Ruby Taylor as a scholar and a gentlewoman without offending most of the whites in their audience, for her bright light shone forth in a black neighborhood; whites need not feel challenged. Neither did Gosden and Correll have to camouflage Ruby in a maid's uniform; there were no white characters around for her to serve. And besides being a black among blacks, she was also a woman.

White contempt for blacks has always been inseparably bound up with fear of them. Over the generations, whites worried about retribution from rebellious slaves, economic competition from black artisans or Afro-American strikebreakers, and the sexual aggressiveness attributed by legend to black men. By their very nature, many of these anxieties—and therefore much of the rawest, harshest racial repression—were directed at black males by white males.[13]

White men have tended to see white women, too, at least partly as adversaries—though the female challenge differs both in kind and in degree from the threat posed by the black male. The theme of the "battle of the sexes"—the alleged desire of the woman to rein in and domesticate the man, to "wear the pants in the family," or to subvert the man's judgment through seductive manipulation—has remained a staple of western culture at least since Old Testament chroniclers wrote of Adam and Eve, Samson and Delilah.[14] Popular entertainment, by and large, has reinforced the network of social customs, religious dogma, and legislation through which men define and defend their dominion over women.

Two closely allied ways to disarm an adversary—or at least to manage one's fear and resentment of him—are to laugh at him and to love him. To portray the Afro-American male as a lazy, shuffling, watermelon-stealing "coon," or as a ridiculous imitator of white sophistication, provided an antidote to white men's fear of him. To make a black male "lovable"—a childlike, fawningly loyal servant, or a kindly, harmless Old Uncle—neutralized him just as effectively. Small wonder that, over the long haul, these supposedly funny and affectionate stereotypes, elements of which became so prominent in *Amos 'n' Andy*, proved far more popular than the frightening black spectres of novelist Thomas Dixon and his ilk.

White men's laughter at women differed from their jokes at the expense of black men, and white women could obviously be lovable in ways that black males could not. Men desired women, and needed them. Men had mothers, sisters, and wives whom they neither could nor would segregate and demean wholesale as they did blacks. As a result, writers and entertainers tended to poke fun not just at women, but also at the institutions that brought men and women together, and even at defeats men supposedly suffered in the battle of the sexes. The fictional white coquette, for instance, however frivolous and bubble-headed, differed from the childlike "coon" in a basic way: unlike "Sambo," she could frequently and openly vanquish the white male—by stringing him along, by transferring her fickle affections to another, or by rebuffing the interested man completely. Other women characters dominated their men much more directly and remorselessly; these were the overbearing, harpylike battle-axes who typically appeared in the role of wife or mother-in-law.

Even though they might wield power over men—and indeed, largely *because* they might—fictional women characters, like black men, were often depicted unflatteringly in popular literature and entertainment. *Black* female characters, however, generally fared better than black males, and in some narrow fields they might equal or surpass even white women. It was primarily the "mammy"—the most prominent and venerable of all black female types—who achieved this feat.

The "mammy" was the female counterpart of the minstrels' Old Uncle. She made her way as a stock character from minstrel shows through the popular literature of the decades after Reconstruction, and thence into comic strips, radio series, and films like *Gone with the Wind*. She was unlettered, unpolished, physically plain at best and extravagantly corpulent at worst. Yet in her own limited but important domain—her white employer's kitchen and nursery—she could be assertive, stubborn, sassy; she governed both her own family and the children of "her" white folks with a heavy but loving hand. Ever ready to give a piece of her mind to anyone—sometimes including white adults—whom she found in need of it, she could be a miracle of domestic skill, industry, and efficiency.[15]

Why did whites give the stage "mammy"—and to some extent, the real-life women on whom she was based—the latitude they did? White men, including those who ran the entertainment industry, did not ordinarily look at black women as competitors or adversaries. As the white male saw things, it was black men, not black women, who might plot revolt, take over white men's jobs, or violate "white men's women." In the meantime, the Afro-American woman posed none of the problems to the white male that the white female did. It was the white woman who supposedly sought to ensnare the male in the web of domesticity, or who, in the role of mother, wife, or mother-in-law, might try to order his life, restrain his behavior, and limit his options. The black woman made no such demands of him.

As a female and an Afro-American, she had always been doubly disadvantaged. If a white man sexually assaulted her under slavery, she had no legal right to accuse or testify against him, for she was black. In the Great Migration, the combination of her color and her gender confined her with rare exceptions to work as a domestic servant or to a few jobs in manufacturing whose conditions and pay could make her envy even the greenest immigrant working woman from Europe.[16]

Yet at the same time, the black woman was spared at least some restrictions and humiliations. The inferiority of her position was so obvious, so complete, that the white man need not rub it in so constantly and in so many ways as he did with the potentially troublesome, threatening black male. Then too, granting certain privileges and immunities to a black woman in real life, or strengthening one in a fictional vehicle, offered a bonus: it could further the cause of humbling her black male counterpart. Gosden and Correll probably had no such conscious goal; but the practice came naturally because it fit a well-established pattern of American race relations. And when the radio team placed a female in the all-black world of *Amos 'n' Andy*, the last shackles fell off her; the limited freedom of action the "mammy" had enjoyed in the world of whites now became almost complete. Ruby Taylor could be young and attractive—unlike the "mammy"—for there were no white men in *Amos 'n' Andy* whose attention she would divert from their "own" women. And she could be intelligent and self-confident, for the only men whom Ruby would outclass were black.

···—◼◉◗—···

Gosden and Correll did present unflattering female images: alongside Amos and Ruby's made-in-heaven relationship, the radio team could focus for weeks at a time on the misfortunes that man might suffer in his encounters with woman. The barbs *Amos 'n' Andy* aimed at women and at married life are remarkable above all for a kind of orthodoxy that transcends race; they bear a striking resemblance to the humor of artists in the same period who portrayed white characters.

The comic strips of 1925–1930 offer an encyclopedia of such humor. The strips often portrayed the young, attractive, poised woman as a headstrong manipulator, playing one suitor against another and making men jump through hoops to win and keep her favor. Male characters often assumed that her ultimate goal—and that of all women—was to catch and tie down a husband. In the strip *Harold Teen*, a young man tells a bartender of his "sensible" girlfriend, who prefers staying home in the evening to going out on an expensive date. "That's just a come on game," retorts the barkeep; "after y' marry 'em they'll run ya ragged!" Another strip, *Larry*, shows how the male prey feels after a woman has snared him and shown her true colors. "Why do they have the aisle roped off in church when folks are getting married?" a boy asks his father, who has just been bawled out by his battle-ax of a wife. "That's so the bridegroom can't get away, m'boy," replies the chastened father.[17]

Gosden and Correll's Andy shared the white bartender's view of women and their designs on men. He finds out all about the marriage trap when he becomes involved with the Widow Parker. "Practiced in the arts of love, graduate of five (financially) successful marriages,"[18] the widow uses Andy's love letters as evidence in a breach-of-promise suit after he backs out of marrying her. A couple of years later, in 1931, a similar debacle with a fortune hunter named Madam Queen— who mistakenly believes Andy is wealthy—monopolized the action in *Amos 'n' Andy* for several months.

If the predatory Mrs. Parker was a "black widow" in the figurative sense, her literal, racial blackness had as little bearing on her character as it did on her speech and her manner in the *Amos 'n' Andy* comic strip. Gosden and Correll depicted her precisely as others portrayed white women who sought a husband by hook or by crook. She and Madam Queen, like Ruby, were *female* characters, whose race was at most secondary.

The stereotypical white wife of the 1920s was not necessarily an out-and-out gold digger like Madam Queen, but her often frivolous desires made her a constant drain on her husband's pocketbook. "How much longer are we going to wait for mummie, daddy?" asks a small child standing with its father in front of a milliner's display window in one cartoon. "Not long now, dear," the father replies as he contemplates some fifteen empty hat stands. "They're just taking the last hat out of the window."[19] Andy likewise asserts that a married man and his money are soon parted; Ruby, he insists, will forget she ever said she could live "in one little room in somebody's attic" if only she could marry Amos. To Amos's statement in another episode that marriage requires one to "give an' take," Andy retorts that the husband must "give de money an' take de back-talk."[20]

In fact, Ruby's values never changed, even after her marriage to Amos some years later. But other wives in *Amos 'n' Andy*, and in the "white" comic strips that ran during the show's early years, did even greater damage to their husbands' pride than to their paychecks. The typical domestic conversation in *Bringing Up Father* revolved around peremptory commands from wife Maggie. "Now I want you to call on Mr. Duffaey—and . . . see that you act like a gentleman," ran one typical harangue. "And if I hear that you didn't go there it won't be good for you—do you hear that?" Her cowed husband Jiggs usually answered with refrains of "Yes, Maggie." Small wonder that, when a friend of Jiggs laments that his wife has lost her voice, Jiggs replies, "Aw, shut up! You don't know when you're well off!"[21]

The sisterhood of such acid-tongued harridans always had plenty of fearsome representation on America's comic pages during and after Gosden and Correll's early years in radio. Moon Mullins summarized their physical charm when he called one of their number a "dizzy-lookin' old crowbait."[22] And frequently their verbal abuse of their men moved on to physical battery. In the popular *Blondie*, for example, Dagwood Bumstead's patrician grandmother—a grotesque mountain of a woman adorned with pearls and pince-nez—tries to force Dagwood's fiancee Blondie to marry her other fop of a grandson instead. She sanctimoniously adds that she has "always made it a point never to interfere in any of my children's affairs—it wouldn't be right." But when the dandy grandson replies, "Quite so, Grandma, quite so," the old lady breaks her cane over his head. "You shut up," she shouts. "I'm running this!"[23]

The Christmas season of peace and love brings even graver consequences for the oppressed husband in another comic strip, *Keeping Up with the Joneses*. A Yuletide argument ends when the hefty Clarice lands a large vase against the head of her diminutive mate Al. But this is only a warm-up for events three days later, when Clarice discovers that the diamonds on the watch Al has given her for Christmas are artificial. In the aftermath, a policeman reports the bad news to one of Al's friends: "They say a couple of his ribs are bent an' both eyes are closed."[24] Given the constant threat to self-esteem and physical well-being that many comic-strip males faced, it is not surprising that the young man in *Harold Teen* could say to the bartender, "Y'know, Pop! There are times when I believe I could almost hate wimmin'!" Or that the barkeep—older and more experienced—could reply, "Times? All the time! That's my motter!"[25]

The theme of domestic violence—that staple of comic strips peopled by white characters—often worked its way into *Amos 'n' Andy* as well. And Gosden and Correll, like the strip artists, played the motif for laughs. The main difference was that violence not only by wives against husbands, but also by men against women, was occasionally discussed in the early *Amos 'n' Andy*. As usual, Andy endorses the extreme position, explaining to Amos how to make Ruby Taylor "so crazy 'bout yo' dat you wouldn't have nuthin' to worry 'bout de rest o' yo' life":

Andy: Boy, de meaneh yo' treat 'em, de mo' dey love yo'. I know a
          man used to hit his gal in de nose ev'vy night—she was crazy
          'bout him.

Amos: Any man dat'd hit a gal in de nose aint got much to do.
Andy: You smack one of 'em in de nose ev'vy night, you'll THINK you got sumpin' to do.
Amos: Whut good is dat goin' to do—hittin' a gal in de nose?
Andy: Dat make 'em think you *is* somebody.

"All yo' gotta do to 'em Amos," Andy concludes, "is to just walk up to 'em once or twice a week . . . an' say 'Baby—sock!—now, be good fo' de next 24 hours.' "

When Andy cites the example of a friend in Atlanta who treated his "gal" this way, Amos reminds him that someone shot the man—"I bet he done hit his gal in de nose once too often." Amos sympathizes with the woman in such a relationship, but he cannot sway Andy:

Amos: If I was a gal an' some man would hit me in de nose I'd pick up a razor or gun or whutever I could [get] my hands on—I'd chase him so fast he wouldn't know whut he was doin'.
Andy: You cant just walk up to a gal an' sock her in de nose. You gotta know how to do it.
Amos: How do yo' do it?
Andy: Well—yo' see a gal an' yo' stand her up in front of yo'—den you say Sock! Right in de nose—den you say "Wait a minute, baby, wait a minute—don't git mad now—papa loves yo'—but dont mess wid papa."[26]

Gosden and Correll hardly advocated the "socking" of women. This is another instance of Andy's bluster, which Amos effectively deflates; indeed, listeners could easily understand the dialogue as a satire on the arrogance of some men. In any case, the radio team's dramas mentioned such male-on-female violence only rarely, especially after the show's early months.[27] Gosden and Correll kept Andy, like their other major characters, from becoming utterly one-dimensional; his aggressive talk concealed a heart that, like Amos's, was romantically vulnerable to feminine charms. He sends flowers to one Rosie Waite;[28] and even after their respective breach-of-promise suits, he falls for the Widow Parker, and later for Madam Queen, all over again.

Even so, Andy's violent pronouncements and his assumption that women are masochists stand out. Indeed, his last line in the exchange about "socking" women ("papa loves yo'—but dont mess wid papa") sounds for all the world like the words of a pimp to one of his prostitutes. In general, *Amos 'n' Andy*'s creators aimed to achieve a "whole-some" appeal to the entire family;[29] that such a line—so coarse and unfunny by today's standards—could find its way into their radio series shows how casually the subject of hostility in male-female re-lations was bandied about in the 1920s. The entire scene also suggests a greater readiness among white writers to portray antisocial behavior, and among white listeners or readers to accept it, when black char-acters were involved.

Andy's occasional incitements notwithstanding, *Amos 'n' Andy* closely paralleled the "white" comic strips in that the female nearly always attacked her defenseless male rather than the other way around. Sometimes the man had it coming—for example, when a libidinous but over-the-hill husband compulsively pursued beautiful young women (or, as one ever-frustrated white comic-strip character in *Keeping Up with the Joneses* called them, "gazelles"[30]). In *Amos 'n' Andy*, the perennial target of wifely mayhem was the Kingfish of the lodge. As so often in the comic strips, the humor revolved as much around the husband's inconstancy and his childish evasion of punish-ment as around his wife's shrewishness.

In one episode, the Kingfish explains that, when you are married, "you is always in trouble"—"an' it's always de woman's fault." He illustrates his point with an account of a recent incident at the home of the Swordfish of the lodge:

Kingfish: . . . I was sittin' dere an' dis heah gal come over to me— knowin' I was de high officer—an' she sit down on de sofa next to me an' she say-a—"How yo' feelin' today, big boy?"

. . .

Andy: Whut did you say?

Kingfish: I say-a—I'se feelin' pretty good baby—how you feelin'. Den she say—gimme a kiss honey—an' I kissed de gal—an' I happened to look up an' my old lady was standin' over in de corner an' she picked up a lamp an' threw [it] at me. Just like I tell yo' boys—you'se always havin' trouble wid yo' wife.

Andy: See dere Amos—de women is always wrong.

Amos: I guess you' right alright. Funny how dey git mad about little things like dat, aint it?[31]

Amos's final remark sounds a false note; Gosden and Correll have consistently portrayed him as too sensitive toward women's feelings to condone the Kingfish's offense. Overall, however, the scene typifies the battle of the sexes as it was waged both in *Amos 'n' Andy* and in nonracial American popular humor of the same era.

Gosden and Correll's black women resembled those of other artists since the days of minstrelsy in one basic way. A fictional black female could be attractive or grotesque, charming or domineering; but whatever she was, her personality—and her stereotyped traits, if any—flowed from her gender as much as from her race. The result was a lessening of the moral distance—a partial leveling—between black and white women as portrayed in popular literature and entertainment.

In fact, some of the virtues that popular artists attributed to the essentially nonthreatening Afro-American woman were denied to her nearest white counterparts. The "mammy," for example, might lack book-learning, physical beauty, and subtlety, but she was often a sympathetic and in some ways an admirable character. There was absolutely nothing pleasant or admirable about Jiggs's Maggie and her like, even when their abrasiveness seemed partly justified by the behavior of their childish husbands.

Moreover, by contrast to the "mammy," the white battle-ax was often presented basically as an idler with no apparent skills other than gossiping and playing bridge.[32] She might even have servants to do her housework; her main physical exercise came from whacking her unfortunate husband on the head with a rolling pin every now and then. The young white coquette, who in the 1920s took the form of the "flapper," might be depicted as a hard worker, typically in the secretarial field. But she also tended to indulge herself at the expense of men, one of whom, she assumed, would eventually marry her and take her away from her temporary way-station in the world of work. The fictional flapper and battle-ax were strong characters, but they used their strength to control their men—the coquette by manipulation, the shrew through intimidation and brute force. The "mammy," too, might push her men around, but she often wielded *her* power for the good of others. So the partial leveling between black and white female characters in comedic writings and performances was a "leveling up" for the black woman and a "leveling down" for her Caucasian counterpart.

Cartoonists, writers, and performers of comedic material portrayed a wide variety of white characters within each gender. They made many of their white males inept or juvenile—ideal types are simply not funny—and they rendered some of their white females sympathetically. The partial leveling between comic black and white women was just that—partial. The overall picture, however, is clear. As a group, white women characters in newspaper humor columns, comic strips, and other popular media might deal some formidable blows, but metaphorically they took a beating. Stereotyping of black female characters was in some ways even narrower, but often less vicious. Black men, meanwhile, remained at the bottom of the heap; even the feckless, henpecked white husband at least looked like a human being, in contrast to the monkey-like "coon." And while popular writing and entertainment outside the realm of comedy did offer white male heroes, the American public saw very few black male characters who were not comic figures.

If Correll and Gosden treated black male characters better than some of their contemporaries did, the pair carried the leveling between black and white females further still. Because the radio team did not portray white women at all, theirs was entirely a "leveling up" of black women. This process had its ironies and its negative side. As the partial elevation of the "mammy" had done, the portrayal of strong and even cultured black women in *Amos 'n' Andy* made the flaws of their men seem even more glaring. Respectful portrayals of women, of course, need not come at the expense of men. But as long as American entertainment humbled the black male in a hundred other ways, any respect accorded black female characters was unlikely to benefit him and might even add to the burdens he already carried.

Then too, given the abundant negative stereotyping of white women in the 1920s and '30s, to present a range of black women characters that paralleled the spectrum of white female types was no pure compliment to the black race. Where Correll and Gosden depicted Ruby Taylor as considerate and sincere, they had the Widow Parker and Madam Queen use shameless trickery to snare the man they wanted. Where Ruby was gentle and trusting, the Kingfish's wife was ever ready to take lamp in hand to keep her man under control. Gosden and Correll's treatment of black women thus yielded an odd, double-edged kind of racial egalitarianism: Ruby equaled the most virtuous white heroines, while *Amos 'n' Andy*'s female "heavies" could be as unpleasant as white ones in other vehicles.

Still, Gosden and Correll deserve credit for some of their portrayals of black women. For the vagaries of the American racial code and the use of an all-black cast of characters might offer writers and performers the hypothetical *option* of portraying dignified black women; but nothing required them to *exercise* this freedom, and most did not. In one story, Octavus Roy Cohen had his male character Florian

Slappey pursue Evva Mapes, a young debutante whom "Mother Nature," in "a giving mood," has rendered "seven ways from the ace in the matter of pulchritude." Asked about her long absence from Birmingham, Evva explains, "I'se been off to a cemetery gettin' educated." When Slappey invites Evva out, she devours innumerable courses of expense fare; "I always craves food," she announces superfluously. Even after Slappey, his funds exhausted by Evva's voraciousness, takes the wheel of the taxicab he has hired and intentionally runs it into a tree to avoid paying the driver, Evva emerges from the wreck with a barbecue sandwich in her hand. The contrast between Evva Mapes and Ruby Taylor could hardly be more striking, even though both women are supposed to represent the black elite. A similar divide separates Amos's view of women from that of Florian Slappey—"a confirmed misogynist" who approaches Evva "not because of any personal interest," but "merely as a fitting complement to his own radiant personality."[33]

Even Correll and Gosden's most negative female characters, then, were no more repellent, and sometimes less so, than many of those—both black and white—that their contemporaries created. This, to be sure, is faint praise; but the character of Ruby, even in the years when listeners never heard her voice, made a real breakthrough, and Amos's attitudes and behavior were depicted as worthy of such a woman. Ruby and her courtship with Amos drew more heavily on old-fashioned sentimentality than on the spirit of the 1920s, but their relationship did provide a counterweight to Mrs. Parker's and Madam Queen's manipulation of Andy and to the state of siege that prevailed at the Kingfish's house. For all Amos's occasional clumsiness and Andy's harangues against matrimony, Gosden and Correll portrayed the love between Amos and Ruby with far more humanity and with greater prominence than other popular writers and entertainers did with black characters at the time.

And although they retained and even widened the conventional gap between the competent black female and the floundering male, Gosden and Correll at least did not suggest that all the dignity and initiative in the race belonged to women. Mr. Taylor, the honest, knowledgeable black professional men whom major characters occasionally consulted, and even Sylvester, though they occupied but a small part of the drama, reared their heads often enough to suggest—to anyone willing to listen—that there was more to the male half of the urban black community than ignorant, shuffling waiters and bellboys.

7

···━●◉●━···

Amos 'n' Andy's *Balancing Act*

The Commonwealth Club was one of the many places in Richmond where whites and blacks came into close but unequal contact every day. The club's members were white business and professional men. Its servants, including those who waited table in clean, pressed white jackets, were black. Early in 1931, a local newspaperman described an evening at the club. "It was 2 minutes of 7," he reported:

> A hundred and sixty-five Richmond merchants in the ballroom . . .
> were just finishing the first course of their annual dinner. Instead of
> removing the plates, the waiters silently drew back and stood in a line
> against the wall. Men looked at their watches. . . . [C]onversation
> lagged. The clatter of the room died out. Musicians laid their instru-
> ments by. A long pause. Expectancy. Perhaps a flutter of impatience.
> Then, from the stage, magnified many times, came a familiar voice—
> *Thursday night, Feb'r'y twenty-sixth, Amos and Andy in person.* Every
> man in the room breathed contentedly and settled back for fifteen
> minutes of undiluted enjoyment.[1]

All across the United States, similar scenes took place. Interest in *Amos 'n' Andy* was especially high at the time of the Commonwealth Club dinner—Andy was embroiled in the suspenseful breach-of-promise suit filed by Madam Queen. But even in more ordinary times, meetings of all kinds were routinely interrupted for *Amos 'n' Andy*'s fifteen minutes. Family dinnertimes, and even factory shifts and church services, had been adjusted to permit people to tune the show in. Movie theaters offered a nightly quarter-hour intermission during which they played the radio broadcast for their patrons. *Amos 'n' Andy* impersonators had become a standard item at costume parties and in amateur talent shows. More remarkable still, the full-blown version of this *Amos 'n' Andy* mania was already nearly a year and a half old and showed few if any signs of abating.

Tens of millions, rich, poor, and in-between, shared the Richmond merchants' "undiluted enjoyment" of this unassuming radio series. The show's appeal even crossed lines of race. The local chronicler may not have been thinking of the Commonwealth Club's waiters, standing mute in the background, when he noted the pleasure of "every man in the room" at the opening sounds of *Amos 'n' Andy*. But many other Afro-Americans were listening to the broadcast in their own homes and neighborhoods with no less attentiveness than the white businessmen at their banquet.

Freeman Gosden and Charles Correll had won their enormous popularity through a combination of finely honed instincts as showmen and plain luck. By using radio to tell a story, they opened a whole new dimension for a medium that had caught the public's fancy even while most of its programming still derived from older genres. Eight months before the debut of *Sam 'n' Henry*, critic Wilson Wetherbee had called on broadcasters to develop programs that would establish some kind of continuity among their various components rather than simply present an agglomeration of unrelated performances. But he believed it would take time for listeners to acquire the ability of "visualizing by sound"—a prerequisite for the rise of radio drama.[2]

Gosden and Correll and the management of station WGN accomplished much more much sooner than Wetherbee had anticipated. By telling a more or less seamless story day after day, the station and its stars achieved a type of continuity that even Wetherbee—who called for harmony *within* each individual broadcast—had not thought of. And the show's creators assumed from the very beginning that their listeners could visualize scenes presented through radio dialogue. Without making their verbal cues to the audience unsubtle or distracting, the pair used words to arouse vivid images: Sam and Henry being propelled high into the skeleton of a building under construction, or Sam fleeing from the bathtub and hiding beneath the bed.

Gosden and Correll demonstrated both the power of the radio audience's imagination and the ability of the medium, when used skillfully, to stir it. They filled a gaping void and won a huge following as a result.

Gosden and Correll exploited the serial format to the full, often building interest and suspense gradually, day after day, until all America seemed to be listening and discussing the action. The Widow Parker's breach-of-promise suit against Andy achieved this effect in *Amos 'n' Andy*'s pre-network days, and the similar affair involving Madam Queen in 1931 moved slowly but intriguingly toward a climax over a period of two and a half months. One fan in Michigan expressed the sentiments of many: "You know I like to listen to Amos & Andy? only just when it gets interesting, then you have to wait until the next night."[3]

The frequency and regularity of Gosden and Correll's broadcasts—the team took no vacations during *Amos 'n' Andy*'s first six years—helped make the show part of many families' daily routine. When the characters mentioned the day of the week, Gosden and Correll took care that it matched the actual day on which that episode was broadcast. This, like their building many stories around particular times of the year—Christmas, "Decoration Day," summer vacation, income tax time—gave the series a flavor of reality and invited listeners to identify with its characters.

In less skillful hands, however, the daily format could just as easily have led to satiation and boredom. That did not happen; *Amos 'n' Andy* stayed on the air as a daily show for a decade and a half, switching to a once-weekly schedule only in 1943. The brevity of Gosden and Correll's dialogues helped prevent oversaturation. And once they moved from the syndicated discs of the "chainless chain" to live network broadcasts, the team profited from writing each show no more than a couple of days ahead of time. If fan mail and the radio columns of the press showed that a given plotline was catching on, Gosden and Correll could build on it to milk the popular interest. If a story idea fell flat, the pair could quickly move on to something new.[4]

The radio team could count on their employers to help keep them in the public eye. Both WGN and WMAQ were owned by metropolitan newspapers, and these gave generous publicity to Gosden and Correll and their series. The Chicago *Tribune*, owner of *Sam 'n' Henry*, and the two men's subsequent employer, the *Daily News*, arranged and promoted stage appearances by the team. The *News* also helped to run the "chainless chain" that made *Amos 'n' Andy* known across much of the United States, and to put together the Rand McNally book about the show in 1929. After the series moved to NBC, the network's publicity department busily issued press releases full of complimentary information about Gosden and Correll and their creations.[5] Show business columnists and fan magazines were only too happy to give *Amos 'n' Andy* frequent and usually favorable attention.

NBC also did its best to keep its hand on the pulse of the listening audience, mainly by collecting thousands of newspaper items about *Amos 'n' Andy*. Its clipping services missed nothing, from passing references to the show in otherwise unrelated articles to lavish, multipart newspaper spreads, and from rural weeklies to the daily papers of New York City. Gosden and Correll took pains to avoid offending even minor elements of their audience. They quickly learned that, if Amos became ill after eating six hamburgers, some mogul of the beef industry might complain; likewise the fish canners if a character happened to mention his dislike for mackerel.[6] Gosden and Correll's spectacular success itself seemed to reinforce their popularity. The pair's six-figure radio and movie contracts won attention in both the news and the editorial columns of the press. Far from stirring resentment—even as the Great Depression deepened—the riches won by Correll and Gosden and by a few other radio stars seemed to evoke fascination and admiration; they offered an upbeat contrast to the dreary post-1929 economy.[7]

Few aspects of *Amos 'n' Andy* won as much approving comment in the press as its "clean," wholesome character. During the first several years of *Amos 'n' Andy*, the film industry became the lightning rod for a reaction against the liberalized social mores—in dress, music, popular dance, and the behavior of women—for which the "roaring" 1920s are still remembered today. In an era when states and localities across America sponsored official boards of censorship, the Hollywood studios defended themselves by adopting their own code forbidding excessive violence, religious and ethnic slurs, and—above all—"obscenity" and "indecency."[8] In such an atmosphere, Gosden and Correll took pains not so much to keep their act "clean"—for *Amos 'n' Andy* by its very nature hardly lent itself to lewdness—but to proclaim it so at every opportunity. By 1931, the year following the establishment of the motion picture code, Gosden was citing his show's wholesomeness as one of two reasons for *Amos 'n' Andy*'s success (the other being the humanity and universality the pair claimed to invest in their characters). Where the early Sam and Henry had smoked and occasionally drunk alcohol and gambled, Gosden now boasted that Amos and Andy neither practiced these vices—except for Andy's "big 'seegar' "—nor swore. "We get many letters from ministers and from mothers commending us for the cleanliness of our work on the air," Gosden declared.[9]

The American press did not need much convincing on this score. An editorialist in Richmond took satisfaction in *Amos 'n' Andy*'s popularity, particularly because it far exceeded that of "the newest filth from Hollywood." Another editor rejoiced that *Amos 'n' Andy* gave the lie to producers of entertainment who allegedly believed "there is a demand for risqué performances that violate the old moralities and decencies."[10] Accolades for the "good wholesome fun" of *Amos 'n' Andy* came in fan letters, newspaper columns, and published letters to editors—including some written by Afro-Americans.[11] As usual, Gosden almost instinctively understood the psychology of his audience. With their conspicuous concern for "decency," he and Correll gave Americans yet another reason to listen to *Amos 'n' Andy* and to praise it: in doing so, listeners could lay claim to good taste and sound values in a time when many worried that old, comfortable verities were under attack.

Amos 'n' Andy spoke reassuringly about another, deeper social issue: the Great Depression. The stock market crashed ten weeks after the debut of the series on NBC, and the economic disaster that followed beset the public mind for years afterward. Amos and Andy called it the "repression," and they occasionally addressed the issue in thinly veiled pep talks, exhorting listeners to face the future with optimism, or even offering economic prescriptions. Amos, having heard a speech on the importance of consumer confidence, laments to Andy that even people with a little money "is 'shamed to buy sumpin' 'cause other people is goin' think funny, an' dey'se afraid dat dey might hurt other people." On the contrary, Amos explains, "Ev'y time you buy sumpin' you he'p de man dat CAN'T 'ford to buy nuthin', 'cause you put people to work."[12]

More typical and subtle was Gosden and Correll's portrayal of Andy as a self-important but inept capitalist. The audience took special pleasure in Andy's entrepreneurial misadventures, judging from the newspaper coverage those segments drew and from the frequency with which Gosden and Correll—ever-responsive to popular demand—resorted to them. These storylines took on a special resonance in the Depression era, when many believed that the capitalists who had ridden high and forecast unlimited growth in the 1920s had in fact helped to wreck the economy through greed, carelessness, and incompetence. A writer in Los Angeles late in 1930 compared "the financial 'experts' or 'wizards' of the country," who offered no way out of the economic slump, to Andy with his impressive-sounding but meaningless financial calculations. The "wizards," he wrote, "have been sitting in their easy chairs emulating Andy in the taxicab office, repeating—'Seven million—ten million—This IS a mess.' "[13]

But Gosden and Correll's portrayal of the taxi company and Amos and Andy's other business ventures satirized more than just the failures of high finance. Andy embodied not only the businessman's fall from grace, but also the greed and hubris in people of all classes. Gosden and Correll saved the overbearing Andy from becoming too unsympathetic a character precisely by having him fail and suffer; listeners could feel both impatience with businessmen as a class and empathy for the struggling individual entrepreneur. Amos, meanwhile, represented the little man trying to better himself and to make the best of a bad situation. An American public that had lost its way and suffered a disaster, yet plodded forward day after day in the hope of better times to come, could identify with both these types—to the degree listeners were prepared to look beyond the characters' race.

Amos 'n' Andy could ease the Depression blues in any number of other ways. The series made the calamity seem momentarily amusing, and therefore more bearable, through Andy's garbled explanations of the Depression's causes; it made sport of Wall Street manipulators through the Kingfish's commentary on their doings; and its characters put in a good word for President Franklin D. Roosevelt now and then.[14] Gosden and Correll dealt so skillfully with the economic crisis, in fact, that many Americans today remember their show as the consummate Depression comedy and consider that achievement to have been the primary reason for *Amos 'n' Andy*'s huge popularity.[15]

In reality, Gosden and Correll had played Andy and his forerunner Henry as flamboyant but hapless businessmen since 1926, and their series became a great hit while the boom of the '20s still seemed likely to go on forever. When hard times did come, the pair did not significantly alter their show. As in their decision of 1926 to depict black characters of the Great Migration, the kind of material that Gosden and Correll were best equipped to perform happened to mesh compellingly with developments that were changing American life in profound ways. The two men dealt cleverly and adroitly with the Depression because they were and always had been good topical satirists.

Their characters frequently discussed the pre-Depression presidential election campaign of 1928, in which New York Governor Alfred E. Smith opposed Secretary of Commerce Hoover. Shortly after the two political parties made their nominations, Gosden and Correll used one installment of *Amos 'n' Andy* to skewer politicians of various stripes.[16] A black ward heeler tries to convince Amos and Andy to vote Republican. One of his "proofs" of Hoover's superiority in fact lampoons the failure of President Calvin Coolidge and Secretary Hoover to ease the economic woes that plagued farmers throughout the period of general prosperity in the 1920s. "Herbert Hoover," says the politico, "knows more 'bout politics dan any other one man in de country. . . . [H]e is done figgerd out de farm relief in such a way dat de farmers is happy an' dey dont know it." As for the Socialists, Andy's misrendering of their party's name as "social-risk" packs an entire political commentary into a single word. Andy proceeds to explain that the Socialists are the party that "puts ev'vybody on de same basin."

Andy: . . . How much money is you got?—I'll show you how to be a social-risk.

Amos: I got four dollars.

Andy: Well, yo' see—I aint got nuthin'—you gimme two dollahs an' you'll be a social-risk.

Amos: I better go back to de democrats—dat's whut I better do.

The episode ends with a trenchant and unmistakable satirical swipe at "Hoovercrats"—those Democrats, especially in the South, who abandoned their party's nominee in 1928 because Smith was a Roman Catholic and an opponent of Prohibition. The Republican political operator assures Amos, who considers himself a Democrat, that he can "vote fo' Herbert Hoover—den after 'lection you kin still be a democrat." "Well, you kin count on me den," Amos replies. "I'll vote fo' Hoover but I just wanna let yo' know dat I'se a democrat—I'll die a democrat."

The colloquy between Amos and Andy and the politician illustrates more than just its authors' early and effective use of topical satire. Gosden and Correll wove the scene out of several threads;

teasing out these different strands reveals much about how *Amos 'n' Andy* won the hearts of a diverse people undergoing rapid, sometimes wrenching social change.

Although Al Smith emerges unscathed from this particular dialogue, the sketch typifies Correll and Gosden's evenhandedness, twitting Democrats and Republicans alike. So does the exchange in which Andy tries to convince Amos to vote Republican:

Amos: Well, de republicans aint ever done nuthin' fo' me.
Andy: Dey is done as much fo' yo' as de democrats is done.
Amos: De democrats aint done nuthin' fo' me yet.
Andy: Well, dere you is.[17]

Gosden and Correll's political impartiality—reinforced by visits to both Hoover and Franklin Roosevelt during their respective administrations—allowed them to use piquant humor like their parody of the Hoovercrat defections without causing resentment.

Still more important, perhaps, Correll and Gosden put their occasional sociopolitical barbs in the mouths, if not of babes, then at least of characters whom they represented as naifs. They inherited that practice from the classical minstrels, who had used the stump speaker in much the same way. Amos and Andy's ignorance and rural naiveté made them good conduits for subtle satirical comment—much as the same qualities, along with his youth, permitted Huckleberry Finn innocently to convey Mark Twain's condemnation of slavery and racism to a mostly white mass readership. Like Twain, Gosden and Correll achieved something further with their indirection: they offered the discerning listener the satisfaction of extracting the satire, each time relishing his or her own perceptiveness and sophistication.

Like the blacked-up stump speaker of the nineteenth century, Amos, Andy, and the others readily addressed issues—such as Hoover's agricultural policy or Coolidge's veto of "de Hogan, Mc-Darry Farm relief bill"—that had nothing to do with race. Indeed, even in *Amos 'n' Andy*'s topical dialogues, Gosden and Correll held firmly to their policy of not discussing the question of color. This prim silence in a series that implicitly raised issues of race in every sentence was part of a more complicated balancing act than that between political parties—a quest for balance that the shifting racial terrain of the times demanded.

As the first performers who gave the American masses a detailed picture of black life in the northern city, Gosden and Correll had their characters do some things that were forbidden to Afro-Americans in much of the South. For example, many southern whites were so intent on excluding their black neighbors from political life that they or their fathers had resorted to fraud, threats, assault, and even murder; yet Correll and Gosden regularly showed Amos, Andy, and other blacks voting and discussing politics. Moreover, the radio team portrayed the black man who solicited the pair's votes for Hoover as "a big politician" who did not hesitate to criticize the Democratic party's delegation in Congress, which was all white and largely southern. In that era—when Hollywood producers usually avoided the slightest hint of racial equality in their films for fear of southern censorship and boycotts[18]—why did performers as obsessive about avoiding controversy as Gosden and Correll feel so free to broadcast these election segments?

The team incorporated a variety of safety valves into their work. By having their characters discuss tariffs and farm bills rather than the race question, Gosden and Correll divorced the political activity of their creations from those realms in which many white listeners saw black participation as a threat. Not content with removing the really hot issues from the table, the pair went so far as to have Amos proclaim himself a dyed-in-the-wool Democrat who had inherited that conviction from his "Gram'pa"[19]—a strange sort of "grandfather clause" for a figure like Amos, whose own race had been disfranchised by the Democrats in the same period his grandpa was supposedly extolling them.

Furthermore, Correll and Gosden portrayed Amos and Andy as innocents easily manipulated by political hacks. "I dont know nuthin' 'bout de 'lection," Amos admits in 1928. "I dont even know who is runnin'." Andy then characterizes the contest as "Al. Smith vesuvius Herbert Hoover." Even the "colored politician," though he may be "big" in influence and more knowledgeable than Amos and Andy, is none too bright: "Brothers," he explains, "we is gotta go back an' look at de his'try of each one of de candidates—den in redition to dat, we is gotta look at dey're platform an' dey're referendum." As for the sanctity of the ballot in Chicago's black precincts, Gosden and Correll have Amos mention that one of his lodge brothers is "countin' on votin' ten times." And a few days later, after Andy—for no particular reason—has proclaimed that he too is a Democrat, he and Amos switch their allegiance immediately upon reading of plans for a Republican parade with a twenty-five-piece band, which will allow them to strut in their new clothes.[20] Gosden and Correll trotted out the old

Zip Coon/dandy routine as if to make up for showing blacks actively involved in politics.

This counterpoise between realism and heavy stereotyping was an essential part of the white team's larger balancing act. So was the way *Amos 'n' Andy* compensated for depicting blacks who had left the South—a development many white Southerners resented and opposed—by painting a benign picture of the conditions Amos and Andy left behind in Georgia. Amos's occasional bouts with nostalgia for the South served the same purpose: lugging his and Andy's suitcases as the two search for a place to live in Chicago, Amos "kind-a wish[es] . . . dat I was standin' on Peachtree street in Atlanta." Yet Gosden and Correll, pursuing the golden mean, employed such lines sparingly enough to avoid the cloying, incredible "longin' for the old plantation" that some minstrel songs had expressed. Within a few days of Amos's reverie about Peachtree Street, Amos and Andy sit in their room, cooking beans and wondering where future meals will come from. A letter from home describing barbecues and chicken dinners makes the pair excruciatingly hungry, yet neither expresses a wish to be back in Georgia.[21]

By the time they launched *Amos 'n' Andy*, Correll and Gosden had already developed a knack for appealing to a nationwide audience that encompassed a variety of notions about blacks and their place in American society. The team's political humor, like the rest of *Amos 'n' Andy*, offered something for almost everyone. For those of either race to whom a portrayal of big-city black life devoid of political activity would have seemed flat and unconvincing, Gosden and Correll depicted their characters electioneering. At the same time, the racist could find the ignorant "coon" he knew and cherished, while listeners of all persuasions could enjoy clever commentary on nonracial political and social issues.

Even the "nonracial" components of *Amos 'n' Andy*, however, were served up by black characters. Of all the factors in *Amos 'n' Andy*'s unprecedented popularity, its creators' use of race is the most complex, coloring every other element of the show's unique appeal. Yes, the broadcasts were "clean." But judging their wholesomeness in the larger sense of the word—as a picture of black people, created by white men for a largely white audience—requires a different, more complicated set of standards. Did the show's high "moral" tone—exemplified by Amos's kindness, conscientiousness, industry, and loyalty, and by his chaste, romantic love for Ruby—prompt the white listener to see its characters as fully human, universal personalities whom he or she could care deeply about?

Gosden and Correll did gain friends by not stepping on the toes of commercial, political, or religious groups. But the "interest" that had by far the most at stake was not the meatpackers, the Bible Belt whites, the Democrats, or the Republicans, but rather the group that the show portrayed every day for every moment it was on the air— Afro-Americans. The radio team poked fun at businessmen in general; but they did it largely through Andy, whose race and "coon"-like ignorance might obscure the universality of the satire. *Amos 'n' Andy*'s catchphrases sprouted in casual American conversation like weeds; but when millions of whites used caricatured expressions based on "black" English, the repartee might carry special social and historical undertones. "I'se regusted" and "Sho', sho' " had resonances that "Wanna buy a duck?" and "T'ain't funny, McGee!"—trademark phrases from other popular radio series—did not.

Gosden and Correll succeeded partly because they and their handlers were masters of publicity, but all the hoopla in the world could not have sold a bland, conventional product year in and year out, as the stars of many canceled shows could attest. RKO Pictures learned this lesson from Amos 'n' Andy's movie, *Check and Double Check*, in 1930, onto which the company grafted a second storyline featuring white characters. (RKO feared that Amos 'n' Andy, whom the public was used to hearing in fifteen-minute doses, would not be able to "carry" an entire movie.) Few films of that time were promoted so extravagantly; screaming headlines in two-page newspaper spreads proclaimed that "A Breathless World Awaits" the "most Unique Entertainment in World History!" Yet the public's initial rush to the moviehouses quickly dissipated as early audiences had little good to say about what they had seen.[22] Fans preferred the pictures that Gosden and Correll created through words alone, without "help" from white characters or from Hollywood executives who tried to market Amos 'n' Andy by diluting its very essence.

There were many reasons for the *Amos 'n' Andy* phenomenon; for such a long-lasting and spectacular success, there almost had to be. But in the end, most of them lead back to a simple truth: no explanation of the *Amos 'n' Andy* sensation is possible without a close look at the question of color.

Gosden and Correll themselves put the race of their characters at the center of their work, and not only by what they did during their daily quarter-hour on the air. The games they played with the color line on the Pantages theater circuit in 1929 were not their last. Using special makeup and spotlights, the pair continued to present their quick-change illusion in personal appearances for some months after joining NBC. In at least one city, a local ice cream parlor recognized the interest that the team's chameleonism had aroused among the public; it vigorously promoted a vanilla-with-chocolate "Amos 'n' Andy sundae" as "A Delight—in Black 'n' White."[23]

Gosden and Correll's publicity had emphasized race all along—though at first without suggesting any racial paradox of the kind that their light-trick later created. The Chicago *Tribune*, whose station WGN broadcast *Sam 'n' Henry*, consistently referred to the team as "two colored boys" and often discussed the characters as though they were real people. The paper ran drawings depicting Sam and Henry as caricatured black men, and for months it did not mention that the actors on the show were white. "For a long time," a newspaper in Tulsa recalled two years later, "many fans . . . believed the entertainers to be colored." Late in Correll and Gosden's first year as Sam 'n' Henry, the *Tribune* finally distributed photos of the two white men; "My, Aren't You 'Sprised?" a headline in one Illinois paper asked readers.[24] Months of subsequent press attention to the white Gosden and Correll could not dislodge from many listeners' minds the images that the pair worked so hard to create over the radio. The very first page after the introduction to the book *All About Amos 'n' Andy* in 1929 answered the four questions that fans still asked most often about Gosden and Correll; one of these was, "Are the boys white or colored?" Nearly a year after *Amos 'n' Andy*'s move to NBC, a columnist in Cincinnati still found it necessary to point out to his readers that the two actors were white.[25]

After Gosden and Correll's true race was revealed, they and their promoters continued to remind listeners that they meant to portray the life of real Afro-Americans—unlike many traditional blackface performers since the Civil War. Even beyond its radio page, the Chicago *Tribune* equated Sam and Henry with the city's real black citizens. The Great Migration had created an important new market of Afro-American consumers, and the paper ran a long news article about a big new store to be built on the black South Side. The *Tribune* proclaimed in a headline and again in the body of the story that "Sam 'n' Henry are to have a complete department store all of their own." That language, though a bit facetious, accorded with the *Tribune*'s claim that Gosden and Correll represented blacks of the South Side pretty much as they really were.[26]

One way that publicity for *Amos 'n' Andy* encouraged such perceptions and reinforced the racial identity of the show's characters was through inflated claims that Gosden and Correll did research among blacks when preparing their broadcasts. Their announcer Bill Hay touted the team's "intimate knowledge of Negro nature" and assured fans that "both men spend as much time as possible among Negroes, making a study of accents and witticisms and garnering ideas for situations." Because Correll and Gosden "go among negroes [and] learn their ways and foibles," a Baltimore paper declared, "their picturization of Southern negroes transplanted to the North" might well be "the most realistic ever accomplished."[27]

When the setting of *Amos 'n' Andy* shifted from Chicago to Harlem for the network premiere of the series in 1929, Gosden and Correll assured the public that they were sensitive to the subtle "difference[s] between the life and habits" of blacks in various cities. Correll announced plans to "do some real research work" in New York before the transition: he and Gosden would "spend a good deal of time in the black-and-tan district, in the cabarets, listening to the negroes talk and picking up atmosphere for a new series of episodes." Some weeks later, a widely published report even asserted that Gosden and Correll, "not content with anything that merely smacked of a sightseeing trip through New York's great Negro district," had actually lived among "the Harlem colored folk."[28]

Much of the team's publicity during the first four years after the debut of *Sam 'n' Henry*, however, reinforced the characters' color in a very different way: it emphasized not only the supposed realism of the broadcasts, but also their kinship to old-style, racially stereotyped images. The Chicago *Tribune* published and distributed photographs of "Sam" and "Henry" in burnt cork, huge white lips, shabby clothing, and comic poses. The paper occasionally discussed the fictional pair in ways that recalled the minstrel shows and "coon" songs. One ad for the radio series referred to Sam and Henry as "these two blots of ink." Another announced a public autographing session by "Henry." "Please don't ask Sam" for his autograph, the paper requested parenthetically; "he can't write, and you'd just hurt his feelings."[29]

Such extreme stereotyping misrepresented Gosden and Correll's work; they had portrayed Sam reading and writing, sometimes fluently, in their radio episodes. But a white public that had been brought up on a diet of "coon" images casually accepted this openly belittling sort of humor—and some people reflexively saw Correll and Gosden as working in that tradition. The pair's subsequent employers, the Chicago *Daily News* and the NBC network, continued to trade on *Amos 'n' Andy*'s links with the past, though less crudely than the *Tribune* had. The *News* supplemented its new, daily *Amos 'n' Andy* programs with a weekly minstrel-show broadcast built around the main characters from the serial.[30] The *Amos 'n' Andy* book of 1929 included photographs of Gosden and Correll in grotesque blackface makeup enacting scenes from their broadcasts. In advertising the volume to booksellers, the publisher referred to the two men as "darky comedians," a term that did little to enhance their credentials as innovators. The press coverage of the transition to NBC in August 1929 recycled the same old photos of the white actors in clownish blackface getup.[31]

Only with the making of *Check and Double Check* in 1930 did photos and drawings of a different kind come to be used frequently. In these, as in the movie itself, Gosden and Correll wore what was meant to be realistic makeup rather than grotesque, conventionalized blackface. That was an important shift. What had not changed, however, was the centrality, the indispensability, of the characters' color.

But which dark image represented the "real" *Amos 'n' Andy*? The traditional, caricatured "coon"? Or the modern, urban Afro-American, whose life Gosden and Correll said they found interesting enough to merit close study and conscientious reproduction in their broadcasts? Either way, of course, the pair aimed to make most of their black characters amusing, often in ways that reinforced racial stereotypes; and besides, many white Americans failed to grasp that there was any essential contradiction between minstrel images and real black life. Gosden and Correll, however, declared that there *was* a difference between hackneyed caricature and semirealism, and they laid claim to authenticity with an earnestness not often heard since classical minstrelsy with its plantation tableaux began to give way to the baroque in the mid-nineteenth century. The radio team's avowed goal—to depict the Afro-Americans of the post-World War I northern metropolis—was, on its face, as new as the minstrel tradition was ancient, as novel as the Great Migration itself.

Jim McIntyre of McIntyre and Heath—one famous, veteran blackface duo that itself claimed to portray blacks authentically—denied that Correll and Gosden were doing anything original. If he and Heath had ever "bothered" with radio, said McIntyre in 1930, they would have demolished the younger team. McIntyre and Heath had "been doing a nigger act for 50 years," the old-timer sniffed, and other blackface performers—especially Amos 'n' Andy—simply copied them.[32]

Was McIntyre right? Were Gosden and Correll, in spite of all their claims, just another "nigger act" that could have been transported back to 1910 or 1880 without having to change anything more than a few stage props and their Harlem backdrop? The content of their broadcasts offers one set of answers. But in the end, the people who tuned in *Amos 'n' Andy* defined the show, and interpreted its messages, for themselves.

8

·····━━●◅━━·····

A Changing Racial Landscape

For people who lived in a racially segregated society, white Americans in the late 1920s and early 1930s spent more than a little of their time thinking about blacks. Those who lived in places with large and longstanding black populations—mainly in the South—knew Afro-Americans as employees, as servants, or at least as a constant and visible part of the daily scene. In the cities that had become destinations for thousands of black migrants from the rural South, whites looked at their new neighbors with interest, amusement, scorn, or resentment. Even whites who lived in areas untouched by the Great Migration heard and read about racial change and conflict in the city and about growing black political assertiveness, and they listened to Afro-American musicians through the new mass medium of radio. White Americans of all regions, classes, and persuasions got a steady diet of black images, which pervaded popular literature, entertainment, and comic strips as they had for years.

And everyone, it seemed, listened to *Amos 'n' Andy*. Because whites thought about blacks in a variety of ways, and because Gosden and Correll sent mixed signals about their intentions and packed such a diversity of elements into their broadcasts, different listeners heard any number of different things there. *Amos 'n' Andy* served as a kind of Rorschach test of each white fan's attitudes; white responses overall trace a map of America's changing racial landscape and the color line that divided it up in ever more complex and ambiguous ways.

Traditional "Negro impersonators" and popular writers had usually portrayed Afro-Americans as peculiar and inferior, though often likable in limited ways. In the years around 1930, there were still many whites who preferred those old images—some in spite of the racial changes in the real world, but others precisely because of them. Such people tended to see the blackness of Gosden and Correll's characters as essential rather than incidental, and to think of real black Americans—and not just those in comedic entertainments—as amusing buffoons. One fan wrote a poem in appreciation of *Sam 'n' Henry*. His concluding lines made it clear that he understood the show as dealing in old-style "coon" stereotypes, and that he endorsed these without reservation: he encouraged Gosden and Correll to "Make poor Sambo's empty noodle/Bring you profits every day."[1]

Of all the incarnations of the fictional "coon," few had been more widely exploited on the stage or in popular jokes than the shiftless black chicken thief. A newspaper in East Texas saw Gosden and Correll's characters as fitting that mold; the paper revealed the arrest of two local black men for stealing chickens by announcing that "Beaumont has it's [*sic*] own Sam an' Henry!" Nowhere did the reporter even mention the full names of the accused, preferring to call the men by the names of the "Chicago radio favorites" throughout the article; the smirking headline read, "Sam An' Henry Plead Guilty In Fowl Theft." The author quoted the defendants as saying they filched the birds "cause we was hungry"—a hearty appetite, along with sleepiness, figuring prominently among the supposed traits of the "coon."[2]

A newspaper article in 1930 noted that a radio station in Fort Worth was regularly broadcasting a comic blackface duo called Honeyboy and Sassafras. The article pictured that team in grotesque blackface makeup, and explained that they combined "the slow drawlings of the 'Blue Gum' negro with the snappy repartee of the 'High-Yellow' darky." The writer of the piece found these old-fashioned and racially insulting radio routines comparable to Gosden and Correll's work; he called Honeyboy and Sassafras "KSAT's 'Amos 'n' Andy.' "[3]

The poetic suggestion that "Sambo's noodle" tended to be empty, whether he was a character in *Amos 'n' Andy* or a real Afro-American, echoed in the comments of other listeners at least as late as the mid-1930s. One paper in California ran a picture of a skydiver posing with "Andy and Amos, the two parachute test dummies," which were headless. Lest any reader miss the intended comparison, the caption explained that this "Amos and Andy have no heads at all which is a charge sometimes leveled at the whole fraternity." The writer did not specify whether he was referring to the Mystic Knights of the Sea or the entire black race.[4]

Fans at a personal appearance by Gosden and Correll in Norfolk, Virginia, in 1935 showed special enthusiasm for a heavily stereotyped secondary figure from *Amos 'n' Andy* called Lightning. A slow-witted, drawling Stepin Fetchit type, Lightning may well have been the purest example of the classic "coon" that Gosden and Correll ever created. His very nickname was a joke, and in at least one episode his creators had portrayed him as unsure even of his own last name. In Norfolk, Lightning was the one "incidental character . . . [who] won a roar of applause and laughter by the mere mention of his name, even before Mr. Gosden sounded his voice."[5]

Sometimes whites pinned the traditional images they enjoyed in *Amos 'n' Andy* onto real Afro-American individuals. An old friend from Freeman Gosden's Navy days remarked that his fellow patients in a veterans' hospital in Virginia had taken to calling "one of the maids who works in an adjoining Ward . . . 'Madam Queen' . . . for good and sufficient reasons." Gosden's correspondent did not state those reasons, but one assumes the appellation was not meant to be flattering. Whites adopted names of *Amos 'n' Andy* characters as joking or even derisive nicknames for real blacks often enough to make this one of the specific grievances against *Amos 'n' Andy* cited by the black Pittsburgh *Courier* and some of its readers during the paper's protest of 1931.[6]

Some white listeners who enjoyed mainly the traditional elements in *Amos 'n' Andy* seemed not to notice the show's innovative urban setting or its concern with the still-unfolding Great Migration. These were often people whose lives the real Migration had not affected much; the South, where Afro-Americans were departing, not arriving in large numbers, apparently had more than its share of them. These listeners' view of the black race did not necessarily grow out of their own immediate concerns; often, they had simply inherited attitudes that had arisen years before out of the racial anxieties and rationalizations of their forebears. A different kind of racist response came *particularly* from northern cities, often from people who did recognize *Amos 'n' Andy* as a pathbreaking treatment of a new arena of black American life. The minstrel-style layers of Gosden and Correll's portrait of the Great Migration helped these whites in the urban North to ease their own uncertainty about racial change and to justify their resentment or disgust at the actual influx of blacks they were witnessing round about them.

Several white newspaper writers in northern cities explicitly equated the characters in *Amos 'n' Andy* with the real denizens of Harlem and then wrote both groups off as eccentric and ludicrous. One man produced a series of stories for the *Radio Digest* and the Washington *Post*, rendering large portions of his text in what was supposed to be black dialect. The writer jokingly claimed to have interviewed Amos and Andy "on 134th street on the dark side of New York" at an hour when "all Ethiopia [was] abroad." While strolling among "dusky citizens" ranging from an "old white-haired darky and several urchins" to a "little tot in kinky braids," the writer had supposedly found Amos and Andy's taxicab—a decrepit vehicle bound together with "hay wire," whose lack of a roof admitted "fresh air everywhere but in the tires!" He went on to give an overt answer to a question that Gosden and Correll always left to the listener: whether Amos and Andy's inadequacies were those of blacks specifically or of humankind at large. This reporter stated in so many words that the "Neanderthal" taxi was pretty much the type of operation one would expect from a "dusky, kinky-haired young industrialist."[7]

A court case involving a black citizen of Harlem in 1930 came to center on *Amos 'n' Andy* and led several white commentators to offer their views of what big-city life was like among Afro-Americans. A white judge summoned a black taxi driver, whom he had sentenced the day before to four months for assault, back from the Tombs prison. The judge told the prisoner that listening to *Amos 'n' Andy* the night before had convinced him "that a cab driver in Harlem has a pretty hard time, after all." As a result, the judge revoked the jail sentence and placed the black man on probation.[8]

The judge—whom one paper quoted as saying he found "some pretty good philosophy in things Amos said" on the radio—may not have intended to mock the defendant or blacks in general. But no benevolent impulses got in the way of several New York papers, whose interest in the case had been aroused by the *Amos 'n' Andy* angle. None failed to mention the black man's specific crime—an assault on a ladyfriend that evoked the image of the impulsive, violent "bad nigger." One reporter in particular could not contain his scornful amusement at the case of this "Negro boy" (in fact a man of thirty-seven) who had discovered that a certain woman, once the defendant's "most intimate friend," had become "someone else's most intimate friend." The writer archly reported that the cabbie "hit her in the left eye, broke her glasses, cut her face, and when she still refused to resume their friendship he kicked her in the right leg." The same writer quoted the cabdriver in caricatured "Negro" dialect, and related the judge's hope that the defendant's religion ("I'm a Babtis, jedge") would help him "to keep away from your women."[9]

Gosden and Correll can hardly be blamed for the racism of the contemporary press. *Amos 'n' Andy*, however, did contain elements that appealed to whites who not only held traditional views of race, but who also felt urgent, real-world racial insecurities. Such listeners found it easy and reassuring to assume that the radio characters and real urban Afro-Americans shared a certain imbecilic inferiority. They held to the century-old idea that city life would magnify the black man's supposed incompetence and antisocial tendencies, but *Amos 'n' Andy* helped them to express that belief politely and comfortably— with a chuckle rather than a sigh or a shudder.

For a century and more, immigrants had typically been quick to absorb the racist attitudes that native-born white Americans grew up with. Fear of competition from cheap black labor always fueled the process, and that worry again became intense in northern cities during the massive black migration. Irish-Americans in particular had a history of antipathy toward blacks, and they had played a prominent role in the massive Chicago race riot of 1919, which was above all a response by whites to the Great Migration of blacks into that city. A desire to be accepted into the ranks of "real," white Americans had also fed immigrant disdain for blacks; blackface entertainment and the "coon" stereotype had long been popular among immigrants, as among natives.

Many immigrants and their children may have enjoyed the universal elements of *Amos 'n' Andy* as much as, or instead of, the show's stereotypical aspects. But the reactions of some of them show how appealing traditional notions about blacks could be to people of various ethnic backgrounds in the early 1930s. Diogene Musacchio of Philadelphia painted the legend "Fresh Air Taxicab Co. of America Inc./Amos 'n' Andy" in intentionally crude letters on the side of his car to show "his appreciation for his favorite entertainers." In Buffalo, Morris Freedman and Joe Vastola donned traditional, grotesque blackface makeup to impersonate Amos and Andy in a student stunt night. As they awaited execution in a prison in Kansas City, "bandits" John Messino, Carl Nasello, and Tony Mangiarcino were reported to be following Amos and Andy's radio adventures with animated interest.

A news item quoted Mangiarcino as giving the guards credit for "treating us white" by letting them tune in the show during their last hours on earth.[10]

The novelist James T. Farrell set his *Studs Lonigan* trilogy of 1932–1935 in *Amos 'n' Andy*'s, and his own, home city of Chicago. With unblinking realism, Farrell depicted the Irish-American Lonigans' bitter flight from their old neighborhood to escape an influx of blacks whom they consider little better than animals. Although *Amos 'n' Andy* depicted the same Great Migration that led to the Lonigans' exodus, the radio series contained enough conventional stereotypes to ease the pain and the fear of people like Studs's immigrant father. "You would have laughed yourself sick at them," he tells Studs, speaking about Amos, Andy, and friends. "They're so much like darkies. Not the fresh northern niggers, but the genuine real southern darkies, the good niggers . . . , lazy, happy-go-lucky, strutting themselves out in titles . . . and honors, just like in real life."[11]

Gosden and Correll's picture of blacks in the North attracted not only people who wished that the race had stayed, mentally if not physically, in the South, but also many whites who seemed to believe blacks had done just that. It did not occur to these listeners that the Great Migration might be changing the Afro-American, and some of them showed no signs of noticing that a massive migration was even taking place. Although the backward-looking, stereotypical components of *Amos 'n' Andy* might appeal to such fans, some of them particularly liked the elements of broader human interest in the series—especially in the South, where the Great Migration did not present the urgent issue that it did in the northern city.

Some praised both *Amos 'n' Andy*'s characters and the black race as a whole in an affectionately patronizing way which recalled the attitude of southern conservatives in Thomas Nelson Page's heyday. One such tribute came from former Governor M. R. Patterson of Tennessee. Rather than seeing the main characters of the radio series as an undifferentiated pair of headless dummies, he emphasized that "one [was] just opposite to the other and both true to life." Still, Gosden and Correll had left enough of the South in their central characters to make them utterly recognizable—and the show's northern backdrop inconsequential—to people like Patterson. Though he judged Andy the perfect example of an "ignorant egotist," Patterson found Amos "at times . . . irresistible in his simplicity, the perfect type of the sweet tempered, trustful and honest negro we have all seen here in the South, and for whom we can not help having genuine interest and affection."[12] Patterson found support in *Amos 'n' Andy* for his view that blacks, like other human beings, ought to be treated kindly, but that they did best when they had white guidance. Some notable political careers in the South had been built on crude appeals to white racism over the preceding decades; Theodore Bilbo and Eugene Talmadge would carry the technique to new lows during the *Amos 'n' Andy* years. Yet all the while, Patterson's brand of "responsible" conservativism claimed many adherents among the South's leading whites.

Ironically, a thinking southern white listener might overlook *Amos 'n' Andy*'s northern setting not out of obliviousness to changes in America's racial landscape, but rather out of an enlightened recognition of change. In March 1930, at the height of the *Amos 'n' Andy* craze, a columnist in the Charlotte *Observer* lauded several local radio broadcasts that featured "colored talent" performing "delightful" and "finely rendered" spirituals, and he gave a serious, respectful summary of a broadcast talk by a black minister. The *Observer*'s writer counted residents of the Charlotte area "privileged to hear the real in negro melody" rather than the "imitation stuff" broadcast by certain Chicago stations. Yet Gosden and Correll's work passed muster for this southern liberal who so valued authenticity; he earnestly suggested that the local black quartet he found so good and so genuine "would make an excellent companion piece to Amos n' Andy."[13]

To the *Observer*'s man, it was irrelevant that the characters he found so engaging played out their daily dramas in a northern city. Cities in the South had long contained large, relatively complex Afro-American communities with a top layer of ministers and other professional people, so Amos and Andy's South Side or Harlem in many ways looked familiar to urban southern whites. The less tradition-bound among these people had even come to believe that black community notables ought to be consulted occasionally by the whites who ran things. Southern liberals such as the *Observer*'s writer, like *Amos 'n' Andy* itself, recognized the human face of the Afro-American and granted him or her a kind of respect. But both the southern white liberal and the Chicago radio team were still defining the New Negro partly in the old ways, and they were both humanizing a segregated system. In the short run, that made things seem more pleasant and civil, but blacks in later years would begin to see efforts to smooth off the rough edges of southern apartheid as a major obstacle on the road to equality.

White Southerners of various persuasions, then, exercised an option that Gosden and Correll's work, in its ambiguity, tendered them: they saw the *Amos 'n' Andy* characters as "their" blacks—as Afro-Southerners. For most of America's history, almost all blacks had lived in the South, and a large majority still did; southern whites had long claimed to have special knowledge of Afro-American character which equipped them to handle their race problem without interference from misguided Yankees. One fan from Arkansas paid Gosden and Correll what he considered the ultimate compliment, proclaiming that Southerners like himself "that know 'the nigger' . . . appreciate the fidelity with which they portray them." Another listener—a Presbyterian minister—assured the broadcasters that his approval of *Amos 'n' Andy* carried special weight: being "a Georgian by birth and rearing," he wrote, qualified him to judge "impersonators of the negro."[14]

That southern whites still thought highly of their own credentials as experts on black people is no surprise. The real news about the Great Migration that emerges from some white responses to Gosden and Correll's show—whose *sine qua non* was its northern, urban setting—is how many Americans in all regions, even a decade or two into the Migration, either had not *got* the news, or did not understand what it meant. Many whites outside the South continued to think of Afro-Americans as a southern group and to accept the notion that southern whites knew everything worth knowing about the black race. When an Illinois paper ran a photo in 1926 that gave away Gosden and Correll's true color, the caption under the two white faces read, "they're not from Dixie, as you see." Of course, Gosden *was* from the South; the carelessly reasoned caption reflects the equally careless but common assumption that blacks were all Southerners. As late as 1935, a northern reporter could refer to the "authentic Harlem, or deep-south accents" in *Amos 'n' Andy* as if those two speech varieties were one and the same.[15]

"Gosden's Southern birth instilled him with an inherent understanding of the Negro," wrote Douglas Gilbert in his twelve-part newspaper series on *Amos 'n' Andy* in 1930. That osmotic knowledge, Gilbert added, ensured that Gosden would be "inherently truthful in his delineations" of "the Negro psychology." Show business journalists remedied Correll's northern origin by stating that Gosden had taught his partner the essentials of Negro character, or by declaring—with great exaggeration—that Correll had "spent many years in the south on vaudeville tours."[16] As a means of effortlessly acquiring insight into the Afro-American soul, simply planting one's feet on southern soil from time to time thus took its place alongside southern birth.

Besides these two paths to omniscience, white radio columnists suggested, and their readers apparently accepted, yet a third: heredity. Correll did, after all, have a southern grandmother. "Without doubt," a writer for the *Radio Mirror* assured her readers, "the Southern heritage of both troupers has been immeasurably helpful in [the] realism" their series achieved. In 1935, the southern credential still looked convincing. "Gosden was the one who supplied the knowledge of negro dialogue [*sic*] and characteristics" for the radio series, wrote one reporter in Iowa, "inasmuch as he is from the south and thoroughly understands the negro."[17] The attention given even in Boston to the exploits of Gosden's father in the Civil War was a variation on the same theme. Many white Americans now saw the Civil War as a romantic if tragic conflict between two gallant opponents; Walter Gosden's history as a Mosby ranger did not alienate Yankee readers, but rather established Freeman's credentials as "a true son of the South,"[18] which in turn qualified him in the eyes of many northern whites to interpret black characters.

To be sure, a high percentage of blacks residing in the North as of 1930 had been born in the South. But these Afro-Americans were now living—and many had lived for years—in a profoundly different situation from the one they had left behind. When northern whites assumed that Gosden's boyhood in the South made him an expert on Harlem or the South Side, they demonstrated something more than a failure to realize that a large and growing part of Afro-America was no longer southern. They also embraced a patronizing view of blacks—that the race possessed a peculiar "psychology" which the all-knowing southern white man comprehended fully. This idea that southern whites "knew the Negro" had deeply affected the fate of Afro-Americans for decades. The North had used that doctrine to justify its abandonment of southern blacks to the mercies of their white neighbors after Reconstruction. The same deference to white Southerners now helped to ensure that the southern states' near-autonomy in matters of race would not be radically challenged until the 1950s and beyond.

White America's response to *Amos 'n' Andy* encompassed much more than racism, inertia, and ignorance, however. Gosden and Correll's most remarkable accomplishment was to produce a show so rich and complex that it won admirers ranging from ultra-racists to outspoken racial egalitarians. Some of the latter could be almost as oblivious as the racists were to the importance of the Great Migration in molding a new Afro-America, and white liberals' understanding of their black fellow citizens was not free of fantasy. But the fantasies were different—sometimes a century old, yet sometimes redolent of the traumatic 1930s.

Some listeners found out-and-out moral paragons in *Amos 'n' Andy*, particularly in the character of Amos, and commended the series as a true-to-life course in Christian precepts. A couple even declared that the virtues of the *Amos 'n' Andy* characters were ones that real Afro-Americans possessed in unique abundance and that whites ought to imitate. Such views were typical of those scattered white church agencies, clergy, and lay persons in the 1920s and '30s, especially in the North, who had begun to press for changes in the conservative racial course that most Protestant churches had long followed. Women, both North and South, were especially active in this limited, often paternalistic, yet significant movement "to work for the 'equal' part of the 'separate but equal' doctrine" during the *Amos 'n' Andy* era.[19]

Lydia Glover Deseo, writing in a Methodist women's magazine published in Chicago, criticized traditional blackface entertainment for lacking "the droll, natural, incomparable humor of the typical Negro" and for "degrading . . . the true spirit of the Negro race." Deseo's description of the "typical" Afro-American was far less condescending than that term would imply today; she found Afro-Americans' own wit, rather than blacks as people, to be amusing. And where even white conservatives sometimes praised black spirituality, Deseo went further. She found in the race an "indefinable spiritual quality which places the Negro on a pedestal, high above those of us who have not suffered as poignantly." She put Gosden and Correll "in a class by themselves" for having captured something of the spirit of real Afro-Americans.[20]

Deseo believed, along with many white opponents of racial oppression over the previous century, that the races, though equal in the eyes of God, had different group characteristics. Most important, blacks were by nature kinder and more sentimental than whites—more "feminine," as some writers put it—and as a result they often made better Christians. Lydia Deseo's opinion of *Amos 'n' Andy* showed the resilience of this "romantic racialism," a reformist worldview that had been important as far back as Harriet Beecher Stowe's time.[21]

In a sermon delivered in 1931, Burris Jenkins, a noted Disciples of

Christ minister in Kansas City, likewise drew religious lessons from *Amos 'n' Andy*. But Jenkins—a New Testament scholar, former college president, and prolific author, especially of works on applied religion—sorted out what he saw as the universal and the specifically "Negro" merits of the show's characters more explicitly than Lydia Deseo had.[22] By and large, Jenkins found the series to be a depiction less of the black race than of general "human nature, grave and gay." "The devoted friendship between Amos and Andy," for example, "[compared] favorably with the historic friendships between any two men, running clear back to the time of David and Jonathan"—who, Jenkins added, "probably . . . were of about the same complexion as Amos and Andy." Amos, "harmless and kindly," possessed of industry and a "clear mind"; the "good and kind" Ruby; the "slow, . . . lazy, . . . futile" Lightning, and all the rest were not racial types. Rather, said Jenkins, they all made up "a picture gallery . . . in which most of us can find ourselves."

Jenkins did not dismiss Amos and Andy's race as irrelevant; the struggles of the "little bunch of Harlemites" reminded him of how much real blacks suffered and how much whites could learn from them. The preacher found vivid social criticism in a recent series of episodes in which "poor little Amos" had been mistakenly arrested and subjected to "what the average Negro dreads beyond anything except a hospital, the bars of a prison." Jenkins decried traditional stereotypes of blacks that depicted them as hedonistic, apathetic, and irresponsible. To the degree the race was in fact "careless and carefree," the attitude of whites "should be not one of condescension but of emulation." Harlem, said Jenkins, "holds more of the real joy of life than our boulevards or Riverside Drive or Park Avenue." He believed whites needed to "catch something of the independence of mere things, something of the joy in song, in human association, in conversation, in worship, that characterizes these humble people who possess so much freer spirits and deeper philosophy of living than we possess. . . . It is a Christian philosophy after all."

Jenkins romanticized the life of blacks in city ghettos; it is easier for the well-off to praise the ability to "be happy with little things" than for the poor to practice it. Moreover, Jenkins accepted certain stereotypes of blacks—though not the inherently negative ones—when he assumed that Afro-Americans as a group were "carefree" and joyous by nature. Still, white Americans were not used to being told that Jesus wanted them to "toss our heads and wear whatever colors [come] to us . . . with the careless brightness of the flowers," as "the

Harlem people" did. In holding up these traits as a model for whites, the pastor at least offered a healthy, respectful alternative to the condescending voyeurism that drew whites to Harlem's cabarets and whorehouses in search of "primitive," uninhibited black life.

As a Jewish rabbi of East European parentage, Jacob Tarshish carried less of the baggage of romantic racialism than did liberal Protestants, who were direct heirs to that tradition. Tarshish devoted one segment in his widely heard series of popular-philosophical radio addresses in 1935 to *Amos 'n' Andy*. He gave a perfunctory nod to the Afro-American's supposed "good humor" and superior "natural-[ness]," but praised *Amos 'n' Andy* mainly for showing the nation "a great race in American life"—"talented" and "heroic in the midst of discrimination and injustice." At the same time, Tarshish located Gosden and Correll's achievement in their creation of characters who, though black, in fact "belong to all nations and races."

The rabbi's only reservation about the show was that Weber City, a New Deal-style model town in which Gosden and Correll involved their characters for a time, was all-black. Tarshish wanted a "mingling of nations, religions, races"—an integrated America in which whites would hear "the Negro's cry for better opportunity and living conditions." This brand of liberalism, which ascribed any differences between the races to environmental factors, was the wave of the future; by 1935, the idea that blacks had special, race-linked personality traits was finally beginning to wither among white liberals in the face of challenges from scientists and black intellectuals.[23] Jacob Tarshish, Lydia Deseo, and Burris Jenkins differed in their quickness to absorb the new thinking. But that each found *Amos 'n' Andy* useful in pleading for racial justice at a time when other whites considered "Amos" and "Andy" the perfect names for a pair of stuffed, headless parachute test dummies, shows how open to varied interpretations Gosden and Correll's work was.

Many other white listeners drew a moral or a bit of social criticism from *Amos 'n' Andy* without couching those lessons in religious terms. A striking feature of such comments is that they typically addressed none of the racial issues that some of the religious commentators raised; many did not mention race at all. These fans, most often from the North and Midwest, found the radio series—as one man put it—"worth while" not only "for chuckles" but also "for truly serious contemplation." Some found trenchant commentary in *Amos 'n' Andy* on the American economy, especially as it sputtered through the Depression. One listener got his "biggest kick" from Andy's custom, when faced by a crisis in his taxi business, "to 'hold a meetin'.' " The fan saw this as "a crack at some of the bushwah of modern business executives"—namely "the unnecessary push-buttoning of bosses and [the] equally futile conference habit." In Amos, "the practical member of the company," he found a prescription for drumming up more business in any firm: real executives had to "[get] off that soft seat in their office and [go] to work," just as Andy should.[24]

Columnist Elsie Robinson extracted a virtual sermon from Andy's conviction at one point that a fortune-telling charlatan named Prince Ali Bendo had put a curse on him. Superstition and fear of the supernatural had long been part of the "coon" stereotype, but Robinson understood Andy's fear of the Prince in universal terms, as a comment on the American spirit flagging after years of economic hardship. "Is Andy any sillier than you, and you, and me?" she asked. "Don't we, too, convince ourselves we're 'living under a curse'?" Robinson insisted that neither Andy's mishaps nor general unemployment and breadlines were foreordained. "If your mind is alert, if your heart is eager and you keep on hustling," she admonished both Andy and her readers, "the thing you need will come your way."[25]

Although Robinson's exhortation brimmed with naiveté and reflected the nation's bewilderment about the causes of the Depression, she was not alone in drawing a lesson from *Amos 'n' Andy* for surviving in hard times. Several years earlier, not long after the stock market crash, the *Christian Science Monitor* was already praising Amos and Andy for a talent that many would have to cultivate in order to get through the crisis: "their ability to wink an eye at misfortune . . . , never to look backward, . . . and always to live just from day to day."[26] For neither the first nor the last time in *Amos 'n' Andy*'s history, yesterday's racist stereotype became, in the mind of some whites, today's model for emulation by people of their own race. To these listeners, the "carefree" acceptance of adversity commonly attributed to Afro-Americans had more to recommend it in a time of economic disaster than it had in the 1920s, when many had believed that anyone with enough competitive drive could wrench personal success out of the American economy.

···—●—···

People who saw *Amos 'n' Andy* as a showcase for the unique virtues of a noble black race were a small minority—though an articulate one that was gaining some influence in the churches and elsewhere. Those who drew secular moral and practical lessons were more numerous. At the other extreme, whites who found nothing more in

Amos 'n' Andy than a humorous confirmation of racist stereotypes also represent a minority of the recorded responses—and probably even of listeners overall. Most commonly, it seems, white fans thought of Gosden and Correll's creations as vivid, human characters whose race was one—but only one—prominent aspect of their makeup. And for many whites in this last category, the color of those fictional personalities apparently made them neither more nor less sympathetic than they might have been had the radio team portrayed them as white.

Columnists and editors, whose business it was to opine and explain, generally concurred with fans on *Amos 'n' Andy*'s superiority to other acts, and with one another on the reasons for it. "These boys are no ordinary black face comics," said one writer of Gosden and Correll. "They have created living characters whose adventures thousands follow with interest." A writer for the *Christian Science Monitor* agreed that Gosden and Correll had far surpassed other blackface teams by eschewing "wise-crack[s]," cheap puns and "vaudeville methods"— all of which were "too remote from life as the listener lives and knows it." *Amos 'n' Andy* offered "human talk" and "character" rather than "mere caricature." Though the series depicted "one strata [*sic*] of life," said the *Monitor*, the "warmth of humanity" it conveyed ensured that, "as we laugh" with its characters, "we think, 'Even as you and I.' "[27]

A white writer in Fort Worth did not overlook the characters' race; for him, Gosden and Correll were realists who never placed their creations "in any situation in which a negro would not naturally find himself." But the writer attributed the show's success primarily to its "humanness" in presenting "characters [who] do things that remind one of persons he has known, whether of the negro race or not." Another columnist found that *Amos 'n' Andy* captured a truth he had learned over "forty years, living along the Ohio River in a town with a large colored population": that blacks "possess the common characteristics of white men," some good and some bad. He praised Amos as a "philosopher" whose "energy, enthusiasm and industry might be a model for many a white man."[28]

Heywood Broun, the popular columnist and racial liberal, took a slightly different tack. He rejected the notion that *Amos 'n' Andy* was "a searching study of Negro life and character," being "farced a whole scale above reality." Yet he took "great delight" in Gosden and Correll's "admirable work," whose "undoubted contact with the world in which we live" prompted listeners to "accept the various characters as living, breathing persons."[29] Broun came closer to capturing the mood of the white public than did those—both liberal and racist—for whom the color of *Amos 'n' Andy*'s characters was the show's single pivotal element.

A listener in Virginia praised the "humor, pathos and logic in the dialogue" and the "comradeship . . . of these two lovable characters," Amos and Andy. He found the series "intensely human": "There are many Andys in this world. . . . Would that there were more like Amos. . . . It would be a better place in which to live." Nothing in this fan's letter suggested that he saw race as an issue in *Amos 'n' Andy*.[30]

Though Gosden and Correll's show was a comedy, its essential appeal seemed to many to lie somewhere other than in its humor. One white columnist insisted that Gosden and Correll's "skits include other elements beside [*sic*] comedy," focusing instead on "the fundamentals of every-day life." If their characters were clowns, he added, so was Shakespeare's Falstaff, whom *Amos 'n' Andy* approached in "appeal" if not in "sublimity." "They are not always funny and never brilliant," wrote radio columnist Charlotte Geer of the radio pair, "but they speak a universal tongue." Amos and Andy's adventures, she wrote, "are natural, they are life itself." "If Amos and Andy were merely amusing," agreed a paper in Massachusetts, "only a small percentage of radios would be tuned for them." Rather, Gosden and Correll had won their unprecedented popularity "because they are playing a drama that might be real. It seems real."[31]

"All of Us Can See Ourselves in the Simple Portrayal of 'Amos 'n' Andy,' " proclaimed the headline of a large article by Charles Tracewell that ran in several newspapers. Far from viewing the schemes and swindles of the Mystic Knights of the Sea as specific to urban black society, Tracewell asserted without regret that "all of us are after every one else's money" in the "often glorious adventure of modern American business life." (Tracewell seemed unperturbed by the Depression.) As Amos, "with his honest simplicity, yet inherently shrewd mind," strove to defend his meager treasure against the Kingfish and others, Tracewell wrote, "each and every member of the wide-flung whole identifies himself" with the beleaguered cabbie.[32]

Others agreed that *Amos 'n' Andy*'s main appeal lay in its ability to capture the essence of day-to-day human existence, but defined that essence more broadly than Tracewell did. One white writer in 1929 compared *Amos 'n' Andy* to Shakespeare, Plato, Aristotle, and Homer, all of whose writings "live" because "they portray life." Correll and Gosden's work possessed "the same wealth of living qualities," he said. "Who does not see his neighbor, or even himself, when he listens to this comic pair before the 'mike.' " Well into the 1930s, as Gosden and Correll began their tenth year on the air, white observers were still praising *Amos 'n' Andy*'s characters for being "so much like the people we know."[33]

A remarkable portion of the praise for *Amos 'n' Andy*'s universality came not from show business journalists, who often praise performers in terms that the stars' own publicists suggest, but rather from editorialists and general feature writers who did not usually find radio programs important enough to comment on. And white radio listeners with no intellectual credentials at all often lauded the same universal elements in Gosden and Correll's characters that the professional scribes did. "I think there could be no better satire of people in general" than *Amos 'n' Andy*, wrote a woman from Illinois. "Each new event can make you think of some person with whom you are in contact with most every day." "Say, Andy puts me in mind of a lot of these fellows in this dump," said a white worker in a Michigan factory, "always waiting for some one else to do the work." In summarizing her co-workers' reactions to Gosden and Correll's characters, the timekeeper who recorded that comment wrote that "some talk of them as if they were really some neighbors they knew."[34]

Many white listeners expressed their empathy with *Amos 'n' Andy*'s characters primarily through the spirited interest they took in the stories that Gosden and Correll presented. Fans might find their own everyday experiences and emotions amusingly reflected in *Amos 'n' Andy*. In one episode, the Kingfish proclaimed that a man must put his foot down when women become too assertive, but then yielded to his wife's demand that the two go out to dinner. A fan in Massachusetts particularly enjoyed Amos's observation that, judging by the results, the Kingfish must have "put his foot down" on a banana peel—"which," wrote the listener, "I have done and slipped." The factory timekeeper in Michigan recorded a number of remarks revealing her co-workers' active emotional engagement in Amos and Andy's adventures: "I'm glad Amos is finely waking up"; "By god, I hope the widow Parker sues Andy again he's such an old fool"; "Say you know that big stiff Andy[,] you just watch & see[,] if Amos gets the co. on its feet, the piker will try to get all the credit"; "Say you know that ape Andy, if I'd meet him I'd sock him a good one on the jaw." The animosity that some fans nursed toward Andy had little to do with his color, but stemmed rather from his exploitation of their cherished Amos. These white fans enjoyed seeing Andy get his occasional comeuppance. "Keep this big fellow in the role of the underdog for at least another year," wrote one man after Andy suffered a setback. "I know we have been following the programs for that long waiting for this to happen, and you can't make it strong enough."[35]

Amos and Andy's amours, both comical and serious, excited the interest of many. A New Hampshire woman whose radio had been in the repair shop asked the broadcasters for an update on Widow Parker's suit against Andy. "Would you tell us kindly the out come of the case and how 'Poppsie Boy' went back to 'Snookums,' " she asked. "Hope Amos is not roped in [by another woman] while Ruby is away at school," the writer added. A better-educated father, speaking on behalf of his whole family, waxed more eloquent. "We have chuckled over Andy's never-failing magnificence and his colossal ability as a business man," he wrote. "We have been inspired by the high aims and rigid honesty of Amos, and we have all been close to tears at times when real trials and tribulations beset either of our beloved friends."[36] Given this kind of lively interest, it is not surprising that a number of newspapers ran a detailed daily summary of the previous evening's episode of *Amos 'n' Andy* for readers who had missed a broadcast.[37] The public's concentration on the storyline rather than simply on the show's humor testifies both to the potency of the serial format and to Gosden and Correll's success in delineating characters who—though they were black and funny—won white listeners' sympathy as human beings.

Never was this achievement more obvious than when Correll and Gosden placed one of their characters in a crisis. "Behind the humor of their difficulties is the shadow of tragedy," said the New York *American*. The fictional world in which Andy became trapped in "the mire of debt" through the overuse of credit was "a world of reality. . . . He gets the sympathy of millions in a like predicament." Amos, of course, won more hearts than his partner. When a family crisis forced Ruby to leave Harlem for Chicago, wrote one listener, "there were thousands of unshed tears—and some that were shed" for Amos. (The parting, of course, turned out to be only temporary; Ruby was too popular a character for Gosden and Correll to jettison.)[38]

Another parting between the two lovers threatened to be irrevocable: Ruby fell ill with pneumonia, and one evening's broadcast closed with Amos's sobs and a line suggesting she had died. "Please read this sof[t] and seriously. Make it real," Correll and Gosden admonished their announcer in a note above the narrative introduction on that night's script. He did, and so did they. For many, the suspense exceeded even that aroused during Andy's breach-of-promise cases. "It's strange, isn't it," wrote one columnist, "how a couple of fellows can create out of nothingness a character so true that you're really and deeply concerned about her pulse beat?" Amos's was "the only radio voice that ever brought tears to our eyes," a white newspaper editor wrote. "When he came out from Ruby's room in the hospital at the crisis, and was led away by Andy and the Kingfish, his voice broadcast grief and anxiety as we never heard it in any tragedy on the stage." Amos's reaction to Ruby's decline was "as true and touching a bit of acting as ever has been done on stage or screen," said another writer. "Radio never before has approached it." The anguish of Amos, "that sincere and true gentleman," was "great acting because it was life," she added. "What one of us, out of sad experience, could not recognize it?"[39]

Gosden and Correll created many situations that were less drastic, but which still tugged at the audience's heartstrings. When Amos adopted a stray dog, one listener wrote that "Amos 'n' Andy, and, of course, the dog" were "too wonderful for words." "The little dog's 'barking' [supplied by Gosden and Correll themselves] and Amos' care for him" and for a stray cat, wrote another fan, "are instances of kindness that should stimulate all children and some grown ups too to care for animals at all times." The climax came when the dog's rightful owner appeared and claimed his lost pet from a heartbroken Amos. The little tragedy struck a chord among listeners. "Ever become attached to a dog and then suddenly lose it?" asked a columnist. "If you have, you know just how Amos felt. . . . Poor, poor Amos." A New Jerseyan was so touched by Amos's loss that he shipped a real dog to Amos and Andy in care of the NBC studios in New York.[40]

Sentimentality, of course, had been part of the minstrels' stock in trade. But the sentimentality of *Amos 'n' Andy*, however bathetic some of it seems today, presented a different picture than that of either the minstrel balladeer or the Old Uncle. The emotions of Amos and Ruby, of supporting characters like Sylvester—and sometimes even of Andy or the Kingfish—largely transcended race. Yet those emotions were never for an instant "de-racialized," for the principal figures' stage dialect and the situations the radio team placed them in constantly reminded the listener of the characters' color. Just as important, the concern and affection they showed was shared among blacks rather than directed to a latter-day Ol' Massa.

Gosden and Correll managed to present characters who aroused empathy among whites without ceasing to be black. One of the most vivid illustrations of that empathy was the naming of white children after the principal figures in the radio series. At least one baby was christened with the given names Charles Freeman, but in every other reported case parents named their children after Gosden and Correll's fictional, black alter egos. The names Amos and Andy were most commonly given to twins—over a hundred pairs of them by 1935—though a single birth posed no obstacle for at least one set of parents who called their son Amos Andy. False rumors that Gosden and Correll gave cash premiums to parents of twins so named may eventually have contributed to this phenomenon. (The team did send a pair of engraved silver spoons to each family.) But the practice seems to have been well established before such rumors began to circulate.[41]

Amos and Andy were not caricatured "black" names, and that made it possible for parents to use them. (Most couples were less venturesome in such matters than the pair of "Kentucky mountaineers" who reportedly named their triplets Amos, Andy, and Madam Queen.[42]) But people would not have *chosen* to give their children the names of characters whom they did not find appealing. White parents who named their twins Amos and Andy knew that others would almost invariably connect the boys' names to those of the fictional radio figures, but that prospect did not trouble them.

Normal-sounding names for black comic characters—Gosden and Correll often borrowed the names of their real-life white friends—were themselves a kind of breakthrough in an age when comic strip artists and writers of popular fiction typically assigned their black creations absurd monikers like Mushmouth, Skeeter Butts, Orifice Latimer, and Caesar Clump. But conventional names were only one of the many "normal" attributes Gosden and Correll gave to their characters. Black though they were, those figures captured the interest and affection of many listeners who found qualities in them that went far beyond color.

···——●◉●——···

A radio series, movie, or other work of fiction does place characters and situations at a safe remove from the audience; the reader or listener may find them deeply engaging but connect them with their counterparts in the real world only in the most limited ways. Some, perhaps many whites enjoyed the innovative, humane, or instructive aspects of Gosden and Correll's work while sharing—and sometimes expressing openly—the least enlightened racial assumptions of the series. One writer in 1926 praised Sam, Amos's predecessor, for being forthright about the gaps in his knowledge and "anxious to learn";

"don't be ashamed to be Sam" in this respect, he urged his readers. But that exhortation did not affect the writer's basic estimate of Sam as "one of those meek and humble coons who . . . [move] ignorantly among the scenes of a but dimly understood world." Freeman Gosden's old friend in the veterans' hospital in Virginia told how keenly his fellow patients had listened to Amos's faltering attempt to deliver a speech at the lodge hall in one episode: "Everyone was suffering in profound sympathy for Amos that night." Yet these were the same patients who also amused the writer by calling a black maid at the hospital "Madam Queen."[43]

The tendency of listeners to comment on *Amos 'n' Andy*'s humanity and to downplay the race of its characters also owed something to the way Gosden and Correll and their white employers promoted the series. The Chicago *Tribune*, though it frequently caricatured its "two colored boys," also played up the "homely, human" side of *Sam 'n' Henry*; announcer Bill Hay, in his introduction to the *Amos 'n' Andy* book of 1929, likewise praised the show's characters for being "so real and human." Correll and Gosden themselves sounded the same refrain. Their show was popular because of its "human, likeable characters," said Correll in 1931. "We have all had, more or less, the same experiences as Amos and Andy."[44]

The team pressed this point even more emphatically as the years passed. "We try to reflect the life of not only the colored people but of the white people as well," they proclaimed on one occasion in the mid-1930s. Correll said that, from the very beginning, he and Gosden had taken care to make their characters "the kind of folks everybody knows. We looked among our friends, our relations, and our wives' relations for them." Gosden compared himself with Amos: "That boy is too good for me. . . . I can't live up to Amos," Gosden said. "He's the real, solid citizen."[45]

By 1929, Gosden and Correll and the journalists who covered them had begun to reinforce that line by distancing the pair from the minstrel and vaudeville traditions. "Neither had ever appeared in 'blackface' before" *Sam 'n' Henry*, one article asserted a few months after the team's debut on NBC. At least until the mid-'30s, writers continued to state that Gosden and Correll "never had done negro characterizations" before 1925.[46] Those assertions, of course, were false; Gosden and Correll *had* portrayed black characters on the stage for years, both before and after they joined the Joe Bren Company.

The misstatements served to promote Gosden and Correll by putting them in a class apart from any traditional, burnt-cork competition. Similarly, the broadcasting industry and radio columnists alike wanted to stress radio's novelty and minimize its debt to earlier forms of entertainment. But these explanations tell only part of the story. To say that whites praised *Amos 'n' Andy* for its universal human interest because Gosden and Correll pitched their show that way explains neither why the team wanted exactly that kind of recognition nor why so many listeners were ready to grant it to them.

The place of blacks in American society was changing, and so were the ways in which they and the white majority thought about race and interacted with each other. Those changes pushed Gosden and Correll, stations WGN and WMAQ, and especially the NBC network to gloss over the team's minstrel-show past and to make their two oft-repeated but contradictory claims: that *Amos 'n' Andy* portrayed people in general rather than a single race, and that its creators took pains to render an authentic picture of Afro-American life.

The basic change on the American racial scene was the very process that Gosden and Correll depicted in *Amos 'n' Andy*: the Great Migration of Afro-Americans from the South and their concentration in northern cities. Urban life altered the way blacks worked, thought, and acted. Afro-American literature, music, and art flowered after World War I in Harlem and far beyond. Black politics and protest took on new vigor and an array of new forms ranging from black candidacies for office and antidiscrimination suits to Marcus Garvey's mass movement for black renewal centered on an Africa freed from colonial rule. An unapologetic acceptance of blackness and pride in the race's character and achievements were integral to much of this ferment.

Some black writers—especially those dependent on white sponsors, influenced by white authors, and writing largely for white audiences—produced work that emphasized the supposed exoticism and primitivism of black life. Others, however, insisted that black artists themselves, rather than white caricaturists and curiosity seekers, should define Afro-American culture, character, and aesthetics. As early as 1915, blacks had organized protests against *The Birth of a Nation*, achieving partial victories in some localities where the film was banned or censored. Although black assertiveness helped shape Gosden and Correll's publicity, however, the pair began distancing themselves from their blackface background and emphasizing the universality of their characters even before serious criticisms of their show by Afro-Americans began to surface around the beginning of 1930.

Several American cities had suffered severe race riots during and after World War I—a time when political reaction and aggressive white racism were on the rise. The riot of 1919 in Chicago—the city from which Gosden and Correll would broadcast from 1925 through 1937—was one of the worst in American history. Whites, as usual, were the main aggressors, but blacks often defended themselves or retaliated against whites. Chicago's white elite may not have loved blacks, but they cherished the civil peace on which their city's prestige and economic advancement depended. So leading figures in the city urged the governor of Illinois to appoint a Commission on Race Relations to study the causes of the riot. The commission brought about few broad, concrete changes, but its long inquiry did yield a frank and exhaustive report on Chicago's racial situation. By spearheading the commission's effort, some of the city's most distinguished citizens demonstrated their genuine desire to avoid further racial conflict.[47]

One of those leaders, Race Commission member Victor F. Lawson, published the Chicago *Daily News*, which went on to broadcast *Amos 'n' Andy* in 1928 and 1929. Another future employer of the radio pair, Colonel Robert McCormick of the Chicago *Tribune*—whose station WGN broadcast *Sam 'n' Henry* beginning in 1926—followed a much more conservative political line than Lawson's *News*. But both papers took steps to cool Chicago's racial climate in the years after the riot—the very period when Gosden and Correll began their radio career.[48]

In its long report published in 1922, the Race Commission showed that the *Tribune*'s coverage of Afro-Americans had been particularly inflammatory during the time leading up to the riot and had remained slanted thereafter. Even more regularly than other local papers, the *Tribune* ridiculed blacks and portrayed them as antisocial, especially through the paper's crime stories.[49] By the time of *Sam 'n' Henry*, the *Tribune* still had not become a model of racial enlightenment; for example, it still consistently identified black criminals by race in both articles and headlines. Yet it at least had begun to give respectful coverage to Afro-American and interracial affairs.

Some items seem cloying or patronizing today; a story on the *Tribune*'s distribution of food baskets to the poor at Christmas in 1927 noted explicitly that "many colored families were visited" by the paper's volunteers. At about the same time, though—at the peak of *Sam 'n' Henry*'s popularity—the *Tribune* reported on a lecture delivered in the city by a white clergyman who attacked the idea of Nordic supremacy. ("If you are boasting of being 100 percent American," the paper quoted him as saying, "why not include the Negroes, for not one of them ever went back on this country.") The *Tribune* also covered events like the week-long exhibition, "The Negro in Art," which was intended to "improve race relationships" by educating whites about black achievements.[50]

Victor Lawson's *Daily News*, Gosden and Correll's subsequent employer, had shown much more respect for blacks than the *Tribune* even before the riot. During the 1920s, its coverage improved further. By 1925, the *News* was running sizable and respectful stories on Afro-American affairs; an article on the convention of the black National Medical Association in Chicago, for instance, quoted the views of the group's new president at length. And in a review of a book on the history of blacks in the Second City, the *News*'s writer proclaimed that "the story of the Negro in Chicago . . . has taken on epic form." Although the *News* still identified black criminals by race, it generally did not sensationalize such stories, and it now capitalized the word "Negro," which it had not done before the Race Commission's study.[51]

Though Victor Lawson died in 1925, the *News* was giving regular, fair coverage by the time of *Amos 'n' Andy*'s debut in 1928 to the activities of black politicians—and there was more and more to cover in that realm. Sheer numbers, geographic concentration, and able leadership had made blacks a political force in Chicago—more dramatically so, in fact, than in any other American city. The South Side had elected its first black alderman and state senators by 1915.[52] Well before 1929, when Chicago's Oscar DePriest became the first Afro-American to serve in the United States Congress in a generation, Chicago's powerful whites were taking the black vote seriously.

Freeman Gosden and Charles Correll probably did not spend their spare time reading the works of the black novelists and poets of the Harlem Renaissance or wrestling with the concept of the "New Negro." But for compelling practical reasons, their employers at the *Tribune* and the *News* had become less inclined to offend blacks or feed racial passions, and that showed in the "spin" that those papers gave to the radio series. The *News* even went so far as to declare *Amos 'n' Andy* an exemplar of the spirit of the black renaissance. The show's popularity among Afro-Americans, said the *News*, proved "the theory of Alain Locke, professor at Howard University, that 'the new Negro' has put away the old sensitiveness about humor which finds its materials in the dialect and character of members of his race."[53] That claim twisted the views of Locke, a leading black intellectual who had recently declared Afro-America's spiritual independence; rejecting "unjust stereotypes" and racial caricatures, Locke probably would not have endorsed Gosden and Correll as interpreters of Afro-American culture and character.[54] Nevertheless, the *News*'s attempt to appropriate Locke's blessing for *Amos 'n' Andy* does demonstrate the paper's desire to cultivate the good will of Chicago's blacks.

To avoid inflaming Afro-Americans, however, was the lesser of two tasks that faced Chicago's newspapers and radio stations as they sought to prevent another race war in their city. Far more serious was the fear of inciting white Chicagoans who felt threatened by the black influx; such people had been the principal actors in the riot of 1919. The threat of future racial pogroms accounts for the *Daily News*'s veiled sermonettes promoting racial good will, which the paper sometimes delivered in the form of praise for *Amos 'n' Andy*'s universality. The same danger makes utterly clear why Gosden and Correll's shows—in which race was of the essence—so rarely referred overtly to color, and why the team completely avoided scenes suggesting, even in the matter-of-fact tone of E. K. Means and Octavus Roy Cohen, that race influenced relations among people.

A scene from *Sam 'n' Henry* illustrates the kind of tightrope walking that this policy sometimes demanded. The Chicago riot had begun with the drowning of a black boy after whites stoned him for swimming into the water off a "white" beach on Lake Michigan. Eight years later, Gosden and Correll placed Sam, Henry, and the Most Precious Diamond of their fraternity at the lakeshore; the three men ogle and comment on women bathers until a young "cookie" whom the Diamond tries to pick up turns out to be lying within earshot of the Diamond's wife, who coincidentally has come to the shore on her own. In the episode's narrative introduction, the announcer mentions in passing that the beach is full of "colored bathers." That one phrase was explicit enough to reassure whites in Chicago that the black trio were neither eyeing white women nor violating the sanctity of a "white" beach, but it was casual enough to avoid reminding listeners—black or white—that Jim Crow beaches were a contentious and potentially deadly issue. Gosden and Correll played it safe in their beach episode, turning the scene of racial hatred and tragedy in 1919 into an arena for an all-black farce in 1927 about a mischievous husband who ends the scene in full flight from an irate wife.[55]

Gosden and Correll became even more careful not to arouse racial passions after their hiring by NBC in 1929. *Amos 'n' Andy* had reached much of the United States even without access to a network, but the move to NBC made the series a truly national program. That posed some problems that were as new as network radio itself. Official state and local censorship boards routinely imposed cuts on movies, each body supposedly enforcing the standards of its own community. Although the threat of censorship had led the studios themselves to set up the motion picture code and to think twice before using material that might prove troublesome, a film producer at least had the option of supplying different versions of his movie to different local markets. By contrast, NBC broadcast programs live to the entire United States. To succeed commercially, the network had to attract as many and offend as few people as possible in all regions and among all social, racial, and ethnic groups. In 1930 as now, the prospect of controversy could strike fear in the heart of a sponsor whose aim was to win the good will of the widest possible public.[56]

Finding a safe yet engrossing golden mean in a show that portrayed a new arena of black life for a multiracial, multiregional audience raised special challenges. The need to appeal to both Northerners and Southerners is only the most obvious of these. Although white Americans far outnumbered blacks, were more likely to own radios, and had more money to spend than Afro-Americans, to include black and racially liberal white listeners in NBC's radio audience improved the network's chances of making a profit. Gosden and Correll's balancing act had begun at WGN and WMAQ—portraying the Great Migration while obscuring the conditions in the South that helped cause it; showing blacks voting and politicking, but only in a humorous manner; depicting Afro-American life while minimizing references to race and categorically ruling out scenes that even implied racial unpleasantness. The need to walk that fine line could even require Gosden and Correll to *break* their general rule against having their characters mention race. Another cab-driver punches Amos in the jaw during an argument in one episode, and Andy retaliates in kind; but the radio team avoid any suggestion of racial strife by having Amos mention that his assailant was "colored."[57]

Even as America's changing racial scene caused publicists to insist that *Amos 'n' Andy* depicted all people regardless of color, those same social changes led to just the opposite—declarations that the show portrayed urban Afro-Americans exactly as they were in real life. That paradox flowed out of a deeper one: throughout the history of American race relations, many whites have harbored both a deep bias against blacks and a certain fascination with black life. The early minstrels played to white Northerners' racial prejudices, but also to their curiosity about the "exotic" folkways of the plantation slave. *Amos 'n' Andy*, too, owed some of its success to the dual mentality of many in its white audience. Millions of white Americans of all backgrounds still felt comfortable with the burnt-cork tradition and found echoes of it in *Amos 'n' Andy*; but many whites were also curious about the Great Migration and the new, urban black communities it was creating.

Gosden and Correll tapped that curiosity when they claimed to make frequent research expeditions into black ghettos. At the very same time they were insisting that they portrayed universal rather than racial characters, the team trumpeted their "insistence on absolute realism" and the "painstaking care" they had devoted to the "study of the Negro tongue." "Sometimes a single phrase or expression will be the subject of months of study and research," said one news item.[58]

Gosden and Correll directed such claims mainly at whites; they surely knew that blacks would judge *Amos 'n' Andy*'s dialect for themselves. And the claims—to put the matter charitably—were greatly exaggerated. Gosden, a born mimic, had long felt secure in his command of black language and lore. Besides, he and his partner had to write half a dozen scripts a week and, after joining the network, to broadcast their show twice each night to accommodate listeners in the western time zones; to this load, they often added six or more daily stage appearances on exhausting road tours. This schedule left little time or energy for sociolinguistic research among Afro-Americans, or even for casual visits to black neighborhoods. But the two stars said otherwise to a white public they perceived as demanding *authentic* portrayals of blacks.

That popular hunger made itself felt at the two termini of the Great Migration—the South on one end, and Chicago, New York, Detroit, and Philadelphia at the other—where race affected everyday life. But newspapers in communities nearly devoid of blacks lavished attention on *Amos 'n' Andy*, too. White civic groups and social clubs in small-town, Main Street America piped the radio show into their meetings; churches, schools, lodges, and YMCAs mounted fund-raising shows featuring Amos 'n' Andy imitators; bridge clubs and neighborhood groups threw parties centered on Amos 'n' Andy themes.

In part, these activities simply continued the home-talent minstrel-show tradition that the Joe Bren Company had once catered to throughout the Midwest and beyond. But like their big-city cousins, small-town and rural whites sensed that the racial picture was changing. They read about Harlem and the South Side in their newspapers (however distorted the treatment might be); they heard Duke Ellington on the radio; they knew of Oscar DePriest's election to Congress and of the flap that ensued when his wife was invited to a reception at the White House. They read prominent newspaper stories and editorials about lynchings in the South, and about the organized efforts of blacks and liberal whites North and South to abolish lynch law. They remembered the race riots after the World War and perhaps even recalled that blacks had begun to fight back. They smelled change in the air, and they were curious.

As always, Gosden, Correll, and their employers did their best to respond to the complex demands of their audience. By claiming credit for both universal and "authentic," "Negro" dimensions in *Amos 'n' Andy*, the broadcasters acknowledged that new questions and new concerns had slowly begun to percolate in the thinking of many whites in a changing American society. But Gosden, Correll, and some of the journalists who covered them went even further than this, frequently and explicitly declaring the radio team's great respect for Afro-Americans and highlighting the black public's supposed hearty approval of *Amos 'n' Andy*.

That "large sprinklings of colored folk who enjoy Amos 'n' Andy" lined Gosden and Correll's parade route in San Francisco in 1929 is interesting enough in its own right. But a white reporter's assumption that his white readers wanted to know about those black fans and be reassured that *Amos 'n' Andy*'s stars "never slur or make fun of the colored race" is even more striking—especially if, as some say, white America has had no conscience at all in its treatment of blacks. According to that theory, there has been no "American dilemma" arising from the conflict between the nation's founding principles and its oppressive practices, but simply a widely shared, rarely questioned determination to exclude Afro-Americans from the promise of freedom and equality.[59] Yet it is hard to understand why the Chicago *Daily News* and others bothered to proclaim the "popularity of *Amos 'n' Andy* among both whites and Negroes"[60] to a white public that was beyond shame over its racial record.

Oddly enough, white expressions of concern over Afro-American feelings in the matter of *Amos 'n' Andy* fit perfectly into the psychological profile of many whites during a period when America could not even muster the moral capital to pass a federal antilynching bill. This paradox, in turn, places the *Amos 'n' Andy* phenomenon squarely in the long, sad history of American race relations just as surely as the show's minstrel roots do.

One can answer the claims of conscience in at least two different ways: by working for justice and decency, or by taking care to *see* oneself as just and decent while still behaving in the old, comfortable manner. By 1929, white Americans had had much practice in the second of these responses. Thomas Nelson Page's romances glorifying the old plantation, for example, had helped satisfy white Southerners' hunger to see their past and present racial practices as benevolent, and had furnished Yankees with a comfortable rationalization for their abandonment of Reconstruction.

Many of the parents and grandparents of Page's Yankee readers had both criticized slavery and rationalized its continued existence. They abolished slavery in each of their own northern states; here, conscience helped change reality. Most were unwilling to risk their Union with southern slaveholders by acting to end slavery at the national level, however, and for years they justified this *failure* of conscience by repeating that slavery was an institution of the southern states which Northerners regrettably had no power to alter.[61]

Some of Page's own forebears in the South during the latter 1700s and even beyond had themselves admitted that slavery was morally wrong. But the northern abolitionists' moral indictment of slavery, the profitability of the institution, and the unwillingness of white Southerners to live alongside a free Afro-American population ultimately led many in the South not merely to defend slavery as a necessary evil but to promote it as morally right—a civilizing influence on the supposedly inferior black race, and a far more humane system than the "wage-slavery" of the industrializing North. When thoughtful whites in the South defended their system in *moral* terms, they showed how deeply the moral strictures of northern fellow-claimants to Christian and American values stung them—and how grotesque their own definition of "morality" could become under that kind of pressure.[62]

To concede that white Americans of the 1930s, the 1880s, or the 1830s had a conscience—or at least shared the common human desire "to be considered decent"[63]—is not to flatter them. In fact, it is a kind of indictment, for the same reason that the law punishes those who know right from wrong and yet do wrong (the legally sane), but not those who cannot make that distinction (the insane). Conscience can serve evil when it leads people to ignore or excuse evil rather than grapple with it, or to prettify their perceptions of reality rather than improve reality itself.

White reactions to *Amos 'n' Andy* tell their own story of conscience and self-delusion. Few aspects of those responses stand out more boldly than the desire to see the radio series as friendly to blacks and to believe that Afro-Americans themselves enjoyed the show. Gosden and Correll and their employers promoted those notions; the press and many in the audience took pains to believe them.

This was white America's conscience talking. Whites of the latter 1920s and the 1930s, like those in antebellum and post-Reconstruction times, did manage to mute and distort the voice of conscience on matters of race. Even if Afro-Americans had risen up as one and passionately condemned *Amos 'n' Andy*, it is unlikely that Gosden and Correll would have changed their profitable show substantially, and almost inconceivable that an appreciable number of whites would have stopped tuning it in. But many whites felt better—could get that last full measure of enjoyment out of *Amos 'n' Andy*—if they could believe that to listen and to laugh was not to disparage the black race.

The need of the press and of some in the radio audience to justify Gosden and Correll's series testifies to something else, too—the same truth that all the concern about the show's authenticity suggests: many listeners saw *Amos 'n' Andy*, unlike the Two Black Crows and others, as representing real Afro-Americans. To those listeners, the series sent an ambiguous message.

In one sense, the very humanization of blacks in *Amos 'n' Andy* could be reactionary. It bolstered the "ghetto system," as historian Erik Barnouw has said, through what it told whites about blacks: that " 'they' were lovely people, essentially happy people, ignorant and somewhat shiftless and lazy in a lovable, quaint way, not fitting in with higher levels of enterprise, better off where they were. . . . It could make South Side poverty somehow charming and fitting. The nation needed the fantasy."[64] That need grew as the Great Migration slowly but inexorably undermined the reassuring assumption that race was a southern question that white Southerners knew how to handle.

In reality, *Amos 'n' Andy* sometimes countered the stereotype of black ignorance and often contradicted those of shiftlessness and hedonism. For a commercial radio series of the late 1920s and the 1930s—and a comedy at that—it was more balanced and humane than one might have expected. To depict black characters—other than "mammies" and Old Uncles—whom whites could care about on a human level at least nibbled at the edges of the society's racist assumptions.

Even at its best, though, *Amos 'n' Andy* did not challenge the *status quo* in a basic way; at its worst, it gave Jim Crow and Jefferson Snowball a new lease on life. The shifts in white Americans' understanding of the race question between the World Wars were slow, tentative, inconsistent—and sometimes negative, as the race riots made clear. Not even the most "modern" of the white public's responses to *Amos 'n' Andy*—neither the readiness of many to empathize with the show's black characters, nor the pronouncements of southern and northern liberals, nor white curiosity about the Great Migration, nor the need of some to be told that the series complimented Afro-Americans—pointed toward deep or imminent racial change, but rather to a low-level ferment in the racial thinking of many whites. *Amos 'n' Andy* contributed to that ferment, but in the end, the series comforted most white listeners more than it challenged them.

Yet the very *need* to be so comforted shows that white America's conscience was neither dead nor entirely at peace. To convince oneself that *Amos 'n' Andy* was true and humane and that blacks liked it was an easy, cheap way to get some moral reassurance—far easier than doing something concrete to establish justice in the real world. Before deep change could occur, America's muted conscience would have to be pricked—indeed, pierced to the quick again and again—by those Afro-Americans who, with a few whites, put their bodies and lives on the line during the mass movement for civil rights in the 1960s. But for that movement to succeed, there had to be a conscience in white America that it could prick. The whisperings, the tentative stirrings, the faint vital signs of that conscience—along with its severe limitations—are to be found among white people's responses to *Amos 'n' Andy*.

9

···━▶◉◀━···

The Black Debate Begins

On the Saturday afternoon following Lincoln's Birthday in 1930, several dozen black women of Baltimore sat at card tables in the local YMCA. The Bridge Coterie was raising money for charity as the contestants played for prizes. Successful players advanced through elimination rounds. The tournament proceeded at a leisurely rate, allowing every woman to greet those of her friends with whom she did not happen to be placed in a foursome. But the women's pace suddenly quickened, and the event came to an abrupt end at 6:55 P.M. *Amos 'n' Andy* would begin at seven, and "many rushed to get home in time to tune in" the adventures of the two taxicab entrepreneurs. A reporter for the *Afro-American* newspaper, herself a fan of the radio series, did not manage to leave the tournament in time to catch the broadcast. "I'se regusted!" she wrote afterward, Andy-style. "I missed 'em."[1]

That same week, halfway across the United States in St. Louis, another black woman wrote down her feelings about *Amos 'n' Andy*. Theresa Smith Kennedy addressed her thoughts to the editor of the daily *Post-Dispatch*.[2] Judging by the articulateness and the ease with which they expressed themselves in writing, Kennedy and her counterpart in Baltimore probably came from similar middle-class backgrounds. And they agreed on the popularity of the radio series among their people. "We, the Negroes," wrote Kennedy, besides listening to various blackface artists on the radio, ". . . wait up and keep our children out of bed to hear the most famous of them all—'Amos and Andy.' " Afro-Americans in Kennedy's circle, she reported, found Gosden and Correll's performances not only entertaining, but also true-to-life. "Those fellows must have been reared with colored people," ran the typical comment. "They have them down so pat."

"All right," Kennedy admitted. "As good imitations . . . they can't be beat." But for her, that was not the issue. *Amos 'n' Andy*, she complained, taught black children and "the world at large . . . that the Negro in every walk of life is a failure, a dead beat and above all shiftless and ignorant." Even Amos, who Kennedy conceded "plays the role of one having good judgment and a little horse sense," could not redeem the show, for he "also plays the fool."

Theresa Kennedy found a useful model in the vocal protests of a few black individuals against recent movies they found demeaning to the race. She herself made a practice of sending complaints to the sponsors of radio shows that featured white imitators of blacks. Ever the realist, Kennedy acknowledged that "letters of protest . . . may not cause [such programs] to cease," but she believed Afro-Americans owed it to themselves and their children to make known their "disgust" at "the illiteracy that these radio programs suggest."

In her letter to the *Post-Dispatch*, Theresa Kennedy helped launch a debate over *Amos 'n' Andy* which had its roots in the emerging black consciousness of the 1920s and 1930s, yet continued as the twentieth century neared its end. Over the years, black dismay about the radio series came to resemble a fire in a peat bog: the issue smoldered constantly just below the surface, bursting forth into open flame on occasion, then disappearing underground again, but never finally extinguished. The frustration of Kennedy and others who shared her views centered almost as much on the many Afro-Americans who rescheduled their meals and truncated their bridge tournaments to listen to Gosden and Correll as on the white team themselves. When blacks praised or attacked *Amos 'n' Andy*, they were arguing over their identity, their condition, and their future in a society dominated by whites.

The first installment of that black debate took place in a time of turbulence—of both frustration and promise. The Great Migration had been underway for half a generation. The number of Afro-Americans living in the North and West had trebled since 1900, to two-and-a-quarter million; one in five blacks lived in those regions by 1930, more than twice the fraction of the earlier year. Almost all blacks in the North lived in urban areas—nearly half in New York, Chicago, and four other very large cities.[3] The Great Depression, just beginning when Theresa Kennedy wrote her letter, quickly deepened, temporarily stanching the northward flow of black humanity and wrecking the dreams of countless Afro-American workers and entrepreneurs alike. At the end of the Depression decade, only one black city-dweller in fifty had finished college; only one in fifteen had a high school diploma. Whites in the city, as a group, had spent almost half again as many years in school as their black neighbors and were four times as likely to have finished college. Even so, urban blacks had more than half again as much schooling as their brethren who remained on the farm.[4]

The political ferment in Afro-America that had begun before World War I continued. The election in 1928 of the first black Congressman in a generation was followed by a landmark victory for the NAACP, which helped to defeat the nomination by President Herbert Hoover of a racial conservative, John J. Parker, to the United States Supreme Court in 1930. The following year, the "Scottsboro boys," a group of black teenagers, were condemned to death in Alabama on apparently perjured testimony that they had raped two young white women. The trial showed how hard a road fighters for racial equality had ahead of them, but it also galvanized black opinion, especially in the North, and led to a dogged fight to save the young men and to end the system of all-white juries in the South.

Almost from the beginning, Gosden and Correll seemed to grasp that the Great Migration which they depicted on the radio had also refashioned the real world in which they worked. By portraying identifiable, well-developed black characters day in and day out in a setting that at least purported to be realistic, they were inviting responses to their work from an ever more sophisticated, urbanized black public. The team did what they could to ensure that those reactions would be friendly. To herald the debut of *Amos 'n' Andy* in 1928, the Chicago *Daily News* published photographs of Gosden and Correll posing with groups of blacks. In one photo, the two white men cuddled several of what the paper called "the younger dusky residents of Shreveport"; in another, the duo shared a hearty laugh with a dozen young black men in the same town. The *News* assured readers that "there was a hot time among the Negro boys" there when Gosden and Correll "tried out their best stories in the Negro neighborhoods of the southern city." The paper's radio editor added that Correll and Gosden had "collected a wealth of material" there and in other southern Afro-American communities to enhance the authenticity of the new *Amos 'n' Andy* series.[5]

Such publicity aimed to do more than bolster Gosden and Correll's credentials as delineators of real black people. The physical intimacy and bonhomie conveyed by the pictures created the powerful impression that Gosden and Correll liked blacks enormously. That message not only reassured those white readers of the *News* whose enjoyment of the radio series would be enhanced by the belief that blacks approved of it. It also proclaimed to blacks themselves the good intentions both of *Amos 'n' Andy*'s creators and of the newspaper that would soon begin broadcasting and publishing their work.

Correll and Gosden had also learned to use institutions in Chicago's Afro-American community to win the good will of the race they portrayed. On Christmas Eve, 1927, the team appeared at a holiday celebration for poor blacks of the South Side. Chicago's black weekly, the *Defender*, ran a photo of " 'Sam 'n Henry,' internationally known radio entertainers," whose presence, the paper reported, had helped to create "a brilliant program" designed to "[make] the poor spectators happy." The picture in the *Defender* showed Gosden holding a little black girl said to be the party's youngest guest, while Correll smilingly stood behind chair of the oldest, who claimed to be 120 years old and a former fugitive slave. The *Defender*'s reporter approvingly quoted Freeman Gosden's proclamation at the party of "how much he loved Race people." And perhaps for the first time in the public prints, Gosden invoked the memory of Garrett Brown; the *Defender* duly noted his statement that "his mother brought up a little Race boy in their home" back in Richmond.[6]

As time passed and their success grew, Gosden and Correll and their employers took care to stay on good terms with blacks both within and beyond Chicago. *All About Amos 'n' Andy*, the book published by Rand McNally in 1929, included some thirty photographs. Nearly half of these showed Gosden and Correll enacting scenes from their show in minstrel-style, white-lipped makeup. But the pair and their publisher also diplomatically included four pictures taken the year before depicting the two, without the burnt cork, in joyous communion with real Afro-Americans.

The Chicago *Daily News*, before launching *Amos 'n' Andy*, had enlisted an officer of the city's Urban League chapter to ask several dozen prominent black Chicagoans whether Gosden and Correll's characterizations were acceptable; he found widespread approval.[7] Two years later, as *Amos 'n' Andy* became a national obsession, Gosden still talked proudly of that straw poll. The *News*, Gosden recalled, not wishing "to condone anything that might be regarded as offensive to the colored people of Chicago," had been assured by the "intellectual leaders of the race" there that he and Correll had always "present[ed] a creditable side to the characters we represented." Gosden and Correll told with similar satisfaction of the ovations they had received from blacks who "packed" Chicago's Regal Theater for their stage act—particularly when they performed the light-trick by which the pair instantly changed color.[8]

A reporter for the respected *Christian Science Monitor* wrote early in 1929, in an article largely free of fan magazine–style puffery, that a telephoned invitation to speak at the Chicago Urban League reached Correll while the *Monitor*'s writer himself was present. The duo received a similar invitation from the Du Sable Club, an organization of black businessmen and professionals in Chicago.[9] *Amos 'n' Andy*'s announcer, Bill Hay, may have exaggerated when he claimed that the pair had "frequently been called upon to speak and perform at meetings of colored people both in the North and in the South," and Gosden and Correll were hardly objective judges of their own success in making Afro-Americans their "best friends," as Gosden called them.[10] Still, the team clearly wished to be known as sympathetic to the race, and they won a number of black friends well before their show's premiere on NBC in 1929.

Within a few months of the pair's network debut, the black columnist Chappy Gardner confirmed reports in the white press that "Negroes in New York go wild with glee when . . . Amos and Andy are announced on the radio." Valdo Freeman, son of the black composer and producer of operas, J. Lawrence Freeman, early in 1930 described *Amos 'n' Andy*'s popularity in Harlem. Many black families there, he wrote, did just what whites did every evening at seven: they laid aside what they were doing, gathered around the radio, and observed fifteen minutes of "absolute silence." In the streets, Freeman added, groups of listeners gathered around Harlem's radio stores and barber shops, even in the rain, "until the entire sidewalk was blocked" (only one urban black household in seven had its own radio in 1930). Each night's episode of *Amos 'n' Andy*, by Freeman's account, provided fodder for conversation the next day among Afro-Americans ranging from ministers and doctors to servants and laborers. Many had at first assumed that Gosden and Correll were themselves black, Freeman wrote; the white pair were often mistaken for

Flournoy Miller and Aubrey Lyles, the team from whom the radio
stars apparently "borrowed" the famous "mulsiflyin'-and-revidin' "
scene. Though Freeman complained of racial insults in many radio
advertisements, his verdict on *Amos 'n' Andy* was just the one that
Correll and Gosden and their employers sought—that "they never
insult nor humiliate the Negro."[11]

Indeed, Gosden had learned enough from Afro-Americans over the
years to produce characters and a brand of humor that struck many
Afro-Americans as authentically black. It helped that the two white
performers, and the millions of white listeners, were invisible to the
blacks who tuned the show in; a roomful of Afro-Americans, picturing
the characters as black, could share and enjoy *Amos 'n' Andy*'s humor as
a kind of in-joke. The black press across the country recognized and
responded to this feeling of engagement. The Kansas City *Call*—
a weekly whose news editor, Roy Wilkins, would eventually serve as
head of the NAACP—recognized that "thousands of Negroes throughout the land" wanted to know more about the radio pair. The paper's
drama editor obliged them, passing on information from the team's
quasi-biography of 1929 and stressing in his headline that " 'Amos 'n
Andy' Credit Much of Their Success to Negro Playmates."[12]

The drama editor told of Gosden's supposed "mammy," and of
his black boyhood friend; the latter, in this black writer's estimation,
was "the direct cause" of *Amos 'n' Andy*'s "remarkable" popularity.
The columnist even endowed Correll with an asset that the radio
team's own publicity never claimed for him: a childhood history of
"fast friendship" with "many . . . Negro boys," from whom Charles
had supposedly "learned a lot of things." Having credited Freeman
Gosden's success to his skill at imitating real blacks, the *Call*'s writer
implicitly exhorted Afro-Americans to emulate Gosden. " 'Amos n'
Andy,' after all[,] is but the results of contact of a white boy with a
Negro lad," the black critic wrote, "only the white boy had the
foresight, ambition and vision to capitalize his . . . knowledge. And
still, it must be a bit of comfort to the colored boy to have been the
inspiration of 'Amos 'n Andy.' "

In the Philadelphia *Tribune*, another black paper, an editorialist
noted that "from coast to coast everybody is talking about Amos 'n
Andy." He urged black performers to match Gosden and Correll's
success in exploiting a growing public hunger for shows and writings
depicting Afro-Americans. "Some of the imitators" of blacks, said the
Tribune, "are better than the original article. . . . Negroes had better

be up and doing before the public reaches the conclusion that a white man with a black face can give them Negro entertainment better than those who are permanently black."[13]

Probably no one knows today how veteran black comedians like Miller and Lyles—who had spent years sweating to build careers in vaudeville and on the musical stage—felt about black editors urging them to "be up and doing" lest skillful white performers outshine them at their own game. Miller and Lyles themselves may have been too busy to notice. Since the triumph in 1921 of *Shuffle Along*, an all-black musical comedy which they wrote and staged with Eubie Blake and Noble Sissle, the pair had appeared in movies and produced and starred in several more musicals—including *Runnin' Wild*, which launched the craze for the Charleston dance.[14] Miller and Lyles did notice, however, that some of Correll and Gosden's radio material resembled their own, and that some of their fellow Afro-Americans confused the two acts.

The "borrowing" of material from one act by another was one of vaudeville's basic traditions. Nevertheless, it rankled to see Gosden and Correll becoming radio superstars while blacks who had inspired or even originated some of the white men's material had to settle for more modest success. Few Afro-Americans had performed on radio during the 1920s, and black musical groups were almost the only representatives of their race who broadcast with any frequency during the Depression era. Those black artists who did perform in radio were largely confined to guest appearances; until about 1937, none appeared regularly in the various new series that followed in the footsteps of *Amos 'n' Andy*.[15] Prominent "black" comic parts on radio were played by whites long after changing attitudes and the cinema's visual constraints caused movies to abandon burnt cork.

Afro-American performers thus formed opinions about *Amos 'n' Andy* based on professional considerations as well as personal tastes. Flournoy Miller objected not to the way Gosden and Correll represented the black race, but rather to their alleged usurpation of his own style of doing so; Miller's attorney announced plans to seek a court injunction against NBC unless it made "amends" for using material on which Miller claimed copyright. The lawyer granted *Amos 'n' Andy*'s popularity among Afro-Americans; but he complained, perhaps with self-interested exaggeration, that "the great majority of the colored people in Harlem" believed as late as the spring of 1930 "that the real names of Amos 'n' Andy are Miller and Lyles."[16]

The Columbia Broadcasting System (CBS), influenced by *Amos 'n' Andy*'s fantastic success, gave Miller and his partner their own show in the summer of the following year; they appeared two evenings a week.[17] But no one of any color could match *Amos 'n' Andy*'s popularity; Miller and Lyles's radio series, despite their talent, became a mere footnote in the medium's history. Whether their threat of legal action led to any compensation from NBC is unclear, but it had no important effect on the content of *Amos 'n' Andy* and none whatever on the show's success. Some years later, in fact, Flournoy Miller made his own peace with Gosden and Correll, playing a major role in the casting and writing of *Amos 'n' Andy* on both radio and television.

Some black performers benefited directly, if modestly, from Gosden and Correll's popularity. The early years of the Great Depression brought even harder times than usual for black performers in the movies, and Afro-Americans appreciated any break they got. *Check and Double Check*, the Amos 'n' Andy film of 1930, featured musical numbers by Duke Ellington's orchestra; at the time, the bandleader-composer called the picture a "crowning point" in his career. Besides appearing with Gosden and Correll at the Chicago *Defender*'s picnic for black children the following year, Ellington's band also played on a special NBC radio broadcast that publicized the premiere of the Amos 'n' Andy movie.[18] A friendly relationship between Ellington and Gosden and Correll continued for some years, and the maestro was happy to publicize it.

Startling as it seems now in light of Ellington's illustrious career and the obscurity into which Gosden and Correll's movie quickly sank, the film actually enhanced the musician's reputation in just the way he must have hoped. Whatever its weaknesses, *Check and Double Check* introduced Ellington's music to many whites who, despite his earlier successes, had scarcely heard of him before. A writer for a Chicago paper, apparently more conversant with the history of the Napoleonic Wars than with the cultural contributions of blacks to his own society, informed readers almost parenthetically that "Duke Wellington" would furnish music for the broadcast honoring Amos 'n' Andy's movie debut. An Ohio newspaper announcing a local performance by the Duke's band evinced greater knowledge of Ellington and his "colored musicians," whom it identified as "dispensers of wild Harlem music." But with all its enthusiasm for the orchestra, the paper still—eight months after the release of *Check and Double Check*—listed the band's performance in that film as one of the group's signal achievements and headlined its article, "Ellington Band Bring Amos 'n' Andy Number." In a story about another impending Ellington concert, a newspaper in Indiana mentioned that the band was "remembered best" for appearing in Gosden and Correll's movie the year before. White America was attracted to the group's music because of its intrinsic quality. But the band's association with *Amos 'n' Andy* and the consequent attention given it by the press helped Ellington to get his foot in the white man's door.[19]

Other black performers likewise welcomed the opportunities that occasionally arose because of *Amos 'n' Andy*'s popularity. An all-black bill, including Cab Calloway's orchestra and Gosden's fellow Richmonder, the famous dancer Bill "Bojangles" Robinson, performed in "Harlem's Salute to Amos 'n' Andy," a half-hour special broadcast on NBC in late summer 1930.[20] If any of these black artists had reservations about the way their race was portrayed in *Amos 'n' Andy*, they could see how many of their own people felt no such qualms. More important, the odds against a performer of any color making the big time and staying there were so enormous, and work of any kind so scarce, that actors and other entertainers rarely turned up their noses at an opportunity to receive pay for appearing before an audience.

Conveniently, black performers like Duke Ellington seem to have felt at least tolerably comfortable with Gosden, and downright friendly toward Correll, on the personal level. When Correll asked prominent friends and acquaintances to send greetings to his father on the old man's seventieth birthday in 1936—more than half a decade after *Check and Double Check*—he included Ellington and Bill Robinson in his request. Both men sent telegrams that showed an easy, even joshing familiarity, but whose dignified tone overall averted the impression of "tomming."[21] Both Robinson and Ellington were established stars by 1936. Furthermore, it was fairly clear that Gosden and Correll were out of the movie business (though they did appear briefly in the film, *The Big Broadcast of 1936*), and they were not yet using well-known guests on their radio show. Ellington and Robinson no longer saw the pair as potential employers. Yet Correll asked the black stars to add their touches to his father's big day, and both men responded with grace and warmth.

Professional considerations did encourage black performers to "play ball" with Gosden and Correll both before and after the mid-'30s, and even the likes of Robinson and Ellington probably thought it wise to keep doors open in all directions—just in case. Some of these entertainers may, like Flournoy Miller, have resented the unique success that the two white stars had attained by doing what blacks had been doing with skill and energy for years. Still, Correll and Gosden not only acquired no permanent, overt enemies, but also built some genuine good will, among that small group of Afro-Americans who earned their living on stage and screen and in dance and concert halls.

Despite *Amos 'n' Andy*'s large following among the black masses—indeed, largely *because* of it—Theresa Smith Kennedy of St. Louis was not alone in her "disgust." Several other Afro-Americans publicly registered their dismay over the show during the balance of the year 1930. None, perhaps, did so more articulately than Clarence LeRoy Mitchell of Howard University in Washington, D.C. (This was not the same Clarence Mitchell who later became the NAACP's top lobbyist in Washington.) Mitchell wrote a long letter to the Baltimore *Afro-American;* the paper published his statement on the very day one of its writers was participating in the ladies' bridge tournament that *Amos 'n' Andy* brought to such a hurried close.[22]

Mitchell asked whether his own people really cared how whites saw them. "Ridiculous portrayals of Negro life" by white writers and entertainers were bad enough, Mitchell thought; similar acts staged by black performers and "free clowning by bell boys, porters and waiters, for their white spectators" made matters even worse. But the real harm came when black patronage of acts like *Amos 'n' Andy* convinced whites of the shows' authenticity as portrayals of Afro-American society. "The average white person does not know as much about our finer qualities as we think he does," Mitchell warned, and he ticked off examples: a leading white businessman who did not realize that Howard University had a black president; a social worker who had never heard of an Afro-American physician; a member of the staff at a hospital in Chicago who did not realize that black medical schools existed. Given this ignorance, Mitchell feared, the white man was "forced to believe" the picture of black life that "comes to him in the way of amusement"; this was the "one big reason why we should protest" against Gosden and Correll's production. When blacks "enjoy hearing Amos 'n Andy tell us how ignorant we are," Mitchell warned, "we are not only as 'patient as a jackass,' but just about as sensible."

Mitchell admitted in passing that Gosden and Correll's portrayal of the ignorant minority among blacks was "realistic," but he feared that *Amos 'n' Andy* encouraged whites to "judge the whole group" according to its less sophisticated members. Protests by Irish-

Americans and Jews had "almost put an end to belittling jokes about the less fortunate in their groups," he wrote, and it was now up to Afro-Americans to do the same. The act of protest itself would show whites the other side of black life—"our better selves. If we care," Mitchell concluded, "there will be no more Amos 'n Andy."

Roy Wilkins of the Kansas City *Call* saw in Mitchell's letter much of what he, Wilkins, thought was wrong with the black elite. Wilkins wrote a blistering retort which appeared five weeks later in the Baltimore *Afro*.[23] The pretensions of Mitchell and others like him had earned the race more scorn "than anything a black-faced comedy team . . . could ever broadcast," Wilkins wrote. The challenge for blacks, he thought, was not to attack productions like *Amos 'n' Andy*, but rather to "present, 'publicize' and propagandize" Afro-Americans' accomplishments. That task, Wilkins added acerbically, lay squarely on the shoulders of "the 'better element' (of which Mr. Mitchell obviously considers himself a part)."

But Wilkins demanded more from the Afro-American elite than just greater publicity for black achievements; he wanted more black achievements to publicize. Mitchell and other "articulate, but non-performing pretenders in the so-called 'better element,' " Wilkins suggested, had "fastened on the development of appearances as an objective rather than on the development of intrinsic worth." If black physicians, for example, would only "give up congregating in large centers for social purposes and devote themselves to medicine where they are needed," Wilkins explained, no white social worker would be ignorant of their existence.

"If Amos 'n Andy, the Two Black Crows and Roy Cohen's stories are true and typical," said Wilkins, "then no amount of glossing over, rarin' and pitching, by Mr. Mitchell or anyone else will be able to suppress them." Afro-Americans, in short, should improve themselves until the caricatures *became* untrue and thus innocuous. And while they were at it, blacks should stop "sniffing about with our heads in the clouds," cast aside "false pride," and start producing Afro-American humor that would earn a share of the hundreds of thousands of dollars that Gosden and Correll and other whites were now pulling in.

Despite Wilkins's contempt for what he saw as Mitchell's shallow elitism, the two men represented the same social class and measured success by the same yardstick of educational, commercial, and professional achievement. Moreover, they shared the belief that whites were open-minded enough to be influenced by the accomplishments of Afro-Americans. Wilkins and Mitchell further agreed that there were plenty of untutored, unsophisticated blacks. Yet where Mitchell spoke of that class with an uneasy amalgam of sympathy and embarrassment, Wilkins warmly embraced the black masses just as he found them.

"How would Mr. Mitchell like to have Amos 'n Andy?" he asked. "In plug hats, with morning coats, striped trousers, glassined hair, spats, patent leather shoes and an Oxford accent? Instead of having them struggling with the immediate and universal problem of how to get and keep a decent and usable spare tire for the taxicab, would he have them prating of mergers, mortgages, international loans and foreign trade balances?" If the problems of the average Afro-American were those of Everyman, then so were his foibles; so Wilkins saw no racism in the laughter at Amos and Andy's ups and downs. Wilkins lauded *Amos 'n' Andy* for containing "no offensive words or titles, not a single 'coon,' 'nigger,' 'darky,' 'spade,' 'inky,' or 'blackie.' " The show "is clean fun from beginning to end," Wilkins wrote. "It has all the pathos, humor, vanity, glory, problems and solutions that beset ordinary mortals and therein lies its universal appeal." Gosden and Correll could not have said it better themselves.

··· ➤➤ ◉ ◄ ···

Clarence LeRoy Mitchell's letter and Roy Wilkins's reply laid out some of the issues that would divide thoughtful blacks who commented on *Amos 'n' Andy*—whether in 1930 or a half-century later. All blacks agreed on the need to elevate Afro-America by overcoming racism and the poverty and ignorance it had produced. But there was much dissension as to whether *Amos 'n' Andy* acted as a brake on black progress. Even those who agreed that the show was holding the race back differed over whether it did this by slandering all blacks—or by portraying accurately, but too prominently, a real Afro-American underclass whose failings embarrassed the entire race. Some opponents of *Amos 'n' Andy* aimed their protests squarely at the show's white creators and their employers, while others lashed out also at the countless blacks who clearly enjoyed the series. Ultimately, the *Amos 'n' Andy* controversy stirred new debate on an old but abiding issue: Which aspects of black life and culture should Afro-Americans display in public and which—if any—should they keep among themselves or abandon altogether?

W. J. Walls of Chicago, a bishop of the African Methodist Episcopal Zion Church, began a long crusade against *Amos 'n' Andy* only a few months after the show's move to NBC in 1929. His effort reached its peak in a magazine article of 1930.[24] Gosden and Correll, Walls said, degraded the race by dealing in "crude, repetitional, moronic mannerisms" and representing black speech as "gibberish"; he worried that the series had a "somnolent effect upon the minds of many of our people, especially of the youth." In fact, black devotees of *Amos 'n' Andy* frustrated Walls at least as much Gosden and Correll did, for the show's popularity among Afro-Americans was one of the black man's myriad signals to whites that he "does not care whether he is respected or debased."

Though Walls, who would later serve on the national board of directors of the NAACP, shared Roy Wilkins's aversion to the word "nigger," he felt that blacks had made such a fetish of it that its mere absence satisfied them; they naively welcomed any entertainment that whites, by avoiding that vulgar term, packaged "soothingly and humorously." In *Amos 'n' Andy*, said Walls, "the only universal note constantly struck, but to a point of repulsion, is a love affair" (that of Amos and Ruby). None of the characters in *Amos 'n' Andy* had a family or showed "the highest intuitions of the civilized man." Andy was "presumptuous, vain and ignorant of his limitations." Amos, Walls wrote, personified "impotent ignorance," and was "a smart-Alec" to boot. Bishop Walls accepted a Darwinian, capitalist economy as a given; only by adopting a neo-Calvinist work ethic could Afro-Americans progress or even survive. Amos and Andy, who lived by "blind accident," their enterprises "never succeeding," offered "a dangerous text for a people seeking to build up confidence . . . in an age of employment competition."

Walls saw many of his fellow Afro-Americans as "crude" and "childlike"—but also as "striving" to fulfill a great potential. So, on the one hand, he pled the cause of the downtrodden: the language of *Amos 'n' Andy*, he said, "misrepresents even the average unlettered black man who has been exposed to urban civilization." That black man had proved himself capable of "decisive deeds and positive wisdom." On the other hand, Walls's brief for average Afro-Americans seemed not to cover those with no exposure to "urban civilization." These he called the "unlettered and mentally imbecilic group of our race"—an element which he believed did, lamentably, exist, but which *Amos 'n' Andy* focused on unduly. Although Walls insisted that this group's numbers were "rapidly decreasing," his own definition seemed to consign hundreds of thousands of Afro-Americans who lived in the rural South to the category of imbeciles.

It was racism, said Walls, that had "distorted" the "imbecilic"

element among blacks and "reduced [it] below the touch of hope."
But beyond hope that group was, and this meant that *Amos 'n' Andy*
did not mainly threaten the most deprived, but rather the intelligent
black strivers and achievers, of whom Walls himself was one. When
blacks avidly tuned in Gosden and Correll's show, they were aiding
that pair in doing what no race could afford to permit: "misrepresent-
ing their better people," and allowing "the crude deeds of [their]
unfortunates to be paraded as the order and pattern of a whole people." Where Roy Wilkins laughed at the insecurities of the "better
element," Bishop Walls found that group's position genuinely pre-
carious and feared for its future.

Walls indicted whites for denying opportunity to Afro-Americans,
for "caricaturing" and "distorting" black culture, and for laughing at
black suffering. Yet it was these same whites whom Walls wanted to
persuade—largely through black protests against presentations like
Amos 'n' Andy—that black Americans, too, had "those finer sensibilities possessed universally by cultured races." His goal of causing the
world to "write the capital 'N' in 'Negro' " depended on a "great
American white audience" which Walls himself, only a few paragraphs earlier, had said was "only interested in having us appear to
them in the capacity of fools."

No wonder, then, that Walls was unsure what black demands to
abolish *Amos 'n' Andy* could accomplish. He cited the precedent of
American Jews, whose protests—and whose investments in theaters—
he said had eliminated the harsh caricaturing of an earlier era. Yet
elsewhere in his article, he admitted that blacks might fail to prevent
"insults" like *Amos 'n' Andy* no matter how strenuously they objected.
The long, painful history of American racism gave good cause for
frustration and pessimism. Those emotions warred in Walls's soul
with the hope and determination that Afro-Americans had always
drawn upon to sustain them in their quest for justice. This inner
tension, always a hallmark of black protest, became especially familiar
to those who struggled against *Amos 'n' Andy*. And with Walls's attack,
that fight had only barely begun.

A few months after Bishop Walls published his condemnation of
Amos 'n' Andy, the Pittsburgh *Courier*, which had a nationwide circulation of over fifty thousand, took up the cause. Robert L. Vann, the
editor of that black weekly, launched a drive in 1931 to obtain one
million signatures on a petition demanding that the federal Radio
Commission ban *Amos 'n' Andy* from the airwaves. Vann's petition
complained that "two white men," by "exploiting certain types of

American Negro for purely commercial gain," were undermining "the self respect and general advancement of the Negro in the United States and elsewhere."[25]

Three categories of Afro-Americans, said the *Courier*'s petition, had suffered particularly "harmful and degrading" treatment in the series. *Amos 'n' Andy*'s portrayal of the Mystic Knights of the Sea suggested that in "Negro Secret Orders . . . money is filched from its [*sic*] members by dishonest methods." The other two specific allegations of slander flowed mainly out of the breach-of-promise series in the late winter of 1931, in which Madam Queen sued Andy for failing to honor his engagement to marry her. Gosden and Correll had Amos save Andy from a $25,000 judgment by discovering and revealing to the court that Madam Queen not only was still legally wed to one former husband, but also had married yet another man before becoming engaged to Andy. The *Courier* charged that the series defamed "Negro womanhood . . . as indulging in bigamy." The petition further alleged that *Amos 'n' Andy* had portrayed black lawyers—here Vann had in mind the first attorney Andy consulted in the breach-of-promise case—"as schemers and crooks."[26]

Like Bishop Walls, Robert Vann seemed uncertain whether *Amos 'n' Andy* did greater harm through its effects on whites or on blacks. The *Courier* complained that the series was "a menace to our self respect." "What sort of stuff are we made of," Vann asked, "when we can laugh at ourselves outraged?" "Self Respect" became the central theme of the *Courier*'s crusade; at one point, the weekly called on five thousand black ministers to preach on that theme on a single night, and to exhort their parishioners to protest against *Amos 'n' Andy*. The effect of the radio series on whites, in Vann's view, was to convince them that all blacks belonged to "one of two types. We are either Amos or we are Andy." Vann feared that blacks' acceptance and even enjoyment of *Amos 'n' Andy* confirmed whites in this conviction.[27]

As the *Courier*'s protest unfolded, it became clear that resentment of *Amos 'n' Andy* was not confined to a mere handful of blacks. The *Courier*'s petition attracted thousands of signatures, most of them gathered by activist readers. The newspaper sometimes published names of signers; in one issue, almost an entire eight-column page was filled with names in small type from eighteen states both North and South. The *Courier* claimed to have received 275,000 signatures by the first of August, 515,000 by mid-September, and 740,000 by late October.[28]

Other black organizations or their leaders endorsed the protest. The National Baptist Convention, in executive session, passed a supporting resolution, as did the annual conventions of the black Elks and the National Association of Colored Waiters and Hotel Employees. National gatherings of several other black fraternal groups took the same stand. The entire staff of the black *Louisiana Weekly* of New Orleans signed Vann's petition. The women's mission convention of the A.M.E. Zion Church in Birmingham endorsed the campaign and lauded their own Bishop Walls as "the first Negro in America to publicly protest" against *Amos 'n' Andy*. The *Courier* proudly announced the signing of its petition by various blacks of at least local prominence: a dean of Virginia Union University in Richmond, two editors of Harlem newspapers, and Bishop Walls himself.[29]

The *Courier* published many letters praising the paper's campaign and lambasting *Amos 'n' Andy*, but some letters from readers who questioned or criticized the effort also appeared. Even much of the friendly correspondence made it clear that *Amos 'n' Andy*'s opponents were fighting a difficult battle on several fronts within their own community. Many readers complained less about the radio broadcasts themselves—though they bitterly opposed these—than about the failure of "so many of our people," as a man in Massachusetts wrote, to "see where [Gosden and Correll] are harming us." A Detroiter remarked that "many of our people [enjoy] this pair better than any other feature [on the radio], and do not seem to care who knows it." "Day after day in the streets," agreed a Virginian, "I hear [favorable] comments on these two scoundrels from Negroes." "It is a shame and a pity," despaired a sixteen-year-old girl from Michigan, "to see how some colored people will almost 'break their necks' to tune in on Amos 'n' Andy."[30]

Even many blacks who were not fans of *Amos 'n' Andy*, some readers found, saw no point in making an issue of it. A man in the *Courier*'s home city had lost all "patience with those Negroes who claim that we should not oppose the program of these two white clowns, and that we should 'laugh it off.' " Other backers of the *Courier* complained that black comedians, far from opposing *Amos 'n' Andy*, were undermining the cause. An Indiana man mentioned "a program from New York by some colored comedians" (possibly Miller and Lyles) who had "said some things that were as bad as" Gosden and Correll's material; "this may cause some trouble when we make our protest," the man warned. Bishop Walls himself noted a related impediment to the black crusade: his own mother, like some other Afro-Americans, disliked the radio series but "thought that Amos n' Andy were Negroes."[31]

More ominous yet were the recriminations that various elements of the Afro-American community now flung at each other over which blacks were supposedly responsible for *Amos 'n' Andy*'s success. Some letters to the *Courier* and other papers targeted uneducated, southern-born blacks—this time not only as real-life models for *Amos 'n' Andy* characters, but also as the alleged mainstay of the show's black audience. A black man of Camden, New Jersey, attacked the radio show and the black lower class with equal venom. "To the progressives of the colored race this stupid, cheap bunk of Amos 'n' Andy is a torture," the man wrote to a Philadelphia paper. Only the black "underworld," "the rabble and riffraff of the race," enjoyed it. Listening to *Amos 'n' Andy*'s "vilifying . . . radio prattle" would cause impressionable black children to become like the "unlearned, illiterate, simple [black] Southerner"—a catastrophe that "no competent father of the colored race" would permit. The pleasure that the southern-born black "riffraff" took in *Amos 'n' Andy*, the writer suggested, showed that "you may bring the man from the country, but you cannot bring the country out of the man."[32]

Other blacks, however, found the chief culprits in the race's alleged self-abasement not among Afro-America's lower strata or its professional comedians, but rather in its elite. A couple in New York State were dismayed by the enthusiasm that many in the black middle class showed for *Amos 'n' Andy* and for the dialect its creators used. "It is surprising," they wrote to the *Courier*, "to hear them at bridge parties saying, 'I's regusted' and 'Sho! Sho!' as well as disgusting." "Some of our leading Negroes, it seems, like to hear themselves burlesqued over the air," complained a man from Detroit. "Instead of criticizing this horrible thing, they will say to you that you hate the truth"—by which those middle-class fans presumably meant the "truth" about lower-class blacks as reflected in *Amos 'n' Andy*.[33]

The *Courier* itself lashed out at another cohort of leading Afro-Americans—editors of black newspapers who opposed or ignored Vann's protest. The *Courier* rarely called its opponents by name, but an editorial in the black Louisville *News* illustrates the sort of attitude that frustrated Vann. The *News* declared that it "yields to none in race pride . . . , but it finds itself utterly unable to work up a sweat over Amos and Andy." "If Bert Williams were living today," asked the editorialist, "would he not be on the air caricaturing the Negro? Sure." This writer was certain that "for every two Negroes that talk like Amos and Andy there are twenty thousand Colored Americans far removed from them in intelligence, in speech and in character. Our white neighbors know this as well as we know it and the race is not affected."[34]

In late August, several months into the petition drive, the *Courier* chastised such black editors for being "too dumb to see" the insult embodied in *Amos 'n' Andy*. At first acknowledging only "one or two" opponents in the Afro-American press, the *Courier*'s editorialist contradicted himself later in the same column by saying he had been "ashamed" to admit to a friendly white newspaper "how many such Negro editors we have."[35]

That same month, the *Courier* reacted bitterly to Gosden and Correll's appearance at the picnic for black children sponsored in Chicago's Washington Park by the weekly *Defender*. "Has the Defender Turned Amos 'n' Andy?" asked the *Courier* in the headline of a front-page article. The piece accused the Chicago paper—which it called the "Chicago Surrender, World's Greatest Weakly"—of insulting all those who had signed the *Courier*'s petitions and all the ministers who had supposedly spoken in support of Vann. The *Defender* had at best let Gosden and Correll manipulate it in order to blunt the Pittsburgh paper's protest, the *Courier*'s writer asserted. Very likely, he suggested, the *Defender* had brought the white pair to the park to "make fun of the kiddies" in the hope of gaining advertising from Pepsodent toothpaste, *Amos 'n' Andy*'s radio sponsor. Through all the *Courier*'s condescension, its frustration at being opposed by the country's most prestigious black weekly—which reached more than twice as many readers as Vann's paper did—was unmistakable.[36]

Readers of the *Courier* who endorsed the campaign of protest criticized still other elements of black leadership. A correspondent from Detroit complained that the drive against *Amos 'n' Andy* "should have been a job for the N.A.A.C.P." From New York State came the wish that the *Courier*, as a follow-up to the protest against Gosden and Correll's radio series, would "wage war against our Amos 'n' Andy ministers because they hinder our race from advancing."[37]

The readiness of some Afro-Americans to fault each other—or themselves—for making the race look foolish revealed a broader self-doubt and divisiveness. American society dangled its promise before Afro-Americans, as before others. The most talented and resolute black men and women had won a share of success—though not as big a share as their ability warranted. And the rest of the race, it seemed, had been left behind. Who was to blame?

A few Afro-Americans, like a black Ohioan who wrote to the *Courier*, let white Americans completely off the hook. With the exception of Dr. George Washington Carver, said this writer, the black man had "contributed nothing of basic importance to our modern life." "The Negro, if compelled to exist wholly on his own attainments," the writer asserted, "would live in a state of little more than high-class barbarism."[38] Many other readers, of course, found their fellow blacks no more flawed than any other human beings and saw the race's problems as stemming primarily from white bigotry.

Still others stopped well short of any blanket indictment of their own people, and condemned white racism, yet still accused *Amos 'n' Andy*'s opponents of "hating the truth" about the foibles of Afro-Americans that were supposedly holding the race back. Those who made this argument usually did so in general terms, resisting any temptation to embarrass Robert Vann by pointing explicitly to the pages of the *Courier* itself. Less forbearing critics could have noted that advertisements for insurance against embezzlement by dishonest lodge officers and sensational stories of black-on-black crime and of domestic scandals among prominent Afro-Americans ran in the *Courier* week in and week out, at the very same time Vann was attacking Gosden and Correll's treatment of the Mystic Knights of the Sea and of Madam Queen. Even some of Vann's own supporters agreed with a woman from Washington, D.C., who wrote that "the Negro has a lot to do with" his own bad image, "as he is always making an Uncle Tom of himself to the white man." Another reader who strongly backed Vann's protest complained that the heavy racial caricaturing in the *Courier*'s own comic strip, *Sunnyboy Sam*, promoted "the very same stereotypes" that *Amos 'n' Andy* did.[39] All this dissension among Afro-Americans themselves over the source of their sufferings, the specific remedies for their plight, and even the character of their own race (or certain elements of it) in the end proved more than Robert Vann could overcome.

One element that added fire to the *Courier*'s campaign yet also limited its effectiveness was the insistence of some protesters that *Amos 'n' Andy* did particular harm to the black middle class. Many complained that black businessmen were special victims of a comedy that revolved largely around Amos and Andy's parlous business ventures and the "investment" scams of various black con men. Some

Nineteenth-century minstrels impersonated comely female characters along with grotesque "old gals" and caricatured male figures (detail from handbill, 1867). *(Harvard Theatre Collection, Harvard College Library)* Gosden and Correll carried that tradition even further: In the *Amos 'n' Andy* comic strip of 1928–1929, the attractive, articulate Ruby Taylor presented a startling contrast to her awkward, heavily stereotyped beau, Amos. *(Chicago* Daily News)

Tune in Tomorrow Night at 10 o'clock on WMAQ and Continue with the Story.

From the beginning, Gosden and Correll understood that their work invited responses from an ever more sophisticated, urbanized black public. The team did what they could to ensure that those reactions would be friendly: appearing at a Christmas party for poor Afro-Americans in Chicago, 1927 (above); visiting a civic group in the same city in 1929 (below). *(Correll Family Collection)*

Though the *Amos 'n' Andy* craze of 1929–1931 slowly subsided, the daily version of the show lasted until 1943. During a contest to name Amos and Ruby's new baby in 1936, a publicity photo showed Gosden and Correll engulfed with entries. The pair celebrated *Amos 'n' Andy*'s 3,500th daily broadcast as the decade of the 1930s ended. Their show would remain on the radio in one form or another until 1960. (*Correll Family Collection*)

After a decade of performing alone, Gosden and Correll began to add other actors to their radio show; *Amos 'n' Andy* became a major employer of black talent during the 1940s. The white team rehearse an episode with (left to right) Amanda Randolph (Mama), Ernestine Wade (Sapphire), Eddie Green, Roy Glenn, and Johnny Lee, about 1951. When the Columbia Broadcasting System (CBS) brought *Amos 'n' Andy* to television in 1951, Gosden handed the role of Amos over to Alvin Childress (left), an experienced stage actor and director. Correll's part as Andy went to Spencer Williams Jr. (right), who had written, directed, and starred in all-black movies. (*Correll Family Collection*)

Walter White, leader of the NAACP, saw the *Amos 'n' Andy* television series as an insult and a threat to the gains that black Americans had begun to make since World War II. *(Yale Collection of American Literature, Beinecke Rare Book & Manuscript Library, Yale University)*

CBS asked Sig Mickelson, a liberal vice-president of the network, to pacify the NAACP. But Mickelson's attentiveness to the NAACP's grievances only inflamed the situation. *(Courtesy of Sig Mickelson)*

Journalist Roy Wilkins had ridiculed *Amos 'n' Andy*'s black opponents in 1930. But two decades later, as a high official of the NAACP, he helped Walter White lead the fight to ban the show from the revolutionary new medium of television. *(Yale Collection of American Literature, Beinecke Rare Book & Manuscript Library, Yale University)*

NAACP activists and others accused TV's *Amos 'n' Andy* of slandering the Afro-American professional classes. Johnny Lee's portrayal of the shyster lawyer, Algonquin J. Calhoun, drew some of the most intense fire. *(Correll Family Collection)*

The Kingfish of the Mystic Knights of the Sea lodge—who was best known for bilking Andy and fracturing the English language—had long been Freeman Gosden's most vivid character. Tim Moore made the role his own on television and took on something of the Kingfish persona in real life. *(Department of Special Collections, University Research Library, UCLA)*

Amos 'n' Andy presented enough dignified incidental characters and human touches to make it an elusive target for the NAACP: Amos (Alvin Childress) interprets the Lord's Prayer to his daughter (Patty Ellis) in the Christmas episode. *(Wide World)*

The century that began with huge Confederate celebrations in Richmond brought civil rights demonstrations to Freeman Gosden's hometown and to scores of other places by 1960. The rising tide of Afro-American consciousness made TV networks shy away from all-black situation comedies until the 1970s. *(Richmond Newspapers, Inc.)*

ERASE

SEGREGATION

THIS BLOT

Even as a new era began in American race relations, the old *Amos 'n' Andy* shows continued to appear in dozens of cities. A generation later, recordings and videocassettes from the series found a brisk market among Americans both black and white. After a remarkable sixty-year history, *Amos 'n' Andy* seemed to have a future as well. *(Correll Family Collection)*

protesters took their cue from the urgent concern expressed by Robert Vann, himself a struggling businessman and an attorney by training, about the image of black capitalists and lawyers.[40] But Vann's influence does not adequately explain either the passion that many of *Amos 'n' Andy*'s middle-class critics brought to the protest, or the solicitude that many protesters of all classes showed for the good name of black entrepreneurs and professionals.

The Afro-American businessman of 1931 found advocates in all sorts of places. The Knights and Daughters of Africa, a fraternal organization, attacked *Amos 'n' Andy*'s "reflections upon the honesty and integrity of Negro enterprise." Even the Association of Colored Waiters and Hotel Employees, hardly a den of capitalists, singled out the radio show's harm to "the best interests of the Negro business men" for particular censure. The California *Eagle*, a black weekly in Los Angeles, took a moderate position on *Amos 'n' Andy* overall but was unhappy with the Chicago *Defender* for making Gosden and Correll guests of honor at its annual picnic. The California editors could not believe that "the world's second Negro city didn't have at least two successful businessmen who would not have had to use burnt cork to darken their faces and who would have made better representatives of racial business enterprise than Amos and Andy."[41]

Like other middle-class opponents of the radio series, the *Eagle* raised issues that went beyond the welfare of the black entrepreneur alone; it especially condemned the *Defender* for having "paraded" images from the show before black children, to whom no "sane Negro wants Amos or Andy to become a hero." Others took special aim at the dialect Gosden and Correll used in their broadcasts. One reader of the *Courier* called the language of *Amos 'n' Andy* "vulgar." The couple who criticized their acquaintances for using the show's catch-phrases also decried *Amos 'n' Andy*'s "bad effect on our 'none too good English' as a race." These writers found the radio characters' speech "especially . . . detrimental to those just above illiteracy, as they pick up such so quickly."[42]

"Correct" use of language—which really means command of a tongue's most prestigious variety—is a classic concern of the middle class and the upwardly mobile of any race; white newspapers of the early *Amos 'n' Andy* era carried daily columns that aimed to improve pronunciation, vocabulary, and usage. Many blacks, like other Americans, saw education as the key to improving one's status. To imitate Amos's or Andy's speech could keep a black American out of the middle class and imperil the gains of those who had already arrived there. No wonder, then, that the protest took hold on at least some black college campuses, whose students and teachers embodied the ethic of advancement through education. One man at Southern University in Baton Rouge sent in three hundred signatures with addresses and promised to send that many more again.[43]

The *Courier*'s campaign won support beyond the black bourgeoisie, however—and not only among delegates to the waiters' convention, who held something approaching middle-class status in the bottom-heavy, Jim-Crowed black labor force of 1931. A housemaid who opposed *Amos 'n' Andy* said that she had left a copy of the *Courier* with the white family who employed her, and that, after reading it, they had stopped listening to the radio series. An inmate at the Leavenworth federal prison asserted that of five hundred black inmates there, "there isn't a one that approves of the Amos 'n' Andy program." Some of those prisoners had shown their "fine spirit of race pride" when, as a test, the writer had pretended to like *Amos 'n' Andy*: "agreeably to my surprise I was challenged to physical combat."[44]

There were clear reasons why at least some blue-collar Afro-Americans would join the *Courier*'s protest despite its preoccupation with the interests of black businessmen and professionals. Amos and Andy themselves were working-class, southern-born characters, whatever their entrepreneurial ambitions. If Gosden and Correll's depiction of them *was* insulting, then the blue-collar man or woman had at least as much cause to complain as the bourgeois did. Then too, black preachers, teachers, and editors had largely working-class constituencies; when one of these leaders censured *Amos 'n' Andy*, people listened, and at least some responded.

Black capitalism still held a special place in the dream of race advancement, even though the Great Depression had tarnished its mystique. Booker T. Washington, whose memory was still revered by many, had promoted the idea through his National Negro Business League. W. E. B. Du Bois, opposed as he was to much of Washington's program, also urged Afro-Americans to found businesses and exhorted the black public to support them as a means of advancing the race. Marcus Garvey, the charismatic black nationalist who won wide support among the Afro-American masses after World War I, was an avid proponent of black entrepreneurship. Black-owned banks and insurance companies had long been among the most conspicuous symbols of black success and black potential. And Afro-American businessmen, being human, were not above cultivating the myth, both to gratify their own egos and to stimulate black patronage of their enterprises. Publishers of black newspapers were by definition businessmen themselves, so their journals tended to promote the mystique of black capitalism even more assiduously than they might have otherwise. In such an atmosphere, even a black worker could see an attack on Afro-American business as a blow against the race as a whole.

Still, the middle-class flavor of the *Courier*'s crusade against *Amos 'n' Andy* probably hindered the campaign's progress among a black population that was overwhelmingly blue-collar, and whose vital concern during the bitter Depression year of 1931 was simply to put food on the table. Even many middle-class blacks gave the protest lukewarm support, ignored it, or opposed it outright. Despite Robert Vann's outraged rhetoric, black discussions of the radio series were by no means always conducted in an atmosphere of crisis; Afro-Americans in Lincoln, Nebraska, staged a debate on *Amos 'n' Andy* as part of a program and bazaar sponsored by a black Methodist church.[45] Statements in a couple of *Courier* articles and in a few white newspapers that "the NAACP" had joined the *Courier*'s campaign were incorrect. Some local officers or even branches may have supported Vann's campaign, but others dismissed or denounced it. The president of the NAACP branch in Cheyenne, Wyoming, said that he and most of his peers considered *Amos 'n' Andy* "good, humorous entertainment"; he had "seen Negroes in the South who really act like Amos and Andy." He dismissed the *Courier*'s protest as a "publicity stunt for Vann's paper" and those who promoted the petition as people who "probably had nothing else to do."[46] In Worcester, Massachusetts, a prominent black attorney could not "see any objection to *Amos 'n' Andy* at all." On the contrary, he said, "I think they're funny"; only "thin-skinned," "super-sensitive" blacks could object to the series. "Amos 'n' Andy are humorous," said a black lawyer in Newport News, Virginia, "but the [*Courier*'s] petition is even funnier."[47]

The natural desire to avoid trouble with the majority race cannot by itself explain the many benign or even friendly statements that middle-class Afro-Americans made about *Amos 'n' Andy* in 1931. As Robert Vann's protest began, J. Thomas Newsome, another attorney in Newport News who edited the black newspaper there, led a delegation to a city council meeting. He demanded and got continued city funding for street paving in black neighborhoods. In a testy exchange with the city's white mayor, Newsome came off as anything but a hat-in-hand accommodationist; at about the same time, he was mounting a legal challenge to the exclusion of blacks in his city from the polls in Democratic primary elections. Yet Newsome told a white journalist that "there is more of good natured banter in the dialogue between Amos 'n' Andy than malicious propaganda." "Many of [the show's] wisecracks," he added, "are true to life and some of them . . . show the Negro as a very subtle philosopher"; only someone hard up for a cause would oppose the program.[48]

Sanguine pronouncements about *Amos 'n' Andy* appeared in the pages of the *Courier* itself, where readers could express their views with no worry about what the white man might think. A woman from St. Louis wrote that the *Amos 'n' Andy* craze "did little harm." She accused both the *Courier* and her people at large of having a strange sense of priorities. If Vann organized a protest against lynching, the woman ventured, "the support you will get will be so small it will make you ashamed." "Anyhow," she concluded, "there are too few good-hearted Amoses among us—let's not expose the fact." Beyond the columns of the *Courier,* blacks mounted more stinging attacks on Vann's weekly. Theophilus Lewis, a columnist for Harlem's *Amsterdam News*, wrote that "the Courier campaign will serve one good end. When they complete their tally of signatures we will know precisely how many halfwits there are in the race."[49]

A black Chicagoan found *Amos 'n' Andy* a positive good for the image of his people. "That lovable character, Amos," the man wrote, with "his deep, loyal love to another fine character, Ruby Taylor, and . . . his undying friendship for shiftless Andy, . . . gives one the impression that the Negro race has and does, in spite of its handicaps, produce people who are worthwhile." He added that *Amos 'n' Andy* achieved symmetry by presenting "the higher type professional" along with "the petty con man."[50]

A man from Philadelphia found *Amos 'n' Andy* "the best comedy on the air today"—"an exact portrayal of my race's amusing lighter side." Far from bewailing *Amos 'n' Andy*'s influence on black children, this man was glad to see his "two little daughters anxiously await[ing] the arrival of 7 o'clock," when they could "enjoy their favorites." The "clean, wholesome" series provided a welcome contrast to the "obscene and vulgar" jokes and dances of "Negro shows playing in this city which I would not think of letting my daughters attend."[51]

With Afro-Americans so divided over the meaning of *Amos 'n' Andy*, it is no great wonder that the *Courier*'s petition drive, even according to the paper's own figures, never approached one million signatures. "No one . . . gave us any support" in the protest, Robert

Vann's widow Jessie recalled years later—albeit with some exaggeration. "We finally had to give it up, because seemingly we were not accomplishing anything, unless it was popularizing [*Amos 'n' Andy*], for the radio program continued to have just as many listeners as before and among our own people."[52] Gosden and Correll kept the loyalty of those black listeners without altering their show noticeably, and without changing their public-relations stance toward the black community significantly. Though the team were well aware of the protest and may have appeared at the Chicago *Defender*'s picnic hoping to discredit Vann's attacks, that event was only one in their series of occasional appearances before black groups extending from *Sam 'n' Henry* days through the *Courier* protest and well beyond.[53]

Robert Vann's failure to unite the black community against *Amos 'n' Andy* had a number of causes beyond the parochial middle-class tone of some of his complaints. Some Afro-Americans questioned Vann's motives. The Depression, which wiped out many black newspapers, had created desperate financial woes for the *Courier* as well; the *Amos 'n' Andy* protest was one of several causes Vann adopted in an urgent effort to attract readers. Even in good times, nationally distributed black papers like the *Courier* had had to compete strenuously for slices of a small pie—the largely poor Afro-American population. That competition sometimes led editors to take stands on issues for reasons that had more to do with scoring points against one another than with principle. Vann allowed the *Courier* to be seen in that light when his campaign at one point began to look less like a moral crusade than like a garden-variety feud with the Chicago *Defender*. Vann's opposition to *Amos 'n' Andy* was sincere, but the commercial dimension of his protest, and unproven accusations of corruption and cynicism that critics had lodged against him well before 1931, made it easy to dismiss the *Courier*'s campaign as a mere publicity stunt.[54]

Vann's extravagant rhetoric and grandiose promises during the *Amos 'n' Andy* affair only added to that impression. A mass protest does require hortatory language, and the folk culture of black and white Southerners and their descendants had a place for rhetoric that was judged as much on grandiloquence as on literal content. Black readers were also thoroughly used to Afro-American papers which, like the "yellow" press of the majority culture, ran huge, melodramatic headlines over breathless prose, often describing sensational instances of violence and carnality.

Even so, Vann outdid himself in the *Amos 'n' Andy* campaign. One million signatures, five thousand black ministers preaching against the radio series on a single day, a nationwide radio broadcast in protest against *Amos 'n' Andy*, a court suit against Gosden and Correll—all this sounded impressive at first; but then months passed, and the *Courier* did not fulfill any of these goals. Overheated accolades from readers, which the *Courier* trumpeted—one letter called the protest "the greatest movement toward the uplift of the race that has ever been attempted"[55]—came to sound hollow. So did the claim that Afro-Americans in "hundreds of cities" had backed the campaign "almost 100 percent." The *Courier* was bordering on self-parody by September, when a large headline proclaimed that a black man in Pennsylvania had killed a white man for calling him "Amos." Both the shooting and the all-white jury's verdict of manslaughter rather than murder, said the *Courier*, showed that the campaign against *Amos 'n' Andy* had changed attitudes among Afro-Americans and whites alike. Only in the second half of the article did the reader discover that the slain white man in fact had provoked the shooting by a whole spate of profane verbal abuse and, above all, by a physical assault on the black.[56]

Even the *Courier*'s supporters differed over the campaign's goals. Many protesters actually wanted to ban *Amos 'n' Andy* from the airwaves and seem to have been convinced by the *Courier* that this was possible—though Robert Vann must have known that the broadcasting and radio manufacturing industries were not about to slaughter their golden goose. These true believers were inevitably disappointed. Other supporters of Vann agreed with a reader in Philadelphia who energetically gathered signatures even though he was "sure there are more important subjects we may protest against"; this man favored anything that could bring together "any considerable number of Negroes to support any movement." Such a reader could drop the *Amos 'n' Andy* campaign without much regret as soon as some new crusade began. By late summer 1931, Bishop Walls probably typified many who had given up hope of banning *Amos 'n' Andy*. He now saw the protest primarily as a means to teach whites "that there is a real Negro culture and that all members of the race are not like Amos n' Andy."[57]

In fact, the *Courier*'s protest did make a little progress toward Walls's goal. White newspapers large and small reported both Walls's and Vann's complaints, generally in one or two short, factual wire-service items under small, neutral headlines. A number of papers went on to discuss the protest in editorials almost as varied as white listeners' views of *Amos 'n' Andy* itself.

At one extreme, some small-town papers—mainly in the Deep South and Southwest—agreed with the Texas editor who called the black protesters "a lot of fool Niggers" and insisted that the white broadcasters "bring out nigger characteristics true to Nigger nature just as it is among the denizens of the colored race in large cities."[58] Such language was highly exceptional, however; other hostile editors simply ran mocking or disparaging headlines over the standard wire-service copy ("Negroes 'Regusted' "; "Ambitious Negro Asks that Amos 'n' Andy Be Barred from the Air"; "Knights of Africa Ban Mystic Knights of Sea From Pale of Approval"[59]). Some southern papers blamed the protest on those blacks who one writer said were "born in the cold north and never got over it." An editor in Shreveport challenged Robert Vann by asserting that Gosden and Correll "know their negro stuff. Not the Pittsburgh lawyer type of darky, perhaps, but the old-fashioned Southern negro."[60]

More numerous were white editors who neither condemned nor made fun of Vann but still found him "Too Sensitive," as the title of an editorial in Oregon put it. Some were disappointed and even a little mystified to find blacks objecting to *Amos 'n' Andy*—whose affectionate characterizations, these editors believed, promoted "human equality and kinship" and were "making the Negro's place in American life easier and safer."[61] Other white editorialists found the black protest "easy to understand" but assured Vann that, in light of the "astonishing progress" that "intelligent, industrious and useful Negro citizens" everywhere had made in the past half-century, whites did not see *Amos 'n' Andy* as a depiction of the race as a whole.[62]

A few white papers fulfilled Bishop Walls's highest hopes, supporting Vann outright. "Colored people rightly insist that the Amos 'n' Andy propaganda helps to paste an undesirable label on the colored folks' pigeon-hole in the white man's mind," wrote an editorialist in Toledo. "The negroes have a hard hill to climb," agreed a St. Louis editor. A small-town paper in Oregon saw merit in the complaint that *Amos 'n' Andy* was "a tiresome revival of the old time minstrel darky who represented nothing but what someone imagined a negro to be." A writer in Fairmont, West Virginia, found the *Courier*'s protest "interesting" and "important," though he suggested that black appeals to "public sentiment" and pressure on *Amos 'n' Andy*'s sponsors would achieve more than petitions or court suits. A small-town Iowa paper "sympathize[d] with the colored folk" but warned them that the protest would only advertise *Amos 'n' Andy*; "Let Them Peter Out" naturally, the writer suggested.[63]

If Vann's protest did not change millions of white minds, it did provoke thought among some whites who were already liberally inclined. But the radio show did not peter out. Afro-Americans reached no consensus on it—and over the long haul, Vann himself sometimes sent mixed signals as to what "real Negro culture" and black pride were. Two and a half years after the demise of the *Amos 'n' Andy* campaign, for example, the *Courier* started another "Nation-Wide Drive for Racial Self-Respect." Each reader was asked to send in one dollar for the legal defense of black defendants like the "Scottsboro boys."

Vann soon joined forces with the NAACP and spoke with typical bombast of raising a million dollars. The first of several fund-raising performances that the *Courier* staged featured Stepin Fetchit, among others. Decades of white racism, rather than an active desire by Fetchit himself to betray his race, had produced the shuffling, drawling "coon" roles that won him his fame; still, he was an odd choice to star in a gala promoting black self-respect. Yet when the *Courier*'s fund drive collapsed after netting only a few thousand dollars, Vann blamed the black masses. He wrote to the NAACP's Walter White in frustration that "the Courier was just a little bit in advance in expecting Negroes to have self-respect."[64]

Vann was wrong. Black Americans were not without self-respect. But the *Amos 'n' Andy* protest had shown that blacks defined self-respect in different ways and chose a variety of means to express it.

The idea that the status of Afro-Americans depended largely on their own concrete deeds and achievements was a powerful one, shared by black leaders whose programs differed sharply on other points. Booker T. Washington, in his Atlanta Exposition address of 1895 and in countless pronouncements thereafter until his death in 1915, had urged blacks to strive, to excel, to spend less time pursuing status symbols and educational frills and more effort acquiring practical skills. By laying protest and political activity aside for the time being, working themselves from the bottom upward, and making themselves indispensable to the general economy, Washington insisted, Afro-Americans would win the respect of whites.

W. E. B. Du Bois, Washington's best-known critic, insisted that talented blacks should pursue liberal university education and confront whites head-on with the demand for immediate racial equality. But Du Bois, too, declared that the advancement of Afro-America depended on deeds, not images or airs. He once upbraided a black high school sophomore who proposed that the term " 'Negro,' or 'nigger,' " be abolished as "a white man's word to make us feel inferior." "Things are the reality that counts," Du Bois retorted. "If a thing is despised, . . . you will not alter matters by changing its name." "Your real work as a Negro lies in two directions," he added: "*First,* to let the world know what there is fine and genuine about the Negro race. And *secondly,* to see that there is nothing about that race which is worth contempt; your contempt, my contempt; or the contempt of the wide, wide world."[65]

Neither continuing racial discrimination nor the Depression's propensity to ruin the industrious along with the improvident killed the ethic of self-help among Afro-Americans. On this score, Roy Wilkins's statement during the *Amos 'n' Andy* controversy of 1930–1931 echoed both Washington and Du Bois. Like Du Bois, Wilkins accused a disgruntled young black man, who in this case assailed *Amos 'n' Andy,* of pursuing "appearances" rather than "intrinsic worth." Wilkins had made the same point a few months earlier in language that sounded almost word for word like Booker T. Washington. Of all ethnic groups, Wilkins wrote in a column on *Amos 'n' Andy,* "only the Negro . . . wants to ride in Packards when he ought to be in Fords; wants to be in mansions when he ought to have cottages; wants to talk French before he can speak English."[66]

Both Washington and Du Bois could have endorsed the prescription that Wilkins urged on Clarence L. Mitchell for pursuing real worth and true progress for the race: "Rest assured that if Howard University does its work well, its products will make it known to the far corners of the land . . . ; that if Emmett Scott [former secretary to Booker Washington and former special assistant to the Secretary of War] be known as a useful citizen, it does not matter what his racial identity may be."[67] For Wilkins, Amos and Andy's struggle to find a good spare tire and keep it repaired was just the opposite of a travesty on black enterprise; it was a metaphoric prescription for black advancement. Afro-Americans should put aside "false pride," roll up their sleeves and—in the words of the black Philadelphia *Tribune*—be "up and doing" to match or surpass Gosden and Correll's success.

Bishop Walls, too, hoped *Amos 'n' Andy* would arouse Afro-Americans to be up and doing—but doing at least some things that Wilkins considered worse than useless. Walls accepted Washington's and Wilkins's premise that Afro-Americans must work their way up the competitive capitalist ladder. And he emphatically agreed with Du Bois that blacks had a duty to let the world know what was fine and genuine about the race. But Walls was convinced that *Amos 'n' Andy* obscured in the mind of the world what was fine about blacks. Just as important, Walls believed that by accepting and even enjoying *Amos 'n' Andy*, blacks invited what Du Bois called "the contempt of the wide, wide world." To fight Gosden and Correll, Walls said in effect, would achieve both of Du Bois's goals: it would show the world the pride and the initiative of Afro-America, and it would help ensure that there was nothing contemptible about the race.

Agreement on certain basics, myriad divisions over what, exactly, those basics implied for an Afro-America facing a maze of intractable problems—both had long prevented black opinion in general, and now about *Amos 'n' Andy* in particular, from dividing neatly into two or three distinct camps bearing convenient labels.[68] The issues of Afro-America's image and of black self-respect were far too complex, too personal and subjective, too fraught with dilemmas, to allow even the most orderly mind to develop a formula that could answer every question. For example, Roy Wilkins accepted Du Bois's proposition that deeds, not words or names, determined the state of the race, yet he especially lauded *Amos 'n' Andy* for avoiding unflattering terms denoting blacks; Du Bois himself found the capitalization of the word "Negro" a cause worth fighting for.

It is precisely the intense feelings that welled up around *Amos 'n' Andy*, and the *lack* of formulaic, party-line positions, that make the black debate over the show so revealing in such profound ways. And if complexities and divisions within Afro-America were the shoal on which Robert Vann's protest ran aground, none played a greater role in the *Amos 'n' Andy* debate than the differences between the veteran black residents of the northern city, who had absorbed urban ways over years or even generations, and the masses of black immigrants from the South who had arrived during and after World War I. That division contained elements of both class and cultural antagonism; white racism and the anxieties it spawned among Afro-Americans only worsened the friction.

By the turn of the century, many black "old settlers" in New York and other cities already looked upon new arrivals from the South as "riff-raff," "illiterate," "lazy," "uncouth," and "undesirable"—a "low element . . . who own a lot of dirty rags and dogs and crowds of children."[69] The Chicago *Defender* frequently urged its many southern readers to move north; yet even it joined older city-dwellers in deploring the black immigrants' way of life, which supposedly was harming the race's reputation and intensifying white bias against all blacks. "Keep your mouth shut, please!" the *Defender* scolded. "There is entirely too much loud talking on the street cars among our newcomers." "In the south a premium was put on filth and uncleanliness," the paper explained on another occasion. "In the north a badge of honor is put on the man or woman who is clean."[70]

Black opinion about *Amos 'n' Andy* did not divide predictably along lines of social class; the show had its fans and its enemies in all economic strata. Yet the gap between middle and working classes, between old guard and newcomers, often reared its head during the debate among blacks over *Amos 'n' Andy*. Bishop Walls's criticism of the show took the interests of the untutored southern immigrant into account, finding that *Amos 'n' Andy* overstated his ignorance and ineptitude. Yet Walls, like Robert Vann, took *Amos 'n' Andy* to task less for caricaturing southern blacks in the big city than for allegedly linking the more advanced elements of the Afro-American community to an all-too-real class of black rustics. Walls and many others showed how ready they were to wash their hands of what they saw as the "imbecilic" elements of the race, the "unlearned, illiterate, simple Southerner," "the rabble and riffraff" who disgraced Afro-America both by providing models for Gosden and Correll and by adoring *Amos 'n' Andy*.

In its more extreme form, identification with "white" standards, or at least the hope of advancement by conforming to them, fueled a brisk market in hair straighteners and skin-bleaching potions—like the one endorsed in large advertisements at the height of the *Courier*'s protest by a "charming . . . club woman," a leader of "society" married to a "celebrated" black doctor.[71] Similar values and concerns fueled the visceral middle-class disdain for non-Standard language, whether in *Amos 'n' Andy* or in real life, that some letters to the *Courier* expressed. But those who rejected the supposed norms of the black masses were by no means all self-haters or "assimilationists." Even those Afro-Americans who saw group solidarity, self-sufficiency, and race pride as the path to equality often approached those goals by adopting values similar to the ones that the northern white majority claimed to believe in: hard work, prudence, studiousness, tidiness, personal modesty, and self-restraint.

The desire to shuck off the "southern" image led some articulate blacks to condemn any popular entertainment containing "cotton scenes" or "southern dialect and customs" as "degrading" almost by definition. Many black critics praised the innovative movies *Hearts in Dixie* and *Hallelujah!* in 1929; featuring all-black casts in southern rural or urban ghetto settings, the films transcended some of the limitations previous movies had imposed on black characterizations. Yet the pictures' locales and subject matter alone made them anathema to other Afro-American observers.[72] Clarence L. Mitchell, the Howard University student, considered *Hallelujah!* just as unacceptable as *Amos 'n' Andy;* Theresa Smith Kennedy of St. Louis likened Gosden and Correll's show to *Hearts in Dixie* and found both deplorable.

Robert Vann's desire to be free of the "southern" label was even more intense than his antipathy toward *Amos 'n' Andy* itself. The *Courier* proudly reprinted an editorial from a white paper in Rochester which noted that, although the radio show's central characters embodied "the stereotyped Negro of the Old South," *Amos 'n' Andy* also featured characters who displayed the " 'white' psychology" of "the new Negro, educated, intelligent, moving up the social scale."[73] The *Courier* itself never admitted that *Amos 'n' Andy* contained *any* sophisticated, nonstereotyped characters. Yet Vann was so gratified to find some whites who dissociated the "new Negro"—fully equipped with a "white" psyche—from his crude southern cousin that he eagerly published the Rochester editorial despite its praise for *Amos 'n' Andy*.

The questionable assumption—which, ironically, the creators of *Amos 'n' Andy* shared with Robert Vann—that the new Negro should be virtually indistinguishable from the better class of northern whites meshed with the limitations of radio to place Vann in yet another awkward situation. The *Courier* highlighted the complaint that Andy, after discharging his crooked, incompetent black lawyer in the breach-of-promise case, had hired an accomplished white advocate who proceeded to call him and Amos "boys" throughout the trial. In reality, Gosden and Correll portrayed both Andy's and Madam Queen's brilliant, dynamic lawyers as Afro-Americans. But radio's lack of a visual image obscured this; since both attorneys were supposed to be highly educated men, the radio team read their lines in Standard English. The Rochester editorialist had caught the contextual signals that the two lawyers were black and understood these characters as exemplars of Afro-American achievement, but Robert Vann had assumed that they must be white and had taken offense.[74]

Meanwhile, those blacks who did not oppose *Amos 'n' Andy* either saw nothing to be ashamed of in the culture of southern-born Afro-Americans, or did not see portrayals—even caricatures—of that culture as reflecting on them. Northern blacks had long supported comedians of their own race—from the black minstrels to Miller and Lyles—who, among other specialties, parodied the unsophisticated Southerner. The enjoyment might come from the bemused recognition of one's own southern roots; and if whites were not present in the hall, Afro-American comedians could play to blacks' sense of humor about themselves, and the audience could enjoy the jokes, without worrying that the majority would misinterpret. On the other hand, "southern" blackface humor could do something for urban Afro-Americans—even those of southern origin—that "rube" or ethnic humor did for Americans in general: make the audience feel superior to the group being portrayed without seeming petty or cruel.

Roy Wilkins and people of like mind saw Gosden and Correll in much the same light as they viewed Miller and Lyles and other black comics. Wilkins does not seem to have based his easy acceptance of Amos, Andy, and similar characters mainly on a feeling of superiority to their supposed counterparts in real life. Rather, Wilkins saw Amos and Andy as representing both universal human types and a real segment of the Afro-American community of whom he was not ashamed and by whose ways he did not feel threatened. That Gosden and Correll, in Wilkins's view, drew their characters with warmth and without undue distortion made the radio comics' whiteness irrelevant —except that blacks could have done the same material better.

Other black fans of *Amos 'n' Andy*, especially in the ranks of the educated and the economically comfortable, may have got more enjoyment than Wilkins did from the superiority they felt to most of Gosden and Correll's characters. When the black reporter who described the bridge tournament in Baltimore wrote "I'se regusted!" in a column for the public prints, she obviously separated herself from those who really spoke non-Standard English. Had it occurred to her that anyone might mistake her for the class of people that Amos and Andy represented, she would not have permitted herself the jest. The same applies to the many educated blacks who bandied about Amos 'n' Andyisms.

A story told by black writer William Branch neatly shows how much could turn on a given black listener's understanding of *which* Afro-Americans *Amos 'n' Andy* depicted. Branch recalled how his family used to sit around the radio laughing heartily at *Amos 'n' Andy*— everyone, that is, except his father. Only later did Branch come to understand his father's brooding silence: "Those people were supposed to be 'us.' "[75]

Troubling questions of racial identity would confront Afro-Americans for decades to come. That each person answered them case by case in his or her own way is clear from the diversity of opinion about almost every vehicle or art form that featured blacks during *Amos 'n' Andy*'s early years. Gosden and Correll, black comic acts like Miller and Lyles, black musicals, Stepin Fetchit, jazz, the blues, various movies featuring black actors or all-black casts—each had both fans and articulate detractors among Afro-Americans.

Bishop Walls had as little use for the efflorescence in popular music and dance that his own race was inspiring and producing—he deplored "jazzy, staccato" shows that exploited "primitive weaknesses" found among the black "lower strata"—as he did for *Amos 'n' Andy*. The backlash against "obscenity" and the other changes of the 1920s spanned the color line; Walls and other influential Afro-Americans joined white social conservatives in the fight against the "sordidness, realism, vulgarity, psychoanalysis, free verse, and staccato writing" that Walls thought World War I had spawned,[76] whether these issued from Harlem nightspots, Hollywood film studios, or northeastern universities. There was also a specifically "black" reason for opposing *Amos 'n' Andy*, black musical revues, nightclub acts, and the blues—that all of these pandered to whites' racist appetite for black "exoticism." At the same time, though, some black Americans echoed Walls's prim condemnation of jazz and black musicals, yet praised Gosden and Correll's show as heartily as the pair's most devoted white fans. The black man in Philadelphia who condemned black musical revues as "obscene and vulgar" found *Amos 'n' Andy* "the best comedy on the air."

Meanwhile, many Afro-Americans who reveled in the "jazzy, staccato" brilliance of black performers like Duke Ellington took similar delight in Gosden and Correll's radio performances. The Chicago *Defender*'s praise of *Amos 'n' Andy* was no more enthusiastic than its accolades for the other guests it had invited to its picnic, Ellington and his fellow black bandleader, Lucky Millinder. The *Defender* proudly reminded its readers that the former was "heralded from coast to coast" as the "king of jazz," and promised that the bands would "play red hot, low down melodies that'll make everybody want to shake their feet"—black music for black people. Columnist Lula Jones Garrett of the Baltimore *Afro* lavishly praised Afro-Americans whose performances were exuberantly black. By "being ourselves," Garrett wrote, "the race brought a stimulation to jaded stageland with its joyous abandon in dancing and joyous crooning melodies." Yet she also enjoyed Gosden and Correll's humor.[77]

That blacks disagreed so sharply over the merits of some of their race's greatest talents shows that the dispute over *Amos 'n' Andy* was part of a much wider debate. True, a confluence of factors made Gosden and Correll something of a special case. They were white, and they performed in a strikingly new medium. They distinguished themselves from many of their white peers by introducing some black figures who were polished and articulate, endowing many of their characters with universal as well as "racial" traits, and spinning stories that the average person of either race might become sympathetically absorbed in. And their series—largely for these very reasons—won vastly greater popularity than other vehicles did. Yet *Amos 'n' Andy* was not so different, so removed from the many other black images in popular entertainment and literature, that the issues it raised and the passions it aroused can be called unique.

The wide-ranging debate among black Americans over images in popular media, and over the potential of those images to accelerate or hinder black progress, was in large part an argument over self-definition. That some Afro-Americans dismissed black popular music, dance, and comedy as "vulgar" manifestations which corrupted black minds and gave whites the wrong idea about Afro-America, while others embraced these forms as expressions of the unique genius of the race, shows how profound these differences in self-definition could be in a society where whites wrote—and rigged—the rules. That those who loved and took pride in black music and humor often enjoyed *Amos 'n' Andy* reminds us how tricky it can be to define black consciousness, black militancy, and the relationship between the two. That social class was so imperfect a predictor of a person's views about *Amos 'n' Andy* raises still other questions, to which the rest of the show's history may suggest some answers.

The fire kindled in 1930 and 1931 by W. J. Walls, Robert Vann, and others died down, but these complexities—in all realms of black life—still confronted Afro-Americans as they struggled to define themselves and their place in American society. The dispute over *Amos 'n' Andy* abated, but without giving any satisfaction to those whom the series had offended. The fire still smoldered beneath the surface; under the right conditions, it might flare up again.

10

···───◉◆◉───···

"This Continuing Harm"

The changes that America went through in the years after the *Amos 'n' Andy* protest of 1931 were even more dramatic than those that had produced and molded the radio series in the first place. Politicians and would-be messiahs of both right and left competed for followers, pushing a dizzying variety of remedies for the Great Depression. Franklin Roosevelt's New Deal energized reformers of all stripes and gave them opportunities that they had lacked during the years since the First World War. Some of those reformers were Afro-Americans. The Roosevelt Administration appointed advisers and specialists on "Negro affairs" in many government departments. FDR's "Black Cabinet," which included the highest-ranking of those officials, gave Afro-Americans a more prominent place in the national government than they had ever had before; the Great Migration had created a northern black vote worth courting.

Congress passed legislation that strengthened labor unions—which by now included pioneering organizations like the black Brotherhood of Sleeping Car Porters and the interracial Committee for Industrial Organization (CIO). The New Deal quickened the Great Migration once again after a slowdown during the early Depression years. Adding a new push to the northward flow of people, the New Deal paid southern landowners not to produce crops and thus helped push sharecroppers who had tilled that land out of their homes. Meanwhile, the fairer administration of New Deal relief programs outside the South created a new northward and westward pull on black Southerners.

World War II began to accelerate many of these changes even before the United States became directly involved. American industry geared up for war, creating hundreds of thousands of new jobs in an economy that was becoming ever more urban and modern; the lingering Depression finally ended. The threat of A. Philip Randolph, leader of the Sleeping Car Porters, to stage a mass march of blacks on Washington, D.C., secured a Presidential order prohibiting the exclusion of Afro-Americans from employment in defense plants. Millions of Americans, both black and white, were exposed to new places and new ideas, whether as wartime industrial workers or as soldiers. Prominent among those in new roles during the 1930s and '40s were American women. Frances Perkins became the first female Cabinet member. Mary McLeod Bethune was the acknowledged dean of the Black Cabinet, and millions of both races filled wartime jobs that had formerly been "men's work."

Amos 'n' Andy, too, changed during the two decades after the Pittsburgh *Courier*'s protest of 1931—not because of black pressure or the reshaping of American life, but because radio broadcasting changed. Gosden and Correll had created a product in the late 1920s that revolutionized a new medium of mass entertainment and reflected a shifting, blurring color line. But the two men had not gone into radio comedy *in order to* do either of these things. As the 1930s wore on, *Amos 'n' Andy* did continue to offer topical commentary as its characters made their way through the Depression. But the novelty of the show wore off; the *Amos 'n' Andy* mania of 1929–1931 gave way to good but less spectacular ratings, and the series ceased to be a hot topic of discussion. *Amos 'n' Andy* was "as established as the grandfather clock on the stairs," one columnist wrote in 1937. "We may not listen to it all the time, but we know it's there."[1] If the show remained a Rorschach test of racial attitudes, few Americans now felt moved to announce their interpretations of the ink blot.

Radio itself was no longer a novelty by the mid-1930s, but rather a major commercial industry. Better-financed, more elaborate shows had introduced a new universe of stars, many of whom skillfully adopted and modified *Amos 'n' Andy*'s situation comedy formula. Gosden and Correll now shared the spotlight with Jack Benny, George Burns and Gracie Allen, Fibber McGee and Molly, and Fred Allen. As always, Gosden and Correll used innovations and gimmicks to help hold their audience. Late in 1935, for example, they slowly began to use other actors in their broadcasts. At first, such outsiders were used in the women's parts that the veteran team could not easily play themselves. Gosden and Correll could hardly portray Ruby Taylor's wedding to Amos in December 1935 without a Ruby to say "I do"; a white actor named Elinor Harriot uttered the line and played the role of the famous Ruby thereafter. The wedding episode also featured a line by Edith Davis—mother of future First Lady Nancy Reagan and a specialist in "black" stage dialect—as the battle-ax wife of one of the lodge brothers. The following year, when *Amos 'n' Andy*'s sponsor used newspaper ads to promote a nationwide contest to name Amos and Ruby's new baby for a $5,000 first prize, a publicity photo showed Gosden and Correll inundated with entries.[2]

Another prominent female character, Andy's secretary, Miss Blue, was played by a white Texan named Madeline Lee. Andy ran an electric buzzer line between his office and Miss Blue's—only to discover that the secretary could buzz him, but not the reverse. Rather than let the system go unused, Andy took to summoning his employee in the only way he could: his recurring shout, "Buzz me, Miss Blue!," became one of *Amos 'n' Andy*'s best-remembered trademark phrases.

Despite such novelties, signs of trouble for Gosden and Correll appeared toward the end of the 1930s. In 1937, one source estimated that 3.2 million radios were tuned to *Amos 'n' Andy* on the average day; even if five people sat before each of those radios, the show's audience was not nearly as large as the forty million who were said to have listened to *Amos 'n' Andy* at the height of its popularity. One radio columnist reported in 1937 that Gosden and Correll had hoped some recent tinkering with the show would revive the ratings, "but, while the punch was there, the audience just wasn't . . . at least not in the former numbers."[3] *Amos 'n' Andy* switched sponsors, from Pepsodent to Campbell's Soup, early in 1938—and networks, from NBC to CBS, a year later; although CBS stock supposedly rose two points when *Amos 'n' Andy*'s move became known, the show's slide in the ratings continued.[4] Meanwhile, Gosden and Correll felt they had little to lose by making still other changes.

The pair moved their show to California from Chicago in 1937–1938, having already broadcast from Palm Springs and Hollywood during long visits there; they soon began hiring other writers to work on their scripts. Hollywood contained a large colony of black actors, and Gosden and Correll were fairly quick to use them. In 1939, they auditioned Ernestine Wade, an Afro-American musician and actress who went on to play a number of roles in the series.[5] The part she made famous was that of Sapphire, the Kingfish's strong-willed wife—who, in the show's early years, had not been referred to by name. Wade was only the first of many black actors and singers who appeared on *Amos 'n' Andy* during the next decade and a half, making the show one of Hollywood's premier employers of black talent. By the mid-1940s, in addition to Wade and comic actors like Eddie Green and Johnny Lee, Afro-Americans often played incidental parts as articulate professionals—ministers, lawyers, doctors, and the like.[6] The series had always included such occasional characters, but their appearances became more frequent as their middle-class counterparts in American society became more visible.

As always, however, *Amos 'n' Andy* proffered its innovations against a deep background of tradition. Late in 1936, Gosden and Correll took a major step backward toward their pre-network days by devoting one broadcast per week to a minstrel-show version of *Amos 'n' Andy*. The *Amos 'n' Andy* minstrel segments emphasized music as much as comedy; the first of them, for example, included a white soloist, an orchestra, a chorus, and a black male quartet.[7] The conceit that the team employed to fit the weekly minstrel shows into the series was less demeaning to Afro-Americans than it might have been: the members of the Mystic Knights of the Sea supposedly put on the shows as fund-raisers. The picture created was thus one of black characters—the lodge brothers—intentionally performing humorous routines, rather than of whites caricaturing blacks. Of course, the real-life stars *were* still white men—in this instance, whites playing blacks playing blacks.

Some critics gave Gosden and Correll credit as "iconoclasts": having recently made Amos and Ruby parents of a baby girl, said one writer, they were "now determined to toss another precedent out the window" as *Amos 'n' Andy* "gets away from tradition and unlaxes" by staging minstrel shows.[8] With the minstrel segments, Gosden and Correll were indeed abandoning their own tradition of steadfastly minimizing their debt to minstrelsy. Yet nothing could have been less iconoclastic than to revert to a genre with a century-long history and an abundance of racially conservative connotations. The *Amos 'n' Andy* minstrel shows, like the old Joe Bren productions, even used an obviously white interlocutor—Bill Hay, the Scottish-American announcer of the series, playing himself.

By 1936, in fact, Gosden and Correll in many ways had already become followers, not leaders, in radio broadcasting. Other shows had located in Hollywood, were broadcast before studio audiences, included their announcers in the plot, and regularly presented famous guests. These programs were slicker and showier than *Amos 'n' Andy*, and each presented an ensemble of actors rather than simply of different characters' voices. Gosden and Correll and their sponsors believed they had to compete or die.[9] That they resorted to minstrel shows flowed naturally from their own background in burnt cork, and from the persistent readiness of many whites to see minstrel routines as a natural outlet for "black" music and comedy.

But Gosden and Correll were adulterating the quasi-realistic fictional world they had so painstakingly created through their characterizations. And the team did this not only in the minstrel segments, but in *Amos 'n' Andy* serial episodes as well. The first guest performer in a regular installment of the show, appearing in 1936, was the actor Lionel Barrymore. Gosden and Correll worked him into the plot of the broadcast through a farfetched device: they had Amos and Andy drive their taxi on a vacation to Hollywood, where the two Harlemites visited movie lots. At one of these, the two happened to meet and talk with a friendly stranger, who turned out to be Barrymore. The major *Amos 'n' Andy* characters began to plug sponsors' products on the air, and Gosden and Correll now felt free to go out of character at the end of a broadcast to wish the audience a happy Christmas or New Year's holiday.[10]

These practices, which further breached the integrity of *Amos 'n' Andy*'s fictional environment, preceded the biggest of all the changes in the series—a shift in its format in 1943. Gosden and Correll left CBS, and when they returned to the air eight months later—now on NBC again under the sponsorship of Rinso laundry detergent—the daily fifteen-minute serial was no more. The team performed only once a week; each show was a self-contained, half-hour situation comedy. More actors joined the cast, and Gosden and Correll, who for years had insisted on complete privacy when broadcasting, now admitted an audience to their studio.

The writers—and there would be a number of them over the next decade—worked closely with Gosden and Correll, who expected them to stick closely to the norms of characterization and language that the two veterans had established over the years. The writers plied their trade with skill: they trotted out the old catchwords ("I'se regusted," "un-laxin'," and the like), kept the characters lively, and concocted comical stories. The new show was a hit.[11] Still, the use of hired staff, along with the loss of the humanizing influence of the daily serial story, promoted a kind of writing-by-formula that has typified broadcast situation comedy up to our own day. The new, disjointed format encouraged outlandish plots, where the stories on *Sam 'n' Henry* and the early *Amos 'n' Andy* had often been simple, unprepossessing, and involving. Gosden and Correll, after years of writing the show, had themselves begun long since to cook up unlikely storylines. But the shift to the weekly sitcom in 1943 exacerbated that tendency and made it much harder to leaven the humor with suspense and melodrama.

The change in format also sealed a change that had begun during the 1930s—a shift in the relative prominence of the three central characters. Amos—precisely as he became more and more estimable as a family man, provider, and always-responsible voice of common sense—lost some of his usefulness as a comic character. He faded in importance, while the Kingfish moved toward center stage. The Kingfish had regularly tried to swindle Andy ever since the lodge-hall potentate first appeared as *Sam 'n' Henry*'s Most Precious Diamond; his schemes could easily be presented in half-hour segments, and they took a prominent place in the new weekly show. The series thus became more predictable, and more focused around two particular stereotypes: the Kingfish's laziness and cupidity and Andy's monumental ignorance and gullibility.

There may have been yet another reason for *Amos 'n' Andy*'s slide into formulaic routine. Gosden and Correll's efforts to drink from the supposed wellspring of their inspiration—the real Afro-American communities of Chicago and Harlem—had always been greatly exaggerated in the press. For years, the white pair had moved in wealthy circles that had little in common with the world depicted in *Amos 'n' Andy*. Then, at the end of the 1930s, Gosden and Correll left Chicago far behind, and the perpetual sunshine of Hollywood and Palm Springs insulated them still further. Freeman Gosden had once pegged his claims of authenticity to a boyhood surrounded by blacks and to continuing contact with ordinary Afro-Americans. By 1942, Correll had built a mansion designed by the noted black architect, Paul Williams, and Gosden still spoke of his Afro-American boyhood friend. But when the pair talked with two black reporters in that year, Gosden was reduced to confessing that his current data on Afro-American character came from a "colored boy working for me."[12]

The new, half-hour, once-weekly *Amos 'n' Andy* of the mid-1940s still had a good deal in common with the original product. It gave occasional work to many black performers and regular employment to a few. It presented more Afro-Americans in nonstereotyped roles than any other radio series—though that was not difficult, given the competition. But for all that, Gosden and Correll's days as path-breakers were pretty well over. *Amos 'n' Andy*, always a blend of the traditional and the new, remained so—except that by now many of its earlier innovations had themselves become traditions in whose well-worn grooves the show could coast along comfortably.

Black Americans had less to say in public about *Amos 'n' Andy* after 1931 than they had before. As years passed, more of them—even some who admitted they enjoyed *Amos 'n' Andy*—seemed to conclude that the radio series presented some antiquated images that were doing the race little good. But the show's old-shoe familiarity, the waning of its cult status among whites after 1931, and its retention of elements that many Afro-Americans had enjoyed all along helped prevent any new explosion of resentment.

What commentary there was, though sometimes lively, broke little new ground. As Gosden and Correll began a series of appearances at New York's Radio City Music Hall in 1933, a resident of Harlem named Samuel Hamilton sued the pair in a local court. Asserting that *Amos 'n' Andy* had exposed all the black people of Harlem to "ridicule, shame, scorn, humiliation and degradation," Hamilton asked the judge to enjoin Gosden and Correll from making "derogatory, defamatory, slanderous" commentary about the race. Like the Pittsburgh *Courier* before him, Hamilton took particular exception to *Amos 'n' Andy*'s depiction of black entrepreneurs, by which he said "the residents of Harlem [had] been irreparably injured in their reputations and businesses."[13]

Just as some racist whites had mocked the *Courier*'s protest in 1931, so at least one newspaper in New York answered Hamilton's complaints with heavy derision. Hamilton, wrote a correspondent for the *Mirror*, was "regusted. He is irrigated beyond condurance. His self-steem is unreparably unruptioned. . . . He is suffered a confront of his hindmost consensibilities." The *Mirror*'s caption-writer got in his own licks, explaining, "It seems that every time you laughed at Amos 'N Andy over the radio, the colored folks in Harlem were near tears. Their feelings have been hurt. . . . Now ain't that sumpin'. . . ?"[14]

Hamilton may have filed his suit to publicize his grievances rather than to achieve any actual legal result. When the case was called for trial, the plaintiff's attorney failed to appear in court and the suit was dismissed. As usual, Gosden and Correll took steps—short of altering their act—to win the good will of blacks. A radio magazine reported that, on the same day the summons arising from Hamilton's suit was served, "a Harlem charity organization sent [the white pair] a special message of thanks for a donation which these boys had made, and for being friends of the Negro race."[15] Word of the impending suit may have prompted Gosden and Correll's charitable donation, and Samuel Hamilton's legal action certainly prompted NBC to publicize the black group's message of thanks and amity. Like the team's many earlier declarations of respect for Afro-Americans, such gestures—besides gratifying Gosden and Correll's humanitarian impulses—deflected black resentment and soothed the conscience of those white fans who wanted reassurance about *Amos 'n' Andy*'s good intentions.

Soon after Hamilton filed his suit, the NAACP quietly complained to Pepsodent, *Amos 'n' Andy*'s sponsors—but not about the series as a whole. Rather, the organization was unhappy with a particular plot-line suggesting that tourist camps in the North were segregated by race. To take issue with such a relatively fine point at least implied that the NAACP accepted the legitimacy of the series overall. Even the Pittsburgh *Courier* had pulled in its horns since the demise of its protest of two years before. The paper covered the NAACP's complaint—including the response of Pepsodent's advertising manager, who thought blacks "imagined" insults where none existed—without great fanfare. For their part, Gosden and Correll continued to cultivate black listeners throughout the 1930s. On more than one occasion, for example, the team donated hogs to be given away as prizes at the convention of the National Federation of Colored Farmers.[16]

Some black voices spoke as favorably of Gosden and Correll after 1931 as any had ever done earlier. In 1934, a black newspaper writer in Chicago was still praising Gosden and Correll's appearances at black charity events and their efforts "to keep from offending the sensibilities of Negroes."[17] Nevertheless, one phrase in the writer's story—"This much must be said in favor of 'Amos 'n' Andy' "—showed that some things had changed since 1930 or so: even black friends of the series recognized that black grumbling about the program had become fairly widespread.

Gosden and Correll's show still retained a sizable following among ordinary Afro-Americans in these years, however. In 1935, a black newspaper in Atlanta announced that the "colored balcony" at a local theater would be open to accommodate hundreds of fans for a series

of personal appearances by Amos 'n' Andy. The management of the
theater was confident enough of black Atlantans' enthusiasm for the
two stars that it raised the price of those Jim Crow seats to twenty-five
cents apiece, with no discount for children. The black newspaper
itself agreed that the presence of "radio's greatest personalities"
would make for a "gala occasion."[18]

Even in the 1940s, the occasional criticism of *Amos 'n' Andy* that
did surface tended to be mild, as when a reader complained to a black
weekly in Ohio that "Radio Programs Misrepresent the Negro." The
writer included *Amos 'n' Andy* in his indictment, although even he
admitted that the series had shown "some improvement" of late.[19] In
1942, Almena Davis, a reporter for the black Los Angeles *Tribune,*
could still praise Gosden and Correll for "a real understanding of
people" that transcended race. The only complaint she and an associate had offered the team during an interview was that their radio
material was becoming "corny" because the stars did not keep up
with black popular culture and slang. "You ain't hipped to the jive,"
Davis told them.[20]

At the same time, though, Davis's article revealed that for her and
for many others, "Amos 'n' Andy" had become a generic term for
shuck-and-jive black buffoons who were holding the race back. She
showed some impatience with Gosden and Correll's admission that a
black employee—who she figured must epitomize "all the Uncle
Toms and 'amos 'n' andys' in the race"—was the main representative
of her people whom the white stars saw regularly. Under a picture of
Correll and Gosden in blackface, a caption noted, with a hint of
dissatisfaction, that the performers had "made a million dollars pre-
tending to be 'us.' " And a sampling of local blacks' opinions of *Amos
'n' Andy* that ran in the same issue of the *Tribune* disclosed that, while
some enjoyed the show, others found it "annoying."

During the same period, the radio series continued to win an
audience among white liberals whose forthright stands on racial matters had won them the enmity of the right wing. In 1935, Eleanor
Roosevelt, the President's wife, spoke on her own radio program of
her devotion to *Amos 'n' Andy* and the Burns and Allen show. And
Samuel S. Leibowitz, the noted defender of the "Scottsboro boys,"
did not hesitate in 1939 to offer a "legal opinion" on an issue that
Gosden and Correll had raised in one of their cliffhanger episodes.
When Andy's wedding was interrupted by gunshots before the minister declared that the hero and his intended were now man and wife,
the press sought Leibowitz's view and he gave it—presumably after

listening to the show. (He said the marriage was valid.)[21] Of course, liberal whites did not always know the minds and hearts of their black friends. But the two groups seem to have had one thing in common when it came to *Amos 'n' Andy:* through the 1930s and beyond, many of them still tuned in the show and enjoyed it.

By the 1940s, *Amos 'n' Andy* was living out a discreet old age—popular, but uncontroversial and indeed little noticed by many Americans. To Gosden and Correll's annoyance, they were still running into people at the end of that decade who politely asked them how they managed to broadcast every single day—years after the team had stopped doing so.[22] *Amos 'n' Andy* would have faded away quietly with the rest of radio comedy and drama in the 1950s, had the series not been adopted by the new mass medium that supplanted radio.

Ever since the 1920s, show business writers, actors, producers, and network executives had spoken of television as if its arrival were imminent. The technology of TV was already being developed during the 1930s, and several widely publicized experimental broadcasts were made toward the end of that decade. One of these, emanating from the New York World's Fair in 1939, featured Gosden and Correll.[23] Only after World War II, however, did commercial TV become a reality.

In 1948, the Columbia Broadcasting System pulled off a coup by raiding NBC's pool of comedic talent. CBS offered large sums to NBC stars, not in the form of salaries to the performers, but rather as buy-outs of their shows. The stars would have to pay only the relatively low capital-gains tax on the sale price rather than the higher rate that applied to wages and salaries. After the purchase, CBS would continue to pay the stars a salary for their services on the shows that the network itself now owned. CBS's offer won over Jack Benny, Edgar Bergen, Red Skelton, Burns and Allen, and Gosden and Correll. The deal boosted CBS's radio ratings and gave it a firm foundation for its new TV division.[24]

For many years, Gosden and Correll had been mulling over the prospect of television and what it might mean to them. At first they assumed that they would continue to play the title roles when their show moved to TV. By the 1940s, that already seemed impractical. Correll was in his fifties, much older than the fictional Andy. Besides, the era in which whites played blacks on the screen had ended long ago. Gosden and Correll began to think that they should hire black actors for the televised *Amos 'n' Andy* but dub in their own voices for the major characters. Ultimately, however, even Gosden began to consider entrusting the parts entirely to others. "If we can find actors with suitable voices we'll let them do the talking," he told an interviewer in 1948. "We'll have to hunt around for just the right talent. It won't be easy."[25]

Gosden was right; the search was long and arduous. After CBS acquired the show, a former advertising executive named James Fonda was assigned to keep Gosden and Correll happy and to seek black actors to play in the televised *Amos 'n' Andy*. The talent hunt continued on and off for at least one year, and it could easily have lasted even longer had it not been for the help of two veteran Afro-American performers, Flournoy Miller and Alvin Childress. Childress, a New York stage actor, had appeared in the successful all-black production of Philip Yordan's *Anna Lucasta* and had directed one of the road companies that took the play on tour. Miller had collaborated with Eubie Blake, Noble Sissle, and his own regular partner, Aubrey Lyles, on several famous all-black musical comedy shows in the 1920s. It was Miller who in 1930 had threatened to seek a court injunction against Gosden and Correll for allegedly stealing his comic material; more recently, though, he had helped with casting and scriptwriting for the *Amos 'n' Andy* radio show.[26]

Childress himself had been the first actor hired for the TV series. Though he feared that his light complexion would hurt his chances, he had practiced all the major roles before his tryout and won the part of Amos. But his immediate task was to travel about the country for CBS, auditioning black performers—including the bandleader Cab Calloway, who read for the part of the Kingfish. Childress used the studios of CBS affiliate stations to record tests of the best prospects, but none of his finds won a major role in the series.[27]

Miller, meanwhile, traveled with James Fonda, and the connections the old trouper had developed during a lifetime in show business paid off. For the part of Andy, Miller located Spencer Williams Jr., a prolific former director, writer, and actor in all-black movies, who had retired to Oklahoma. Miller also suggested Harry (Tim) Moore—a former horseracing jockey and boxer, and retired star of medicine shows, vaudeville, and all-black revues like Lew Leslie's *Blackbirds* shows—for the role of the Kingfish. In 1950, Gosden himself conducted auditions at a theater in Richmond during his first visit to his old home town in many years.[28] But nothing came of this; in the end, the TV show was built around Miller's two candidates, along with Childress and several black members of Gosden and Correll's radio series—Johnny Lee as Calhoun the lawyer, Ernestine Wade as the Kingfish's wife Sapphire, Amanda Randolph as Sapphire's mother, and Lillian Randolph (Amanda's sister) as Madam Queen. The new cast's skill as comic actors convinced even Gosden that they could "do the talking" in the series for themselves.

The initial *Amos 'n' Andy* television film was produced in October 1950. The new series was one of the first to be filmed rather than broadcast live. CBS had not finished building its Television City in California, so the network rented facilities from the Hal Roach movie studio. James Fonda oversaw production for CBS, and Charles Barton—an experienced director of movie comedies starring Abbott and Costello, Ma and Pa Kettle, and others—was hired to direct *Amos 'n' Andy*. Both these choices proved felicitous in maintaining good human relations on the set. Fonda, a white Mississippian, had, as an adult, seen much of the wider world. He had outgrown the racial norms of his boyhood home, and he treated his black employees with respect. Barton, who had far more day-to-day contact with the cast, had never been pushed to grapple with the issue of race as Fonda had. Barton, indeed, was naive about white racism: he found Alvin Childress's recollections of a lynching during the black actor's youth in Mississippi literally unbelievable. At the same time, however, Barton was an amiable man who treated actors considerately. He showed no signs of racial prejudice and became friendly with members of his cast.[29]

CBS did everything it could to reproduce the radio series as faithfully as possible for TV. This was no mere gesture to Gosden's pride. CBS had bought the show because it was a winner on radio (where Gosden and Correll continued to play the leads even after the debut of the television series); the network had no inclination to tamper with a successful formula. Gosden and Correll's longtime head writer, Bob Ross, turned out the TV scripts with two other veterans of the radio series, Joe Connelly and Bob Mosher. The strength of these white writers did not lie in any intimate knowledge of Afro-Americans. A subsequent partner and close friend of Ross later recalled Ross's admitted lack of personal acquaintance with blacks.[30] And Connelly and Mosher would make their mark by writing TV situation comedies, including *Leave It to Beaver*, which were about as remote as one could get from the Afro-American experience. But these men were highly skilled professionals who had mastered Gosden and Correll's formulas and could turn out polished variations on a few central themes week in and week out. Their fidelity to the post-1943 weekly *Amos 'n' Andy* sitcom extended to the use, with minor alterations, of some plots that had already been employed on the radio.

CBS, having chosen the cast for its ability to replicate the radio show, wanted its new black principal actors not to interpret their roles so much as to deliver performances as close as possible to those of Gosden and Correll. Alvin Childress, for example, was expected to render Amos's lines not in his natural resonant baritone, but rather in the higher-pitched, gravelly voice that Gosden used in the role. At first, Childress was even "blacked up" somewhat so that he would look more distinctly "Negro," a situation he protested—successfully, by his own account.[31] Gosden, ever the brooding *auteur*, appeared on the set with Correll in the early days of filming and did not hesitate to offer advice to the actors.

Different versions of these encounters, told over the years by alumni of the show, have entered the folklore of black Hollywood. But all witnesses agree that Gosden's interventions led to friction on the set. By most accounts, Spencer Williams (Andy) bristled at receiving direction from the white star. Williams later said he told Gosden, "I *ought* to know how Negroes talk. After all, I've been one all my life." A white writer on the show recalled Tim Moore (Kingfish) not attacking Gosden directly but fuming on the sidelines after an impromptu, unsolicited coaching session. One remark attributed to Moore, and uttered in almost identical terms by Childress many years later, captures the feeling: some veteran black performers were not happy with the idea of "a white man teaching a Negro how to act like a white man acting like a Negro."[32]

William Walker, a black actor who played incidental parts on the TV *Amos 'n' Andy*, recalled the climactic dispute as having arisen between Gosden and Charles Barton—and indeed, the director would likely have resented intervention between him and his actors by Gosden or anyone else. Walker's story depicts Barton verbally attacking Gosden in the studio, walking out, and threatening to resign unless the radio star were barred from the set. Whatever the specific truth, it is clear that Gosden had differences with Barton, and that he ceased to attend filmings—whether perforce or by choice—at a fairly early stage.[33] But Gosden's basic conception of the show's major roles continued to prevail even in his absence.

The title of the *Amos 'n' Andy* television series, like that of its radio predecessor in the later years, gave an inaccurate picture of the show's content. The central character remained the Kingfish, and many episodes revolved around his attempts to con Andy out of money. Tim Moore brought the Kingfish to the TV screen with extraordinary vividness. Moore himself, then in his early sixties, was a man of lively humor and expansive manner who seemed to his Afro-American colleagues to have been born for the role he now assumed. The bald-headed actor had the same talent for swagger and inspired gibberish that his new, fictional alter ego did, and he wore his trademark broad-brimmed hat off the set as well as on. As the Kingfish, Moore proved himself a master of the con man's toothy but hollow smile. At the same time, though, his rubbery face, which seemed to lengthen visibly in moments of distress, could make him look forlorn and storm-tossed when his schemes got him into trouble—as they usually did. Moore filled his role so perfectly that friends took to calling him "Kingfish" even outside the studio.

The stocky, dark-skinned Spencer Williams played Andy, the second most prominent character in the series, as an amiable dunce. For the Kingfish's schemes, the staple of the TV series, to work, the writers had to make the character of Andy spectacularly ignorant and gullible. Various episodes showed the Kingfish easily convincing Andy that he, Kingfish, was a qualified surgeon, ophthalmologist, flying instructor, and tutor of French. In selling his myriad schemes, the Kingfish had long since displaced Andy as the radio show's Mr. Malaprop, and so he remained in the TV version; yet even the most garbled pitch could ensnare Andy. For any viewers who generalized about Afro-Americans based on the television series, Andy conveyed an impression of black intelligence comparable to the image that the Kingfish presented of the race's honesty and industry. (Neither character held a regular job.) Andy's other salient qualities included warm-heartedness toward true friends like Amos and a rakish love of pretty young women.

Johnny Lee as Calhoun the lawyer was a past master of the stem-winding speech delivered in inflated pseudo-legalese. Although he did not usually initiate swindles, he was not above aiding the Kingfish in his—as in one episode where Calhoun helps the Kingfish convince Andy that there is oil beneath a worthless piece of property the Kingfish wants to unload. Calhoun's credentials as an attorney were suspect, his rhetoric often extravagant and always non-Standard, his vehemence in defending a friend or client no match for his readiness to retreat in the face of danger, and his given name (Algonquin J.) eccentric in a style more typical of Octavus Roy Cohen than of Gosden and Correll. Few characters in *Amos 'n' Andy* surpassed Calhoun in conforming to racial stereotypes, and Johnny Lee—a highly skilled comic actor who had performed with Flournoy Miller after Aubrey Lyles's death—played him to perfection.

The show's most important female character, the Kingfish's wife Sapphire, embodied the same paradox that she and figures like her had presented in the radio series. Sapphire was strong-willed and decisive. Her stage dialect was never as exaggerated as that of Andy and the Kingfish, and she often spoke cultivated English with characters other than the Kingfish himself. Ernestine Wade portrayed Sapphire as a bright woman, much of whose scolding of her husband was understandable in view of his laziness and dishonesty. Yet her assertiveness often took on the shrill tone of the shrew, and the couple's relationship conformed closely to the stereotype of the female-dominated black family—*sans* children in this case. "Sapphire," in fact, had already become a generic folk term among Afro-Americans for a domineering wife.

Where Sapphire typically assailed the Kingfish with withering small-arms fire, her "Mama" rolled out the heavy artillery. Much of Mama's nagging—though she, too, was often sorely provoked by her son-in-law—seemed gratuitous. Like certain other women characters throughout the history of *Amos 'n' Andy*, she epitomized both the race-transcending battle-ax and the hard-edged version of the familiar black "mammy." Amanda Randolph's considerable heft, baleful stare, and enormous hats rendered that image even more vivid on television than it had been on radio. Lightning, the janitor at the Mystic Knights of the Sea lodge hall, appeared in some episodes. Horace (Nick O'Demus) Stewart played him in the slow-drawling, slow-moving, slow-witted mold so firmly established in the popular mind by Stepin Fetchit, Willie Best, Freeman Gosden in the radio version of Lightning, and many other specialists in "coon" roles.

Moore, Williams, Lee, Randolph, and the other comic actors in *Amos 'n' Andy* made the television series into something beyond what the weekly radio show of the 1940s had been, even though the content of the scripts had not changed. They drew on a rich common fund of experience in the folk culture of Afro-America and the traditions of black popular entertainment; they played superbly off each other, and they made the most of the visual dimension that TV provided. Each could use a glance, a gait, a grunt, a pause, a cock of the head, or any number of other ephemeral, hard-to-define elements to say things that the lines by themselves could not convey. As the literary scholar Henry Louis Gates Jr. has written, the *Amos 'n' Andy*

TV ensemble at its best "transformed racist stereotypes into authentic black humor."[34]

As he always had in the radio series, Amos Jones personified honesty, good intentions, and loyalty to his friends, mixed with a healthy skepticism about the Kingfish's schemes; he still drove the Fresh Air cab to support his wife Ruby, his daughter Arbadella, and two younger children. Alvin Childress took the character farther than ever down the path Gosden had chosen for Amos during the radio show's later years: he played the television role calmly, with dignity and intelligence, in a dialect that was identifiably Afro-American but not heavily caricatured. Childress's Amos was therefore exceptional among black characters in popular comedy up to that time; he exemplified all the classic American virtues without having his racial identity laundered out in the process. Meanwhile, following the time-honored custom of depicting some black women characters as smoother and more sophisticated than their men, Ruby and Arbadella spoke Standard English no different from that of middle-class whites. But *Amos 'n' Andy* was a comedy, and the Jones family were not comic characters. As a result, Amos appeared only sporadically on the show, and his wife and daughter rarely.

Through its incidental black characters, *Amos 'n' Andy* furnished other contrasts to the various stereotypes represented by Andy, the Kingfish, Calhoun, Lightning, Sapphire, and Mama. Some of the young women Andy dated, for example, were attractive and articulate, though a few were also silly or coquettish in a manner that was not race-specific. These women also tended to be relatively light-skinned, and thus conformed to the traditional correlation between beauty and whiteness. Moreover, as in the *Amos 'n' Andy* comic strip two decades earlier, the gravitation of such graceful and sophisticated characters to a caricatured male ignoramus, even as it partly humanized Andy, also created a jarring effect. The juxtaposition threw Andy's weaknesses into even sharper relief and made the women seem naive or eccentric in their choice of male companionship.

Other peripheral figures in TV's *Amos 'n' Andy* made a less ambiguous impression. A given episode might include interaction between one or more of the central characters and a black doctor, minister, teacher, detective, real estate broker, nurse, or other professional person. Roy Glenn, William Walker, Ernest Anderson, Vince Townsend and other Afro-American actors followed the precedents they themselves had set on the *Amos 'n' Andy* radio series during the 1940s: they played such roles with dignity, in language that was not merely Standard but resonant and often elegant, though not stilted in delivery. Here *Amos 'n' Andy* offered something that no other series in television's first two decades did: brief but frequent glimpses of blacks functioning as educated practitioners of prestigious occupations. Actors in *Amos 'n' Andy* took pride in these roles; they considered the series, in Bill Walker's words, to be the only program "that shows Negroes in every walk of life—legitimately, not as . . . character[s] to be laughed at."[35] Although *Amos 'n' Andy* concentrated on Andy and the Kingfish, the show gave white viewers at least some opportunity to grasp that these figures did not typify the entire black race—that the competent black professionals shown on *Amos 'n' Andy* might have counterparts in real life.

Several of the actors who frequently played these dignified roles were dark-skinned, and this tempered the impression one might draw by comparing the Amos Jones family with the darker Andy and Kingfish—that poise, intelligence, and responsibility came in proportion to Caucasian features. Here television drove home a point that radio could not. The Standard English of incidental characters on the radio series might sometimes leave listeners unaware that those characters were meant to be black at all, but the TV picture made that realization—a surprising one for some prejudiced white viewers—unavoidable. Of course, the television series would have offered these mind-broadening suggestions more forcefully if it had included more such roles, and if—as in real life—the speech of more characters had been both identifiably black *and* articulate.

Amos 'n' Andy also included white incidental characters now and then. Interaction between them and the black central figures of the series—like almost every other aspect of the show—followed rules established years earlier by Gosden and Correll. The team's comforting but unrealistic reluctance since *Sam 'n' Henry* to have their characters mention race or experience its consequences had become complete during the later years of the radio show. In the television series, too, white characters talked to blacks as they would to other whites. Occasionally, a white character might express annoyance with a black one, or even threaten him, but nothing suggested that race played a role in the transaction. In one episode, a group of whites rent the basement of the Mystic Knights of the Sea lodge hall. Although the Kingfish's lines do include one "Yes Sah," the segment still portrays black men becoming landlords to white men—a situation not especially common in Harlem, and more foreign still to many southern viewers. Even when the whites (a shady lot, as the opening scene reveals) talk about Andy and the Kingfish in the black pair's absence, they refer to them only as "those two birds"—nomenclature even more prim than the nonracial references to "rubes," "yokels," and "dumb bells" in *Sam 'n' Henry* and the early *Amos 'n' Andy*.[36]

This episode and a few others, moreover, included white characters who were ignorant, devious, or downright criminal. The men who rent space in the lodge hall turn out to be counterfeiters; one gang member speaks a lower-class white dialect. The Kingfish becomes obsequious to the counterfeiters only when the ringleader menaces him after mistakenly concluding that Kingfish and company have stolen his fake money. Yet even as the segment portrays these whites as crooks, it also draws on the stereotype of the cowardly, quaking black man: on finding out what the counterfeiters are up to, Andy and the Kingfish "run around the room in panic" and mistakenly flee into the closet rather than out the door. When they run back out of the closet to the exit, they collide there in their haste and get stuck.[37] Such a scene could be played by white characters, but the Kingfish and Andy were black men exhibiting what some whites considered negative "black" traits. Moreover, here as elsewhere, the broad and sometimes slapstick visual style of the televised *Amos 'n' Andy* accentuated the show's other caricatured features.

Two other components of the *Amos 'n' Andy* television series contributed notably to the show's atmosphere. One of these—vaudeville-style repartee, some of it incompatible with the situation or the personalities of the characters who delivered it—had been present since the birth of *Sam 'n' Henry*. Professional writers composing weekly, self-contained comedies found themselves particularly tempted. When Sapphire leaves home in one episode, the woebegone Kingfish confesses to Andy how much he misses "her gentle smile, de sound of her voice, de way de mornin' sun glances off dat bald spot on de back of her head." Describing Mama, Kingfish says, "Andy, you take de venom of a cobra, de disposition of a alligator and de nastiness of a rhinoceros." "Yeah?" prompts Andy. The Kingfish replies, "Put 'em all together dey spell Mother!"[38]

A second salient feature of the new *Amos 'n' Andy* addressed an issue that had never confronted the radio series. Television would present visual images of scenes and characters rather than simply evoking imaginary ones in the mind of each listener. CBS now had to decide what kinds of pictures *Amos 'n' Andy* would offer.

Gosden and Correll had always considered the good will of blacks and of white liberals worth cultivating to the extent this could be done without altering important features of their show. If anything, that concern was even stronger among CBS television executives, who inherited the desire of the national radio networks to avoid alienating segments of their potential audience. Then too, black demands for social change had become increasingly persistent and vocal in the 1940s; network decision-makers were more aware than before of the need to take into account what they supposed black sensibilities to be. CBS therefore made a conscious decision that sets and wardrobe on the new TV series would reflect middle-class tastes as indulged on middle-class budgets.[39]

Amos's taxi became a shiny late-model sedan, boasting a roof, a windshield, and the Fresh Air Company's name professionally lettered on the door. The cabbie's tattered, ill-matched clothing—a standard feature of Gosden and Correll's publicity photos over the years—gave way to a snappy driver's uniform. The Kingfish's apartment, though by no means opulent, contained attractive furnishings neatly arranged within adequate space. Andy's perennial derby remained, but without the prominent dent of the early 1930s. In the TV series, the characters wore clean, well-fitted clothes, though the Kingfish with his three-piece suits and Mama with her massive, sculpted hats dressed a bit eccentrically. The show's producers understood, at least vaguely, how revolutionary the addition of the video image could be, and they tried to ensure that it would arouse only comfortable, friendly feelings among *Amos 'n' Andy*'s viewers, white or black.

When these men considered Afro-American sensibilities, they thought of little beyond the issue of sets and wardrobe; after all, *Amos 'n' Andy* had played successfully on the radio for over twenty years. CBS executives may have been aware of some black dissatisfaction along the way. In 1939, a black journalist in New York had written that it would be "suicide" to move the series from radio to television. At one point during the postwar years, Langston Hughes had his famous black comic character Jesse B. Semple praise an old black intellectual who "has always played the race game straight and has never writ no Amos and Andy books nor no songs like 'That's Why Darkies Are Born' nor painted no kinky-headed pictures." Beginning in 1948, occasional publicity about preparations for *Amos 'n' Andy*'s move to television had led to what one black columnist called a "steady flow" of grumbling among Afro-Americans.[40] But complaints had remained muted and unorganized; few remembered the black debate of 1930–1931 or the protest of the Pittsburgh *Courier* in the latter year. The possibility that any major black organization would attack the new TV series was not considered either in programming meetings at CBS's corporate headquarters in New York or in discussions among network executives in Hollywood, who assumed they would sail smoothly to a hit series.[41]

They were only half right. *Amos 'n' Andy* did win high ratings, placing among the season's top fifteen TV series. In an era of mostly half-hour shows, when more prime-time series were broadcast than today, that ranking indicated an even greater success than it would now. But the sailing was anything but smooth; the show's troubles began immediately.

Nothing more clearly demonstrates CBS's misplaced confidence than the timing of *Amos 'n' Andy*'s TV debut. The network screened previews for television columnists just a few days before the annual national convention of the NAACP, and it scheduled the on-air premiere for the very week that organization would be meeting in Atlanta. The screenings generated newspaper reviews of the series, which meant that any NAACP delegate who strongly objected to the idea of a televised *Amos 'n' Andy* might well arrive in Atlanta with the show on his or her mind. In fact, the NAACP's New York City branch and the conference of its chapters in New York State sent a letter of protest to the chairman of Schenley Distillers—owners of Blatz Beer, which sponsored *Amos 'n' Andy*—shortly after the preview screenings and just before the first broadcast. Though written in polite terms, the letter hinted that blacks might boycott Schenley's products unless the series were canceled.[42] The premiere broadcast of the show, in turn, allowed NAACP delegates from all over the Untied States to watch together, reinforcing each other's negative responses and influencing the views of members who otherwise might not have reacted or even tuned in.

Inaugurating the TV series a few weeks later might not have prevented the executive officers, individual branches, or the national board of the NAACP from protesting, as the formal complaint from the New York chapters showed. But it would have denied the Association the weapon of a resolution, passed unanimously by a national congress, condemning *Amos 'n' Andy* and calling for pressure by branches against CBS's affiliate stations and local Blatz Beer distributors. By the time of the NAACP's next annual convention, *Amos 'n' Andy* would have had a full year to establish itself on television, and it would have been old news.

The unanimous vote to censure *Amos 'n' Andy*, however, concealed problems that would undermine the NAACP's protest just as they had the campaign of the Pittsburgh *Courier* exactly two decades earlier: lack of agreement among Afro-Americans that *Amos 'n' Andy* was offensive, and discord even among the show's critics over how to proceed. Letters exchanged shortly after the convention between Pearl Mitchell, an NAACP activist in Cleveland, and Gloster B. Current, director of branch affairs for the national organization, show how concerned the protesters were about overcoming black indifference to, and even approval of, the new TV series.

Mitchell recalled that some convention delegates had opposed the resolution against *Amos 'n' Andy* behind closed doors. Feelings had run high at times between the two sides, though the dissenters in the end had not embarrassed Walter White, national executive secretary of the NAACP, by standing in the way of a unanimous vote against the television series. Mitchell had met open resistance to the protest on returning to her home city. In fact, disagreements among blacks over the issue were being aired in the "white" daily, the Cleveland *Plain Dealer*. Such debate was already widespread enough that Mitchell could refer to "the usual" argument that blacks presented against the protest. That argument apparently was the same one heard during the *Courier*'s protest in 1931: that the series did not libel blacks as a race, that it was wholesome and amusing, and that black opposition would only—and perhaps deservedly—make the protesters look ridiculous. Gloster Current agreed with Pearl Mitchell that "we are going to have to work hard to educate our own people. . . . The insidiousness of the Amos and Andy show is apparent when we realize that so many intelligent people see no harm in it."[43]

Meanwhile, Walter White found further signs that not everyone reacted to the TV series with the anger and concern that he felt. White hoped that a ringing protest from his friend Ralph J. Bunche, the Afro-American United Nations official who had won the Nobel Peace Prize the year before, would carry particular weight, so he asked Bunche to comment. Yet Bunche sent White only a laconic—indeed apathetic—three-sentence statement about *Amos 'n' Andy*. "I have never watched the 'Amos 'n' Andy' show on television," Bunche wrote. "In fact, I seldom turn on anything, radio or TV, except for sports events. I never cared for Amos 'n' Andy on the radio when I heard it years ago." This response was particularly disappointing since it came in answer to an urgent appeal in which White warned that *Amos 'n' Andy* was winning many black fans. With obvious distress, White told Bunche that he was writing shortly after "Viola, our maid, came in ecstatic over the show saying it's very funny because it's just like some colored folks she knows in Harlem."[44]

White also faced confusion within the NAACP itself. Jessie M. Vann, successor to her late husband Robert as head of the Pittsburgh *Courier*, was not the only one who recalled that "not even the NAACP . . . gave us any support" during the protest of 1931. Yet now the annual convention had "urged and directed" NAACP branches and members to take drastic action—to mount a consumer boycott—against sponsors of *Amos 'n' Andy* and other "stereotyped programs" if this should become "necessary." Hobart LaGrone, president of the Albuquerque branch, sought an explanation from Roy Wilkins, national administrator of NAACP.[45] LaGrone could not have chosen a more appropriate person to ask; although no one seemed to remember it, Wilkins had, after all, written the most elegant black defense of *Amos 'n' Andy* in 1930.

Wilkins acknowledged that "many persons" were asking the same questions LaGrone was.[46] "They never liked 'Amos 'n' Andy' and never tuned it in as a radio show," Wilkins wrote, but "they do not recall the Association having become excited about it and they are inclined to wonder why we now are so vigorous in opposition to the television show." Wilkins gave several reasons for the change in attitude. The radio series, "while objectionable, did have some very human elements in it," Wilkins wrote, chief among which was Amos, who "always was a relieving character, decent, law abiding, family man, human, and understanding." But in later years, with the addition of other actors to the nucleus of Gosden and Correll, Wilkins said, "a pure burlesque was dragged in." Wilkins seemed to grasp how the Hollywoodizing of the radio *Amos 'n' Andy* and the shift from a serial to a weekly format had detracted from the show's appeal to general human interest. Remarkably, however, he seemed to be saying that Gosden and Correll themselves had caricatured Afro-Americans less blatantly than the black actors they hired in the 1940s. And why, one might ask, had the NAACP not protested the "pure burlesque" of the weekly radio show long before *Amos 'n' Andy* came to television?

Two other reasons Wilkins gave for the NAACP's new stand got closer to the heart of the matter. For one thing, he told LaGrone, "The visual impact is infinitely worse than the radio version. . . . The television brings these people to life—they are no longer merely voices and they say to millions of white Americans who know nothing about Negroes, and to millions of white children who are learning about life, that this is the way Negroes are." Furthermore, Wilkins believed, "both Negroes and whites have 'grown up' considerably" since *Amos 'n' Andy*'s early days on radio. "What was endured then and even chuckled over is now seen in its true colors," he asserted, "and resentment is evident on all sides."

Wilkins selectively forgot that he and other Afro-Americans had done far more than simply "endure" and occasionally "chuckle over" *Amos 'n' Andy* two decades before. But he understood that blacks as a group—in part because of the work of the NAACP itself—had become impatient for change and quicker to see insults in white behavior and gestures that had once been "endured" in silence. America as a whole, and black America in particular, had changed, while *Amos 'n' Andy*—a pathbreaker in 1928—still portrayed Andy and Kingfish much as it had twenty-three years earlier. Turning the show into one of the first situation comedies on television had jarringly, and literally, placed that disparity before the eyes of White, Wilkins, and others who had stopped noticing the radio show years before.

At the same time, Wilkins could "not pretend that the sentiment among Negroes is unanimous" on the subject of *Amos 'n' Andy*, and he had already concluded that the NAACP could not "legally, officially, and openly, as an organization, advocate a boycott" of Blatz Beer. The Association would have to make do with "word of mouth suggestions" that blacks shun Blatz, while it continued to protest publicly and seek allies.

The NAACP's leaders did win some vocal black support. After "the slow and steady poison of 20 years of Amos and Andy on the radio," wrote the theatrical editor of the California *Eagle*, the show "just doesn't belong on TV or anywhere else." But the NAACP's sallies against *Amos 'n' Andy* ran up against very different views expressed by other black newspaper writers. In one of the many ironies surrounding *Amos 'n' Andy* over the years, the pages of the Pittsburgh *Courier*—the radio show's most vehement opponent in 1931—now carried some of the warmest black praise for the television series. Show business columnist Billy Rowe recognized the "unhappy circumstance" that critics had to evaluate *Amos 'n' Andy*—the sole all-black series on TV—not only as entertainment, but also as a depiction of the race. But Rowe maintained that Gosden and Correll's radio show had always centered on a "true representation of personality types, not necessarily racial types. The fact that Amos and Andy and all their friends are Negroes is incidental." Television viewers, too,

Rowe predicted, would tune in *Amos 'n' Andy* simply "because it is a cute and amusing show."[47]

Yet even Rowe acknowledged that "seeing [the *Amos 'n' Andy* characters] in the flesh as Negroes might affect some people," and that "to many children across the nation this show will be their idea of how Negroes behave." Indeed, Rowe's attitude was as much one of "great hope" as of actual confidence in *Amos 'n' Andy*. He admitted that the show could "fall into an unfortunate mold," and he appealed to its sponsors to "use their medium to demonstrate the wide panorama of every-day activities in which Negroes are found." To achieve this, he said, the series would have to "grow." But Rowe was so happy to see a group of veteran Afro-American performers proving that they "could hold their own anywhere" that he offered no real criticisms of what he had seen so far. Sharing a point of view typical of black entertainment writers over the years, Rowe would consistently oppose protests against *Amos 'n' Andy* as both futile and harmful to the interests of black performers and black audiences.

Almena Lomax (formerly Davis) of the black Los Angeles *Tribune* had published friendly words about Gosden and Correll's radio work in 1942 even as she expressed her wish to break the neck of the black servant who supposedly inspired it. Now, in 1951, the protesters found themselves diverting some of their firepower from *Amos 'n' Andy* into an attempt to refute Lomax's public complaint that "Walter White has got the NAACP way out on the limb in this matter." An article in an advertising industry journal quoted Nell Russell of the black Minneapolis *Spokesman* as saying that *Amos 'n' Andy* simply showed what much of black life really was, with an added dash of comedy. Even some of the show's black critics expressed only mild or partial disapproval which contrasted sharply with the fighting words of the NAACP resolution. Al Monroe of the Chicago *Defender* "didn't care for the show," finding that the video element made the action seem race-specific and therefore not good for the image of Afro-Americans. He preferred the radio version and—inexplicably—Gosden and Correll's old blackface movie, *Check and Double Check*.[48]

The Los Angeles *Tribune*'s reservations about the NAACP protest were not surprising. Many blacks in that city held jobs connected with Hollywood's entertainment industry, and they tended to see the *Amos 'n' Andy* question as a bread-and-butter issue. First on radio and now on TV, the series had provided work for black actors in media that otherwise used Afro-Americans only sparingly. With encouragement and a spirited introduction from Ronald Reagan, the racially liberal

president of the Screen Actors Guild, actor Bill Walker defended the
TV *Amos 'n' Andy* to the union's executive board as an employer of
blacks, many of them in nonstereotyped roles. In New York, a new
group called the Coordinating Council for Negro Performers organized to oppose the NAACP's campaign against *Amos 'n' Andy*.[49]

The actors in the series itself saw the NAACP leadership as a
naive bunch of do-gooders three thousand miles away who cavalierly
put the performers' livelihood in jeopardy for the sake of a questionable principle. "The NAACP might have been sincere in their protests," Spencer Williams (Andy) said later, but he complained that
the organization had lacked "a qualified person who was familiar with
show business." This, Williams believed, called the Association's
"right to squawk" into question. Maggie Hathaway, who later
founded the Hollywood–Beverly Hills branch of the NAACP itself,
said years afterward that "the National [Association] was never too
interested in Hollywood because they didn't understand Hollywood."
Hathaway and others, "being actors ourselves, didn't see very much
wrong with *Amos 'n' Andy*. We weren't too concerned with stereotyping. We felt if an actor didn't want to be stereotyped, he shouldn't
take the role." Besides, Hathaway believed with Nell Russell of
Minneapolis that "at that time, our [black] culture was what Amos 'n'
Andy were showing."[50]

As it became clear how many Afro-Americans of all social classes—
including some of the NAACP's own activists—were indifferent or
even hostile to the protest against *Amos 'n' Andy*, the Association's
leaders reacted with frustration and impatience. At the end of July,
Mabel K. Staupers, an NAACP stalwart who had won professional
recognition for black nurses from the American medical establishment, spoke condescendingly about blacks who did not embrace the
Association's position. "We have to work with the Negro community," she wrote to Walter White, "in order that they will stop having
a false sense of values and realize the importance of cooperating with
organizations that are doing everything possible to give them full
status as American citizens." The NAACP's director of branches,
Gloster Current, still hoped that the protest would turn out to be
"educational not only for white people but for a number of our own
people who naively accepted the show because they felt it did not
apply to them."[51]

Though it seemed obvious to Current that the characterizations in
Amos 'n' Andy "applied to" all Afro-Americans, other people no less

intelligent than he reached different conclusions on that subject. The question of *which* black Americans, if any, *Amos 'n' Andy* made sport of had already become as central to the protest of 1951 as it had been in Robert Vann's campaign a generation earlier.

In a letter to NAACP branches,[52] Current and the rest of the Association's leadership indeed accused the show of slandering an "entire race of 15,000,000 Americans." "Every character in this one and only TV show with an all-Negro cast is either a clown or a crook," the Association alleged. "All Negroes," the letter added, "are shown as dodging work of any kind." But not all the offenses for which the NAACP condemned *Amos 'n' Andy* were so general; the protesters saw several groups as having been particularly maligned.

Here the NAACP echoed Robert Vann's manifesto of 1931. The Association complained about *Amos 'n' Andy*'s treatment of black women characters, who it said were "shown as cackling, screaming shrews, in big-mouth close-ups, using street slang." And the organization devoted two of the twelve items in its indictment to the injuries allegedly suffered by Afro-American professionals—specifically doctors ("shown as quacks and thieves") and lawyers (portrayed "as slippery cowards, ignorant of their profession and without ethics"). Another item—the NAACP's charge that *Amos 'n' Andy* made "millions of white Americans . . . think the entire race is the same"— surely indicated concern for the reputation of all Afro-Americans of good character, whatever their social class. But it was easy to see in the protest a special resentment of the harm that the series might do to the image of the Afro-American middle class and to black professionals in particular. That focus was not surprising, since many of the delegates to the Atlanta convention, like the NAACP's national leadership, were themselves members of those very groups.

Ironically, the efforts of *Amos 'n' Andy*'s white producers to avoid giving offense through unsavory visual images only fueled this kind of resentment. Now that Andy and the Kingfish were respectably clothed—now that they and their friends frequented a well-maintained lodge hall and the Kingfish was ensconced in a middle-class apartment—viewers tended to *see* them as middle-class. But although the former blue-collar migrants, Amos and Andy, now looked prosperous, only the rarely seen Amos talked and acted differently than he had in 1929. Tidy scenery and tidy characters on the video screen may have avoided one kind of racist insult, but they also made it more difficult for the middle-class black viewer to indulge in a comforting response—writing off the characters' foibles as products of lower-class origins. And what conclusions must whites be drawing from this buffoonery in bourgeois clothing?

Nevertheless, as Gloster Current said, many middle-class black viewers still believed that the television portrayal of Andy and the Kingfish—not to mention Lightning, the janitor—"did not apply to them." And in fact, the NAACP was mistaken if it assumed, as its literature implied, that the series would make a practice of caricaturing the black physicians and other professionals who made their way into many episodes. But there was one glaring exception to *Amos 'n' Andy*'s policy of treating the professional classes with respect: Calhoun, the shyster lawyer, appeared frequently on the show, and he quickly became a lightning rod for complaints. The executive secretary of the Columbus, Ohio, NAACP branch was far from alone when he cited as his main concern the fact that "the Negro lawyer is portrayed in a most unfavorable, professional light."[53]

Arthur B. Spingarn, a white man who held the mostly symbolic office of president of the national NAACP, did not rule out a compromise with CBS. But one of his three minimum demands was "that some decent Negroes such as an upright and inteligent [*sic*] doctor, lawyer or undertaker be among the characters each week." The idea that adding an upright and intelligent janitor or construction worker would help preserve the honor of the race apparently did not occur to Spingarn, or to many other NAACP activists. This, as in Robert Vann's protest, was the blind spot of the campaign's well-educated, professional leadership.[54]

At the same time, middle-class Afro-Americans' objections to *Amos 'n' Andy* could transcend parochial, bourgeois fastidiousness and self-interest. One of Walter White's staffers voiced some classic concerns of the upwardly mobile: she decried the show's "barely intelligible dialogue," such as the Kingfish's "constant mispronunciation of the word 'legitimate' " as "legitirit," and she was unhappy that one episode had "the Negro lawyer . . . go in and out of a series of offices without once removing his hat." But the staffer found "even more dangerous" an implication she discerned in the same episode—"that Negroes are poor financial risks and generally unable to establish good credit ratings for business purposes."[55]

On one level, this, too, was a narrow, middle-class issue; securing a loan to open a business was hardly a pressing personal concern for the great majority of people in either race. Yet discriminatory "redlining" by banks was a policy with serious practical consequences not only for Afro-American entrepreneurs, homeowners, and would-be home-buyers, but for the economic welfare of entire black communities as well. Criticism of any influence that encouraged such redlining was not merely petty or elitist.

Furthermore, objections to *Amos 'n' Andy*'s portrayal of lawyer Calhoun were not confined to leaders of the NAACP or to blacks of the professional class. The reactions of Afro-American workers to the series seldom made their way into the written record, but there had been indications during and since the Pittsburgh *Courier*'s protest of 1931 that social class did not necessarily determine one's opinion of the show. Early in World War II, the Los Angeles *Tribune* had published a collection of brief comments by local blacks about the *Amos 'n' Andy* radio series; a physician pronounced the show devoid of racial overtones, while several blue-collar workers expressed objections much like those the NAACP would advance in 1951. A porter complained that "the Negro uses as good English as any other race," but that *Amos 'n' Andy* suggested otherwise. A car washer found the show "annoying" because "it makes white people look at you as a joke."[56]

Nine years later, similar comments could be heard among working-class blacks who found less to cheer about in the new *Amos 'n' Andy* than Walter White's maid did. Actor Bill Walker often discussed the series with men he characterized as plain "John Does"—in the barber shop, at the race track, or on the street in Los Angeles. Walker defended the show then and afterward, but he met many ordinary blacks who accused *Amos 'n' Andy* of mistreating the race's bourgeoisie. Such people saw the Afro-American professional class as a symbolic vanguard in the struggle to advance the race, and they resented what they considered the short-changing of that class through outdated caricatures in *Amos 'n' Andy*. "We're past that time, man," some said. "That handkerchief-head stuff is no good for us. We want to see some [black] lawyers and doctors."[57]

When Walker would point out that *Amos 'n' Andy* did not caricature incidental black professional characters, it became clear that the discontentment of many ordinary Afro-Americans, like that of the elite, revolved in large measure around Johnny Lee's recurring role as lawyer Calhoun. "I don't like that," ran a typical comment, " 'cause we have very smart [attorneys]." In the face of such criticism, even Bill Walker had to admit that Calhoun was "a fly in the ointment." "I'd argue like hell, . . . and I'd win a few of them," Walker recalled years later. "I won more than I lost; but Johnny Lee would throw me right back on my face, 'cause they'd bring up Johnny Lee every time, and I didn't know how to fight it to save my neck." Even those who otherwise enjoyed the series echoed this one complaint, Walker remembered: " 'Now, the old Kingfish I like, and Andy I like, but that goddamn lawyer, . . . that goddamn Calhoun. They ought to take him off there. Now if you took out Calhoun, I'd go for 'em.' A lot of them said that."

Beyond the impulse to defend black professionals as symbols of the race's progress, some working-class Afro-Americans had a more practical, more personal objection to *Amos 'n' Andy*. They believed the show mocked their own strivings and undermined their struggle to equip their children to advance. One black garbage man told Bill Walker of his struggle to shepherd his fourteen-year-old son through four years at a rough high school and to keep the desire for self-improvement alive in the boy. "I've been telling him and telling him and telling him all the time—preaching to him" to aim high in life, the man related, and "I'm on this goddamn garbage truck working" every day to make it possible for him to do so. When the garbage man heard his son and some friends in the street one day imitating Calhoun and the Kingfish, it was more than the father could bear. "I snatched him in the house . . . and I started to hit him in his mouth," the man told Walker; he had barely managed to confine himself to a verbal reprimand.

No one knows just how widespread such sentiments were; it was impossible for the NAACP to document what Walker recalled as "general discontent" over Calhoun. Then too, there was evidence of support for *Amos 'n' Andy* among ordinary Afro-Americans. When the black *Journal and Guide* of Norfolk conducted "man in the street" opinion surveys after *Amos 'n' Andy* had been running on television for several weeks, seven of ten Afro-Americans in one sample and eleven of sixteen in another said they enjoyed the new TV series. Even the dissenters in these mini-polls—at least some of whom by then must have known of the NAACP's protest—expressed criticisms that sounded mild when compared with the Association's Atlanta resolution. A survey conducted by the Advertest Research company among 365 Afro-American adults in New York and New Jersey found over seventy percent making "favorable comments" about *Amos 'n' Andy* and a full three-quarters disagreeing with the proposition that the series reinforced stereotypes of blacks. Although Walter White contended that the survey was biased—Advertest had presumably been hired by *Amos 'n' Andy*'s sponsor—this could not explain away the large number of blacks who saw the show differently than White did.[58]

As in the Pittsburgh *Courier*'s campaign two decades before, middle-class and well-off individuals set the terms of the formal protest in 1951, and bourgeois Afro-Americans may have been more likely than others to disapprove of *Amos 'n' Andy*. But the latter generalization, if valid at all, again was riddled with exceptions—middle-class blacks who liked the series and blue-collar people who resented it. The failure of some black Americans—like Ralph Bunche—to take television seriously as a social influence, the tendency of many avid TV viewers to separate what they see on television from real life, and the belief of some who disliked *Amos 'n' Andy* that other social issues were far more important—these were only a few of the obstacles that the NAACP faced, and they, too, cut across lines of class and education.

A person's opinion of *Amos 'n' Andy* depended less on actual social status than on feelings of security or insecurity about his or her own position, or that of the race as a whole, in American society. Both individual personality and objective circumstances mold people's expectations for the future. In 1951, as in 1930, some middle-class blacks felt secure enough in their status to see *Amos 'n' Andy* as not affecting them. As long as only the "riff-raff" of the race were the object of the jokes, many of these people not only took no offense but indeed could join heartily in the laughter. Others may have not scorned their simpler brethren, laughing instead with some affection at the TV characters' malapropisms and misadventures—but even these viewers laughed from afar. The bridge-playing Afro-American newspaper columnist who jokingly wrote of her "regust" at missing a broadcast in 1930 belonged to the secure middle class. Similarly, in 1951, Maggie Hathaway of Hollywood and Nell Russell of Minneapolis calmly saw *Amos 'n' Andy* as representing "much of Negro life"— but probably not their own circles.

At the same time, many blue-collar Afro-Americans at the beginning of the 1950s saw little improvement in their own lot. Court victories had produced only token integration in a few southern postgraduate schools; the Supreme Court's decision in *Brown v. Board of Education* was still three years away. Black Americans by and large still held "Negro jobs." The mass movement for civil rights had not yet begun; the Montgomery bus boycott would start only at the end of 1955. Most Afro-Americans in 1951 hoped for a brighter future, but the shortage of tangible progress for ordinary blacks produced, in the minds of some of them, a kind of "security"—or more accurately, a level of certainty about life: things did not change much in either direction, and therefore there was little damage that *Amos 'n' Andy* could do. The ironic result may have been that blacks who believed their status was stable—both those who felt they had "made it" and many of those who didn't expect to—together furnished *Amos 'n' Andy* with a large and appreciative black audience.

Those who felt less sure of the future tended to see the TV series differently. This category, too, included both well-off and working-class Afro-Americans. The NAACP's leadership came mostly from the educated middle class, and the organization, by its very nature, attracted those who were less resigned to the status quo than the average person. The activists of the Association knew history—or at least the history of the American race question—better than most other people, white or black. They looked at the hard-won progress of the past decade or two, which they themselves had largely brought about through dogged effort, and realized all too well how modest and tenuous those improvements were. The more thoughtful among them recalled the rolling back of the gains of Reconstruction by the conservative regime that followed it and by the ultra-racism of the 1890s and early 1900s. They remembered the period of racist reaction after World War I. These were people who, even as they expressed optimism, fully understood that no gain was guaranteed to last.

Walter White epitomized the type. He had seen racism at its most feral as a small boy during the Atlanta race riot of 1906. As white mobs swarmed through the city beating and killing Afro-Americans, one such group—egged on by a young man whom the Whites had known for years—marched on the family's house and nearly burned it down. For White—who looked Caucasian and whose father, a mail carrier, maintained a substantial and well-kept home—the ordeal was a unique formative experience. "In that instant," White later wrote, "there opened up within me a great awareness; I then knew who I was. I was a Negro," whom whites would see as inferior and worthy of "excision, expulsion, or extinction" no matter what he looked like or what he achieved.[59]

White's attitude may have included a trace of resentment, found among strivers in all oppressed groups, at being lumped together with less talented, industrious, or sophisticated members of the same group. But his views encompassed something broader, too: the idea that, if all Afro-Americans were the same in the eyes of the majority, then an attack or insult aimed at any black threatened all blacks. White—who could have exempted himself from discrimination by simply "passing" for Caucasian—spent much of his career fighting lynching, even though in adult life he and his circle were not personally and directly menaced by that practice. And he believed that *Amos 'n' Andy* did not merely insult some remote part of his people, but rather attacked the entire race. The lovable side of some of the show's characters offered no palliative for White, because an "imbecile good nature"—as he wrote several years before the protest of 1951—was part of an indivisible stereotype that included "the skin, the odor, the dialect, the shuffle . . . traditionally attributed [by whites] to Negroes."[60] If the stereotype was indivisible and white prejudice categorical, then the Afro-American struggle against that prejudice must be equally so.

Such attitudes were no more confined to the black middle class than was the feeling that *Amos 'n' Andy* did *not* pose a threat. The garbage man who talked to Bill Walker in Los Angeles led a life radically different from that of the famous, affluent Walter White. Yet his worldview, like White's, comprised both insecurity and hopeful, dogged determination. The garbage man had devoted half a lifetime to an uphill struggle to make better things possible for his son. He saw that goal threatened on all sides: by a substandard, violence-infested school, by the questionable group with whom his son associated, by his own humble status, and by white racism. In this man's mind, *Amos 'n' Andy* posed one more challenge to his hard-won achievements and to his hopes for the future. He moved passionately and decisively to resist the threat.

All in all, black resentment of *Amos 'n' Andy* by 1951 was probably more widespread than in 1931. A black columnist—himself a moderate on the issue of Gosden and Correll's radio series—could write on the eve of the TV premiere that *Amos 'n' Andy* had come to be "frowned upon" by black radio listeners, who were "tired of . . . stereotyped roles."[61] Roy Wilkins's analysis a few weeks later, the recollections of William Walker, and the defensive tone of Billy Rowe and other black friends of the new TV series all point in the same direction. So does the colloquial use among Afro-Americans, emerging long before Gosden and Correll's show moved to television, of the term "Amos 'n' Andy" as an adjective describing fellow blacks whom one held in disdain—as in "Amos 'n' Andy politicians."

The Great Migration and urban life, the Scottsboro case, industrial unionism, the March on Washington movement of 1941, the creation of the federal Fair Employment Practices Committee, the war of bullets and propaganda against Nazi race-hatred, the NAACP's success in nibbling away at segregation through the courts, President Truman's endorsement of civil rights legislation and his integration of the armed forces—these and many other developments since 1931 had raised the expectations of many blacks. More Afro-Americans of all social classes than in any other period since Reconstruction looked at the whole web of racial discrimination and prejudice and said, with Bill Walker's friend, "We're past that time." Even so, fatalism was far from dead among Afro-Americans in 1951, nor was overt militancy widespread; the race as a whole had yet to rediscover what epochal deeds it was capable of.

Afro-Americans were still not of one mind on *Amos 'n' Andy*, as they were on lynching or job discrimination. Even if the NAACP could have enlisted every black citizen in the *Amos 'n' Andy* fight, the Association would have had trouble winning its campaign of protest outright, for only one American in ten was black, and many of those other nine persons were fans of the show. A narrower bloc—no matter how solid—comprising only the black middle class and workers with middle-class aspirations would have faced even greater odds. Still, such a protest might have won some concessions from CBS, for the campaigners would have included the best-educated, best-connected, most articulate Afro-Americans, at least some of whom had valuable experience in confronting white decision-makers with black grievances.

In the real world of 1951, the NAACP—like the Pittsburgh *Courier* before it—could put together neither a true mass protest nor a united front among the Talented Tenth. Some, perhaps many, Afro-Americans in every social stratum grumbled about *Amos 'n' Andy* or certain aspects of the show, but few protested publicly—in part, perhaps, because they knew that many of their peers disagreed with them. The NAACP could state its objections articulately and expect much of its activist element to endorse them, at least for a time. But the Association could not convincingly claim to represent an Afro-American consensus, and its threat of a boycott thus rang hollow from the first.

Nevertheless, the leaders of the NAACP let their hopes outrun their doubts. They urged the Association's branches and youth organizations to continue the battle by sending delegations to local newspapers, CBS television affiliates, and distributors of Schenley products; by persuading other groups, white and black, to complain to the network and the sponsor; and by encouraging local bar owners to apply pressure on Schenley.[62] Meanwhile, the NAACP's national leaders themselves sought support from other organizations, and they hedged their bets by taking their complaints to the friendliest ear they could find at CBS.

···——◉•——···

Sig Mickelson was a white liberal who served as head of news and public affairs for CBS television. Part of his job was to communicate on the network's behalf with religious, civic, and educational groups, including the NAACP and the National Urban League. In the summer of 1951, there was a great deal of communication between the NAACP and CBS—most of it of a distressing nature for all concerned. The absence of a black mass protest left the *Amos 'n' Andy* affair to play itself out as a drama of interest-group politics and network responses. The storm that *Amos 'n' Andy* had kicked up now swirled around the unlikely figure of Mickelson, a quiet-spoken, racially enlightened Norwegian-American from the Midwest, in an unfunny real-life comedy of naiveté and miscalculation on both sides of the divide. In particular, the controversy became a test of the mostly black NAACP's alliance with liberal white individuals and groups; *Amos 'n' Andy* exposed fault lines in that coalition that have opened wider in the years since.

In 1947, while working for CBS's affiliate station in Minneapolis, Sig Mickelson had overseen the production of a documentary series called "Neither Free Nor Equal," an exposé of racial discrimination in the Twin Cities. The shows seemed especially bold at a time when the political right had already begun to attack liberals with the red-baiting methods Senator Joseph McCarthy would later perfect. The local branch of the NAACP cooperated with Mickelson on the documentaries, and the series made a name for him at the Association's national office. After moving to New York, Mickelson got to know Walter White at an all-day conference at White's home in Connecticut and at other meetings.[63]

When the *Amos 'n' Andy* protest of 1951 began, both Mickelson's job description and his acquaintance with White made him the logical person for CBS's top management to turn to. A week or so after the NAACP's Atlanta convention condemned the new TV series, Mickelson got a call from Lawrence Lowman, a vice-president of CBS. Lowman, Mickelson later recalled, told him that the network had "a problem" concerning *Amos 'n' Andy*, and he asked Mickelson to "see what could be done to ease" it. Mickelson translated Lowman's request to mean, "Now, see if you can't talk to your old friend Walter and . . . get him to back off."[64]

Walter White accepted a request from Mickelson to discuss the NAACP's complaints, and the two men met on July 10, less than two weeks after *Amos 'n' Andy*'s television premiere. Mickelson immediately exceeded his mandate from Lowman: rather than simply try to pacify White without making any concessions, he asked the NAACP head for suggestions as to how *Amos 'n' Andy* could be made "acceptable." That invitation gave White the impression that CBS might be persuaded to respond concretely to the Association's grievances; so did Mickelson's remark that CBS and Schenley were "greatly disturbed" by the NAACP's protest.[65]

White essentially told Mickelson that the series was unredeemable—it portrayed blacks as "lazy, amoral, dishonest and stupid," and it committed an especially grave offense by having lawyer Calhoun speak the same dialect as Andy and the Kingfish. Nevertheless, because of what White considered CBS's "rather consistently liberal attitude" in treating the race issue and employing Afro-Americans, he offered to invite "a small but select group" to view one or two segments of the show at CBS headquarters and "discuss frankly . . . what changes, if any . . . would make the film acceptable."[66]

White invited some twenty people to the screening—prominent blacks with connections to the NAACP, and a few white activists and friends of the Association as well. In addition to Arthur Spingarn, the NAACP's president, the whites included Norman Cousins, editor of the *Saturday Review*, and Edwin J. Lukas, civil rights director for the American Jewish Committee (AJC), an organization that often worked closely with the NAACP.[67]

Lukas had asked White to include him in the group; the two men had discussed the *Amos 'n' Andy* protest at length on July 10—the same morning White first spoke with Sig Mickelson of CBS. Lukas told White candidly that he had a special interest in the issue: Lewis S. Rosenstiel, chairman and president of the Schenley corporation —*Amos 'n' Andy*'s commercial sponsor—was a major contributor to the AJC. Lukas now wanted to help Rosenstiel out of the embarrassment that the protest had created.[68] Lukas was doing for Schenley what Mickelson had been assigned to do for CBS—as friends of Walter White, possessing strong civil rights credentials, they were expected to damp the fire ignited in Atlanta and protect the tens of thousands of dollars that CBS and Schenley had invested in *Amos 'n' Andy*. Lukas resembled Mickelson in another way as well: he felt some sympathy for the NAACP's position and hoped for a genuine compromise—which, of course, would involve real concessions by CBS.

Some at the American Jewish Committee seem to have had a deeper concern than simply to help their friend Lewis Rosenstiel out of a jam. Like many of the NAACP's own members, they found it puzzling that the Association mercilessly attacked the televised version of *Amos 'n' Andy* after leaving the radio series in peace for more than twenty years; indeed, the NAACP was still not condemning the radio show, which continued to be broadcast each week. For such people, this inconsistency raised the question of why the NAACP lifted up its voice and threatened a boycott only when *Amos 'n' Andy* appeared under "Jewish sponsorship."[69]

In his meeting with White on July 10, Lukas offered a suggestion that he hoped would satisfy the NAACP: that three academics, including the black psychologist Kenneth Clark, study the *Amos 'n' Andy* films and recommend changes that would "make them acceptable." White was not interested. He told Lukas "that instead of social scientists, what was needed were script writers with imagination and information . . . [and] with authority to make changes," and that even then "it was difficult to see how [the show] could be made acceptable." White added that "infuriated" blacks could make a real dent in the Schenley company's sales even if the NAACP could not mount a formal boycott.

White further alleged that Rosenstiel had been told by a black "public relations counselor" in Philadelphia that Afro-Americans would find an *Amos 'n' Andy* TV series unacceptable. Schenley Distillers had responded not by aborting the show, White went on, but rather by trying to appease the Afro-American public with ads in black papers and donations to black organizations. Lukas should explain to Rosenstiel, White said, that the good will of black Americans was "not a purchasable product like advertising space or alcohol."[70]

In reality, Rosenstiel had been a benefactor of the National Urban League even before he found himself in need of Afro-American help in the *Amos 'n' Andy* fight; the League's black executive director, Lester Granger, considered him "a mighty good friend."[71] But Schenley did run specially designed, full-page advertisements in black newspapers to herald the new TV show. In Chicago, one of these ads was blatantly aimed at softening up Afro-American public opinion: it featured a picture of "the only Negro distributor of a nationally-known beer in the country," a Chicagoan who lauded the

Blatz Brewery's "cooperation in building our territory" over the years. The ad claimed that the black distributor found *Amos 'n' Andy* to be "simple, American humor" like Mutt and Jeff or Blondie and Dagwood—"good, clean, wholesome entertainment" that should "be accepted in the spirit in which it is presented."[72]

Schenley's management, in short, was using the same methods that Gosden and Correll had employed in the 1920s and 1930s to preempt or moderate any resentment among Afro-Americans. Having built a record of philanthropy toward black organizations, Schenley now declared its high regard for Afro-Americans, cloaked its TV show in the mystique of the black entrepreneur, and wrapped the series in the banner of good, clean fun. In fact, the sponsor hoped not merely to prevent complaints from black Americans, but even to recruit many of them into the audience for a show "enacted entirely by Negro entertainers." Some major black newspapers fed those hopes by running, in addition to the revenue-producing advertisements for the new show, a series of laudatory feature stories on *Amos 'n' Andy*'s cast members, presumably based on CBS press releases aimed specifically at black readers.[73]

But if Schenley's time-honored public relations gestures still worked in some quarters, they only inflamed Walter White, who accused the sponsor of attempting to bribe black Americans. Edwin Lukas responded by pulling out another big gun that had worked for *Amos 'n' Andy* before. Two decades earlier, Gosden and Correll had pointed with pride to the endorsements they won from Urban Leaguers and other Afro-Americans; Lukas now asserted that the Urban League had "read and approved" *Amos 'n' Andy* TV scripts, and that the Pittsburgh *Courier* "and one other Negro newspaper" had endorsed the show. White masked his surprise with expressions of skepticism. He returned to his office and fired off letters to the heads of the Urban League and the *Courier* asking for denials that they approved of *Amos 'n' Andy*.[74] Both quickly complied—but their answers to White reflected some of the disarray among leading Afro-Americans in the face of the new TV series.

Jessie M. Vann of the *Courier* responded with a dig at the NAACP for failing to back her late husband Robert in his fight against *Amos 'n' Andy* in 1931, and she reaffirmed her long-standing dislike of the series. "How anyone who has been a constant reader of our paper could say that The Courier approved of the television version of the 'Amos 'n' Andy' show is beyond me," Vann intoned, "and I certainly would be interested in learning the source of their information." Her reply to White, if sincere, suggested that Vann did not read the entertainment pages of her own newspaper, for these had praised *Amos 'n' Andy* lavishly. Although Vann told White that "the position of The Courier would be the same as twenty years ago," her editorial page in fact had not taken issue with its show business editor. When the *Courier*'s columnists finally did comment more than two weeks later, one writer's attack on *Amos 'n' Andy* was offset by a front-page column in which the paper's famous associate editor, George S. Schuyler—an opponent of the radio series in 1931—ridiculed the NAACP for attacking *Amos 'n' Andy* while leaving more offensive productions untouched.[75]

Lester Granger of the Urban League called the claim that the League had approved *Amos 'n' Andy* scripts "a flat falsehood." Granger assured White that he had stated both in New York's black *Amsterdam News* and directly to the Schenley corporation that "I wouldn't like 'Amos 'n' Andy' if it was good, and I've never thought the show was good." Indeed, one of Granger's colleagues confidentially sent polite but firm expressions of her disappointment to Lewis Rosenstiel and to CBS. But Granger's own letter to Walter White also contained a veiled and very different message to the NAACP. Granger backed up his denial that the League had endorsed the TV series by declaring that "we stick to our job of finding employment for Negro workers and opening up other forms of economic opportunity." The Urban League was not about to join a public crusade against one of its own corporate benefactors, especially over an issue that had no direct bearing on the economic lot of Afro-Americans.[76] The Schenley corporation now found itself with no Urban League card to play. But so did the NAACP, which would have to carry on its fight without a great deal of help from other organizations.

Toward the end of July, Sig Mickelson gave Walter White and associates their private screening of *Amos 'n' Andy* at CBS headquarters. About half of the twenty-odd people White had invited actually attended.[77] CBS management wanted Mickelson to calm the NAACP, but the screening had just the opposite effect. White's own mood had hardly improved during his visit to the scene of an antiblack riot in Cicero, Illinois, a few days earlier. As for the members of White's delegation, some—busy, highbrow people that they were—had probably not seen *Amos 'n' Andy* before, and might never have done so if White had not invited them to the special showing. Now, as the film ran, members of the NAACP group—seated in front of a glass imitation TV screen onto which the show was projected—began to comment audibly and bitterly about what they were seeing. Mickelson watched helplessly as the anger of the show's opponents deepened by the minute and sharpened the feelings of the people who had thus far been less committed to the protest.[78]

In the tense atmosphere that prevailed after the screening, Mickelson was loath to suggest to the group that the problem "really [wasn't] serious," he later recalled; "I couldn't do anything to ease their pain, nor could I promise any changes, because I had absolutely no authority whatsoever" to function as anything other than an "intermediary." In fact, after Mickelson submitted a written report on the meeting to his superiors, they took the matter out of his hands entirely. Mickelson got the distinct impression they were "upset" with him: "I think they regarded it as a tactical error to bring all these people in and incite them, to exacerbate their responses" to *Amos 'n' Andy*.[79] CBS's fireman had poured gasoline onto the fire.

Walter White left the screening room more convinced than ever that *Amos 'n' Andy* must be destroyed. Although there were other depictions of blacks on radio and television that he found objectionable,[80] *Amos 'n' Andy* was the most prominent purveyor of the images that irked the NAACP. The lead elephant might be the toughest of them all, but to fell him might stop the entire herd of stereotyped portrayals. White still took pride in some modest concessions he had wrung from the Hollywood movie studios in the 1940s; he now believed that the fate not only of *Amos 'n' Andy*, but also of "future presentations of the Negro on television," might depend on the outcome of this particular struggle.[81]

Immediately after the screening at CBS, White pressed several key figures of the NAACP to put their views on *Amos 'n' Andy* in writing. Most echoed White's position that no compromise was possible. The "established 'Amos 'n' Andy' pattern," wrote Henry Lee Moon, the NAACP's director of public relations, "can no more be cleaned up and made acceptable than, say, the word 'darky.' " Thurgood Marshall, the Association's special counsel, had already expressed a similar view, writing three weeks earlier that "we should stick to our guns that 'Amos 'N' Andy' and everything like it has to go and that there is nothing that CBS, Blatz Beer, Schenley or anyone else can do to remedy this continuing harm."[82]

The exchange of memos within the NAACP showed, however, that there were some cracks in the Association's wall of unconditional opposition to *Amos 'n' Andy*. Even before the screening, Marshall had qualified his own hard line, intimating that he might settle for "a complete and, I mean complete, change" in the TV series rather than outright cancellation. While Mabel Staupers saw no solution other than to cancel *Amos 'n' Andy*, she understood that CBS had contractual commitments to Schenley, and she sympathized with the network's "position in not wanting to withdraw the show." Roy Wilkins, although he saw no way the series could be "doctored up to be palatable," admitted he was "no expert at revision of scripts." He therefore did not rule out the possibility that "the experts in matters of rewriting" could find ways to improve the show. And Arthur Spingarn, recognizing that Schenley would not simply throw away the money it had invested in *Amos 'n' Andy*, was prepared to consider a compromise. If the series would incorporate some prominent, respectable black professional characters, Spingarn could settle for a promise that the show would be canceled after its first year, along with "an announcement . . . before each show that Amos and Andy does not represent real conditions but is merely a burlesque."[83]

Spingarn was not the only party seeking a compromise that would include announcements of this type. While Walter White was busy rounding up written comments, Edwin Lukas of the American Jewish Committee offered the network a detailed set of suggestions for improving *Amos 'n' Andy*.[84] The writers should "minimize" the role of Kingfish, said Lukas, concentrating instead on Amos and Andy, who Lukas believed could offer "consistently unobjectionable entertainment." Future scripts should also eliminate any "stereotyped corruption of the English language" and "unnecessary slap-stick violence and shouting."

Lukas proposed further that the actors playing Amos, Andy, and perhaps one additional character should gather around a table onscreen for "a moment or two" at the end of each episode. They would "converse with each other in acceptably correct English, and with perfect diction, exchanging a few good-natured comments concerning the program just ended." This, said Lukas, would make clear to the audience that *Amos 'n' Andy* was "a deliberate caricature," and that neither its cast nor real Afro-Americans in general behaved like the figures in the TV series. Lukas also suggested that the network run "clever, one-minute jingles" along with the *Amos 'n' Andy* broadcasts to promote "good intergroup relations." Lukas thought these spots would do more good if they were postponed for a month or two; that way they would not seem "too obvious . . . an effort to 'neutralize' the criticism."

Lukas sent a copy of his suggestions to Walter White, suggesting that they could make *Amos 'n' Andy* "infinitely less offensive to your group than it is at the moment." But White now regretted that he had ever allowed Lukas to join the NAACP delegation to the screening at CBS; White was certain that "CBS and Blatz Beer will gladly seize upon these 'constructive' suggestions" to deflect the NAACP's demand that *Amos 'n' Andy* simply be taken off the air. White sent each of his colleagues a copy of Lukas's proposals and asked them to write comments—or more accurately, rebuttals.[85]

That move, like so many others on both sides of the controversy, led to some undesired results. William Hastie, the country's first black federal judge, wrote that to make *Amos 'n' Andy* acceptable would require CBS "to write an entirely different show." Yet he praised Lukas's "thoughtfully conceived" suggestions and admitted they "would lessen the bad impact of the show." Mabel Staupers embraced the Lukas proposals outright, provided only that CBS accept them in their entirety. Where only eleven days earlier she had written that she "just [could] not make myself believe that there is a compromise," Staupers was now saying "that this show could be presented in a manner to bring amusement to people and yet at the same time not be a misrepresentation" of Afro-Americans. Lukas's proposals had undercut White not only in his dealings with CBS, but also in his effort to maintain a hard-line consensus within the NAACP leadership itself.[86]

White's real problem, however, was simpler, though Sig Mickelson's solicitous demeanor obscured it: CBS management had no intention of altering or eliminating *Amos 'n' Andy* no matter what White did. Both the network and Schenley Distillers had invested heavily in the series, contracts with its personnel and with Hal Roach Studios were in force, a number of episodes had been filmed even before the Atlanta protest, and the show's ratings were high. The whole idea in producing *Amos 'n' Andy* had been to take a proven winner from radio, keep it as close to the original as possible, and thus produce a hit television series that would run in prime time for seven or eight years. If there was one thing broadcasting networks were less inclined to do than to court controversy, it was to tamper with success. As for Edwin Lukas's proposals, it was ludicrous to suppose that any TV series would present cast members out of character for the express purpose of destroying the atmosphere the show attempted to create in the first place. The idea that CBS would "bump" a minute of each episode— or forgo some of its commercial time, an even greater taboo—for public service spots promoting good human relations was only a little less farfetched.[87]

Although CBS and Schenley were unhappy about the protest, nothing had happened between June and mid-August to convince them that the NAACP represented a black America that was united on the issue of *Amos 'n' Andy*, much less that large numbers of Afro-Americans who had drunk Blatz Beer before had now ceased to do so. And if anyone at CBS besides Mickelson bothered to read the comments Walter White had assembled from his colleagues, the lack of full unity even among NAACP figures must have reinforced the network's conviction that the benefits of proceeding with *Amos 'n' Andy* outweighed the risks.

Besides, influential white people both inside and outside broadcasting had other things on their mind in 1951—things that seemed, even to racial liberals, more worrisome than an all-black TV situation comedy or the uproar it might generate. The red-baiting purges of Joe McCarthy and of the House Un-American Activities Committee were becoming a national preoccupation. Blacklisting of performers with alleged connections to Communist or "Communist-front" organizations had moved from the motion picture industry into the realm of broadcasting.

A book called *Red Channels* had appeared in 1950, naming 151 writers, performers, and others who had supposedly helped to "transmit pro-Sovietism to the American public" over the airwaves. The station, network, sponsor, or advertising agency that employed persons whose loyalty had been questioned faced threats of boycott that seemed far more convincing than any the NAACP could conceivably mount over *Amos 'n' Andy*. Not to employ any of the scores of people accused of subversion, however, made it difficult to put good programs together. The main victims of the Great Reaction, of course, were not broadcasting moguls or sponsors, but rather the blacklisted writers and performers themselves. Still, the victims' erstwhile employers, too, were beleaguered and afraid. Compared with these problems, the protest against *Amos 'n' Andy* looked like a minor flap.[88]

Even some of Walter White's best white friends hedged their support for the NAACP's protest partly or entirely because of the threat they perceived in McCarthyism. However frustrated White may have been with the American Jewish Committee, the group had worked faithfully with the NAACP on many occasions and even now was asking CBS for major changes in *Amos 'n' Andy*. But the AJC feared that, if right-wing boycotting, blacklisting, character assassination, and demands for political censorship went unchecked and further undermined civil liberties, minorities—including both Jews and blacks—might be the next groups singled out for abuse.

The AJC had therefore adopted a formal policy in response to "the present climate of opinion" several months before the *Amos 'n' Andy* controversy. The statement opposed all "attempts to interfere with free expression through the arts" unless a work posed a "clear and present danger" of violence or oppression against a group. Jews, like Afro-Americans, resented negative depictions of their people, but the AJC felt it had to combat McCarthyism by opposing censorship and boycotts—even against works that "[offend] sensibilities" and "have an undesirable effect on attitudes." Such works should be fought only by appeals to "reason and right feeling," the Committee declared, not by "coercion."[89] The AJC's subsequent unwillingness to support a boycott of *Amos 'n' Andy*, in short, arose not only from its concern about Lewis Rosenstiel's money, but also from the Committee's fear of a right-wing tyranny.

Norman Cousins of the *Saturday Review* drafted a statement at Walter White's request which emphatically condemned *Amos 'n' Andy*. But Cousins's manifesto also included more than three full paragraphs that did not even mention *Amos 'n' Andy*, denouncing instead all attempts to make producers, broadcasters, and publishers like Cousins "conform to the particular desires of private blocks [*sic*], groups and agencies." Rather than justify the red-baiters by emulating them, Cousins wanted the NAACP not merely to forswear the boycott and any hint of "censorship," but to do so in the very statement it would present to CBS. Censorship of *Amos 'n' Andy*, of course, was precisely what Walter White wanted; he or one of his allies in the national office proposed to strike Cousins's entire disquisition on freedom of expression before passing the editor's statement along to Sig Mickelson. Cousins apparently refused, for the remarks stayed in with only one word altered.[90]

Racism was the most important problem in the world to Walter White, to many—probably most—other Afro-Americans, and even to some whites. But to many white liberals, racism was only one of several grave threats to Americans' freedom; one had to respond to all these perils, balancing the demands of each against all the others. Such differences of perspective between the NAACP's black leaders and their white friends were nothing new; the American Civil Liberties Union had jousted with the Association over NAACP demonstrations aimed at suppressing racist movies at least as far back as the mid-1930s. By 1951, there were more white racial liberals than in any earlier period of American history, and a few liberal, labor, and leftist groups issued statements supporting the NAACP's *Amos 'n' Andy* fight; but a bit of lobbying and information-gathering by an official of the United Auto Workers was one of the rare instances of practical help from predominantly white organizations.[91]

In the end, the struggle against *Amos 'n' Andy* in 1951 amounted to a spirited protest lodged by some prominent elements of a ten-percent minority of the American population, imperfectly supported by a small, besieged cohort of white liberals, against a background of widespread but inchoate grumbling among ordinary Afro-Americans. Such a campaign could not outweigh the money already sunk into *Amos 'n' Andy* or the profits yet to be made from the show, and the protest fizzled during the fall of 1951. By Thanksgiving, Walter White was complaining that Schenley's advertising agency would not even answer his letters.[92]

The NAACP's protest won little attention in the white press and less than the Association must have hoped for even in the major black weeklies. Many white critics gave the TV series favorable reviews, and industry analysts cited *Amos 'n' Andy* and *I Love Lucy* as exemplars of a new wave of well-produced episodic series. Even the NAACP itself—perhaps out of discouragement over its lack of success—mentioned the *Amos 'n' Andy* protest only twice, and then very briefly, in its report summarizing the year 1951. In 1952, a white columnist could write that "no minority group, however touchy, has ever found anything offensive" in *Amos 'n' Andy*.[93] It is likely that the author of that statement knew of the NAACP's activities the year before and conveniently decided not to mention them; but he could hardly have taken such liberty with the facts had the protest made much of an impression on his potential readers.

The NAACP campaign led to few if any changes in the content of *Amos 'n' Andy*. Years later, the show's producer thought he recalled some effort to tidy up the female characters' speech. But these women were not *Amos 'n' Andy*'s central figures, and besides, Ernestine Wade for years had been playing Sapphire in a dialect that often approximated Standard English. Later, when CBS hired several additional writers to work on the show, they were instructed to stick as closely as possible to the patterns that had kept *Amos 'n' Andy* popular for years.[94] The famous Christmas episode—whose highlight was an inspirational exposition of the Lord's Prayer, delivered by Alvin Childress as Amos to the cabbie's young daughter Arbadella—has been pointed to for years as an example of *Amos 'n' Andy* at its most human and universal. Yet even this segment was no departure from precedent, much less a gesture designed to appease the NAACP. Gosden had performed Amos's Christmas talk annually on the radio throughout the 1940s, and other episodes of the radio series had used incidental black characters to deliver serious, uplifting, quasi-religious monologues.[95]

CBS renewed *Amos 'n' Andy* for a second year's run in prime time. The show's sponsor chose to buy twenty-six episodes for 1952–1953; a new episode would be shown every other week, and these *Amos 'n' Andy* broadcasts would alternate with those of a different biweekly series. (The network had shown the previous year's thirty-nine segments on a weekly basis, with thirteen weeks of reruns.) The decision for alternate-week scheduling seems to have been a routine one; some other series of the period ran on a similar schedule. A sponsor concerned about black disapproval of *Amos 'n' Andy* would have shunned the program entirely; merely reducing the number of episodes would not affect the potential for controversy. At most, the NAACP's agitation may have made other potential sponsors skittish enough to prevent their considering a joint sponsorship of thirty-nine segments. But it is not clear that CBS even sought such an arrangement; networks and sponsors did not yet realize that biweekly scheduling could put a series at a disadvantage in attracting a steady audience.[96] *Amos 'n' Andy*'s second season suggested that viewers were indeed creatures of habit, preferring programs they could watch week in and week out. Although the show was nominated for an Emmy award as best comedy series, its ratings fell, and it was not renewed for a third year.

Harry Ackerman, the head of CBS television entertainment, perceived a general hesitancy among sponsors after the protest of 1951 toward *Amos 'n' Andy* or any other comedy that might feature blacks,[97] and to this extent the NAACP may have achieved something of what it wished. But the Association wanted to eliminate *Amos 'n' Andy* from America's TV screens, and in this it failed utterly, not only for the two years of the network run but for more than a decade to come. As it had always intended to do, CBS syndicated the *Amos 'n' Andy* films to local television stations across the country, each of which lined up its own sponsors.

From that point on, to ban the show would have required separate campaigns in dozens of cities. The NAACP was not remotely capable of waging such a fight. The effectiveness of its local branches varied widely; for every chapter of the Association that had joined the crusade of 1951, a number of others had remained inactive. Resentment of Walter White's alleged peremptoriness had been brewing within the NAACP long before the summer of 1951, and those feelings had hobbled the protest. Even some branch leaders who ardently joined White's fight against *Amos 'n' Andy* had felt isolated and thwarted, or had problems of their own: the officers in Columbus were having trouble collecting dues even from some of their executive board members, while the branch leader in Milwaukee chided the national office for failing to pay attention to her letters or even to know who the branch's current officers were.[98]

To make up what was then considered a full syndication package, CBS ordered thirteen more episodes of *Amos 'n' Andy* after the prime-time cancellation. By late 1954, the series was appearing on more than a hundred local stations—twice as many, ironically, as it had reached over the network. Moreover, CBS began preparations for a new series, a virtual carbon copy of *Amos 'n' Andy* featuring the same cast. The plan was to produce the films directly for syndication—although even a new network run was considered for a time. Far from toning down those elements of *Amos 'n' Andy* that had most offended the NAACP, CBS proposed at one stage to title the new version, with perfect frankness, *The Adventures of the Kingfish*. The series never came to pass—but not because of black opposition. Rather, CBS determined that the new show would cost so much to produce that it could not turn the desired profit.[99]

The NAACP fired occasional shots at *Amos 'n' Andy* even after the show's network cancellation; the Association complained in 1954 when the British Broadcasting Company announced plans to buy *Amos 'n' Andy* shows for presentation in the United Kingdom.[100] The American racial atmosphere was changing more swiftly now than in 1951. The Supreme Court declared school segregation unconstitutional in 1954, and the black boycott of city buses in Montgomery, Alabama, in 1955 and 1956 followed other, less well-publicized local protests against the Jim Crow system. The NAACP by 1955 found support in a surprising new place—the Coordinating Council for Negro Performers. The Council, an ardent defender of *Amos 'n' Andy* as an employer of blacks four years earlier, now joined the NAACP and the Urban League in condemning the "Amos and Andy image" of blacks that the popular media allegedly presented.[101] A more militant atmosphere in Afro-America was not the only reason for this new consensus. Because *Amos 'n' Andy* had ceased production, its black actors' jobs were no longer at stake, and the Urban League could speak up without any fear of offending a corporate friend.

Amos 'n' Andy's run in TV syndication went on unchecked, however. In the decade after its departure from prime time, the series appeared at one time or another in 218 markets in the United States— and in Australia, Bermuda, Kenya, and western Nigeria (where, the New York *Times* reported, most TV sets were owned by whites). A dozen years after the NAACP protest of 1951, *Amos 'n' Andy* was still running on more than fifty local stations.[102] This may have been the NAACP's worst disappointment in the entire affair, given the Association's special worry about the show's effect on white children who had no contact with real Afro-Americans. Many stations broadcast the *Amos 'n' Andy* reruns during daytime hours when, especially during school vacations, the children of the first TV generation sat glued to the small screen. The images of blacks they saw in *Amos 'n' Andy* were not simply ones the NAACP found harmful. They were images produced in 1951–1954—before the Brown decision, the Montgomery boycott, the sit-ins, and the freedom rides—pictures from a bygone era, preserved intact and disseminated year in and year out among the youth of a new age.

The NAACP protest did help to ensure that no other network TV series would put a black actor in a central role until Bill Cosby's debut on *I Spy* in 1965. It would be unfair, however, to put the primary blame for that state of affairs on the NAACP. The central goal of network broadcasting—to please as many and to alienate as few people as possible all across America—prevented any serious, sustained portrayal of Afro-American characters on the tube during the civil rights era. The white South was on the defensive, many of its people fighting to the last ditch to preserve their old way of life; nerves had been rubbed raw. To present blacks except as musicians, comedians, or players in comic series like *Amos 'n' Andy* seemed to pose more dangers of backlash than ever-cautious sponsors or networks were willing to risk. In the radio era, the comedic images of blacks that *Amos 'n' Andy* traded in had offered a safe, comfortable framework in which network series could employ black actors. But now the NAACP, and an evolving consciousness among Afro-Americans in general, had made those images controversial, too, so the networks largely avoided them. If the Association achieved anything it could call a victory in its fight against *Amos 'n' Andy*, this was it.

It would have been hard to convince many black actors—

especially those who had appeared on *Amos 'n' Andy*—that the aftermath of the protest of 1951 represented a victory at all. Like the show's producers and the management of CBS, the cast had expected a long and profitable network run for the series. The actors received only limited residual payments from the syndication of the shows—but not, apparently, because of racial discrimination. Rather, the precedent for paying substantial residuals had not been firmly established in the new business of TV syndication when they signed their contracts. At least twice after production of *Amos 'n' Andy* ceased, former cast members made personal appearance tours in their old TV roles—but by their own account, CBS stepped in to halt these.[103]

Still, there was little truth in the popular legend of later years that pictured the former stars of the series living out their lives brokenhearted and impoverished. Spencer Williams had come out of retirement to play the role of Andy; when the show was cancelled, he lived on income from Social Security and a military pension. Amanda Randolph (Mama) went on to play the maid in Danny Thomas's long-running situation comedy series. Ernestine Wade (Sapphire) played the organ in funeral parlors, worked as a legal secretary and bookkeeper, and occasionally appeared on radio and television. Jester Hairston, who had filled the minor role of Henry Van Porter, a self-styled socialite, continued his principal career as a well-known director of black choral groups; years later, he provided music for Robert Schuller, the television minister, and returned to series TV in the mid-1980s as a supporting actor in the popular all-black sitcom, *Amen!* Alvin Childress (Amos) worked as a civil servant and sometime actor in movies and TV.[104] Nick Stewart (Lightning), with his wife Edna, ran a theater in Los Angeles which they had founded earlier; plays were still being produced there in the 1980s.

Tim Moore (Kingfish), *Amos 'n' Andy*'s best-known alumnus, appeared several times on Jack Paar's *Tonight* show and served as master of ceremonies in a Los Angeles nightclub. To his friends and to the world, he had become almost inseparable from his role in *Amos 'n' Andy*. He made headlines in 1958 when, having remarried after the death of his first wife, he fired a gun during an argument with members of his new spouse's family, whom he accused of eating a beef roast he had left in his refrigerator. The local papers had a field day, with the prize for punning doubtless going to the worthy who headlined the story, "Police Hook Kingfish for Beef Over Roast." "I'm the old Kingfish," Moore reportedly told the police when they reached the scene. "You should have seen the in-laws scatter when I fired that gun." Eleven months later, Moore was dead of tuberculosis. At his funeral, the church overflowed with "thousands of his friends and fans." Freeman Gosden and Charles Correll served as honorary pallbearers, but it was Moore's black colleagues, including Alvin Childress, Johnny Lee (lawyer Calhoun), Spencer Williams, and Flournoy Miller, who carried his remains to their final destination. [105]

Gosden and Correll themselves did not suffer greatly from the controversy over *Amos 'n' Andy*. Though by turns perplexed, hurt, and angered by the protest of 1951, they continued to appear on radio until 1960. In a concession to the now-dominant format in commercial radio, the team in their last few years on the air mostly played popular records, with Amos, Andy, and the Kingfish as virtual disc jockeys. In 1962, after the failure of *Calvin and the Colonel*, a TV cartoon series in which the two supplied voices for animal characters, Gosden and Correll retired for good. Now in their early sixties and seventies respectively, they were wealthier than ever and, by most accounts, far from preoccupied by the criticism they had received over *Amos 'n' Andy*. [106] The pair's network employers hardly qualified as pitiable victims of the controversy either. CBS had some unpleasant moments in 1951 and made a good deal less money from *Amos 'n' Andy* than it had expected to, but the company still earned a healthy income by syndicating the TV show for more than ten years.

···—●●—···

By 1966, demonstrations for civil rights had begun to be punctuated with calls for black pride and black power. Protests against the continued local showing of *Amos 'n' Andy* had already taken place in Chicago, and CBS finally withdrew the films from syndication. [107] But by then, the shows had been circulating for a period that would have been remarkable even for a former network hit with two or three times as many episodes available. Having squeezed all but the last possible penny out of its investment, CBS now locked the films away and declined to talk about them further. In fact, well-placed sources at the network stated that management had imposed an ironclad prohibition on discussing the *Amos 'n' Andy* affair with outsiders.

Not surprisingly, most observers concluded that CBS was afraid of renewed controversy. Though there was some truth in this, one highly knowledgeable source reported that CBS chairman William S. Paley had squirreled away the films for fear not of agitation by the NAACP, but rather of pirating by film bootleggers. Moreover, CBS applied for a new copyright on the bulk of the films in the late 1970s, and a few years later it asserted its proprietary rights in court against a man who wanted to make a Broadway musical using the *Amos 'n' Andy* characters. People do not ordinarily exert themselves to prevent the theft of something they do not consider valuable. Some evidence suggested, in fact, that CBS was awaiting an auspicious moment to reintroduce the old shows—on videocassettes for home viewing, or perhaps even on television.[108] At least half the episodes—themselves probably bootlegged, and many of less than mint quality—were already available for sale or rental on cassettes by the early 1990s; these found a market among both blacks and whites. Meanwhile, the management of a black cable TV channel announced that a poll of its viewers had revealed widespread interest in *Amos 'n' Andy* among Afro-Americans; the company talked openly of bringing the old series back.[109]

The NAACP remained vigilant, and its opinion mattered in commercial broadcasting circles—probably more than it had to CBS in 1951. When Michael Avery, an attorney from San Diego, proposed to make a nostalgic, hour-long television special on *Amos 'n' Andy* for syndication or cable showings, he found the major national outlets to which he offered his project unwilling to risk a protest; they would buy only if the NAACP approved of the program in advance. Avery later claimed to have won the tacit acquiescence of the National Association on condition that he turn his production into a quasi-documentary, downplaying praise and giving full play to criticism of *Amos 'n' Andy*. When Avery announced his plan to the press, it turned out that the NAACP was not budging after all. Executive secretary Benjamin Hooks lamented "the devastating effects of 'Amos 'N' Andy's' scurrilous stereotypical treatment of blacks" and announced that the Association's opposition to a revival of any sort had not changed.[110]

Despite the NAACP's complaints, Avery produced his show, and it appeared on a number of local TV stations beginning in late 1983. Some speculated that CBS was watching reactions to all this with interest as it considered how it might use its *Amos 'n' Andy* films in the future. The home video market would offer a formidable buffer against criticism should the company decide to market high-quality copies of the shows. A neighborhood video store may seem a more vulnerable target for protesters than a billion-dollar national network; but the NAACP could hardly picket or boycott thousands of video outlets, especially since the physical presence of a few *Amos 'n' Andy* cassettes in such a store would not wave the kind of red flag that a weekly TV broadcast in prime time would. CBS could even sell its original films of the shows *en bloc* to some videocassette company, take its money in a lump sum, and run. In any case, that *sine qua non* of commercial television, the sponsor—typically the weak link in the face of a protest—would be eliminated from the picture.

America and the world had changed greatly since 1951. Yet the NAACP was still fighting the same old war against the same old *Amos 'n' Andy*. And it still feared it was losing, as Ben Hooks's vehement but largely unsuccessful attack on Michael Avery's show demonstrated. As the twentieth century's last decade began, Gosden and Correll's *Amos 'n' Andy*, in addition to its remarkable sixty-year history, seemed to have a future as well. And the fire of resentment in at least some quarters smoldered on.

Epilogue

...━●━...

A New Day?

A mos 'n' Andy became a national sensation partly because it played to whites' curiosity about the changing life of their black fellow citizens. But neither that curiosity nor the novel features of the show itself ever made much of a dent in the racial fantasy-world in which most white Americans lived. The urban, northern setting of *Amos 'n' Andy* did not erase the tendency of many to see Afro-Americans mainly as a southern group—an appendage to American society rather than part of its essence. And the series actively bolstered the related assumption that all was well among Afro-Americans in the North and West, for it almost never showed its characters' race having any effect on their lives. That notion largely survived among whites until the urban riots of the mid- and late 1960s shattered the illusion.

The white press's general inattention to the black debates about *Amos 'n' Andy* arose partly out of the very lack of a single, clear "black" line on the subject. But it also typified white America's age-old habit of seeing blacks, if at all, as a "problem" rather than as a people *confronting* and thrashing out complex problems of their own. At the same time, many white responses to *Amos 'n' Andy* evinced an embryonic readiness, in the face of profound social change of all sorts, to think about Afro-Americans and the color line in some new ways. But when whites insisted that America's favorite radio show—and by

245

implication, the nation as a whole—dealt kindly with blacks, they displayed the self-serving contortion of conscience that they and their forebears had proved so adept at for a century and more. The *Amos 'n' Andy* story reveals a society less and less comfortable defending the most obvious flaw in its democratic order—the color line—yet still unwilling to erase it. Profound racial change would not come through concessions offered spontaneously by a repentant majority, but rather would be delayed until blacks forced the issue in the latter 1950s and the 1960s.

Even the black unity and purposefulness of the civil rights years, though real, were imperfect; beneath them lay a diversity of views which had always existed within Afro-America, and which pervaded a quarter-century of debate over *Amos 'n' Andy*. When the show came to television in 1951, on the eve of the civil rights era, black Americans as always were seeking advancement in a myriad of ways. A few courageous Afro-Southerners and their NAACP lawyers were fighting their way through the courts, demanding what was unthinkable to much of the white South: desegregation of schools. Elsewhere, small groups, including a little-known organization called the Nation of Islam whose voice would one day be heard throughout the land, were calling on blacks to renounce any desire to integrate into an evil white society. Meanwhile, educated, middle-class leaders of the NAACP saw *Amos 'n' Andy* as a negation of everything they and their race had achieved, and they militantly demanded its removal from the air. But other Afro-Americans of similar background considered their attainments secure enough that a mere television series could not threaten them. Columns in black newspapers—like those in the white press of an earlier era— instructed the upward mobile Afro-American in "proper" English usage and pronunciation. And even in this era of increasing black assertiveness, manufacturers of skin-lighteners and hair-straighteners still made plenty of money, playing on some Afro-Americans' insecurities with ads that asked, "Too Dark to Be Loved?"[1] Wherein, then, lay the race's salvation?

Some goals won much more support than others: most blacks, for example, agreed that schools, public accommodations, and opportunities for employment should not be segregated. By contrast, the *Amos 'n' Andy* story illustrates how hard it was to achieve a black consensus on the fictional portrayal of Afro-American characters. Divergent black reactions to almost every depiction of blacks on screen, stage, radio, or television during and since the *Amos 'n' Andy* era reinforce the point.

Afro-Americans disagreed over *Hearts in Dixie, Hallelujah!*, the 1927 film of *Uncle Tom's Cabin*, and the original stage version of *The Green Pastures*—a fantasy about an all-black Heaven as imagined by a child—at about the time of the first great debate over *Amos 'n' Andy* itself. Those disagreements pointed to a deeper lack of accord as to which blacks those productions depicted or reflected upon; how one felt about groups within Afro-America other than one's own; and whether the goal of advancing the race demanded that its members imitate whites exclusively, or permitted them also to glory in their people's unique culture and achievements and to contribute these to American society at large. Even those who believed in the latter course often could not agree on which aspects of black culture were worth preserving and which ought to be disavowed or even suppressed. The problem of what it meant to be black in a society dominated by whites emerges as the most striking and constant theme of the *Amos 'n' Andy* story.

America's racial caste system ensured that few blacks could attain power and prestige, and rivalries among black leaders and opinion-makers over the generations have sometimes become highly personalized, bitter, and destructive.[2] The *Amos 'n' Andy* controversy —especially during Robert Vann's protest of 1931—offers examples of this pattern. But the vituperativeness of the debate among Afro-Americans extended far beyond the elite, coloring the discourse of those ordinary people who sent their views to be published in the Pittsburgh *Courier* and in other papers. The harshness of these clashes reflected the widespread frustration produced by a system that offered blacks in general no clear path to advancement.

Not least among the sources of that frustration was the burden of always having to react to whites' attitudes, actions, and demands. In the case of *Amos 'n' Andy*, a vehicle of entertainment produced *by* whites mainly *for* whites, and the possible or actual reactions *of* whites to the show, defined a deeply felt controversy over black identity and destiny that engaged many Afro-Americans over a long period. But any philosophy, any program of action for an oppressed minority, *has to* react to the majority. This is no less true of agendas that reject "white" values and advocate separation than it is for assimilationist programs. How to interpret the standards and demands of the white majority, which of these if any to accept and to what end, are crucial questions. As the history of *Amos 'n' Andy* shows, debate on these points can therefore be stimulating and productive even though it also produces ambiguity, divisiveness, and bitterness.

The Swedish social scientist Gunnar Myrdal suggested about midway through *Amos 'n' Andy*'s lifetime that exclusion from most forms of participation in political and social life had impaired the development of coherent worldviews among Afro-Americans. "Instead of organized popular theories or ideas, the observer finds in the Negro world, for the most part, only *a fluid and amorphous mass of all sorts of embryos of thoughts*," Myrdal wrote. He found Afro-Americans susceptible to "*a great number of contradictory opinions* . . . depending upon how they are driven by pressures or where they see an opportunity." In other words, a person might embrace Garveyan black nationalism in one set of circumstances, yet espouse some version of interracial socialism in another. The same person might, on a different occasion, go to war for the United States and thus stake a claim to the democracy it claimed to be fighting for—or, under yet other conditions, adopt "a passive cynicism toward it all."[3]

Anyone who reads the editorial pages of black American newspapers in the 1930s can indeed find—on the subject of *Amos 'n' Andy* and on many other topics—petty jealousies, eclectic concatenations of ideas, and internal contradictions sometimes bordering on incoherence. Yet the reader also finds a ferment, a searching and candid intensity that could be fruitful even in its disorder and its abrasiveness. This debate was ultimately about self-definition, and thus about worldview as well. No wonder, then, that many of the editorials and letters to the editor on all subjects in black papers of 1930–1931 are even today more thought-provoking than much of what one finds in the white press of the time.

White Americans, too, have been by and large less coherently ideological during the twentieth century than Europeans, and the 1930s in particular were a turbulent decade in which many a white individual, with little regard for traditional political logic, embraced a variety of panaceas and self-proclaimed saviors. Adversity often breeds such eclecticism, and the Depression years saw the gap between white and black experience narrow somewhat in this as in other respects. In that decade and in general, the variegation, the adaptiveness—or "opportunism"—of Afro-American attitudes and behavior demonstrates blacks' connectedness to general American patterns as much as it does divergence from those norms.

Again and again, black responses to *Amos 'n' Andy* and to other challenges during the same decades illustrated the *American* component in Afro-America. Blacks showed their "American-ness" not only in an ideological individualism that for some shaded off into eccentricity, but also in their allegiance to the gospel of self-improvement; in their emphasis on education and geographic mobility as means to that end; in the tension between ethnic identity and the desire to feel oneself a part of the nation as a whole; and in the rejection by many in the middle class and the ambitious working class of rural and blue-collar norms. In all these ways, blacks—notwithstanding the unique obstacles they faced—were among the most American of Americans. And in their struggle for real democracy and equality, they were the truest Americans of all.

The center of gravity in black opinion about *Amos 'n' Andy* did shift over the years. *Sam 'n' Henry* drew few black protests. By 1930–1931, attacks by blacks against *Amos 'n' Andy* had begun in earnest. In 1951, as two decades before, no single black view of the series emerged, but this time the complaints seemed more widespread than in 1931. Many Afro-Americans, though not seeing in *Amos 'n' Andy* the same burning issue Walter White did, were not happy with the precedent the series was setting for the portrayal of blacks in the medium of the future. By the 1960s, television producers and the networks were convinced that blacks simply would not tolerate a show like *Amos 'n' Andy*.

Even so, dilemmas and disagreements within the black community over media images have persisted to the present day. Many blacks excoriated *Amos 'n' Andy* and several television series of the 1970s for allegedly showering attention on the race's low-life; but in 1968, some Afro-Americans condemned Diahann Carroll's television series *Julia* for "selling out"—portraying a black woman as what Carroll called a "white Negro,"[4] exempt from the problems that most real blacks faced. In the 1960s and afterward, many praised the most successful black film star of the era, Sidney Poitier, as a dignified role model for blacks; yet some accused him of playing overly "sanitized" roles. In the 1970s, many Afro-Americans deplored the "blaxploitation" movie genre, in which black antiheroes consistently and violently vanquished whites, but large black audiences—especially young people of the inner city—cheered.

In the 1980s, Afro-American men and women locked horns over the depiction of black males in Steven Spielberg's film of Alice Walker's *The Color Purple* and in Oprah Winfrey's adaptation of Gloria Naylor's *The Women of Brewster Place* as a TV miniseries. The films of writer-producer-director Spike Lee won plaudits from many blacks for their candor, style, and originality, while others grimaced at Lee's readiness to air in public what they considered to be the race's dirty linen—including antagonisms over color, class, and gender among Afro-Americans themselves.

Also in the 1980s, blacks often asked why *The Jeffersons*—a TV comedy series about a wealthy but crude black entrepreneur, his wife, and his sassy maid—should be permitted to run year after year while *Amos 'n' Andy* was barred; some thought both should be banned, others that both should be broadcast. Many had raised the same question about Redd Foxx's rough-edged portrayal of a junkman in the television series *Sanford and Son*. The quarter-century following *I Spy* brought sharp differences of opinion among Afro-Americans over shows and stars—especially but not exclusively comic ones— including Flip Wilson, Jimmie Walker on *Good Times*, Eddie Murphy, and Mr. T of *The A-Team*.

When Bill Cosby made a ratings-leading sitcom about an Afro-American family beginning in the mid-1980s, he engaged an eminent black psychologist as a regular consultant; the show incorporated such subtle but significant touches as a portrait of Frederick Douglass posted in the room of a teenage daughter, whose list of potential colleges includes two traditionally black schools along with two Ivy League universities. Another daughter longs to spend a summer in Paris, in part because so many great writers from the United States worked there; the two she mentions are Richard Wright and James Baldwin. A popular *Cosby* spinoff series, *A Different World*, depicted life on the campus of a black college—another TV first. Yet some Afro-Americans found Cosby's TV family—which was portrayed as well-educated, affluent, and immune to all but the most tractable of problems—to be "too white."

Still other television series showed that issues from the *Amos 'n' Andy* years had life in them yet. In 1951, the bourgeoisification of sets and costumes had made crude characters like the Kingfish seem more, not less, offensive to some Afro-Americans, especially those in the middle class. Nearly four decades later, the same problem still arose. In 1988, an episode of *Frank's Place*—an imaginative new half-hour drama/comedy, or "dramedy"—revolved around a battle of spells and potions between two black female practitioners of voodoo in New Orleans. Did the presentation of one of these women as stylish, well-spoken, affluent, and understated challenge an offensive stereotype? Or did it create a new one by implying that even the most sophisticated Afro-American exterior may but thinly veil the primitivism and superstition commonly ascribed to blacks in a less enlightened era?

The old questions about media images persisted in a new age

because of a more basic continuity in American life. White racism has been a critical shaper of the lot of Afro-Americans throughout their history; the changes of the latter twentieth century have lightened that burden in some important ways but have come nowhere near eliminating it. As long as black Americans suffer inequality—indeed, as long as they are a conspicuous minority—they are required, whether they wish to or not, to consider actively who they are, how to view their fellow blacks, and how to deal with the white majority. Blacks have answered these questions in a great variety of ways, but shifting, mutually contradictory demands by whites have ensured that no single course clearly, incontrovertibly "works." Small wonder that, while there are some issues that most Afro-Americans substantially agree on, there is no unanimity on how to define blackness and on what, exactly, blacks must do in order to become free, equal, and secure.

Consciously or unconsciously, black viewers often see depictions of Afro-Americans in the media as suggested answers to some of these complex questions. Television and movies affect or offend partly according to what the viewer thinks they are saying about reality; the viewer's response to a given portrayal may in fact be a reaction to the "position" it seems to take. Because the chronic dilemmas of Afro-American life—Du Bois called them "the curious cross currents that swirl about the black American"—generally do not have obvious, unambiguous solutions, consensus remains elusive when blacks respond to portrayals of the race in popular entertainment as well. Inevitably, this proved at least as true of the diverse work of rising black *auteurs* in TV and movies of the 1980s and 1990s—which ignited some of the most heated debates in memory within the Afro-American community—as it had ever been of productions mounted by whites.

Amos 'n' Andy offers the earliest and longest-lived example of these principles in the annals of American broadcasting. The dilemmas that pervade the show's history will continue to apply as long as those of race in general do, and as long as the media portray Afro-Americans at all. The waning of the white backlash of the 1960s permitted what the potency of the black consumer market and a wealth of black talent now ensure: movies and television—in soap operas, dramatic series, and situation comedies alike—will indeed continue to present a large number of black faces.

For all their missteps and disappointments in 1951, the leaders of the NAACP helped mold the relationship between the new television industry and the public into a shape we still recognize today. Groups that oppose depictions of violence, sexuality, the use of alcohol or drugs, and stereotypes based on ethnicity, gender, or sexual preference have joined Afro-American organizations in monitoring TV broadcasting. But protests often end up swelling the audience for the very productions the protesters object to. In any event, popular entertainment and people's responses to it mainly reflect rather than create social realities; repairing media images at best makes only a dent in society's problems. In the latter 1980s, the blossoming of cable channels and the advent of a fourth national network, Fox, sharpened the competition for TV ratings; some new series, such as Keenen Ivory Wayans's *In Living Color*, now sought to grab the viewer's attention by blatantly turning race, sex, and homosexuality into comic mainstays. For Afro-American individuals, black organizations, and broadcasters alike, the future promises its share of confusion and bruised feelings.

···➡◉◗━···

At noontime one Wednesday in mid-August 1981, a group of white men gathered at Richmond's Commonwealth Club for lunch.[5] Where a roomful of 165 club members and a staff of servants had listened silently to the broadcast of Madam Queen's breach-of-promise suit exactly half a century before, only fifteen were present today. One was a Richmond city councilman, another the son of one of Freeman Gosden's partners from the old amateur minstrel shows in the days before World War I. The rest of the group were businessmen, civic boosters, and others who had some connection with Gosden or interest in him.

The fifteen had gathered to celebrate Freeman Fisher Gosden Day, an observance ordained by Richmond's city council the week before. The council consisted of five blacks and four whites who frequently divided on issues along racial lines. This time, however, had been different. When white Councilman Steve Kemp introduced a resolution paying tribute to Gosden and designating August 19—the anniversary of *Amos 'n' Andy*'s debut on NBC—in his honor, four Afro-American councilmen joined with the four whites in approving the proposal, and the inscribed proclamation was signed by the city's black mayor. "Holy mackerel, Sapphire!" marveled a Richmond newspaper in reporting the passage of the resolution with black support.[6]

Some of the black councilmen may have had an easier time voting for the proclamation since its proponents were careful not to mention

Amos 'n' Andy even once, referring only to an unnamed "comedy act" Gosden had broadcast with Charles Correll. Asked about Afro-American criticisms of the old *Amos 'n' Andy* show, the originator of the commemorative resolution admitted, "I just hoped that wouldn't come up."[7] Still, one black councilwoman could not bring herself to vote for the proposal. "I had nothing against Mr. Gosden personally," she explained later, "but I feel that he became wealthy and famous depicting us in a negative fashion." Yet even she, rather than voting against the resolution, simply left the room when the council was polled. Incensed even by so isolated and subdued a dissent, Larry Bonko, a white columnist for a Norfolk paper, blamed Richmond's blacks—who had dominated the city council for all of five years—for the city's failure to honor Gosden during the previous fifty. To Bonko, black sensitivity to perceived racial slights had no place in a society where white racism was supposedly a thing of the past. "I would like to remind the blacks of Richmond," the columnist scolded, "that this is a new day in America."[8] Reading his column, one had to wonder.

On Freeman Gosden Day, Councilman Kemp and several others rode through downtown Richmond in a 1913 Model T Ford bearing the legend, "The Fresh Air Taxi Co." Here there *was* some evidence, however modest, of a new day. In contrast to the cars so decorated on Gosden and Correll's Pantages tour of 1929, the lettering on this sign was correct and professional, and the word "Incorpulated" nowhere in evidence. Many passersby, unaware of the occasion that was being so discreetly observed, either glanced at the car in bewilderment or did not notice it at all.

The Model T eventually took its occupants to the Commonwealth Club. There, an old oil portrait of Colonel John S. Mosby, who had commanded Freeman Gosden's father during the Civil War, looked down upon the gathering. A telephone connection was established with Gosden's residence in Beverly Hills. Gosden was eighty-two and in poor health. Sixteen months later, he would be dead; Charles Correll had died nine years earlier. But Gosden, who had last visited Richmond more than thirty years before, was still alert and verbally adroit. He thanked the city of Richmond and those at the luncheon for honoring him. And then he performed some of his most famous routines from *Amos 'n' Andy*, still in good voice and, according to one of those who attended the gathering, as "comical" as ever.[9]

A couple of weeks later, the Richmond *Afro-American*, a black weekly, asked ten ordinary black Richmonders, most of them apparently under thirty-five, "how they felt about" *Amos 'n' Andy* and whether they thought the TV show "should be revived." An auto body worker replied, "I didn't like it, . . . because the majority of the blacks I know are decent"; he apparently found the TV characters to be the opposite. A male college student also disapproved of the old television series. But the rest of those interviewed, except for one person who had no opinion, praised *Amos 'n' Andy*. A female cashier remembered the show as "good, nice and funny." "I think it's cool," said a salesman; "I enjoyed them as a kid coming up." A middle-aged seamstress, who especially liked Sapphire, believed that *Amos 'n' Andy* "accurately portrayed blacks." "I really think it should be revived," said a young female clerk. "I'd love to see it," agreed a young assistant manager. "I think it's a nice and productive show for the community," he added. "If there are any blacks in it, I'm all for it."[10]

A new day in America? Again, one had to wonder. Perhaps recollections of *Amos 'n' Andy* had taken on the rosy glow that often swaths childhood memories. Or perhaps friendly feelings about the series were still linked, as they seem to have been in 1951 and 1931, to a black person's sense of certainty about his or her prospects—whether for comfort or deprivation—in American society. If so, and if some Afro-Americans were ready for a comeback of *Amos 'n' Andy*, one could only hope that more of them felt confident of their future, and that fewer took it for granted that nothing much would improve, than had been the case thirty or fifty years before.

A Personal Postscript

I grew up on *Amos 'n' Andy*, and it taught me some things that have shaped the rest of my life.

My *Amos 'n' Andy* was the television situation comedy, which was broadcast on weekdays by a local station during my childhood and adolescence in Richmond, Virginia. The series had left prime time in 1953, when I was a year old, and the shows my younger brother and I saw were the syndicated episodes from that era. Like most young Americans who watched *Amos 'n' Andy* on TV, I had never heard the radio show that preceded it for a quarter-century.

For me, *Amos 'n' Andy* was the funniest show on television—and the most interesting. I knew almost nothing of the Afro-American folk traditions that equipped those unforgettable actors to impart life to the material that the white scriptwriters gave them. But it seemed obvious that Tim Moore, Amanda Randolph, Johnny Lee, and the rest were bright and funny in a way that was specifically, inimitably black. I "learned" two things from this, one correct, the other tragically distorted.

I concluded that there was something unique and compellingly attractive about the black world; as the years passed, and I became a student of that world, I found out how right—and yet how ignorant—I had been. The second lesson I took from *Amos 'n' Andy* was not merely that Afro-Americans could be funny, but that being funny was one of their chief functions in life. There were few black images in the media of popular entertainment to tell me otherwise. My encounters with real black individuals were relatively few, and some of those people "wore the mask that grins and lies"—to negotiate the twists and turns of a skeptical, even dangerous white-ruled society, I now realize.

There was yet another, equally fascinating lesson for me in *Amos 'n' Andy*. The show was set in Harlem. Much of the action in the series revolved around the substantial lodge hall of the Mystic Knights

255

of the Sea order; dignified black doctors, nurses, lawyers, policemen, and others appeared around the edges of the show's stories. I was quietly astonished. I lived in a segregated society in which it was possible—almost inevitable—for a middle-class white boy to have no inkling that there were Afro-Americans with college degrees and professions, who spoke like network anchormen, or that there were Afro-American communities whose busy streets were filled with black faces and with institutions owned and run by black people themselves.

The nighttime New York skyline over which the opening and closing credits of *Amos 'n' Andy* appeared, and much of what I saw in between, made me dream of a great city within which lay a great black metropolis. The humor that constituted ninety-five percent of the show—the genuine Afro-American elements, the universal human touches, and the exploitative white fantasies of what blacks were like—did not diminish, and even complemented, the wonder that the metropolis aroused in me. I hoped to see it for myself one day.

All this gradually took on new meaning because of the civil rights revolution that swirled around me during the latter part of my childhood in the South. Ironically, the televised pictures of that revolution joined with images of *Amos 'n' Andy* to furnish my sharpest video memories of that time. On the evening news, as in the Harlem of *Amos 'n' Andy*, I saw pictures of Afro-Americans doing things I had never dreamt they did. Again the seeds of a consuming wonder were planted—a wonder that in later years molded my spiritual, intellectual, and professional life.

But it was too much for a white boy of ten or twelve to comprehend. As I watched the civil rights demonstrations on television, what I later came to appreciate as African-American bravery, eloquence, and grace often seemed to me odd and confusing. My brother and I sometimes handled our nervous puzzlement by laughing at or parodying the impassioned speeches we heard from Birmingham and Selma. Our mother's Christian teaching that those protesters were right had to compete with pressures in the opposite direction from peers—and from some adults, whom I still find it hard to forgive. There was a period of several years, around junior high school age, in which we yielded to those pressures more readily and frequently than I like to remember, indulging in endless, mindless jokes and wisecracks about blacks. Eventually, the tension between what was easy and what we knew to be right became unbearable. The Afro-American friends I came to know in high school helped to free me from it; so, in time, did the study of history.

Amos 'n' Andy gave me simple pleasure and began to open up a new world to me, for which I am still grateful. But the show also conveyed some of those countless messages emanating from the white America of my youth that taught me to laugh at black striving, at Afro-Americans *as* Afro-Americans. Though I never felt the race hatred that consumed some of those around me, I still grieve for the opportunities deferred or lost forever to love my neighbor *as myself*.

A sense of irony and a sensitivity to tragedy may be useful to any historian; they are indispensable for a historian of the South and of Afro-America, and for any thinking person who belongs to either or both of those cultures. At the beginning of my fourth decade as a Southerner and my second as a student of history, conversations with my brother and with a childhood friend made me see more clearly than ever how many-layered the story of *Amos 'n' Andy* was. Piecing that story together, I realized, would draw heavily, through the overlay of remembered laughter, on the feeling for irony and tragedy that lay at the center of my adult identity.

That twenty-five years of radio history preceded the television series I had known lent the subject an added dimension of mystery. Yet even here there was a glimmer of familiarity: I recalled childhood hearsay, confirmed by a line in my grammar-school Virginia history text, that Freeman Gosden, one of *Amos 'n' Andy*'s two creators, had been a fellow Richmonder—which somehow did not surprise me in the least.

This book is the result of my effort to rediscover and understand a monument of American popular entertainment, which for years has been hidden from view for fear that a second look will inflame emotions and upset our comfortable view of ourselves. It will be clear by now that, if emotional engagement with the subject disqualifies one from writing its history, then I am not fit for the task. But I am convinced that good history requires an emotional investment as surely as it does measured analysis. The story of *Amos 'n' Andy* is a story of who we are as a nation. It has been my sometimes painful pleasure to try to tell it.

M.P.E.

Notes

1. White Men, Black Voices

1. Charles Correll and Freeman Gosden, *Sam 'n' Henry* radio script #1, January 12, 1926, in Gosden–Correll Collection, Cinema–Television Library and Archives of Performing Arts, Doheny Library, University of Southern California (hereafter cited as GC–USC).
2. This and the following description of the *Defender* parade and picnic are based, except as noted below, on articles in the Chicago *Defender*, August 1, 8, 15, 22, and 29, 1931. The *Defender*'s coverage leaves one with some uncertainty as to the respective roles of the Ellington and Millinder bands.
3. *Time*, August 31, 1931, in scrapbook, "General Publicity (1928–32)," GC–USC. The Pittsburgh *Courier*, a black weekly which was critical of the event, gave the same estimate of the crowd's size as *Time* did (and indeed was probably the source of the figure that appeared in the newsmagazine). (*Courier*, August 22, 1931, in scrapbook C, GC–USC.)
4. Cooperative Analysis of Broadcasting ratings, cited in Edgar A. Grunwald, "Program-Production History, 1929–1937," *Variety Radio Directory, 1937–1938* (n.p., 1937), pp. 19–20; and J. Fred MacDonald, *Don't Touch That Dial! Radio Programming in American Life, 1920–1960* (Chicago: Nelson-Hall, 1979), pp. 27–29.
5. Newark (New Jersey) *Union-Gazette*, February 21, 1930, in scrapbook #1; and Hammond (Indiana) *Times*, May 29, 1931, in scrapbook #11; both in GC–USC.
6. Walter White, "Negro Leader Looks at TV Race Problem," *Printers' Ink*, August 24, 1951.
7. Resolution quoted in Herbert L. Wright, letter to NAACP Youth Councils, College Chapters and State Youth Conferences, July 19, 1951, in National Association for the Advancement of Colored People Papers, II, A, 479, Manuscript Division, Library of Congress.
8. Interviews with William and Peggy Walker (August 22, 1983, Los Angeles), Maggie Hathaway (August 1, 1982, by telephone), and Alvin Childress (July 14 and 31, and August 7, 1982, Los Angeles); *Journal and Guide*, Virginia edition, July 21, 1951; and *Printers' Ink*, August 3 and 17, 1951.
9. Al Monroe in Chicago *Defender*, June 16, 1951.
10. Billy Rowe in Pittsburgh *Courier*, July 7, 1951.
11. Interview with Alvin Childress, July 14, 1982, Los Angeles; and Leonard C. Archer, *Black Images in the American Theatre: NAACP Protest Campaigns—Stage, Screen, Radio & Television* (Brooklyn: Pageant–Poseidon, 1973), pp. 242–243 (accompanied by a puzzling footnote).
12. Los Angeles *Times*, November 27, 1960, in Los Angeles *Examiner* morgue file, "Gosden, Freeman F.," courtesy of Ned Comstock, Department of Special Collections, Doheny Library, USC.

13. Statements published or broadcast within a single year in the early 1980s which condemned *Amos 'n' Andy* as a purveyor of racist images included those of Phil Donahue on *Donahue* television show, April 15, 1982; Cal Thomas, public relations chief of the Moral Majority, on Jim Bakker TV show, May 8, 1982; Willis Edwards, head of the Hollywood–Beverly Hills Branch, NAACP, on *Entertainment Tonight*, NBC-TV show, September 8, 1982; *Tony Brown's Journal*, PBS-TV, four-part series on blacks in television (show titles: "Blacks in White TV," "Goodbye, Sgt. Ross?" "Black Soap," and "Is TV Off-Color?"), November 1982; J. Fred MacDonald, *Blacks and White TV: Afro-Americans in Television Since 1948* (Chicago: Nelson-Hall, 1983), pp. 21 and 26–33 (although MacDonald does concede that a few "humanizing qualities" were "occasionally" included in the *Amos 'n' Andy* TV series); and Benjamin Hooks, national secretary of the NAACP, quoted in *Variety* (daily), May 3, 1983.

2. Boyhood Dreams and Racial Myths

1. Charles J. Correll, typewritten preface to notes on early life, n.d., whence the quotation; description of house and grounds from Peoria *Star*, July 27 and 28 [1939], and clipping, source unidentified, n.d.; all in Correll family collection, Los Angeles. (In this and later notes, dates and other information that are missing from cited newspaper clippings are supplied in brackets whenever possible.)
2. J. R. Milne in Boston *Post*, March 2, 9, and 23, 1930; *All About Amos 'n' Andy and Their Creators Correll and Gosden* (New York, Chicago, and San Francisco: Rand McNally, 1929), p. 107; Office of Provost Marshal, Louisville, Kentucky, parole for Sarah Correll, October 12, 1864, in Correll family collection; and Rosalind K. Shaffer in Richmond *News Leader* (syndicated item), March 16, 1942.
3. Peoria *Star*, January 27, 1935, in scrapbook #12, Gosden–Correll Collection, Cinema–Television Library and Archives of Performing Arts, Doheny Library, University of Southern California (hereafter cited as GC–USC); and Milne in Boston *Post*, March 2, 1930.
4. *Encyclopaedia Britannica*, 1972 ed., vol. XI, pp. 1086–1086A, citing census of 1900.
5. Charles J. Correll, notes on early life, n.d. [c. 1970?], Correll family collection.
6. Conversations with Richard Correll; and see Philadelphia *Record*, March 21, 1930, in scrapbook #8, GC–USC. Although the *Record* article contains some factual errors, on this particular point it is consistent with the accounts cited in note 7 below.
   Among those shown in an old photograph of Correll as an adolescent with a group of playmates, one boy may be black, although the poor quality of the picture's reproduction in a newspaper of 1930 leaves much doubt. (Miami *Herald*, April 6, 1930, in scrapbook #10, GC–USC.)
7. *All About Amos 'n' Andy*, p. 35; Jeremy Woods in *Screen and Radio Weekly* section of Detroit *Free Press*, August 6, 1939, in Correll family collection; and the following articles in GC–USC: in scrapbook #8: Philadelphia *Record*, March 21, 1930; *Time*, March 3, 1930, reprinted in Watertown (New York) *Times*, March 3, 1930; Bridgeport (Connecticut) *Herald*, March 30, 1930; and in scrapbook #9: New York *American*, March 17, 1930; El Paso *Post*, April 9, 1930.
8. Correll, notes on early life, Correll family collection. Except as noted, the information and quotations in the rest of this section come from this source.
9. Correll, notes on early life, and invitation, Peoria High School commencement

exercises, class of 1907, both in Correll family collection; and J. R. Milne in Boston *Post,* February 23, 1930 (whose assertion that Correll took piano lessons for three years is inconsistent with Correll's own recollection), and March 2, 1930.

10. Correll, typewritten preface to notes on early life, Correll family collection.

11. Interviews with Alvin Childress, July 14, July 31, and August 7, 1982, Los Angeles; interview with William and Peggy Walker, August 22, 1983, Los Angeles.

12. Ann Webb in Winston-Salem *Journal and Sentinel,* May 4, 1930 (which mistakenly asserts that Freeman Gosden's father had immigrated from England), in scrapbook #10, GC–USC; *All About Amos 'n' Andy,* p. 21; Richmond *Times-Dispatch,* November 6, 1911; gravestones, Gosden family plot, Hollywood Cemetery, Richmond, Virginia; Richmond *Times-Dispatch,* January 9, 1949; *Richmond City Directory* (Richmond and Norfolk: Chataigne Directory Co.; in later years, Richmond: Hill Directory Co.), 1882–1917 inclusive. On Emma Gosden's parents, see Richmond *Times-Dispatch,* November 6, 1906, and September 27, 1909. On employment of Gosden sons, *City Directory,* issues of 1895–1896, 1898, and 1915 as compared with Gosden family gravestones. See also interview with Claude M. Monteiro, April 17, 1984, Richmond; interview with Jane Gosden, August 14, 1983, Beverly Hills; and MS. Census returns, Richmond, 1900 and 1910.

13. *Richmond City Directory,* 1902; Helen Johnston Skinner, "A Childhood in Early Richmond, 1899–1910," *Richmond Quarterly,* VII, 1 (Summer 1984), 34. See also Mary Wingfield Scott, *Houses of Old Richmond* (New York: Bonanza Books, 1941), pp. 206–207, 220–223, 248–253, and 286–287; and Paul S. Dulaney, *The Architecture of Historic Richmond* (Charlottesville: University Press of Virginia, 1968), pp. 131, 134, 136–137, and 138.

14. *Richmond City Directory,* 1902–1912 inclusive; Monteiro and Gosden interviews; and Richmond *Times-Dispatch,* June 22, 1950, whence the quotation. Thanks to Charles McDowell Jr., writer of the last-named item, for bringing it to the author's attention.

15. Virginius Dabney, *Richmond: The Story of a City* (Garden City, N.Y.: Doubleday, 1976), p. 248.

16. Dabney, *Richmond,* p. 275.

17. Richmond *Times-Dispatch,* November 6, 1911; Milne in Boston *Post,* February 23, 1930, and also March 16, 1930 (with yet another picture on the Mosby theme); and Richmond *News Leader,* February 23 and 25, 1933, in file, "Gosden, Freeman F.," Richmond Public Library (hereafter cited as FFG–RPL). Milne's biography of Gosden and Correll, which appeared in six long weekly installments, was more frequently reprinted and excerpted in other newspapers than most other specimens of its kind. See, for example, Albany (New York) *Knickerbocker Press,* March 23, 1930, in scrapbook #10; and Buffalo *Courier-Express,* March 28, 1930, in scrapbook #9; both in GC–USC.

18. Gosden and Monteiro interviews, and visit to Gosden home, Beverly Hills; Monteiro, letter to Freeman F. Gosden, November 24, 1982, and handwritten reply from Gosden on same sheet, courtesy of Mr. Monteiro; clipping, "Shows and Show People According to Hoyle," source unidentified [1934], in scrapbook #12, GC–USC; Shaffer in Richmond *News Leader,* March 16, 1942; Charlottesville (Virginia) *Daily Progress,* June 14, 1961, in FFG–RPL; and John S. Mosby, testimonial to war service of W. W. Gosden, courtesy of Jane Gosden.

19. Michael B. Chesson, *Richmond After the War, 1865–1890* (Richmond: Virginia State Library, 1981), p. 192; and Dabney, *Richmond,* pp. 236 and 294–295.

20. Dabney, *Richmond*, pp. 237 and 256–257; Virginius Dabney, *Virginia: The New Dominion* (Garden City, N.Y.: Doubleday, 1971), pp. 413–414; and Chesson, *Richmond After the War*, pp. 157 and 191–192.

21. See George M. Fredrickson, *The Black Image in the White Mind: The Debate on Afro-American Character and Destiny, 1817–1914* (New York: Harper & Row, 1971), pp. 256–262. Pp. 228–255 offer an enlightening discussion of the development of "racial Darwinism."

22. The extent to which Populists "blamed" blacks for Populist defeats and acquiesced in the subsequent disfranchisement of Afro-Southerners has been the subject of some disagreement. See C. Vann Woodward, *Origins of the New South, 1877–1913* (1951; reprint edition, Baton Rouge: Louisiana State University Press, 1971), p. 323; and J. Morgan Kousser, *The Shaping of Southern Politics: Suffrage Restriction and the Establishment of the One-Party South, 1880–1910* (New Haven: Yale University Press, 1974), pp. 5–6, 246–247, and *passim* (which, however, caricatures Woodward's position somewhat).

23. See Dabney, *Richmond*, pp. 237, 257, and 270; and Chesson, *Richmond After the War*, pp. 157–158 and 183–184.

24. Dabney, *Richmond*, pp. 271–272.

25. A similar point is made by Fredrickson in *Black Image*, p. 262.

26. Gaines M. Foster, *Ghosts of the Confederacy: Defeat, the Lost Cause, and the Emergence of the New South, 1865–1913* (New York and Oxford: Oxford University Press, 1987), pp. 119, 140, and 194.

27. But not entirely absent before the late 1880s. Black militia units had marched in at least some Confederate memorial parades in Richmond prior to 1887. (Chesson, *Richmond After the War*, p. 195. See also Foster, *Ghosts*, pp. 136 and 140.)

28. Robert Deane Pharr, *The Book of Numbers* (New York: Avon, 1970), p. 11.

29. Gravestone, Willie B. Gosden, Gosden family plot, Hollywood Cemetery, Richmond; Richmond *Dispatch*, March 11, 1902 (see also March 12, 1902); and Richmond *Times-Dispatch*, November 6, 1911.

30. *Richmond City Directory*, 1912–1917 inclusive; Vera Duke, letter to Edward A. Leake Jr., August 21, 1981, in FFG–RPL; Richmond *News Leader*, February 23, 1933, in FFG–RPL; Richmond *Times-Dispatch*, September 12, 13 (editorial and separate news article on coroner's inquest), and 14, 1917; and Monteiro interview.

31. Richmond *Times-Dispatch*, January 9, 1949; Ann Webb in Winston-Salem *Journal and Sentinel*, May 4, 1930, in scrapbook #10, GC–USC; and Gosden interview. Gosden had spent time away from home before, briefly attending school in Atlanta as an adolescent, apparently while living with his sister and brother-in-law there. (Atlanta *Constitution*, May 19, 1935, and [January 1936?]; and Atlanta *Georgian*, March 8, 1934; all three in box, "Amos & Andy—Loose Scrapbook Pages by Year— 1930–35," GC–USC.) But Atlanta in those days was not very different from Richmond in atmosphere.

32. *All About Amos 'n' Andy*, pp. 22–23; Monteiro interview; Allentown (Pennsylvania) *Chronicle and News and Evening Item*, February 1, 1935, in box, "Amos & Andy— Loose Scrapbook Pages by Year—1930–35," folder "1935," GC–USC; Arthur Frank Wertheim, *Radio Comedy* (New York: Oxford University Press, 1979), p. 19; Richmond *Times-Dispatch*, April 14, 1936, in FFG–RPL (which, however, gives the wrong year for Gosden's hiring by the Bren organization).

33. Richmond *News Leader,* June 21, 1950, in FFG–RPL; Peoria *Star,* January 27, 1935, in Correll family collection; and Gosden interview.

34. Gosden and Monteiro interviews.

35. *All About Amos 'n' Andy,* p. 22; Monteiro interview; and Boston *Post,* December 22 [1929], in scrapbook #8, GC–USC.

36. For mention of a supposed Gosden "mammy," see Bridgeport (Connecticut) *Herald,* March 30, 1930, and Philadelphia *Record,* March 21, 1930, both in scrapbook #8, GC–USC; and Watertown (New York) *Times,* April 26, 1930, in scrapbook #9, GC–USC. See also *All About Amos 'n' Andy,* p. 21. On Gosden's not reminiscing about a "mammy," see Gosden and Monteiro interviews.

   When a relative of Freeman's wrote an account of his childhood for a North Carolina newspaper, she included a detailed description of a black child who she said had worked in the Gosden home—but not one word about a woman servant. (Ann Webb in Winston-Salem *Journal and Sentinel,* May 4, 1930, in scrapbook #10, GC–USC.) The same is true of a long article credited to Gosden and Correll, "as told to" a newspaper feature writer; although it discusses Gosden's early contact with blacks, it does not mention a "mammy." (Boston *Post,* December 22 [1929], in scrapbook #8, GC–USC.) At least in his very early childhood, however, Freeman did have a black nurse. (MS. Census returns, Richmond, 1900.)

   In the present work, the term "mammy" will be used in quotation marks to denote the specific category of servant so designated in the documents cited. This implies no endorsement of the use of the term, which is generally considered offensive in our own time, in other connections. Likewise, the author prefers in most cases to dispense with the marker *sic,* even when a quoted phrase does not conform to modern standards of correct or respectful usage (for example, the word "Negro," especially when spelled without the initial capital).

37. Gosden and Monteiro interviews; *All About Amos 'n' Andy,* pp. 21–22 and 47–48. See also Boston *Post,* December 22 [1929], in scrapbook #8, GC–USC; and Buffalo *Evening News,* April 5, 1930, in scrapbook #10, GC–USC.

38. Sources for Brown's real name: Monteiro interview; and Wertheim, *Radio Comedy,* p. 24. Despite the offensive quality of the appellation, this work will occasionally use the nickname "Snowball," in quotation marks, when directly or indirectly quoting a source that uses the name, or when referring specifically to the personality depicted—accurately or not—in such a source. Otherwise, this book will use Brown's real name, even though almost no other document—and none of the early ones at all—do so.

39. On whites hiring black children, see, for example, Skinner, "A Childhood in Early Richmond," 32. *All About Amos 'n' Andy,* p. 21, asserts that Brown lived with the Gosdens. See also Buffalo *Evening News,* April 5, 1930, in scrapbook #10, GC–USC; and Pawtucket (Rhode Island) *Times,* December 20, 1929, in scrapbook #8, GC–USC.

   On the two boys' ages and the duration of Garrett Brown's stay with the Gosdens, compare Almena Davis in Los Angeles *Tribune,* March 22, 1942, in box, "Amos & Andy—Loose Scrapbook Pages—1936–44, 1946–48, 1954," folder "1942," with Wertheim, *Radio Comedy,* p. 24. Ann Webb in Winston-Salem *Journal and Sentinel,* May 4, 1930, in scrapbook #10, GC–USC, likewise implies that the two boys were of about the same age. Garrett Brown's name began to appear in the *Richmond City*

Directory, at addresses different from the Gosdens', by 1910, however, which suggests that he was several years older than Freeman.

40. Ann Webb in Winston-Salem *Journal and Sentinel*, May 4, 1930, in scrapbook #10, GC—USC. See also Philadelphia *Record*, March 21, 1930, in scrapbook #8, GC—USC.

3. Jefferson Snowball, Traveling Minstrel

1. Except as noted, the following account of the UDC convention is based on Fredericksburg *Daily Star*, April 25, 26, and 27, 1917.
2. Fredericksburg *Free Lance*, May 1, 1917.
3. Fredericksburg *Daily Star*, April 24 and 25, 1917; and handbill, Billy Burke Minstrels, Fredericksburg, April 27, 1917, located (despite its date) in scrapbook, "General Publicity (1928–32)," Gosden–Correll Collection, Cinema–Television Library and Archives of Performing Arts, Doheny Library, University of Southern California (hereafer cited as GC–USC).
4. Fredericksburg *Daily Star*, April 28, 1917.
5. Fredericksburg *Daily Star*, April 28, 1917; handbill, Billy Burke Minstrels, Fredericksburg, April 27, 1917, in scrapbook, "General Publicity (1928–32)," GC–USC; and Virginius Dabney, *Richmond: The Story of a City* (Garden City, N.Y.: Doubleday, 1976), pp. 320 and 354.
6. Fredericksburg *Daily Star*, April 28, 1917; and Richmond *Times-Dispatch*, May 22, 1950, in file," Andrews, T. Coleman," Richmond Public Library.
7. Hans Nathan, *Dan Emmett and the Rise of Early Negro Minstrelsy* (Norman: University of Oklahoma Press, 1962), p. 50; and Robert C. Toll, *Blacking Up: The Minstrel Show in Nineteenth-Century America* (New York: Oxford University Press, 1974), pp. 26–28. The minstrels were not the first whites to portray Afro-Americans; minor black characters occasionally appeared in plays staged for American audiences in earlier decades.
8. See Nathan, *Dan Emmett*, pp. 50–57. See also Toll, *Blacking Up*, p. 28.
9. Nathan, *Dan Emmett*, pp. 57–59; and Toll, *Blacking Up*, pp. 68–69. On the role of antebellum minstrelsy in reassuring whites of their supposed superiority to blacks, see Toll, pp. 67 and 78.
10. See Toll, *Blacking Up*, chapter 5, in which p. 135 offers a handy summary of the postwar changes in minstrel shows, pp. 147–148 describe two specific Haverly productions, and pp. 152–154 discuss the waning of blackface. See also Frank Costellow Davidson, "The Rise, Development, Decline, and Influence of the American Minstrel Show" (doctoral dissertation, New York University, 1952), pp. 112 and 118.
11. Douglas Gilbert, *American Vaudeville: Its Life and Times* (New York and London: Whittlesey House, 1940), pp. 79–80. On blackface minstrels in white "ethnic" roles, see Toll, *Blacking Up*, pp. 161–162.
12. Harry Tucker in Richmond *Times-Dispatch*, November 2 [1930?], in file, "Gosden, Freeman F.," Richmond Public Library (hereafter cited as FFG–RPL). On Joe Cook, see Gilbert, *American Vaudeville*, pp. 255–258. (In this and later notes, dates and other information that are missing from cited newspaper clippings are supplied in brackets whenever possible.)
13. W. R. Stith, letter to editor, Richmond *Times-Dispatch*, January 18, 1949, in FFG–RPL; Allentown (Pennsylvania) *Chronicle and News and Evening Item*, February 1, 1935, in box, "Amos & Andy—Loose Scrapbook Pages by Year—1930–35," folder

"1935," GC–USC; *All About Amos 'n' Andy and Their Creators Correll and Gosden* (New York, Chicago, and San Francisco: Rand McNally, 1929), p. 22; clipping, source unidentified [syndicated item? late 1935 or first half of 1936?], in scrapbook #12, GC–USC; Tucker in Richmond *Times-Dispatch*, November 2 [1930?], FFG–RPL; Milne in Boston *Post*, March 2, 1930.

14. Stockton Earp in Richmond *Times-Dispatch* Sunday Magazine Section, January 15, 1939, in FFG–RPL; and Milne in Boston *Post*, March 2, 1930.

15. Hazel Canning in Boston *Post*, December 22 [1929], scrapbook #8, GC–USC; and *All About Amos 'n' Andy*, p. 16.

16. See Sterling Brown, *The Negro in American Fiction* (1937; reprint edition, New York: Atheneum, 1969), especially pp. 6–10, 15, and 45–46.

17. Toll, *Blacking Up*, pp. 90–97.

18. Robert C. Toll, *On with the Show! The First Century of Show Business in America* (New York: Oxford University Press, 1976), pp. 152–155.

19. See Brown, *Negro in American Fiction*, pp. 64–69, 71–75, and 78–82. Even among relatively liberal writers, the aspect of black suffering considered most frequently from the antebellum period until World War I and beyond was the plight of the "tragic octoroon," often a female, white in appearance but relegated by blood to the scorned black race. Some of these works seemed to suggest that desirable qualities inhered in direct proportion to the number of one's white ancestors, and that miscegenation— and indeed blackness itself—were a curse. See Sterling Brown, *Negro Poetry and Drama* (1937; reprint edition, New York: Atheneum, 1969), p. 113.

20. Brown, *Negro in American Fiction*, pp. 77–78 and 100–114; and Brown, *Negro Poetry and Drama*, chapter 3, especially pp. 32–36, 37–38, and 42.

21. See Carl Wittke, *Tambo and Bones: A History of the American Minstrel Stage* (Durham: Duke University Press, 1930), pp. 123–132 and 257; Davidson, "American Minstrel Show," pp. 208–210; and Joseph Boskin, *Sambo: The Rise & Demise of an American Jester* (New York and Oxford: Oxford University Press, 1986), pp. 85–90 and 93. See also Joseph Csida and June Bundy Csida, *American Entertainment: A Unique History of Popular Show Business* (New York: Billboard, 1978), p. 157.

22. Toll, *Blacking Up*, chapters 7 and 8.

23. Brown, *Negro Poetry and Drama*, p. 91. On the constraints and dilemmas that faced black minstrels—and, by extension, other black performers—see Toll, *Blacking Up*, pp. 196, 202, and 228.

24. See Lawrence W. Levine, *Black Culture and Black Consciousness: Afro-American Folk Thought from Slavery to Freedom* (New York: Oxford University Press, 1977), pp. 360–361.

25. Peoria *Journal and Transcript*, January 22, 1935, and [Davenport, Iowa, late January 1935], " 'Andy,' of Famous Radio Team . . . ," both in scrapbook #12, GC–USC; and Milne in Boston *Post*, March 2 and 9, 1930.

26. Milne in Boston *Post*, March 9, 1930; and [Davenport, Iowa, late January 1935], " 'Andy,' of Famous Radio Team . . . ," in scrapbook #12, GC–USC.

27. Milne in Boston *Post*, March 9, 1930; Peoria *Journal and Transcript*, January 22, 1935, and [Davenport, Iowa, late January 1935], " 'Andy,' of Famous Radio Team . . . ," both in scrapbook #12, GC–USC; and Moline (Illinois) *Dispatch*, March 14, 1930, in scrapbook #6, GC–USC.

28. Program, Jollies of 1918, Davenport Elks, directed by Joe Bren Company, November 1, 2, and 3, 1917, in Correll family collection; Milne in Boston *Post*, March 2 and

9, 1930; *All About Amos 'n' Andy*, pp. 16–17; program, Benefit Minstrel and Revue, Arsenal Workers Clubs of Davenport and Rock Island, December 5, 6, and 7, 1918 (in which Correll directed his fellow munitions workers, perhaps in his first assignment for the Bren Company), in Correll family collection; and Peoria *Journal and Transcript*, January 22, 1935, in scrapbook #12, GC–USC (whence the quotation from Correll).

29. Log of performances, seasons of 1919–1920 and 1920–1921, in Charles J. Correll's scrapbook of his career with Joe Bren Company (hereafter cited as Correll/Bren scrapbook), Correll family collection; Milne in Boston *Post*, March 16, 1930; and John C. West in *Chicago Today* magazine, February 6, 1972, in Correll family collection.

30. Correll/Bren scrapbook; and Dolly Dalrymple in Birmingham (Alabama) *Age-Herald*, February 19, 1922, located (despite date of item) in box, "Amos & Andy—Loose Scrapbook Pages by Year—1930–35," (hereafter cited as box, "Scrapbook Pages—1930–35"), folder "c. 1933–35," GC–USC.

31. Correll/Bren scrapbook, in particular the following: [Kewanee, Illinois, December 1920?], " 'Jollies of 1920' Scores Highly . . ."; [Warren, Pennsylvania, fall 1920?] (whence the quotation); [Kewanee, Illinois, December 1920?], "All Ready for Curtain . . ."; and [Independence, Kansas, fall 1920?].

Many of the items in the Correll/Bren scrapbook were clipped in such a way as to obliterate publication dates or names of newspapers. Information given in brackets in this and other notes has been determined from the content of each article or from comparisons with Correll's schedule for 1919–1921. Where other elements of a standard citation are not available, this and many later notes include one or more of the following: a full or partial headline, the title of the Bren show discussed in a given press item, or the name of the organization sponsoring the show.

32. Dalrymple in Birmingham *Age-Herald*, February 19, 1922, in box, "Scrapbook Pages—1930–35," GC–USC.

33. On Gosden and Correll's "clowning," see [Kewanee, Illinois], December [1920?], "Three Wild Men Stop Traffic . . . ," in Correll/Bren scrapbook. On minstrel parades, see Charlotte *Observer* [September 16, 1920?], American Legion Jollies of 1920, and [Warren, Pennsylvania, fall 1920?], "Minstrels Unable to Parade," both in Correll/Bren scrapbook; and Milne in Boston *Post*, March 23, 1930.

34. Milne in Boston *Post*, March 9 and 16, 1930 (which describes the recruitment of Bren directors); *All About Amos 'n' Andy*, p. 22; Richmond *Times-Dispatch*, January 9, 1949; Richmond *Times-Dispatch*, April 14, 1936, and Richmond *News Leader*, May 15, 1946, both of which are found in FFG–RPL (both these chronicles, however, err as to the year Gosden joined the Bren Company); Peoria *Journal and Transcript*, January 22, 1935, in scrapbook #12, GC–USC (quoting Correll himself); Jeremy Woods in *Screen and Radio Weekly*, a section of the Detroit *Free Press*, August 6, 1939, in Correll family collection (a later rendition of Correll's own version of the story); and Jerry Lazarus in Richmond *Times-Dispatch*, August 20, 1981, FFG–RPL (based on a telephone interview with Gosden in 1981, more than six decades after his first meeting with Correll). These accounts differ somewhat in narrative detail and chronology; but the best evidence, from the Correll/Bren scrapbook and elsewhere, suggests that Gosden caught the Bren Company's eye in 1919–1920 and was sent to join Correll at the beginning of the 1920–1921 tour.

35. On Gosden's role at Durham, see [Durham, North Carolina], February 17 [1935], in scrapbook #12, GC–USC. On Correll and Gosden's joint participation in later engagements, see Charlotte *Observer*, September 17, 1920, and two clippings, [Warren, Pennsylvania, fall 1920?], all in Correll/Bren scrapbook; West in *Chicago Today* magazine, February 6, 1972, in Correll family collection; and *All About Amos 'n' Andy*, pp. 27–28. That Correll and Gosden's duets included humorous patter is suggested by the description of a similar appearance in another town by pianist Correll and Joe Bren himself. (Two clippings, [Bellefontaine (Ohio) *American*, c. February 16–18, 1920], Elks Jollies of 1920, in Correll/Bren scrapbook.)

36. [Kewanee, Illinois, December 1920?], Jollies of 1920, in Correll/Bren scrapbook; Milne in Boston *Post*, March 23, 1930; Ashland (Ohio) *Times-Gazette* [c. March 9–11, 1921], "Comedy Revue Presentation," and [Winston-Salem, North Carolina? early spring 1921?] (with quotation on Gosden's monologue), both in Correll/Bren scrapbook.

37. Correll/Bren scrapbook, particularly the following: [Bellefontaine *American*, c. February 16–18, 1920], Elks Jollies of 1920; Charlotte *Observer*, September 17, 1920; Ashland *Times-Gazette* [c. March 9–11, 1921], "Comedy Revue Presentation"; [Warren, Pennsylvania, fall 1920], " 'Jollies of 1920' . . . Is Enjoyed by a Capacity Crowd"; [Winston-Salem, North Carolina? spring 1921?]; and [Nashville, c. February 1921], "Legion's 'Jollies of 1921' Proves Wonderful Success." Also, advertising circular, Joe Bren Production Co. (1925), located (despite its date) in "Freeman F. Gosden— Scrapbook (1926–30)," GC–USC. [Morgantown, West Virginia] *Post*, October 3, 1923, in Correll/Bren scrapbook, shows that the basic elements of the first act remained the same three years later, although their specific setting and the devices used to introduce them had changed.

38. Toll, *Blacking Up*, pp. 161–162, 53–54, 76, and 77.

39. Correll/Bren scrapbook, particularly Ashland *Times-Gazette* [c. March 9–11, 1921], "Comedy Revue Presentation."

40. Toll, *Blacking Up*, pp. 66, 80–82, and 84 (on some early minstrels' portrayals of the inhumanity of slavery), and pp. 87–88 and 97 (on the abandonment of such themes by the minstrels, who Toll says hated abolitionism and feared disunion).

41. See Toll, *Blacking Up*, pp. 78–79 and 187.

42. [Kewanee, Illinois, December 1920], " 'Jollies of 1920' Scores Highly . . ."; [Morgantown] *Post*, October 3, 1923; Charlotte *Observer*, September 17, 1920; and two clippings, [Bellefontaine *American*, c. February 16–18, 1920], Elks Jollies of 1920; all in Correll/Bren scrapbook.

43. Program, Jollies of 1922, Elks Lodge, Logansport [Indiana], January 2–3, 1922, in Correll family collection; Dalrymple in Birmingham *Age-Herald*, February 19, 1922, in box, "Scrapbook Pages—1930–35," GC–USC; and the following items in Correll/ Bren scrapbook: n.p. [c. January 3, 1922], Elks Jollies of 1922; [Beaumont (Texas) *News*, 1921 or 1922], "Shriner's [sic] Show Pleases Large Audience Here"; Columbus (Georgia) *Ledger*, May 21, 1922; [Rock Island, Illinois, fall 1920].

44. [Beaumont *News*, 1921 or 1922], "Shriner's Show Pleases Large Audience Here," in Correll/Bren scrapbook.

45. See Toll, *Blacking Up*, pp. 55–56, 70–71, and 162.

46. [Beaumont *News*, 1921 or 1922], "Shriner's Show Pleases Large Audience Here," in Correll/Bren scrapbook.

47. Columbus *Ledger,* May 21, 1922; and [Rock Island, Illinois, fall 1920]; both in Correll/Bren scrapbook.
48. [Kewanee, Illinois, December 1920], " 'Jollies of 1920' Scores Highly . . . ," in Correll/Bren scrapbook.
49. Charlotte *Observer,* September 17, 1920, in Correll/Bren scrapbook.
50. Ashland *Times-Gazette* [c. March 9–11, 1921], "Comedy Revue Presentation," in Correll/Bren scrapbook.
51. On nineteenth-century minstrels' jaundiced view of "modern" women of their own time, see Toll, *Blacking Up,* pp. 162–163 and 183–184; and Davidson, "American Minstrel Show," pp. 113–114.
52. West in *Chicago Today* magazine, February 6, 1972, in Correll family collection; Dalrymple in Birmingham *Age-Herald,* February 19, 1922, in box, "Scrapbook Pages—1930–35," GC–USC (source of the quotation on "young . . . matrons"); [Durham, North Carolina, c. September 1, 1920?] (whence the "bevy" quotation), and [Morgantown] *Post,* October 3, 1923, both in Correll/Bren scrapbook; and advertisement [Clinton, Iowa], n.d., Elks show, in Correll family collection (which contains the final two phrases quoted in this paragraph).
53. [Morgantown] *Post,* October 3 and 4, 1923, in Correll/Bren scrapbook.
54. Milne in Boston *Post,* March 16, 1930.
55. [Morgantown] *Post,* October 3 and 4, 1923, in Correll/Bren scrapbook.
56. See Toll, *On with the Show,* pp. 118 and 121; and Brown, *Negro Poetry and Drama,* pp. 111–112.
57. Advertisement [Clinton, Iowa], n.d., Elks show, in Correll family collection; and the following items from Correll/Bren scrapbook: Kankakee (Illinois) [*Republican*], November 6, 1919, Follies of 1920; Morgantown (West Virginia) *New H*[——?] (remainder of newspaper's name cut off), October 2, 1923; [Bellefontaine *American,* c. February 16–18, 1920], Elks Jollies of 1920; Waterloo (Iowa) *Evening Courier and* [——?] (remainder of name cut off), [fall 1920], "Elks Star Again as Minstrel Men."
58. West in *Chicago Today* magazine, February 6, 1972, in Correll family collection. See also [Winston-Salem, North Carolina? spring 1921?], in Correll/Bren scrapbook; and Milne in Boston *Post,* March 16, 1930.
59. [Winston-Salem? spring 1921?]; and Morgantown *Post,* October 4, 1923; both in Correll/Bren scrapbook. See also [Morgantown, 1922–1923 season], "Kiwanis Show Is Repeated," in Correll/Bren scrapbook.
60. Correll, log of performances, seasons of 1919–1920 and 1920–1921, in Correll/Bren scrapbook; notes on fragment of another notebook cover, in Correll family collection; Dalrymple in Birmingham *Age-Herald,* February 19, 1922, in box, "Scrapbook Pages—1930–35," GC–USC; and the following in "Freeman F. Gosden, Scrapbook (1926–30)," GC–USC: advertising prospectus, Joe Bren Production Co. (1925), and [Ottawa, Ontario] *Journal,* March 25, 1925.

4. Inventing Radio and Toying with Color

1. See Rosalind K. Shaffer in Richmond *News Leader* (syndicated item), March 17, 1942, in file, "Gosden, Freeman F.," Richmond Public Library (hereafter cited as FFG–RPL).
2. J. R. Milne in Boston *Post,* March 23, 1930; [Warren, Pennsylvania, fall 1920?], "Minstrels Unable to Parade," in Charles J. Correll's scrapbook of his career with Joe

Bren Company (hereafter cited as Correll/Bren scrapbook); Peoria *Journal and Transcript*, January 22, 1935, in scrapbook #12, Gosden–Correll Collection, Cinema–Television Library and Archives of Performing Arts, Doheny Library, University of Southern California (hereafter cited as GC–USC); *All About Amos 'n' Andy and Their Creators Correll and Gosden* (New York, Chicago, and San Francisco: Rand McNally, 1929), p. 28; and Shaffer in Richmond *News Leader*, March 17, 1942, in FFG–RPL. (In this and subsequent notes, dates and other information that are missing from cited newspaper clippings are supplied in brackets whenever possible.)

3. Jenkintown (Pennsylvania) *Times-Chronicle*, April 24, 1930, in scrapbook #10, GC–USC. On Correll's first marriage, see [Elizabeth City, North Carolina, c. March 1921?], "Introducing," in Correll/Bren scrapbook.

4. Charles J. Correll, notes on early life, and John C. West in *Chicago Today* magazine, February 6, 1972 (whence the quotation), both in Correll family collection; Milne in Boston *Post*, March 30, 1930; and advertising prospectus, Joe Bren Production Co. (1925), in "Freeman F. Gosden—Scrapbook (1926–30)," GC–USC.

5. Jeremy Woods in *Screen and Radio Weekly* section of Detroit *Free Press*, August 6, 1939, in Correll family collection (whence the quotation); Milne in Boston *Post*, February 23, 1930; and log of performances, 1920–1921, in Correll/Bren notebook (which would seem, by contrast to Woods, to place the New Orleans broadcast in the spring of 1921.)

6. Woods in Detroit *Free Press*, August 6, 1939, in Correll family collection; Milne in Boston *Post*, February 23 and March 30, 1930; advertising prospectus, Joe Bren Production Co. (1925), and [Ottawa, Ontario] *Journal*, March 25, 1925, both in "Freeman F. Gosden—Scrapbook (1926–30)," GC–USC; and Arthur Frank Wertheim, *Radio Comedy* (New York: Oxford University Press, 1979), p. 20.

7. Chicago *Evening Post Radio Magazine*, April 9, 1925, and [Chicago? early April 1925?], both in "Freeman F. Gosden—Scrapbook (1926–30)," GC–USC; Wertheim, *Radio Comedy*, pp. 20–21; radio logs, Chicago *Daily News*, May and June 1925; Peoria *Journal and Transcript*, January 22, 1935, in scrapbook #12, GC–USC; and the following two items in Correll family collection: West in *Chicago Today* magazine, February 6, 1972, and Bill Irvin in Chicago *American*, May 25, 1968.

8. Chicago *Daily News*, June 16, 1925.

9. See Chicago *Daily News*, May 10 and 31, June 7, and July 8, 1925. On Hoover's role, see Erik Barnouw, *A History of Broadcasting in the United States*, vol. I: *A Tower in Babel* (New York: Oxford University Press, 1966), pp. 174 and 177–180 (quotation from Zenith Corporation, *The Zenith Story*, p. 8, cited in Barnouw, p. 180); and Joan Hoff Wilson, *Herbert Hoover: Forgotten Progressive* (Boston and Toronto: Little, Brown, 1975), pp. 112–113.

10. Chicago *Daily News*, May 31, 1925, characterized the pact of silence as a "gentlemen's agreement." See also Barnouw, *A Tower in Babel*, pp. 93 and 207.

11. Chicago *Daily News*, January 4 ("Dialog" column, on problems of reception and other trials of "radio life"), May 3 (advertisement for Statichoke), June 14 (whence the quoted headline), and June 28; all 1925.

12. Chicago *Daily News*, June 28, July 10, and October 9, 1925; and Barnouw, *A Tower in Babel*, p. 180 (on changes in the broadcasting press).

13. See Barnouw, *A Tower in Babel*, pp. 148–150; and William Hedges in Chicago *Daily News*, December 26, 1925.

14. By 1927, the anticipated early arrival of television was discussed almost offhandedly; see Quin A. Ryan in Chicago *Daily News*, November 13, 1927. On the Klan's ambitions, see Chicago *Daily News*, July 3, 1925.

15. Chicago *Tribune*, May 3, 1925.

16. Chicago *Evening Post Radio Magazine*, April 9, 1925, in "Freeman F. Gosden— Scrapbook (1926–30)," GC–USC; photograph of Correll and Gosden with promotional caption in *Radio Magazine*, August 12, 1925, cited by Esther Shultz, Chicago *American* [mid-August 1935], in scrapbook #12, GC–USC; and packet of Correll and Gosden sheet music, in Correll family collection.

17. *All About Amos 'n' Andy*, pp. 31–32.

18. George T. Simon, *The Big Bands* (New York: Macmillan, 1967), p. 503 (whence the characterization of Ash's band); and Chicago *Daily News*, October 30 and December 16, 1925.

19. See motion picture columns, Chicago *Daily News*, August–December 1925, in particular September 26, October 17, and November 5.

20. Chicago *Daily News*, September 12, 1925 (cf. Chicago *Tribune*, July 15, 1927); Abel Green and Joe Laurie Jr., *Show Biz from Vaude to Video* (New York: Henry Holt, 1951), p. 217; and *Radio Digest*, September 1925, in "Freeman F. Gosden— Scrapbook (1926–30)," GC–USC.

21. Carl Sandburg in Chicago *Daily News*, September 17, 1925; and *Daily News*, September 12, 21, and 23, 1925.

22. *All About Amos 'n' Andy*, p. 32; and Chicago *Daily News*, October 3 (whence the quotation) and October 7, 1925.

23. *All About Amos 'n' Andy*, p. 32; and Richmond *News Leader* [c. November 1925– early January 1926], "Richmond Lad Is Heard over Radio," in "Freeman F. Gosden— Scrapbook (1926–30)," GC–USC.

24. Wertheim, *Radio Comedy*, pp. 21–23 (citing interview with Correll, *Same Time . . . Same Station*, KRLA radio broadcast, Los Angeles, January 10, 1973, and Les Tremayne, interview with Henry Selinger, January 10, 1973, Pacific Pioneer Broadcasters); Peoria *Journal and Transcript*, January 22, 1935, in scrapbook #12, GC–USC (citing Correll himself); Milne in Boston *Post*, March 30, 1930; Shaffer in Richmond *News Leader* (syndicated item), March 18, 1942, in FFG–RPL; *All About Amos 'n' Andy*, pp. 32–34; James R. Crowell in *American Magazine*, April 1930, in box, "Scrapbook Pages—1930–35," GC–USC; Jerry Lazarus in Richmond *Times-Dispatch*, August 20, 1981, in FFG–RPL; and the following two items in Correll family collection: Daniel D. Calibraro (ed.) (text by John Fink), *WGN: A Pictorial History* (Chicago: 1961), pp. 28–30; and West in *Chicago Today* magazine, February 6, 1972. These accounts differ as to details; the narrative given here contains those facts that emerge from careful comparison of the sources.

25. Richmond *News Leader* [c. November 1925–early January 1926], "Richmond Lad Is Heard over Radio," and Rockford (Illinois) *Register-Gazette*, October 4, 1926, both in "Freeman F. Gosden—Scrapbook (1926–30)," GC–USC; and Brian Rust (compiler), *The Victor Master Book* (Pinner, Middlesex, England: published by compiler, 1969), vol. II, p. 41.

26. Chicago *Tribune*, July 10, 1927; Wertheim, *Radio Comedy*, p. 23; Woods in Detroit *Free Press*, August 6, 1939, Correll family collection; Shaffer in Richmond *News Leader*, March 17 and 18, 1942, in FFG–RPL; and Rust, *Victor Master Book*, vol. II, pp. 26, 33, and 41. In GC–USC: *Microphone*, March 1930, in box, "Scrapbook

Pages—1930–35," folder "1930"; C. B. (Bud) Kingston in Bridgeport (Connecticut) *Herald,* March 20, 1930, in scrapbook #8; and Ruth Geri, "The Woman Behind Amos and Andy," *Radio Mirror* [late 1934 or 1935], in scrapbook #12, all of which contain more than the usual number of factual errors or confuse parts of the story, but which all concur on Gosden and Correll's use of the "Kinky Kids" act on WGN.

27. Woods in Detroit *Free Press,* August 6, 1939 (which wrongly places McCanna's proposal in March 1926), Calibraro and Fink, *WGN: A Pictorial History,* pp. 28–30, and West in *Chicago Today* magazine, February 6, 1972, all three in Correll family collection; and Wertheim, *Radio Comedy,* pp. 23–24. See also Shaffer in Richmond *News Leader,* March 18, 1942, in FFG–RPL (which, however, wrongly states that WGN could not adapt any already existing comic strip owing to copyright laws; the Chicago *Tribune,* Gosden and Correll's employer, itself owned rights to *The Gumps*).

28. *All About Amos 'n' Andy,* p. 35; West in *Chicago Today* magazine, February 6, 1972, in Correll family collection (which quotes Correll as saying that, "since we'd done minstrel material in the home talent shows, we settled on two Negro characters from Birmingham" for the radio series); and Gosden, quoted by Jerry Lazarus, Richmond *Times-Dispatch,* August 20, 1981, in FFG–RPL.

29. Peoria *Star,* February 6, 1928, in scrapbook, "Sam 'n' Henry (1926–27)," GC–USC, and Peoria *Journal and Transcript,* January 22, 1935, in scrapbook #12, GC–USC, state that the actors' identities were kept secret for four months or more. But in fact, a Victor Company list of new record releases identified the actors behind the radio characters somewhat more than three months after the premiere of *Sam 'n' Henry.* (Scrapbook, "Sam 'n' Henry [1926–27]," in GC–USC.) The first quoted phrase in this paragraph is Correll's. (West in *Chicago Today* Magazine, February 6, 1972, in Correll family collection.)

30. Calibraro and Fink, *WGN: A Pictorial History,* pp. 28–30, in Correll family collection; and the following in scrapbook, "Sam 'n' Henry (1926–27)," GC–USC: Quin A. Ryan in Chicago *Tribune,* January 2, 1927; Chicago *Tribune* [c. February 2, 1926]; [*The Trib* magazine], April 1926, "Sam 'n' Henry Go East . . ."; and letter, F. J. Ashley to L. M. Schrieber (*sic*), March 28, 1927. The *Tribune*'s story of a rush of phone calls in response to *Sam 'n' Henry*'s absence from the air is consistent with more objective indications of the show's popularity, some of which are cited in this and later notes.

31. Chicago *Tribune,* September 18, 1927; and the following in scrapbook, "Sam 'n' Henry (1926–27)," GC–USC: Chicago *Tribune,* January 9, 1927; and two press releases [Chicago *Tribune* Company, early September 1926]. At the Radio Industries Banquet of 1926, Gosden and Correll performed a "song-and-patter" routine as well as *Sam 'n' Henry* dialogue.

32. Chicago *Tribune,* September 18, 1927, and the following in scrapbook, "Sam 'n' Henry (1926–27)," GC–USC: Chicago *Tribune,* May 23, 1926, and May 1, 8, 15, and 29, 1927; Chicago *Tribune Sports Almanac,* 1927.

33. Newspaper advertisement, Corley Company [Richmond, c. April 1926], located (despite its actual date of publication) in box, "Scrapbook Pages—1930–35," folder "c. 1933–35"; Rockford (Illinois) *Register-Gazette,* October 5, 1926, in "Freeman F. Gosden—Scrapbook (1926–30)"; and the following in scrapbook, "Sam 'n' Henry (1926–27)": circulars titled "New Victor Records," reprints of Victor newspaper advertisements, and other Victor promotional material, 1926; circulars, "Sam 'n'

Henry," Philadelphia Victor Distributors Inc. and Werlein's Victrola Service (New Orleans) [both 1926 or 1927]. All these items are in GC–USC.

34. Charles J. Correll and Freeman F. Gosden, *Sam 'n' Henry* (Chicago: Shrewesbury Publishing Co., 1926); report, "Investigation of the Metropolitan Section," in scrapbook, "General Publicity (1928–32)," GC–USC; and the following in scrapbook, "Sam 'n' Henry (1926–27)," GC–USC: numerous advertisements for Metropolitan Section, Chicago *Tribune*; promotional circular, "Now They're in the Newspapers!" issued by Chicago *Tribune* Newspapers Syndicate (1927); Louisville *Courier-Journal*, April 15, 1927; Montgomery Ward & Co. Spring and Summer Catalogue, 1927. The *Sam 'n' Henry* column ran in the Sunday *Tribune* from February to October 1927.

35. Advertisement, C. & S. Specialty Co., reprint from *Junior Home Magazine* [1926 or 1927]; promotional materials, candy wrapper, etc., Shotwell Mfg. Co. (1927); and *International Confectioner*, February 1927; all in scrapbook, "Sam 'n' Henry (1926–27)," GC–USC.

36. On Gosden and Correll's weekly salary, see Crowell in *American Magazine*, April 1930, in box, "Scrapbook Pages—1930–35," GC–USC. On radio revues, see [Correll and Gosden], script for WGN Radio Revue, n.d. [fall 1926], and Elgin (Illinois) *Courier*, October 2, 1926, both in "Freeman F. Gosden—Scrapbook (1926–30)," GC–USC. On Gosden and Correll's other personal appearances, see numerous clippings in "Freeman F. Gosden—Scrapbook (1926–30)," and scrapbook, "Sam 'n' Henry (1926–27)," both in GC–USC. On their earnings from those appearances, and Correll's metaphor for them: West in *Chicago Today* magazine, February 6, 1972, in Correll family collection.

37. West in *Chicago Today* magazine, February 6, 1972, in Correll family collection, (whence the quotation); and *All About Amos 'n' Andy*, pp. 36–40.

38. Woods in Detroit *Free Press*, August 6, 1939, in Correll family collection (whence the quotation); numerous clippings from personal appearance tour of February–March 1928, in scrapbook, "General Publicity (1928–32)," GC–USC; William S. Hedges in Chicago *Daily News* [c. February 25, 1928], in scrapbook, "Sunday Tribune 1/2 Page 1927—Transition Sam 'n' Henry to Amos 'n' Andy," GC–USC; and *All About Amos 'n' Andy*, pp. 109–110.

39. Charles Correll and Freeman Gosden, *Amos 'n' Andy* radio scripts #1–4, March 19, 20, 22, and 23, 1928, GC–USC, with rejected names marked out and the names "Amos" and "Andy" interpolated by hand; *All About Amos 'n' Andy*, p. 52; Wertheim, *Radio Comedy*, pp. 35–36; and interview with Richard Correll, July 16, 1982, Hollywood.

40. Gosden quoted by Woods in Detroit *Free Press*, August 6, 1939, and Correll quoted by West in *Chicago Today* magazine, February 6, 1972, both in Correll family collection; and *Amos 'n' Andy* radio script #2, March 20, 1928.

41. Gosden quoted by Woods in Detroit *Free Press*, August 6, 1939, and Correll quoted by West in *Chicago Today* magazine, February 6, 1972, both in Correll family collection.

42. See Barnouw, *A Tower in Babel*, pp. 143–150; and William Hedges in Chicago *Daily News*, December 26, 1925.

43. This and the following information on the "chainless chain" come in part from three items in Correll family collection: Woods in Detroit *Free Press*, August 6, 1939; San Francisco *Examiner*, May 2, 1929, in folder, "Pantages Publicity, San Francisco, California" (hereafter referred to as Pantages SF); and Correll, notes on early life.

Other information on the "chainless chain" comes from Peoria *Journal and Transcript*, January 22, 1935, in scrapbook #12, GC–USC; Jerry Lazarus in Richmond *Times-Dispatch*, August 20, 1981, FFG–RPL; and *All About Amos 'n' Andy*, pp. 39, 91–94, 110–111, and 115.

44. New York *Telegram*, July 27, 1929, in "Freeman F. Gosden—Scrapbook (1926–30)," GC–USC (whence the quotation); and San Francisco *Chronicle*, May 11, 1929, in Pantages SF. For examples of misidentifications and a misspelling in two papers in one city on a single day, see Curran D. Swint in San Francisco *Daily News*, and A. Fulton Gillaspey in San Francisco *Bulletin*, both May 6, 1929, in Pantages SF.

45. Correll, notes on early life, in Correll family collection; and see Minneapolis *Journal*, June 28, 1929, and Minneapolis *Tribune*, June 30, 1929, located (despite their dates of origin) in box, "Scrapbook Pages—1930–35," folder "c. 1933–35," GC–USC.

46. New York *Telegram*, July 27, 1929, in "Freeman F. Gosden—Scrapbook (1926–30)," GC–USC; Correll, notes on early life, in Correll family collection; and the following, all in Pantages SF, all 1929: San Francisco *Chronicle*, May 11, and *Examiner*, May 5; Gillaspey in San Francisco *Bulletin*, May 6; J. Clarence Myers in San Francisco *Call and Post*, May 2; Oakland *Post-Enquirer*, May 2.

47. Accounts of these events that vary slightly in emphasis or detail but agree on the major points are found in the following items in the Correll family collection: Correll, notes on early life (according to Correll's recollection, the chainless chain "was growing continuously" at the time NBC made its offer); Jay Stewart, quoted by Bill Kennedy in Los Angeles *Herald-Examiner*, July 25, 1973; and Woods in Detroit *Free Press*, August 6, 1939. Yet another account is in Wertheim, *Radio Comedy*, p. 36. Whether Gosden and Correll themselves took any initiative in bringing about Lord & Thomas's proposal to NBC is no longer clear.

48. Correll, notes on early life, in Correll family collection; and New York *Telegram*, July 27, 1929, in "Freeman F. Gosden—Scrapbook (1926–30)," GC–USC.

49. Myers in San Francisco *Call and Post* (whence the quotation), and Oakland *Post-Enquirer*, both May 2, 1929, in Pantages SF; Wertheim, *Radio Comedy*, pp. 50–51; see also San Francisco *Examiner*, May 5, 1929, in Pantages SF. The decoration of cars as Fresh Air taxis by local people was not motivated solely by love of *Amos 'n' Andy*; a prize was offered for the best version.

50. Myers in San Francisco *Call and Post*, May 2, 1929, Pantages SF.

51. Oakland *Post-Enquirer*, May 2, 1929, in Pantages SF.

52. George C. Warren in San Francisco *Chronicle*, May 4, 1929, Pantages SF.

53. Warren in San Francisco *Chronicle*, May 4, 1929, Pantages SF.

54. Warren in San Francisco *Chronicle*, May 4, 1929, Pantages SF, offers the most careful and detailed account of an Amos 'n' Andy performance in San Francisco. See also the following items in other San Francisco papers, Pantages SF: *Call*, May 13, 1929 (which differs from Warren's story in the *Chronicle* only in offering less detail); Swint in *Daily News* and Gillaspey in *Bulletin*, both May 6, 1929 (which differ from the preceding pieces as to details—owing either to careless reporting or to actual changes made by the performers from one show to the next—but which agree on the general outlines of the performances).

55. Warren in *Chronicle*, May 4; *Call*, May 13 (whence the first quotation); and Gillaspey in *Bulletin*, May 6, 1929 (source of the second quotation); all of San Francisco, in Pantages SF.

56. See Swint in San Francisco *Daily News*, May 6, 1929, in Pantages SF.

5. The Great Black Migration into America's Living Room

1. Allan H. Spear, *Black Chicago: The Making of a Negro Ghetto, 1890–1920* (Chicago and London: University of Chicago Press, 1967), p. 141.
2. Charles Correll and Freeman Gosden, *Sam 'n' Henry* radio script #1, January 12, 1926, in Gosden–Correll Collection, Cinema–Television Library and Archives of Performing Arts, Doheny Library, University of Southern California.
3. Charles Correll and Freeman Gosden, *Amos 'n' Andy* radio script #1, March 19, 1928.
4. *Amos 'n' Andy*, script #2, March 20, 1928.
5. Gosden and Correll portrayed Amos as turning thirty during *Amos 'n' Andy*'s first year on the air. (*Amos 'n' Andy*, script #183, October 25, 1928.)
6. *Amos 'n' Andy*, script #5, March 24, 1928.
7. Gilbert Osofsky, *Harlem: The Making of a Ghetto: Negro New York, 1890–1930*, 2nd edition (New York: Harper & Row, 1971), pp. 30–32. For examples of the same phenomenon in the 1930s, see two advertisements in New York *Amsterdam News*: September 16, 1931 (for "Back Home Excursion" by bus to Richmond, Virginia), and September 17, 1931 (for United Sons of Georgia Association Annual Ball).
8. *Amos 'n' Andy*, script #1, March 19, 1928. In *Sam 'n' Henry*, Gosden and Correll did not show their principal characters on the farm at all, and the two migrants mention only incidentally that they have worked as cotton pickers. (*Sam 'n' Henry*, script #6, n.d. [January 17, 1926?].)
9. *Sam 'n' Henry*, script #1, January 12, 1926.
10. *Amos 'n' Andy*, script #11, April 2, 1928.
11. E. K. Means, "The Ten-Share Horse," in *Further E. K. Means* (New York and London: G. P. Putnam's Sons, 1921), pp. 267 and 274.
12. Octavus Roy Cohen, "The Fly and the Ointment," in *Black and Blue* (1926: reprint edition, Freeport, New York: Books for Libraries Press, 1970), p. 42.
13. *Sam 'n' Henry*, scripts #1 and 2, January 12 and n.d. (January 13?), 1926.
14. *Sam 'n' Henry*, scripts #2 and 3, n.d. (January 13 and 14, 1926?).
15. *Amos 'n' Andy*, script #5, March 24, 1928.
16. *Amos 'n' Andy*, script #6, March 26, 1928.
17. *Sam 'n' Henry*, script #2, n.d. (January 13, 1926?).
18. *Sam 'n' Henry*, scripts #4 and 5, n.d. (January 15 and 16, 1926?); and *Amos 'n' Andy*, scripts #7 and 10, March 27 and 31, 1928.
19. *Sam 'n' Henry*, scripts #3 and 5, n.d. (January 14 and 16, 1926?). In *Amos 'n' Andy*, too, the narrator announces in an early episode that the principals' search for a room has taken them to the South Side. (*Amos 'n' Andy*, script #8, March 29, 1928).
20. *Amos 'n' Andy*, script #10, March 31, 1928.
21. *Amos 'n' Andy*, scripts #13, 14, 119, and 133, April 5 and 6, August 11 and 27, 1928.
22. *Amos 'n' Andy*, scripts #125–132, August 18–26, 1928.
23. Cohen, "The Fly and the Ointment," p. 49, and "The Lady Fare," p. 32, both in *Black and Blue*.
24. Thomas Cripps, *Slow Fade to Black: The Negro in American Film, 1900–1942* (New York: Oxford University Press, 1977), p. 122.
25. "The Two Black Crows," Columbia Records #1-219, n.d., in Recorded Sound Division, Performing Arts Research Center at Lincoln Center, New York Public Library.

26. *Amos 'n' Andy*'s dramatic richness so far surpassed anything in vaudeville-style black-face acts that even Thomas Cripps, a modern expert on black performers and black images in entertainment, assumes that the Two Black Crows were second-rate *imitators of* Amos 'n' Andy. (*Slow Fade to Black*, p. 269). In fact, the Crows became widely known well before the debut of *Sam 'n' Henry*. (For a sketch of the Crows' background, itself written before *Sam 'n' Henry* existed, see Chicago *Daily News*, November 20, 1925.)

27. Newport News (Virginia) *Daily Press*, May 9, 1931.

28. On rare occasions, however, a strip might include an incidental black character who, though serving whites and physically caricatured, spoke Standard English. See the waiter in *Somebody's Stenog*, Chicago *Daily News*, September 3, 1925. (But even here the black bellboys speak in "black" dialect.)

29. One writer-entertainer who had given black characters something like a legitimate place in a fictional northern urban environment was Edward Harrigan, creator of multiethnic musical-comedy cityscapes on the stage beginning in the 1870s. But Harrigan had concentrated his attention on Irish-Americans, not on the Afro-Americans who interested Gosden and Correll. See Robert C. Toll, *On with the Show! The First Century of Show Business in America* (New York: Oxford University Press, 1976), pp. 183–189; and Sterling Brown, *Negro Poetry and Drama* (1937; reprint edition, New York: Atheneum; 1969), p. 111.

30. See Spear, *Black Chicago*, pp. 5–126.

31. This chapter and the one that follows, which intensively analyze the content of Gosden and Correll's work, concentrate on *Sam 'n' Henry* and the first year of *Amos 'n' Andy*. This was the period in which the radio team established the central characters and themes of their series. Later chapters will refer to the content of *Amos 'n' Andy* in subsequent years.

32. *Sam 'n' Henry*, script #4, n.d. (January 15, 1926?).

33. *Amos 'n' Andy*, scripts #1 and 2, March 19 and 20, 1928.

34. The traits of Amos and Andy correspond closely to those of Sam and Henry respectively. At some points in the opening episodes of the hastily invented *Sam 'n' Henry*, Gosden and Correll's characterizations were simply confused. But the characters became more consistent and the differences between them more sharply defined in the later episodes of *Sam 'n' Henry* and in its successor series, *Amos 'n' Andy*.

35. *Sam 'n' Henry*, script #2, n.d. (January 13, 1926?).

36. *Amos 'n' Andy*, scripts #2 and 6, March 20 and 26, 1928.

37. *Sam 'n' Henry*, script #5, n.d. (January 16, 1926?).

38. *Sam 'n' Henry*, script #6, n.d. (January 17, 1926?).

39. *Amos 'n' Andy*, script #12, April 3, 1928.

40. *Amos 'n' Andy*, script #1, March 19, 1928.

41. *Amos 'n' Andy*, script #1, March 19, 1928.

42. *Amos 'n' Andy*, script #2, March 20, 1928.

43. *Amos 'n' Andy*, scripts #6 and 8, March 26 and 29, 1928.

44. *Amos 'n' Andy*, scripts #106 and 109–111, July 27, 30, and 31, and August 2, 1928.

45. *Amos 'n' Andy*, script #133, August 27, 1928.

46. Robert C. Toll, *On with the Show*, p. 291.

47. *Amos 'n' Andy*, script #161, September 29, 1928.

48. *Sam 'n' Henry*, scripts #279 and 280, January 4 and 5, 1927.

49. Chicago *Tribune*, April 17, 1927.

50. *Amos 'n' Andy*, script #1, March 19, 1928.

51. *Amos 'n' Andy*, script #5, March 24, 1928.

52. *Amos 'n' Andy*, script #11, April 2, 1928.

53. Arthur Frank Wertheim, *Radio Comedy* (New York: Oxford University Press, 1979), p. 32.

54. *Amos 'n' Andy*, script #97, July 16, 1928.

55. *Amos 'n' Andy*, script #14, April 6, 1928.

56. *Amos 'n' Andy*, script #11, April 2, 1928.

57. *Amos 'n' Andy*, script #120, August 12, 1928.

58. *Amos 'n' Andy*, script #107, July 28, 1928; and selections from "The Two Black Crows," Columbia Records, March 14–December 3, 1927, in Historical Sound Recordings Collection, Yale University Library.

59. *Amos 'n' Andy*, script #165, October 4, 1928.

60. *Amos 'n' Andy*, script #33, May 3, 1928.

61. *Amos 'n' Andy*, scripts #31 and 32, April 30 and May 1, 1928.

62. *Amos 'n' Andy*, script #24, April 20, 1928. One's ability to describe a given character's speech is limited when—as in Charlie's case—recordings of the broadcasts in which the character appeared have not been preserved. Yet Gosden and Correll consistently wrote "Negro dialect" semiphonetically in their radio scripts and adhered closely (though not absolutely) to the scripts when broadcasting. The team wrote the lines of most white characters, and of upper-class (and a few other) black characters, with standard spellings. Especially in Gosden and Correll's early years, there was almost no middle ground between Standard and non-Standard speech, except on the rare and brief occasions when a white immigrant character appeared.

63. *Amos 'n' Andy*, script #38, May 8, 1928.

64. *Amos 'n' Andy*, scripts #175–188, October 15–30, 1928.

65. *Amos 'n' Andy*, script #163, October 1, 1928.

66. "Cupidity/stupidity," it seems, is a turn of phrase so apposite that it almost writes itself; the author disclaims any right of ownership in the formulation, having encountered it elsewhere since writing this passage.

67. Many whites, however, were perfectly capable of laughing at the supposed eccentricities of blacks while overlooking their own. See, for example, the quotation from James T. Farrell's chronicle of Studs Lonigan early in Chapter 8 of this book.

68. *Amos 'n' Andy*, script #81, June 28, 1928.

69. *Amos 'n' Andy*, scripts #93 and 94, July 12 and 13, 1928.

70. *Amos 'n' Andy*, script #58, June 1, 1928.

71. *Amos 'n' Andy*, scripts #151, 122, and 152, September 17, August 14, and September 18, 1928.

72. *Amos 'n' Andy*, script #84, July 1, 1928.

73. *Amos 'n' Andy*, scripts #98 and 99, July 17 and 19, 1928.

74. *Amos 'n' Andy*, script #151, September 17, 1928.

75. *Amos 'n' Andy*, script #12, April 3, 1928. In this and the following long quotation, semicolons have been inserted editorially to facilitate reading. As in other quotations in this work, punctuation has also been partially regularized and some typographical errors corrected for the same purpose.

76. *Amos 'n' Andy*, script #114, August 5, 1928.

77. *Amos 'n' Andy*, script #3, March 22, 1928.

78. See Miller and Lyles, "Traveling," Okeh Records #40118 (recorded 1924), in His-

torical Sound Recordings Collection, Sterling Memorial Library, Yale University; and Thomas Cripps, *Slow Fade to Black*, pp. 225–226.

79. *Amos 'n' Andy*, script #142, September 7, 1928.

6. The Mystic Knights and Their Ladies

1. Jacqueline Jones, *Labor of Love, Labor of Sorrow: Black Women, Work, and the Family from Slavery to the Present* (New York: Basic Books, 1985), pp. 180–181.

2. Jones, *Labor of Love*, pp. 154, 162, and 192–193.

3. Charles Correll and Freeman Gosden, *Amos 'n' Andy*, radio scripts #90–92, July 8–10, 1928.

4. *Amos 'n' Andy*, script #119, August 11, 1928.

5. *Amos 'n' Andy*, script #142, September 7, 1928.

6. Thomas Cripps, *Slow Fade to Black: The Negro in American Film, 1900–1942* (New York: Oxford University Press, 1977), pp. 157 and 160. The quoted phrases are Cripps's.

7. Chicago *Daily News*, August 8, 1928, in scrapbook, "Chicago Daily News Cartoons (1928–29)," Gosden–Correll Collection, Cinema–Television Library and Archives of Performing Arts, Doheny Library, University of Southern California.

8. Similarly, whenever cartoonists juxtaposed heavily caricatured black characters with whites who were caricatured only lightly if at all, that contrast alone sent a potent message. Conceivably, one might look on the caricatured black figures in, say, an advertisement for a minstrel show as mere conventionalized figures not intended to represent a real race of people. A cartoonist effectively denied the reader this option when he placed a bizarre-looking black character in an otherwise relatively realistic setting.

9. *All About Amos 'n' Andy and Their Creators Correll and Gosden* (New York, Chicago and San Francisco: Rand–McNally, 1929), pp. 109–110, states that Gosden and Correll furnished the actual dialogue for the strip. Whether or not this is strictly accurate, Gosden and Correll's decision not to have their women characters speak in the show's early years makes the comic strip especially important as evidence of how the team imagined them.

10. Robert Toll attributes the appeal of these minstrel "yaller gals" to their combination of Caucasian features and light skin with "the exoticism and 'availability' of Negroes." (*Blacking Up: The Minstrel Show in Nineteenth-Century America* [New York: Oxford University Press, 1974], p. 76.) Since the songs sung to, by, and about the "yaller gals" were typically chaste and sentimental rather than "exotic" or erotic, however, it is questionable whether they conveyed enough of a sense of sexual "availability" for this to constitute a major part of the "gals' " appeal. More likely, minstrels portrayed the "yaller gals" as they did for lack of an acceptable alternative: the blacked-up balladeers' romantic songs "worked" only if the "gals" to whom they sang were both black and reasonably comely.

11. This hypothesis deserves to be tested by extensive analysis of documents that survive from the era of minstrelsy. The whole issue of minstrels' portrayals of women, and of male characters in relation to those "women," is one that Toll frames intriguingly, but about which much remains to be discovered.

12. Chicago *Daily News*, September 12, 1925.

13. White women's resentment of their husbands' sexual attentions to black women was no less real; but as the southern diarist Mary Boykin Chesnut noted in the Civil War

era, this resentment did little to circumscribe the lives of white men in a man's world.

14. Disdainful satire of "modern" (white) women, by the way, had been a mainstay of nineteenth-century minstrel-show humor, as Robert Toll shows (*Blacking Up*, pp. 162–163 and 183–184).

15. On "Aunt Dinah Roe," an early "mammy" figure described in a minstrel song of 1850, see Toll, *Blacking Up*, p. 79; on the minstrels' depiction even of the "mammy" and other sympathetic types as racially inferior, see Toll, p. 67.

16. Jones, *Labor of Love*, pp. 166–168 and 177–179.

17. *Harold Teen*, in Chicago *Tribune*, November 27, 1927; and *Larry*, in Chicago *Daily News*, September 3, 1925.

18. *All About Amos 'n' Andy*, pp. 46–47; see also pp. 61–75.

19. Chicago *Tribune*, December 4, 1927. Although the cartoon is British, the *Tribune* found it worthy of prominent display.

20. *Amos 'n' Andy*, scripts #165 and 86, October 4 and July 3, 1928.

21. New York *American*, October 22, 1930.

22. Chicago *Tribune*, November 27, 1927.

23. New York *American*, October 22, 1927.

24. Chicago *Daily News*, December 23 and 26, 1925.

25. Chicago *Tribune*, November 27, 1927.

26. *Amos 'n' Andy*, script #150, September 16, 1928.

27. Amos's faithless former love Mamie does write from Atlanta that her husband has given her a ring with a fake jewel, stolen from her, and "hit [her] in de nose." Andy is pleased to hear of the latter action, but Amos—even after the mistreatment he has suffered at Mamie's hands—is not. (*Amos 'n' Andy*, script #142, September 7, 1928).

28. *Amos 'n' Andy*, scripts #104 and 105, July 24 and 26, 1928.

29. On Gosden and Correll's claims to "wholesomeness," the reasons for those claims, and the meaning of the term in this connection, see Chapter 7.

30. See *Keeping Up with the Joneses*, Chicago *Daily News*, late August and early September, 1925.

31. *Amos 'n' Andy*, script #141, September 6, 1928.

32. But not always; right up to our own day, the *Moon Mullins* comic strip depicted Mamie as an industrious, working-class woman who could wield a rolling pin with the best of them when her husband Willie stepped out of line.

33. Octavus Roy Cohen, "The Lady Fare," in *Black and Blue* (1926; reprint edition, Freeport, New York: Books for Libraries Press, 1970), pp. 3–36.

7. *Amos 'n' Andy*'s Balancing Act

1. Richmond *News Leader* [c. February 27, 1931], in scrapbook, "General Publicity (1928–32)," Gosden–Correll Collection, Cinema–Television Library and Archives of Performing Arts, Doheny Library, University of Southern California (hereafter cited as GC–USC). (In this and subsequent notes, dates and other information that are missing from cited newspaper clippings are supplied in brackets whenever possible.)

2. Chicago *Tribune*, May 3, 1925.

3. Fan letter, Mary Justine Dutt (St. Joseph, Michigan) [February 1929?], in scrapbook, "General Publicity (1928–32)," GC–USC.

4. See Charles J. Gilchrest in [Chicago] *Daily News* [c. 1934], "Two Letters of Criticism

Mean 'Out' . . . ," in scrapbook #12, GC–USC. See also Douglas Gilbert in New York *Telegram*, March 29, 1930.

5. See scrapbook #4, GC–USC, *passim*.

6. Gilchrest in [Chicago] *Daily News*, "Two Letters . . . ," in scrapbook #12, GC–USC; and interview with Elinor Harriot Nathan, July 26, 1983, Beverly Hills.

7. See, for example, Eileen Creelman in New York *Sun*, reprinted in Atlanta *Journal*, April 10, 1930; Duluth *Herald* and Charlotte *Observer*, both April 12, 1930; and Sault Ste. Marie (Michigan) *News*, April 15, 1930; all in scrapbook #9, GC–USC. Arthur Frank Wertheim, *Radio Comedy* (New York: Oxford University Press, 1979), p. 48, makes a similar point about the value of stars' financial coups as a symbolic antidote to the public's Depression blues.

8. See *The Motion Picture* (trade monthly of Motion Picture Producers and Distributors of America), May 1930. The term "indecency" appears in the headline of an article on the new movie code in Boston *Post*, April 1, 1930.

9. Kansas City *Star*, August 30, 1931, in scrapbook C, GC–USC. Gosden and Correll had been announcing that "we want our fun to be clean" since the days of *Sam 'n' Henry*. (Decatur [Illinois] *Review*, January 31, 1928, in scrapbook, "Sam 'n' Henry (1926–27)," GC–USC.)

10. Richmond *News Leader* [c. February 27, 1931]; and unidentified clipping [latter 1930?]; both in scrapbook, "General Publicity (1928–32)," GC–USC.

11. Fan letters in scrapbook, "General Publicity (1928–32)," GC–USC: Frank H. Levell (Bloomington, Indiana), February 24, 1930; Saml. [?] G. Danforth (Arlington, Massachusetts), February 9, 1930; and Octavia Miller (Galesburg, Illinois), February 19, 1929. For similar comments from blacks, see Roy Wilkins, letter to Baltimore *Afro-American*, March 22, 1930; and Philadelphia *Record*, August 14, 1931, in scrapbook C, GC–USC.

12. Quoted by Charles J. Gilchrest in Chicago *Daily News*, July 19, 1932, in scrapbook, "General Publicity (1928–32)," GC–USC.

13. *Bantagrams* (Los Angeles), December 1930, in scrapbook, "General Publicity (1928–32)," GC–USC.

14. See Wertheim, *Radio Comedy*, pp. 36–45, a detailed and subtle treatment of *Amos 'n' Andy* as a Depression comedy.

15. For example, see liner notes, "3 Months with Amos 'n Andy" (record album with selection of radio episodes from February to May 1945), Murray Hill Radio Theatre, Murray Hill Records, 1979. Even Wertheim, a careful and perceptive analyst, implies that *Amos 'n' Andy* owed its popularity above all to its interplay with the real experience of the Depression. He writes, for example, that the radio series made its network premiere "ten months [actually it was ten weeks] before the stock market crash," and that "a year later . . . [it] was a national craze"—which suggests that the crash largely accounts for the craze. (*Radio Comedy*, p. 36.)

16. Charles Correll and Freeman Gosden, *Amos 'n' Andy* radio script #118, August 10, 1928.

17. *Amos 'n' Andy*, script #123, August 16, 1928.

18. See Thomas Cripps, "The Myth of the Southern Box Office: A Factor in Racial Stereotyping in American Movies, 1920–1940," in James C. Curtis and Lewis L. Gould (eds.), *The Black Experience: Selected Essays* (Austin: University of Texas, 1970), pp. 116–144.

19. *Amos 'n' Andy*, script #118, August 10, 1928. It later develops that Ruby Taylor and

her father, too—unlike most black Chicagoans before the 1930s—are Democrats. (*Amos 'n' Andy*, script #123, August 16, 1928.)

20. *Amos 'n' Andy*, scripts #118 and 121, August 10 and 13, 1928.

21. *Amos 'n' Andy*, scripts #7 and 10, March 27 and 31, 1928.

22. On the unexpected drop-off in the movie's drawing power after an initial flood of business, see *Motion Picture News*, November 8, 1930, pp. 35 and 39, and November 15, 1930, pp. 38 and 40; and especially *Exhibitors Herald-World*, November 22, 1930, pp. 19 and 61.

23. *Christian Science Monitor* [mid-January 1930]; unidentified clipping [early October 1929]; and placard advertising Amos 'n' Andy sundae; all in "Freeman F. Gosden— Scrapbook (1926–30)," GC–USC.

24. [Tulsa, Oklahoma, c. March 1928], in scrapbook, "General Publicity (1928–32)," GC–USC; and Rockford (Illinois) *Daily Register-Gazette*, September 29, 1926, in "Freeman F. Gosden—Scrapbook (1926–30)," GC–USC.

25. Advertisement for *All About Amos 'n' Andy*, Chicago *Daily News* [c. March 1929], in scrapbook, "General Publicity (1928–32)," GC–USC; *All About Amos 'n' Andy and Their Creators Correll and Gosden* (New York, Chicago, and San Francisco: Rand McNally, 1929), p. 13 (and again on p. 107); and Mark Barron in Cincinnati *Enquirer*, July 6, 1930, in scrapbook, "General Publicity (1928–32)," GC–USC. See also the item that ran in many small-town papers early in 1930, which contradicted the belief of "thousands of . . . listeners" that Gosden and Correll were black. (Groveland [Florida] *Graphic*, March 27, 1930, and other clippings in scrapbook #10, GC–USC.)

26. Chicago *Tribune*, July 24, 1927, in scrapbook, "Sam 'n' Henry (1926–27)," GC– USC. See also a similar reference to South Side blacks in Decatur (Illinois) *Review*, January 31, 1928, in the same scrapbook. For the complaint of a black Chicagoan who, four years later, still remembered—and resented—the *Tribune*'s equation of her people to Sam 'n' Henry in the department-store article, see Pittsburgh *Courier*, July 18, 1931.

27. [New York?] *Evening World* Radio Section, January 4, 1930, in "Freeman F. Gosden— Scrapbook (1926–30)"; and Baltimore *News Sun* [?], August 3, 1929, in scrapbook, "General Publicity (1928–32)"; both in GC–USC. (The author of the latter item did not identify any other acts that had focused on the Great Migration.)

28. Louisville *Herald*, August 30, 1929, in scrapbook #3; unidentified clipping [Minne-apolis], June 28, 1929, in "Freeman F. Gosden—Scrapbook (1926–30)"; Syracuse *American*, March 28, 1930, in scrapbook #9; and *Saturday Night* (Detroit), August 31, 1929, in scrapbook #3; all in GC–USC. The item from the Louisville *Herald* appeared in a number of other papers as well.

29. Two unidentified clippings [Chicago *Tribune*, both 1927?; one—containing the longer quotation—from December of the year in which it appeared], in scrapbook, "Sam 'n' Henry (1926–27)," GC–USC.

30. See two clippings [Chicago *Daily News*, 1928 or 1929], "Preparing WMAQ Minstrel Show" and "Stars on Fair Hour Tonight," in scrapbook, "Sunday Tribune 1/2 Page— 1927—Transition Sam 'n' Henry to Amos 'n' Andy," GC–USC; and *All About Amos 'n' Andy*, p. 109.

31. Rand McNally Company, advertising circular addressed to book dealers, n.d. [1929], in scrapbook, "General Publicity (1928–32)," GC–USC. See photographs in Chi-cago *Daily News* [July or August 1929], "Amos 'n' Andy Are Going on the Chain";

in Cleveland *Plain Dealer*, July 28, 1929; and in C.D.N. *Circle*, August 20, 1929; all in scrapbook, "General Publicity (1928–32)," GC–USC. See also similar items in many other newspapers, GC–USC.

32. Jim McIntyre quoted in column, "Inside Stuff—Vaudeville," *Variety*, October 29, 1930, in Correll family collection, Los Angeles.

8. A Changing Racial Landscape

1. "A.W.B." in column, "In the Wake of the News," source unidentified, May 18 [1927?], in scrapbook, "Sam 'n' Henry (1926–27)," Gosden–Correll Collection, Cinema–Television Library and Archives of Performing Arts, Doheny Library, University of Southern California (hereafter cited as GC–USC). (In this and subsequent notes, dates and other information that are missing from cited newspaper clippings are supplied in brackets whenever possible.)

2. [Beaumont (Texas?)], n.d., in scrapbook, "Sam 'n' Henry (1926–27)," GC–USC.

3. Niagara Falls *Gazette* (dateline: Fort Worth), July 19, 1930, in scrapbook #6, GC–USC.

4. [Palm Springs, California? February or March 1935?], in scrapbook #12, GC–USC.

5. [Norfolk, February 16 or 17, 1935], in scrapbook #12, GC–USC. Lightning admits he "aint sure" of his last name while giving testimony in the trial of Madam Queen's breach-of-promise suit against Andy. (Charles Correll and Freeman Gosden, *Amos 'n' Andy* radio script #917, March 2, 1931.)

6. Ward [last name not given], letter to Freeman F. Gosden, April 22, 1930, in scrapbook, "General Publicity (1928–32)," GC–USC; and Pittsburgh *Courier*, June 6, 13, and 27, and September 5, 1931.

7. Chatt Campana in Washington *Post*, April 27, 1930, in scrapbook #10, GC–USC. The same author's writings on *Amos 'n' Andy* appeared in the *Radio Digest* under the byline Mark Quest; one of these is cited in Chapter 9, note 8.

8. Two clippings, n.p. [April 1930], "Saved from Prison by Amos 'n' Andy" and "Amos and Andy Soften Judge; Driver Freed," in scrapbook, "General Publicity (1928–32)," GC–USC.

9. New York *Sun*, April 17, 1930, in scrapbook, "General Publicity (1928–32)," GC–USC.

10. Philadelphia *Evening Public Ledger*, March 1, 1930, in scrapbook #1; Buffalo *News*, March 29, 1930, in scrapbook #10; and Springfield (Missouri) *Press*, July 23, 1930, in scrapbook #6; all in GC–USC.

11. James T. Farrell, *Judgment Day* (1935), in Farrell, *Studs Lonigan* (New York: Modern Library, 1963), p. 99.

12. M. R. Patterson in Memphis *Commercial Appeal*, reprinted in Montgomery (Alabama) *Advertiser*, April 4, 1930, in scrapbook #9, GC–USC, and in other papers.

13. Charlotte *Observer*, March 15, 1930, in scrapbook #10, and March 24, 1930, in scrapbook #9, both in GC–USC.

14. Fan letters: W. G. Furry (Van Buren, Arkansas), February 13, 1929; and Julian S. Sibley (Shelbyville, Tennessee), February 25, 1929; both in scrapbook, "General Publicity (1928–32)," GC–USC.

15. Rockford *Daily Register-Gazette*, September 29, 1926, in "Freeman F. Gosden—Scrapbook (1926–30)"; and [Davenport, Iowa, or Rock Island, Illinois, January 27, 1935], in scrapbook #12; both in GC–USC.

16. Douglas Gilbert in New York *Telegram*, March 29 and 31, 1930; and [Tulsa, c. March 1928], in scrapbook, "General Publicity (1928–32)," GC–USC.

17. Maris Anne Lane in *Radio Mirror* [early 1934?]; and Rex Ballard in [Davenport (Iowa) (*Times?*), January 28, 1935]; both in scrapbook #12, GC–USC.

18. Washington *Evening Star*, December 21, 1931, in scrapbook, "General Publicity (1928–32)," GC–USC.

19. See David M. Reimers, *White Protestantism and the Negro* (New York: Oxford University Press, 1965), pp. 51–108; the quotation comes from p. 95.

20. Lydia Glover Deseo in *Epworth Herald* (Chicago: Methodist Book Concern), December 6 [1930], in Correll family collection. Although the movie *Check and Double Check* was hardly the pinnacle of Gosden and Correll's popular or artistic success, it was in a review of that film that Deseo made her comments.

21. See George M. Fredrickson, *The Black Image in the White Mind: The Debate on Afro-American Character and Destiny, 1817–1914* (New York: Harper & Row, 1971), chapter 4.

22. Burris Jenkins, "Amos 'n' Andy, Sermon in the Community Church, Kansas City, Sunday morning, December 13 [1931]," published in *The Christian* (Kansas City), December 19, 1931, in scrapbook #12, GC–USC.

23. Jacob Tarshish, printed transcript, "The Lamplighter" broadcast, January 13, 1935, located (despite its date) in box, "Amos & Andy—Loose Scrapbook Pages—1936–44, 1946–48, 1954," folder "1937," GC–USC.

    Fredrickson, *Black Image*, pp. 327–331, offers a brief look at the waning of romantic racialism in the 1930s and 1940s. The intellectual trend of the '30s is perceptible in the work of Jacob Tarshish himself, who made more of the supposed positive racial traits of blacks in an earlier version of his talk on *Amos 'n' Andy* in 1931 than he would only four years later. See Columbus (Ohio) *Dispatch*, February 2, 1931, in scrapbook, "General Publicity (1928–32)," GC–USC.

24. Francis Roberts in column by Nick Kenny, [New York] *Daily Mirror*, March [7?, 1930], in scrapbook, "General Publicity (1928–32)"; and "Clericus" in Brooklyn *Standard Union*, April 8, 1930, scrapbook #10; both in GC–USC.

25. Elsie Robinson in column, "Listen, World!," newspaper unidentified [c. 1934], scrapbook #12, GC–USC.

26. *Christian Science Monitor* [mid-January 1930], in "Freeman F. Gosden—Scrapbook (1926–30)," GC–USC.

27. New York *News*, [latter] 1929; and "L.A." in *Christian Science Monitor*, April 12, 1930; both in scrapbook, "General Publicity (1928–32)," GC–USC.

28. Robert Randol in Fort Worth *Star-Telegram*, April 29, 1934, in box, "Amos & Andy—Loose Scrapbook Pages by Year—1930–35," folder "1934"; and W. G. Sibley in column, "Along the Highway," newspaper unidentified [early 1930?], in scrapbook, "General Publicity (1928–32)"; both in GC–USC.

29. Heywood Broun in New York *Telegram* [early 1930?], in scrapbook, "General Publicity (1928–32)," GC–USC.

30. John G. Triplett in [Norfolk *Ledger-Dispatch*, late March or early April 1930], in scrapbook, "General Publicity (1928–32)"; both in GC–USC.

31. Denver *Morning News*, April 8, 1930, in scrapbook #10; [Charlotte Geer in] Newark (New Jersey) *News*, February 18, 1930, in scrapbook #7; and Newton Centre (Massachusetts) *Town Crier*, April 4, 1930, in scrapbook #9; all in GC–USC.

32. Charles E. Tracewell in Washington *Star*, reprinted in Kansas City (Missouri) *Star*, February 26, 1930, scrapbook #7, GC–USC.

33. Clipping, n.p. [late 1929?], "Why the Amos 'n' Andy Craze?" in "Freeman F. Gosden—Scrapbook (1926–30)"; and [Atlantic City, c. April 1935], "Amos 'n' Andy On Steel Pier," in scrapbook #12; both in GC–USC.

34. Fan letters: Octavia Miller (Galesburg, Illinois), February 19, 1929; and Mary Justine Dutt (St. Joseph, Michigan) [c. February 1929?]; both in scrapbook, "General Publicity (1928–32)," GC–USC.

35. *Amos 'n' Andy*, script #566, January 14, 1930, and fan letters: Saml. [?] G. Danforth (Arlington, Massachusetts), February 9, 1930; Mary Justine Dutt (St. Joseph, Michigan) [c. February 1929?]; and Chas. L. Hall (Chicago), February 14, 1929; all in scrapbook, "General Publicity (1928–32)," GC–USC.

36. Fan letters: Mrs. Karl E. Allen (Lebanon, New Hampshire), February 26, 1929; and F. M. Hausler [?] and family (Oakland, California), August 19, 1929; both in scrapbook, "General Publicity (1928–32)," GC–USC.

37. Many such synopses are to be found in scrapbook #6 and elsewhere in GC–USC.

38. New York *American* [early 1930?], in scrapbook, "General Publicity (1928–32)"; and "West Orange" in Charlotte Geer column, Newark *News*, April 4, 1930, scrapbook #9; both in GC–USC.

39. *Amos 'n' Andy*, script #971, May 4, 1931; Jack Foster in New York *World-Telegram*, May 5, 1931, in scrapbook, "General Publicity (1928–32)"; Gallipolis (Ohio) *Tribune*, June 11, 1931, in scrapbook #11; Newark *News*, May 5, 1931, in scrapbook, "General Publicity (1928–32)"; all in GC–USC.

40. "A Great Radio Fan" in Charlotte Geer column, Newark *News*, April 4, 1930, scrapbook #9, GC–USC; fan letter, Saml. [?] G. Danforth (Arlington, Massachusetts), February 9, 1930, in scrapbook, "General Publicity (1928–32)," GC–USC; Portland *Oregonian*, April 13, 1930, in scrapbook #9, GC–USC; and J. R. Milne in Boston *Post*, April 27, 1930.

41. [Columbus, Ohio? 1930?], "Named for Amos and Andy," in scrapbook, "General Publicity (1928–32)"; Esther Shultz column, Chicago *American*, October 7, 1935, and two clippings [Youngstown, Ohio, 1934; and n.p., February 10, 1935? (syndicated cartoon)], all in scrapbook #12; and clipping [fall 1929?], "Greensburg Baby Named 'Amos Andy,' " in "Freeman F. Gosden—Scrapbook (1926–30)"; all in GC–USC. See also a number of clippings in scrapbook, "General Publicity (1928–32)," and Port Chester (New York) *Item*, July 21, 1930, in scrapbook #10, both GC–USC.

In at least one case, black twins were christened Amos and Andy, although a white intern at the hospital where they were born was credited with suggesting the names. (Holland [Michigan] *Sentinel*, May 5, 1931 [UP item], in scrapbook #11; and Chicago *Daily News*, February 20, 1931, in scrapbook, "General Publicity [1928–32]"; both in GC–USC.)

42. Clipping, n.p. [c. 1933?], "Ain't 'At Sumpin?," in scrapbook, "1930–34," GC–USC.

43. *American Appraisal News*, quoted on dust jacket, Charles Correll and Freeman Gosden, *Sam 'n' Henry* (Chicago: Shrewesbury Publishing Company, 1926), in scrapbook, "Sam 'n' Henry (1926–27)"; and Ward, letter to Freeman F. Gosden, April 22, 1930, in scrapbook, "General Publicity (1928–32)"; both in GC–USC.

44. [Chicago *Tribune*, early February 1926], "Sam 'n' Henry, W-G-N's Comic Story Makes Hit with Fans," in scrapbook, "Sam 'n' Henry (1926–1927)," GC–USC; Bill Hay, foreword to *All About Amos 'n' Andy and Their Creators Correll and Gosden* (New York, Chicago, and San Francisco: Rand McNally, 1929), p. 8; and Correll quoted by A. B. McDonald in Kansas City *Star*, August 30, 1931, in scrapbook C, GC–USC.

45. Clipping, n.p. [c. 1934 or 1935]; Correll quoted in [Norfolk, Virginia, February 16, 1935], "Amos 'n' Andy, Popular Radio Entertainers . . ."; Gosden quoted in Baltimore *American* [October 28, 1934], "Amos and Andy Here For Week at Theatre"; all in scrapbook #12, GC–USC.

    A word about the term "boy" is in order here. When used by a white person to address a black man, the term has long been understood as deprecatory and patronizing. On the other hand, adult males of both races were often called "boys" in past decades without intent to belittle. For example, Correll and Gosden—in their real-life, white identities—were commonly referred to and addressed as "boys" by columnists, employers, wives, and others. As late as the 1950s, the executives involved in producing the *Amos 'n' Andy* television show referred to the now aging pair of writer/actors as "the boys"—reflecting the usage of the time. (See interview by telephone with James Fonda, August 7, 1982.) While trying always to be sensitive to signs of racist attitudes, then, the historian must not blindly apply today's norms to yesterday's usage.

46. [New York?] *Evening World* Radio Section, January 4, 1930, in "Freeman F. Gosden—Scrapbook (1926–30)"; and Randol in Fort Worth *Star-Telegram*, April 29, 1934, in box, "Amos & Andy—Loose Scrapbook Pages by Year—1930–35"; both in GC–USC. See similar statements in Baltimore *News* [-? (newspaper name cut off)], August 3, 1929, in scrapbook, "General Publicity (1928–32)," GC–USC; and in two items found in scrapbook #12, GC–USC: Gosden and Correll writing in Esther Shultz column, Chicago *American*, October 7, 1935; and clipping, n.p. [c. 1934 or 1935]. The article in the *Evening World* Radio Section went so far as to say that, when Correll and Gosden began broadcasting in 1925, "neither had ever been before an audience, although their profession was the theatre."

47. Arthur I. Waskow, *From Race Riot to Sit-In, 1919 and the 1960s* (Garden City, N.Y.: Doubleday Anchor, 1967), pp. 60–62. (See also p. 103, on the appointment of a mayoral commission on race relations in the 1940s owing to the fear of another riot.) A concise, useful interpretive summary of the Race Commission's work after the riot of 1919 is Waskow's chapter 5, pp. 60–104.

48. See Waskow, *From Race Riot to Sit-In*, pp. 100–101, on the Race Commission's assumption that the fear of future riots would provide the motivation for any progressive changes Chicago's elites might bring about.

49. For a comparison of the treatment of blacks by the major white papers in 1918, see Chicago Commission on Race Relations, *The Negro in Chicago: A Study of Race Relations and a Race Riot* (Chicago: University of Chicago Press, 1922; Arno Press and New York Times edition, 1968), p. 532. See also William M. Tuttle Jr., *Race Riot: Chicago in the Red Summer of 1919* (New York: Atheneum, 1970), pp. 104–105.

50. Chicago *Tribune*, December 25, October 5, and November 20, 1927. Similarly, the *Tribune*'s allegations that the mayor's political machine manipulated the black vote

had become less racially insulting than those before the riot. (See *Tribune*, December 18, 1927; cf. *The Negro In Chicago*, pp. 527–528.)

51. Chicago *Daily News*, August 31 and July 11 (Final Edition), 1925. On the *News*'s policy prior to 1922 regarding use of the term "Negro," see Victor F. Lawson, quoted in *The Negro in Chicago*, p. 549. For other substantial stories about Afro-American affairs appearing in the *Daily News* within a single two-week period shortly after Gosden and Correll left the employ of that newspaper, see issues of January 6, 17, and 18, 1930.

52. Allan H. Spear, *Black Chicago: The Making of a Negro Ghetto, 1890–1920* (Chicago and London: University of Chicago Press, 1967), pp. 77–79 and 122–124.

53. Chicago *Daily News*, March 7, 1929, in scrapbook, "General Publicity (1928–32)," GC–USC.

54. See Alain Locke, "The New Negro," in Locke (ed.), *The New Negro: An Interpretation* (New York: Albert and Charles Boni, 1925), especially pp. 4 and 9.

55. Charles Correll and Freeman Gosden, *Sam 'n' Henry* radio script #417, July 10, 1927, in GC–USC.

56. See J. Fred MacDonald, *Don't Touch That Dial! Radio Programming in American Life, 1920–1960* (Chicago: Nelson-Hall, 1979), pp. 104–109.

57. *Amos 'n' Andy*, script #303, March 14, 1929. Amos and Andy's move to Harlem and to NBC in 1929 was accompanied by a temporary upswing in overt references to characters and institutions as "colored"—especially in the brief narrative introductions to episodes. As in the early Chicago scenes in *Sam 'n' Henry* and the original *Amos 'n' Andy*, these references served notice to listeners that the world of this radio series was an all-black one—a world in which race would never become an issue.

58. [Toledo, Ohio, December 1, 1929], "Radio Celebrities In Person At Paramount," in "Freeman F. Gosden—Scrapbook (1926–30)," GC–USC.

59. Charles E. Silberman, *Crisis in Black and White* (New York: Vintage, 1964), pp. 9–10; and Stokely Carmichael and Charles V. Hamilton, *Black Power: The Politics of Liberation in America* (New York: Vintage, 1967), pp. 5 and 77.

60. Chicago *Daily News*, March 7, 1929, in scrapbook, "General Publicity (1928–32)," GC–USC.

61. For a concise and compelling analysis of how northern whites mediated the conflict in their own minds between the values of freedom and Union, see David M. Potter, *The Impending Crisis: 1848–1861* (New York: Harper Torchbooks, 1976), pp. 36–50. See also William W. Freehling, "The Founding Fathers and Slavery," *American Historical Review*, LXXVII (February 1972), 81–93.

62. A classic discussion of these issues—which draws some conclusions that the author of the present work considers highly debatable—is Charles G. Sellers Jr., "The Travail of Slavery," in Sellers (ed.), *The Southerner as American* (Chapel Hill: University of North Carolina Press, 1960), pp. 40–71. Ronald T. Takaki, *A Pro-Slavery Crusade: The Agitation to Reopen the African Slave Trade* (New York: Free Press, 1971), roots the proslavery ideology of the antebellum white South largely in "moral anxiousness" about slavery itself.

63. Eugene D. Genovese, *Roll, Jordan, Roll: The World the Slaves Made* (New York: Vintage, 1974), p. 48.

64. Erik Barnouw, *A History of Broadcasting in the United States*, vol. I: *A Tower in Babel* (New York: Oxford University Press, 1966), p. 230.

9. The Black Debate Begins

1. Baltimore *Afro-American*, February 22, 1930, in scrapbook #7, Gosden–Correll Collection, Cinema–Television Library and Archives of Performing Arts, Doheny Library, University of Southern California (hereafter cited as GC–USC).

2. St. Louis *Post-Dispatch*, February 21, 1930, in scrapbook #7, GC–USC.

3. Gunnar Myrdal (with Richard Sterner and Arnold Rose), *An American Dilemma: The Negro Problem and Modern Democracy* (New York, Evanston, and London: Harper & Row, 1944), pp. 192 and 183.

4. Myrdal, *American Dilemma*, pp. 943–944.

5. Chicago *Daily News*, February 25, March 7 and 19, 1928, and several clippings with dates cut off, from the same paper, same period, all in scrapbook, "Sunday Tribune 1/2 Page—1927—Transition Sam 'n' Henry to Amos 'n' Andy," GC–USC.

6. Chicago *Defender*, two clippings [c. January 1, 1928?], one in scrapbook, "Sam 'n' Henry (1926–27)," and the other in scrapbook, "General Publicity (1928–32)," both GC–USC. (In this and subsequent notes, dates and other information that are missing from cited newspaper clippings are supplied in brackets whenever possible.)

7. Charles I. Bowen in [Chicago *Defender*, c. 1934], "Here's How Race Aided Start of Amos 'n' Andy," in box, "Amos & Andy—Loose Scrapbook Pages by Year—1930–35," folder "1934," GC–USC.

8. Mark Quest in *Radio Digest* [March 1930?], in "Freeman F. Gosden—Scrapbook (1926–30)," GC–USC.

9. *Christian Science Monitor*, February 20, 1929; and Chicago *Daily News*, March 7, 1929; both in scrapbook, "General Publicity (1928–32)," GC–USC.

10. *All About Amos 'n' Andy and Their Creators Correll and Gosden* (New York, Chicago, and San Francisco: Rand McNally, 1929), p. 9; and Quest in *Radio Digest* [March 1930?], in "Freeman F. Gosden—Scrapbook (1926–30)," GC–USC.

11. Chappy Gardner quoted by Lula Jones Garrett in Baltimore *Afro-American*, January 25, 1930, in scrapbook #5; and Valdo Freeman in New York *Evening World*, reprinted in Hartford *Courant*, April 6, 1930, in brown scrapbook (lacking cover), "Pepsodent"; both in GC–USC. On black radio ownership: J. Fred MacDonald, *Don't Touch That Dial! Radio Programming in American Life, 1920–1960* (Chicago: Nelson–Hall, 1979), p. 333.

12. Kansas City *Call*, December 13, 1929. That many Afro-Americans found *Amos 'n' Andy* authentic and engaging emerges strikingly from contemporary sources; long conversations with Professors Henry N. Drewry (April 5, 1985) and Norman Hodges (February 27, 1985) made this point even clearer and more vivid for the author.

13. Philadelphia *Tribune*, March 20, 1930, in scrapbook #10, GC–USC.

14. Langston Hughes and Milton Meltzer, *Black Magic: A Pictorial History of the Negro in American Entertainment* (Englewood Cliffs, N.J.: Prentice-Hall, 1967), p. 103.

15. Estelle Edmerson, "A Descriptive Study of the American Negro in United States Professional Radio, 1922–1953" (unpublished master's thesis, University of California, Los Angeles, 1954), pp. 19–32, 35, 132–133, 198, 213–216, and 314. On radio's exclusion of jazz performances—and thus of many black musicians—in the early and mid-1920s, see Erik Barnouw, *A History of Broadcasting in the United States,*

vol. I: *A Tower in Babel* (New York: Oxford University Press, 1966), pp. 128–129 and 130–131.

16. Boston *Daily Record,* April 29, 1930, in scrapbook #10, GC–USC.

17. Memphis *Press-Scimitar,* July 9, 1931, in scrapbook #11, GC–USC; and Chicago *Defender,* August 22, 1931.

18. Thomas Cripps, *Slow Fade to Black: The Negro in American Film, 1900–1942* (New York: Oxford University Press, 1977), p. 106 (whence the quotation); and Chicago *Daily News,* October 24, 1930, in scrapbook #11, GC–USC (one of many newspaper stories on the movie premiere show).

19. Chicago *Daily News,* October 4, 1930; Youngstown (Ohio) *Telegram,* June 23, 1931; and Michigan City (Indiana) *Dispatch,* August 8, 1931; all in scrapbook #11, GC–USC. See in addition Buffalo *Evening Times,* May 4, 1930, in scrapbook #10, GC–USC.

20. Chicago *American,* August 29, 1930, in scrapbook #11; and [Chicago] *Examiner,* August 29, 1930, in scrapbook #8; both in GC–USC. Of course, it was white network officials who named this "salute," and the implication in publicity for the broadcast that Harlem saw Amos 'n' Andy as "Its Ambassadors" came from a headline-writer in Chicago who surely was white.

21. Scrapbook from 70th birthday of Charles Correll's father, in Correll family collection, Los Angeles. "We uns wish you the happiest of birthdays," wrote Ellington on behalf of his band. "May each be more happy[,] more healthy than its predecessor."

22. Baltimore *Afro-American,* February 15, 1930, in scrapbook #7, GC–USC. In his response to Mitchell's protest—which is discussed below—Roy Wilkins assumed that Mitchell was a student at Howard, although the latter had not explicitly stated his relationship to the university.

23. Baltimore *Afro-American,* March 22, 1930, in scrapbook, "General Publicity (1928–32)," GC–USC.

24. W. J. Walls in *Abbott's Monthly,* December 1930, pp. 38–40 and 72–74. In that same year, a wire service dispatch from Hot Springs, Arkansas, reported that another black minister, Rev. Arthur D. Williams, had begun protesting against *Amos 'n' Andy,* not because the program's depiction of black life was utterly inaccurate, but rather because it lacked balance and harmed the interests of the race. (New York Evening *Sun,* July 16, 1930, in scrapbook #10, GC–USC.)

25. Pittsburgh *Courier,* August 1 and September 12, 1931; and see Andrew Buni, *Robert L. Vann of the Pittsburgh Courier* (Pittsburgh: University of Pittsburgh Press, 1974), pp. 223 and 228.

26. Pittsburgh *Courier,* September 12, 1931; and *Courier,* May 16, 1931, quoted in Buni, *Vann,* p. 228.

27. Pittsburgh *Courier,* September 12, 1931; and *Courier,* May 16 and April 15 [sic], 1931, quoted in Buni, *Vann,* p. 228. (The latter citation in Buni seems to be in error; April 11 and 18 are the nearest dates on which issues of the *Courier* appeared).

28. Pittsburgh *Courier,* August 1 and September 12, 1931, in scrapbook C, GC–USC; *Courier,* October 10, 1931, cited in Buni, *Vann,* p. 229; and Arnold Shankman, "Black Pride and Protest: The Amos 'N' Andy Crusade," *Journal of Popular Culture,* XII, 2 (1978), 241.

29. Toledo *Times* (Associated Press item), September 14, 1931; Pittsburgh *Courier,* August 22 and 29, and September 5, 1931; Oklahoma City *Times* (AP item), August

7, 1931; and New Bedford (Massachusetts) *Times*, August 28 and 29, 1931; all in scrapbook C, GC–USC.

30. Pittsburgh *Courier*, August 1, 1931, in scrapbook C, GC–USC.

31. Pittsburgh *Courier*, August 1, 1931; and New Bedford *Times*, August 29, 1931; both in scrapbook C, GC–USC.

32. Philadelphia *Record*, August 30, 1931, in scrapbook C, GC–USC.

33. Pittsburgh *Courier*, August 29, 1931, in scrapbook C, GC–USC.

34. Louisville *News*, reprinted in Kansas City *Call*, August 28, 1931.

35. Pittsburgh *Courier*, August 29, 1931, in scrapbook C, GC–USC.

36. Pittsburgh *Courier*, August 22, 1931; and Buni, *Vann*, pp. 229–230. Buni reports that the circulation of the *Courier* was 50,000 or more as of 1930 (p. 223); that of the *Defender*—though declining from some 200,000 in 1925—did not fall as low as 100,000 until 1933 (p. 227).

37. Pittsburgh *Courier*, August 1, 1931, in scrapbook C, GC–USC.

38. Pittsburgh *Courier*, August 1, 1931, in scrapbook C, GC–USC. Although the author of this letter wrote during the *Courier*'s campaign against *Amos 'n' Andy*, he did not comment on the radio series, but only on his race's attainments as a general issue.

39. Pittsburgh *Courier*, August 1, 1931, in scrapbook C, GC–USC; and *Courier*, July 4, 1931. On the issue of stereotyping in *Sunnyboy Sam*, see Shankman, "Black Pride and Protest," 247.

40. See Buni, *Vann*, pp. 40–41 and 231.

41. St. Louis *Times* and Oklahoma City *Times*, both August 7, 1931; Pittsburgh *Courier*, August 22, 1931; and California *Eagle*, September 4, 1931; all in scrapbook C, GC–USC.

42. California *Eagle*, September 4, 1931; and Pittsburgh *Courier*, August 29, 1931; both in scrapbook C, GC–USC.

43. Pittsburgh *Courier*, August 29, 1931, in scrapbook C, GC–USC.

44. Pittsburgh *Courier*, August 1 and 22, 1931, both in scrapbook C, GC–USC.

45. Lincoln (Nebraska) *Star*, September 1, 1931, in scrapbook C, GC–USC.

46. On a supposed NAACP role in the protest, see Pittsburgh *Courier*, May 16 and 30 and June 13, 1931; and also Paoli (Indiana) *News*, July 8, 1931, in scrapbook #11, GC–USC. On the failure of the national NAACP to come to Robert Vann's aid, see Jessie M. Vann, letter to Walter White, July 17, 1951; and Roy Wilkins, letter to Hobart LaGrone, July 25, 1951 (in which Wilkins refers to the NAACP's not "having become excited about" the radio version of *Amos 'n' Andy*); both in National Association for the Advancement of Colored People Papers, II, A, 479, Manuscript Division, Library of Congress. On the Cheyenne NAACP: Cheyenne *Eagle*, August 14, 1931, in scrapbook C, GC–USC. For details of another local NAACP branch's decision not to join the *Courier*'s protest, see Casper (Wyoming) *Tribune*, August 11 and 14, 1931, and Lander (Wyoming) *Post*, August 21, 1931; both in scrapbook C, GC–USC. For an endorsement of Vann's protest by an officer of the NAACP branch in Memphis, see Pittsburgh *Courier*, May 23, 1931.

47. Worcester *Gazette*, August 7, 1931, in scrapbook C, GC–USC; and Newport News *Daily Press*, June 28, 1931. The Worcester lawyer did say that Gosden and Correll for a time had used "a slang word for Negro" that had caused him "some annoyance," but that even this had "been pretty well eliminated." He did not say what the offending term was, and this particular complaint, muted though it was, is a bit puzzling in light of the radio team's reluctance to mention race in their broadcasts.

See also Ottumwa *Courier,* August 10, 1931; Gorry (Pennsylvania) *Evening Journal,* August 12, 1931; and Springfield (Massachusetts) *News,* August 8, 1931; all in scrapbook C, GC–USC.

48. Newport News *Daily Press,* May 12 and June 28, 1931; and Pittsburgh *Courier,* August 8, 1931.
49. Pittsburgh *Courier,* August 29, 1931, in scrapbook C, GC–USC; and Theophilus Lewis in *Amsterdam News,* July 22, 1931. See also Romeo L. Dougherty in *Amsterdam News,* July 15 and August 5 and 12, 1931.
50. Chicago *Daily News* [c. mid-1931], in scrapbook, "General Publicity (1928–32)," GC–USC.
51. Philadelphia *Record,* August 14, 1931, in scrapbook C, GC–USC.
52. Jessie M. Vann, letter to Walter White, July 17, 1951, NAACP Papers, II, A, 479.
53. In the spring of 1932, for example, the *Defender* announced that Gosden and Correll had accepted an invitation to appear with Ethel Waters and other black performers at a benefit performance staged by the local black physicians' association. (Chicago *Defender* [May 1932], in scrapbook, "General Publicity (1928–32)," GC–USC; and *Defender,* May 21, 1932.) The pair politely turned down the *Defender's* invitation to its annual picnic in 1932, however, pleading a conflict with their travel schedule. (*Defender,* July 9 and 16, 1932, in scrapbook, "General Publicity (1928–32)," GC–USC.) For another appearance by the pair, see *Defender,* December 17, 1932.
   Although NBC's newspaper-clipping services monitored the *Courier's* protest closely, Gosden, Correll, and the network never felt compelled to alter their policy of not acknowledging any protests publicly. (See radio column in Boston *Record,* August 8, 1931, scrapbook C, GC–USC.)
54. Buni, *Vann,* pp. 222–227 and 161–170; and for Vann's sniping at the *Defender,* Pittsburgh *Courier,* August 22, 1931, in scrapbook C, GC–USC.
55. Pittsburgh *Courier,* August 1, 1931, in scrapbook C, GC–USC.
56. Pittsburgh *Courier,* September 5, 1931, in scrapbook C, GC–USC, which also contains the quoted phrases laying claim to "almost 100 percent" black support for Vann.
57. Pittsburgh *Courier,* August 1, 1931; and New Bedford *Times,* August 29, 1931; both in scrapbook C, GC–USC.
58. Sterling City (Texas) *News Record,* August 14, 1931, in scrapbook C, GC–USC.
59. Oklahoma City *Oklahoman,* June 28, 1931, in scrapbook #11, GC–USC; Denison (Texas) *Herald,* August 6, 1931, and Waco (Texas) *News Tribune,* August 8, 1931, both in scrapbook C, GC–USC. The disproportionate number of papers from Texas and Oklahoma among clippings hostile to Vann in GC–USC may be partly the product of an especially thorough clipping service employed by NBC for that region; those two states certainly held no monopoly on racism. Many southern newspaper stories on *Amos 'n' Andy* are free of derogatory language and characterizations of blacks. On the other hand, when blatant expressions of racism do occur in coverage of *Amos 'n' Andy,* they are found largely in southern papers.
60. Oklahoma City *Times,* August 11, 1931; and Shreveport *Journal,* August 10, 1931; both in scrapbook C, GC–USC.
61. Portland (Oregon) *Advocate,* August 29, 1931; and Philadelphia *Record,* August 10, 1931; both in scrapbook C, GC–USC.
62. Springfield (Massachusetts) *Union,* August 10, 1931 (see also Springfield *News,* August 8, 1931) in scrapbook C, GC–USC.
63. Toledo *Times,* August 8, 1931; St. Louis *Star,* August 8, 1931; Hillsboro (Oregon)

Independent, August 14, 1931; Fairmont *West Virginian,* August 8, 1931; and Indianola (Iowa) *Register,* August 27, 1931; all in scrapbook C, GC–USC.

64. Buni, *Vann,* pp. 239–243. When Vann wrote his letter to White, he may well have been thinking not only of his recent failure, but also of his disappointments in the earlier fight against *Amos 'n' Andy.* (On what Thomas Cripps calls blacks' "love-hate" for Stepin Fetchit, see Cripps, *Slow Fade to Black: The Negro in American Film, 1900–1942* [New York: Oxford University Press, 1977], pp. 100 and 105–106.)

65. *Crisis,* March 1928, pp. 96–97.

66. Kansas City *Call,* November 29, 1929.

67. Baltimore *Afro-American,* March 22, 1930.

68. Even the New York–based *Negro World*—a classic "movement" newspaper founded by the now-exiled Marcus Garvey—found its clientele no less fractious on the issue of *Amos 'n' Andy* than the rest of black America. The paper endorsed Robert Vann's protest in one editorial, but then dropped the issue quickly and awkwardly in the face of mixed reactions from its readers. (*Negro World,* June 20 and July 11, 1931.)

69. Gilbert Osofsky, *Harlem: The Making of a Ghetto: Negro New York, 1890–1930,* 2nd ed. (New York: Harper & Row, 1971), pp. 43–44.

70. Allan H. Spear, *Black Chicago: The Making of a Negro Ghetto, 1890–1920* (Chicago and London: University of Chicago Press, 1967), p. 168. Spear has found the "myth" (Spear's term) that the behavior of black newcomers brought on racial discrimination repeated in the *Defender* at least as late as 1939 (p. 168, n. 2).

71. Chicago *Defender,* August 15, 1931.

72. Cripps, *Slow Fade to Black,* pp. 236–253, especially pp. 240–242, 249, and 250–253 (the quoted phrases beginning with "cotton scenes" are from p. 242); and Kansas City *Call,* February 7, 1930 (on *Hallelujah!*).

73. Rochester *Times-Union,* reprinted in Pittsburgh *Courier,* June 6, 1931, in scrapbook #11, GC–USC.

74. Pittsburgh *Courier,* May 16, 1931; and Rochester *Times-Union,* reprinted in *Courier,* June 6, 1931. For examples of how Gosden and Correll's broadcasts indicated that the two skilled lawyers were black, see Charles Correll and Freeman Gosden, *Amos 'n' Andy* radio scripts #875 and 893, January 12 and February 2, 1931.

75. Barnouw, *A Tower in Babel,* p. 230.

76. W. J. Walls in *Abbott's Monthly,* December 1930, p. 74. The phrase about "sordidness" comes from the black critic Benjamin Brawley, whom Walls quoted approvingly. See also the condemnation of "vulgar" acts, "shaking . . . hips," and "fiery tongues" in black stage shows by Chappy Gardner, a black entertainment writer, in Pittsburgh *Courier,* January 10, 1931.

77. Chicago *Defender,* August 1 and 15, 1931; and Baltimore *Afro-American,* January 25, 1930, in scrapbook #5, GC–USC.

10. "This Continuing Harm"

1. Unidentified clipping [1937], "Amos or Andy," with illustration by Henry Major, in scrapbook #12, Gosden–Correll Collection, Cinema–Television Library and Archives of Performing Arts, Doheny Library, University of Southern California (hereafter cited as GC–USC). (In this and subsequent notes, dates and other information that are missing from cited newspaper clippings are supplied in brackets whenever possible.)

2. See Don Foster in Chicago *Times,* December 29, 1935, in scrapbook #12; Larry

Wolters in Chicago *Tribune*, December 26, 1935, in box, "Amos & Andy—Loose Scrapbook Pages by Year—1930–35" (hereafter cited as box, "Scrapbook Pages— 1930–35"), folder "1934" (despite date of item); and two clippings, sources unidentified [fall 1936], in scrapbook #12: Pepsodent ad promoting baby-naming contest, and photograph of Gosden and Correll; all in GC–USC.

3. [Vancouver, British Columbia], August 11, 1937, "And They're Still Going Strong"; and Darrell V. Martin in [Pittsburgh?] *Post-Gazette*, May [1937] (whence the quotation); both in scrapbook #12, GC–USC.

4. *Daily Variety*, March 10, 1939, in box, "Amos & Andy—Loose Scrapbook Pages— 1936–44, 1946–48, 1954" (hereafter cited as box, "Scrapbook Pages—1936–54"), folder "1939," GC–USC (on the rise in CBS stock); and Arthur Frank Wertheim, *Radio Comedy* (New York: Oxford University Press, 1979), p. 268, citing ratings figures from Harrison B. Summers, *A Thirty-Year History of Programs Carried on National Radio Networks in the United States, 1926–1956* (Columbus, Ohio, 1958).

5. Lonny Brooks in Los Angeles *Times*, June 17, 1977, in file, "Ernestine Wade," Margaret Herrick Library, Academy of Motion Picture Arts and Sciences, Beverly Hills (hereafter cited as AMPAS). Elinor Harriot said years later that Gosden and Correll had not used black actors earlier in part because there had been few of them available in Chicago. (Interview with Elinor Harriot Nathan, July 26, 1983, Beverly Hills.)

6. Of course, without the cue of dialect, some in the radio audience might assume these characters were white. Yet sometimes an actor managed—with the help of the storyline itself—to suggest such a character's race through oral clues that did not impair the elegance and grace of his or her performance. See the long, dignified monologue of the minister in the episode of December 29, 1944, in which the "dropping" of a few "g's" is the only non-Standard feature. (Record album, "Amos 'n' Andy Classics," Murray Hill Records.)

7. Don Foster column [early December 1936]; and Larry Wolters column [Chicago *Tribune*], December 5, [1936]; both in scrapbook #12, GC–USC.

8. Two unidentified excerpts from newspaper columns [one December 4, 1936, the other slightly earlier], both in scrapbook #12, GC–USC.

9. Wertheim, *Radio Comedy*, pp. 268–269.

10. On the Barrymore appearance: Larry Wolters column [Chicago *Tribune*?], July 31, 1936, in scrapbook #12, GC–USC. An example of a holiday greeting: Charles Correll and Freeman Gosden, *Amos 'n' Andy* radio script #2489, December 31, 1936.

11. See *Variety*, January 5, 1944, in box, "Scrapbook Pages—1936–54," folder "1944," GC–USC.

12. Almena Davis in Los Angeles *Tribune*, March 22, 1942, in box, "Scrapbook Pages– 1936–54," folder "1942," GC–USC. This article does not specify whether it was Gosden or Correll who spoke of having a black employee, but the direct quotation of Gosden in the paragraph that immediately follows suggests that he made this comment as well.

13. James Whittaker in [New York] *Mirror* [first half of February 1933?], in scrapbook, "1930–34," GC–USC.

14. Whittaker in *Mirror*, in scrapbook, "1930–34," GC–USC.

15. Wilson Brown in *Radio Stars*, July [1933?], in scrapbook, "1930–34," GC–USC.

16. Pittsburgh *Courier*, September 2, 1933, on microfiche, "Amos 'n' Andy," in Schom-

burg Center for Research in Black Culture, New York Public Library (hereafter cited as Schomburg); and unidentified clipping, "Amos 'n' Andy Announce Prize Hogs for Farmers" [mid- or late 1930s], in box, "Scrapbook Pages—1930–35," folder "1935," GC–USC.

17. Charles I. Bowen in [Chicago *Defender*, c. 1934], "Here's How Race Aided Start of Amos 'n' Andy," in box, "Scrapbook Pages—1930–35," folder "1934," GC–USC.

18. Unidentified clipping [Atlanta *World?* c. 1935], "Amos 'n' Andy to Be At Georgia," in box, "Scrapbook Pages—1930–35," folder "1935," GC–USC.

19. Unidentified clipping [Ohio], December 26, 194? (last digit cut off), "Says Radio Programs Misrepresent the Negro," on microfiche, "Radio," in Schomburg.

20. Almena Davis in Los Angeles *Tribune*, March 22, 1942, in box, "Scrapbook Pages— 1936–54," folder "1942," GC–USC.

21. Norman Siegel in unidentified clipping, May 21, 1935, "Comedy Programs Highly Favored by Wife of President," in box, "Scrapbook Pages—1930–35," folder "1934" (despite date of item); and Richmond *Times-Dispatch*, May 3, 1939, in box, "Scrapbook Pages—1936–54," folder "1937" (despite date of item); both in GC–USC.

22. Florabel Muir in *Redbook*, March 1948, p. 110.

23. Erik Barnouw, *A History of Broadcasting in the United States*, vol. II: *The Golden Web* (New York: Oxford University Press, 1968), p. 126.

24. Barnouw, *Golden Web*, p. 245.

25. Earl Wilson in clipping, source unidentified, October 27, 1944, in box, "Scrapbook Pages—1936–54," folder "1942" (despite date of item), GC–USC; Muir in *Redbook*, March 1948, p. 110 (whence the quotation); and Howard C. Heyn (Associated Press item) in Richmond *Times-Dispatch*, January 9, 1949, in file, "Gosden, Freeman F.," Richmond Public Library (hereafter cited as FFG–RPL).

26. Interview by telephone with James Fonda, August 7, 1982; interviews with Alvin Childress, July 14 and 31, and August 7, 1982, Los Angeles; and Estelle Edmerson, "A Descriptive Study of the American Negro in United States Professional Radio, 1922–1953" (master's thesis, University of California, Los Angeles, 1954), pp. 19, 30, and 375.

27. Childress interviews; and various letters between executives of CBS and Alvin Childress, in Childress's possession.

28. Fonda interview; Edward T. Clayton in *Ebony*, October 1961, pp. 66–73; K. Lewis Warren in Richmond *News Leader*, June 21, 1950, in FFG–RPL; Charles McDowell Jr. in Richmond *Times-Dispatch*, June 22, 1950, and conversations with McDowell.

29. *Amos 'n' Andy* television audition script (filmed October 6, 7, and 9, 1950), in Theater Arts Library, University of California, Los Angeles (hereafter cited as TAL–UCLA); David C. Phillips, John M. Grogan, and Earl H. Ryan, *Introduction to Radio and Television* (New York: Ronald Press, 1954), pp. 258–261; and interviews with the following: Sig Mickelson (August 11, 1983, San Diego), Childress, Fonda, William and Peggy Walker (August 22, 1983, Los Angeles), and Jester Hairston (August 19, 1983, Los Angeles).

30. Interview with Harry Ackerman, August 17, 1983, Hollywood, concluded by telephone, August 21, 1983; interview with Dave Schwartz, August 7, 1982, Beverly Hills.

31. Ackerman and Childress interviews.

32. Edward T. Clayton in *Ebony*, October 1961; Childress and Schwartz interviews.

33. Walker interview; interview with Jane Gosden, August 14, 1983, Beverly Hills.

34. Henry Louis Gates Jr. in New York *Times*, November 12, 1989.
35. Walker interview.
36. *Amos 'n' Andy* television script #2, "The Counterfeiters Rent the Basement," TAL–UCLA. Thomas Cripps makes a similar point, but without noting a crucial fact: Gosden and Correll themselves established the policy of minimizing racial references a quarter-century before *Amos 'n' Andy*'s move to television—that is, nearly a generation before the post-World War II coming of age of the black middle class that Cripps considers pivotal in the *Amos 'n' Andy* story. See Cripps, "*Amos 'n' Andy* and the Debate over American Racial Integration," in John E. O'Connor (ed.), *American History, American Television: Interpreting the Video Past* (New York: Frederick Ungar, 1983), p. 45. An apparent oversight in a note (n. 36) in Cripps's article also suggests that the "birds" quotation comes from an episode other than the one cited here.
37. *Amos 'n' Andy* script #2, TAL–UCLA. (Scripts of shows #2 and 3 were compared with TV films, Motion Picture Division, Library of Congress.)
38. *Amos 'n' Andy* TV script #3, "Kingfish Has a Baby," TAL–UCLA.
39. Ackerman interviews.
40. Julius Adams in New York *Amsterdam News*, August 12, 1939, quoted in Cripps, "*Amos 'n' Andy*," p. 38; Langston Hughes, "Banquet in Honor," in *The Best of Simple* (New York: Hill and Wang, 1961), p. 44; and Al White in Chicago *Defender*, June 23, 1951. See also Edmerson, "Negro in Radio," pp. 189 and 191–193.
41. Mickelson, Ackerman, and Fonda interviews.
42. *Variety*, July 4, 1951.
43. L. Pearl Mitchell, letter to Gloster B. Current, received July 16, 1951; Mitchell, letter to editors, Cleveland *Plain Dealer*, July 12, 1951; and Gloster B. Current, letter to Mitchell, July 17, 1951; all in National Association for the Advancement of Colored People Papers, II, A, 479, Manuscript Division, Library of Congress (hereafter cited as NAACP Papers).
44. Walter White, letter to Ralph J. Bunche, July 13, 1951; and Bunche, letter to White, July 20, 1951; both in NAACP Papers, II, A, 480.
45. Jessie M. Vann, letter to Walter White, July 17, 1951; Herbert L. Wright, letter to NAACP Youth Councils, College Chapters, and State Youth Conferences, July 19, 1951; and Hobart L. LaGrone, letter to Roy Wilkins, July 21, 1951; in NAACP Papers, II, A, 479.
46. Roy Wilkins, letter to Hobart LaGrone, July 25, 1951, in NAACP Papers, II, A, 479. *Variety*, July 4, 1951, quotes Wilkins as predicting shortly before the premiere of the series that the video version of *Amos 'n' Andy* would be "far worse than it ever was on radio."
47. California *Eagle*, August 23, 1951, quoted in Edmerson, "Negro in Radio," pp. 393–394; and Billy Rowe in Pittsburgh *Courier*, July 7, 1951. Chester Washington, an associate editor of the *Courier* who covered show business and entertainment, had already written that "the video version of 'Amos 'n' Andy' will be making a potent bid to become the greatest television show on earth." (See *Courier* magazine section, June 30, 1951, and Chester L. Washington in *Color*, June 1951, both in CBS-TV publicity packet, GC–USC. See also Washington in *Courier*, June 23, 1951.)
48. Almena Lomax quoted in Gloster B. Current, draft, "Why NAACP Opposes *Amos 'n' Andy* on TV," in NAACP Papers, II, A, 479; Nell Russell quoted by Arnold M.

Rose, "TV Bumps into the Negro Problem," *Printers' Ink,* July 20, 1951; and Al Monroe in Chicago *Defender,* June 16, 1951.

49. Walker interview; *Printers' Ink,* August 17, 1951, on microfiche, "Amos 'n' Andy," in Schomburg.

50. Williams quoted by Edward T. Clayton in *Ebony,* October 1961; Childress interviews; interview by telephone with Maggie Hathaway, August 1, 1982.

51. Mabel K. Staupers, letter to Walter White, July 30, 1951, in NAACP Papers, II, A, 480; and Gloster B. Current, letter to Ardie Halyard, August 10, 1951, in NAACP Papers, II, A, 479.

52. Circular, "Why the 'Amos 'n' Andy' TV Show Should Be Taken Off the Air," attached to Gloster B. Current, letter to NAACP Branches, Youth Councils, and College Chapters, August 16, 1951, in NAACP Papers, II, A, 479.

53. Barbee William Durham, memorandum #11 to Executive Committee and Advisory Board members, Columbus Branch, NAACP, July 7, 1951; and Durham, letter to Blatz Beer Company, July 12, 1951; both in NAACP Papers, II, A, 479. See also Mabel K. Staupers, memorandum to Walter White, August 10, 1951, NAACP Papers, II, A, 480.

54. Arthur B. Spingarn, letter to White, August 1, 1951, in NAACP Papers, II, A, 480. Cripps, *"Amos 'n' Andy,"* emphasizes the middle-class character of the 1951 protest as its main defining element.

55. Miss [Lucille] Black, memorandum to Walter White, December 5, 1951, in NAACP Papers, II, A, 480.

56. Los Angeles *Tribune,* March 22, 1942, in box, "Scrapbook Pages—1936–54," folder "1942," GC–USC.

57. Walker interview.

58. *Journal and Guide,* July 14 (Home Edition) and July 21 (Virginia Edition), 1951; *Printers' Ink,* August 17, 1951, on microfiche, "Amos 'n' Andy," in Schomburg.

59. Walter White, *A Man Called White* (New York: Viking Press, 1948), pp. 3–12; quotation from p. 11.

60. White, *White,* p. 4.

61. Al White in Chicago *Defender,* June 23, 1951.

62. Herbert L. Wright, letter to NAACP Youth Councils, College Chapters, and State Youth Conferences, July 19, 1951; and Gloster B. Current, two letters to NAACP Branches, Youth Councils, and College Chapters, August 16 and September 14, 1951; all in NAACP Papers, II, A, 479.

63. Mickelson interview. For a reference to Mickelson's attendance at the meeting at White's house, see Walter White, letter to Ralph J. Bunche, July 13, 1951, in NAACP Papers, II, A, 480.

64. Mickelson interview.

65. Mickelson interview; and Walter White, memorandum to the files on conference of July 10 with Sig Mickelson, July 11, 1951, in NAACP Papers, II, A, 480.

66. Walter White, memorandum to the files on conference of July 10 with Mickelson, July 11, 1951, and White, memorandum to Algernon D. Black and 17 others, July 11, 1951, both in NAACP Papers, II, A, 480; and Mickelson interview.

67. Walter White, memorandum to the files on conference of July 10 with Mickelson, July 11, 1951; and White, memorandum to Algernon D. Black and 14 others, July 19, 1951; both in NAACP Papers, II, A, 480.

68. Walter White, letter to Edwin J. Lukas, July 9, 1951; and White, memorandum to

the files on conference of July 10 with Lukas, July 10, 1951; both in NAACP Papers, II, A, 480.

69. Gloster B. Current, letter to L. Pearl Mitchell, July 17, 1951, in NAACP Papers, II, A, 479.

70. Walter White, memorandum to the files on conference of July 10 with Lukas, July 10, 1951, in NAACP Papers, II, A, 480.

71. Lester Granger, letter to Lewis Rosenstiel, May 24, 1951, in National Urban League Papers, VII, A, 1, file "Amos 'n' Andy," Manuscript Division, Library of Congress (hereafter cited as Urban League Papers). See also Schenley's full-page advertisement in National Urban League 40th Anniversary Yearbook: 1950 (New York, 1951), p. 118. Unlike Schenley's later advertising (see below), this ad gives no indication whatever that the company perceived any need to justify its sponsorship of Amos 'n' Andy, whose pilot episode had already been filmed, to the League.

72. Chicago Defender, June 23, 1951; and see Journal and Guide, June 23, 1951.

73. See Chicago Defender, June 23, 1951; and Journal and Guide, June 16, 23 and 30 (including a small "news item" on two black sales representatives who worked for Schenley), and July 7 and 14, 1951.

74. Walter White, memorandum to the files on conference of July 10 with Lukas, July 10, 1951, in NAACP Papers, II, A, 480; and White, letters to Jessie Vann and to Lester Granger, both July 10, 1951, both in NAACP Papers, II, A, 479.

75. Jessie M. Vann, letter to Walter White, July 17, 1951, in NAACP Papers, II, A, 479; and Joseph D. Bibb and George S. Schuyler in Pittsburgh Courier, August 4, 1951. A Courier reporter revealed in the same issue that the majority of Afro-Americans he had approached in Pittsburgh had enjoyed Amos 'n' Andy's TV debut.

76. Lester B. Granger, letter to Walter White, July 16, 1951, NAACP Papers, II, A, 479; and Ann Tanneyhill, letters to Frank Stanton, Lewis Rosenstiel, and William Chase, all August 10, 1951, in Urban League Papers, VII, A, 1, file, "Amos 'n' Andy." Edwin Lukas's comments to White upon hearing of Granger's denial suggest that one or more Urban League figures, perhaps at the branch level, may indeed have expressed approval of Amos 'n' Andy, but that they were no longer willing to admit this. (Lukas, letter to White, July 23, 1951, NAACP Papers, II, A, 480.)

On Granger's avid cultivation of Rosenstiel earlier in 1951, before the Amos 'n' Andy controversy, see Granger, letter to Rosenstiel, May 24, 1951, and also [Ann Tanneyhill], letter to William Chase, August 10, 1951, both in Urban League Papers, VII, A, 1, file, "Amos 'n' Andy."

77. Walter White, letter to William H. Hastie, August 9, 1951, NAACP Papers, II, A, 480.

78. Mickelson interview.

79. Mickelson interview.

80. The NAACP convention had also censured Beulah—a comedy series on ABC-TV which featured several black characters—as well as other unnamed radio and TV shows that the Atlanta resolution said contained "stereotyped characterizations." But the Association stopped mentioning Beulah shortly after the Atlanta meeting, and it did not take on any other series in either of the electronic media—not even Gosden and Correll's own radio show. The Association's annual report for 1951 mentioned no show other than Amos 'n' Andy in its references to the resolution of protest. (NAACP Annual Report, 1951, pp. 11 and 71.)

81. On the "bull elephant" theory, see Ackerman interviews. On White's dealings with Hollywood studios, see Thomas Cripps, *Slow Fade to Black: The Negro in American Film, 1900–1942* (New York: Oxford University Press, 1977), pp. 375–379 and 385–387. The quotation from White comes from Walter White, memorandum to Algernon D. Black and 14 others, July 19, 1951, in NAACP Papers, II, A, 480. (White's full sentence is somewhat ambiguous because of garbled syntax, but his intended meaning seems to be that suggested here.) See also White, letter to Roy Norr, July 11, 1951, in NAACP Papers, II, A, 479.

82. Henry Lee Moon, memorandum to Walter White, August 1, 1951; and Thurgood Marshall, memorandum to White, July 11, 1951; both in NAACP Papers, II, A, 480.

83. Thurgood Marshall, memorandum to Walter White, July 11, 1951; Mabel K. Staupers, letter to White, July 30, 1951; Roy Wilkins, memorandum to White, August 1, 1951; and Arthur B. Spingarn, letter to White, August 1, 1951; all in NAACP Papers, II, A, 480.

84. Edwin J. Lukas, letter to Walter White, August 7, 1951, NAACP Papers, II, A, 480.

85. Walter White, memorandum to [Roy] Wilkins, [Arthur] Spingarn, and [Mabel] Staupers, August 9, 1951; and White, letter to William H. Hastie, August 9, 1951; both in NAACP Papers, II, A, 480.

86. William H. Hastie, letter to Walter White, August 10 [1950]; Mabel K. Staupers, memorandum to White, August 10, 1951; Staupers, letter to White, July 30, 1951; and White, letter to Sig Mickelson, August 16, 1951; all in NAACP Papers, II, A, 480.

87. Ackerman interview; and Richard Bruner, "Amos 'n' Andy Hassle Won't Stop TV Show," *Printers' Ink*, July 20, 1951. White understood Mickelson to say in a telephone conversation in mid-August that CBS had conferred with Gosden and Correll about changing future TV scripts and had "found them amenable." Mickelson had indeed suggested that CBS officials talk to Gosden, but he recalled years later that he got "no response whatsoever on that." (Walter White, memorandum to the files on telephone call from Sig Mickelson, August 20, 1951, in NAACP Papers, II, A, 480; and Mickelson interview.)

88. Mickelson interview; *Red Channels* (New York, 1950), quoted in Barnouw, *Golden Web*, p. 265. For a treatment of blacklisting and red-baiting in the broadcasting industry, see Barnouw, *Golden Web*, pp. 253–283.

89. Ann Lowe to Walter White, n.d., copy of American Jewish Committee, "Statement on Censorship" (date of promulgation: March 29, 1951), in NAACP Papers, II, A, 480.

90. [Norman Cousins], proposed NAACP statement on *Amos 'n' Andy*, n.d. [late July 1951], with suggested changes interpolated [by Walter White?] in longhand; Cousins, telegram to White, August 1, 1951, quoted on cross-reference sheet, "Amos 'n' Andy, August 1, 1951—Telegram"; and (minimally) revised version of Cousins's statement, enclosure accompanying White's letter to Sig Mickelson, August 9, 1951; all in NAACP Papers, II, A, 480. Where Cousins had originally written that the NAACP would "take no action against" *Amos 'n' Andy*, the revised version renounced only "*organized* action" (emphasis added).

91. On the ACLU: Cripps, *Slow Fade to Black*, p. 68. On a similar case of conflicting

priorities during the *Birth of a Nation* controversy of 1915, see W. E. Burghardt Du Bois, *Dusk of Dawn: An Essay Toward an Autobiography of a Race Concept* (1940; reprint edition, Millwood, N.Y.: Kraus-Thompson, 1975), p. 240. On the UAW: Francis A. Henson, letters to Walter White, August 7 and 10, 1951, in NAACP Papers, II, A, 479; and New York *Times*, September 21, 1951. On support for the NAACP from other organizations in 1951: Edmerson, "Negro in Radio," pp. 390–391; letters to White from G. Faber et al., NAACP Papers, II, A, 479.

92. Walter White, letter to Sig Mickelson, December 5, 1951, NAACP Papers, II, A, 480.

A decision by the CBS-TV affiliate in Milwaukee to limit *Amos 'n' Andy*'s run in that city temporarily cheered NAACP activists. But joy gave way to deepening frustration when the station soon reversed itself. See Ardie A. Halyard, letter to Gloster P. (*sic*) Current, July 27, 1951; unidentified clipping [Milwaukee? c. early August 1951], attached to Francis A. Henson, letter to Walter White, August 10, 1951; and Ernestine [O'Bee], letter to Ann [last name not given], n.d. [c. September 1951]; all in NAACP Papers, II, A, 479.

93. See very small articles on the protest in New York *Times*, July 10, 1951 (p. 35, col. 7), and September 21, 1951 (p. 36, col. 7); and see *Newsweek*, July 9, 1951; Pittsburgh *Courier*, July 7 and 28 and August 4, 1951; and *Journal and Guide*, June 30 and July 7, 14, 21, and 28, 1951.

For reviews, see CBS-TV publicity packet, GC–USC. On *Amos 'n' Andy* as part of a new wave in TV: Phillips, Grogan, and Ryan, *Introduction to Radio and Television*, p. 260.

NAACP Annual Report, 1951, p. 11, devotes only one sentence to the resolution condemning *Amos 'n' Andy*; p. 71 has another five-word reference to the issue. On the supposed lack of opposition to *Amos 'n' Andy* from "touchy" minority groups: Victor O. Jones in unidentified clipping [November 16, 1952], "Amos 'n' Andy—Iron Men of Broadcasting," located (despite its date) in scrapbook, "Sam 'n' Henry (1926–27), GC–USC.

94. Fonda and Schwartz interviews; interview with Jay Sommers (July 29, 1982, Beverly Hills); and interview by telephone with Paul West, November 5, 1982.

95. See, for example, the speech of the black preacher in the *Amos 'n' Andy* radio show, December 29, 1944, on record album, "Amos 'n' Andy Classics," Murray Hill Records.

96. Fonda interview.

97. Ackerman interviews.

98. Barbee William Durham (executive secretary, Columbus branch), Memorandum #11, July 7, 1951; and Ardie A. Halyard (president, Milwaukee branch), letter to Gloster P. [sic] Current, July 27, 1951; both in NAACP Papers, II, A, 479.

99. Sommers and Ackerman interviews; New York *Times*, December 20, 1954, on microfiche, "Amos 'n' Andy," in Schomburg; and numerous documents in "*Amos 'n' Andy* Master File," Hal Roach Studios, courtesy of Mark Lipson.

100. New York *Times*, April 9, 1954, on microfiche, "Amos 'n' Andy," in Schomburg.

101. New York *Times*, February 21, 1955, on microfiche, "Coordinating Council for Negro Performers," in Schomburg.

102. New York *Times*, September 21, 1963, in file, "Amos 'n' Andy," Performing Arts Research Center at Lincoln Center, New York Public Library.

103. Childress interviews, as well as various clippings and other documents, and one personal appearance script, in Alvin Childress's possession; Walker, Fonda, and Ackerman interviews; Lubbock (Texas) *Morning Avalanche*, January 28, 1956; Lubbock *Evening Journal*, January 27 and 30, 1956; and Edward T. Clayton in *Ebony*, October 1961.

104. Edward T. Clayton in *Ebony*, October 1961; Lonny Brooks in Los Angeles *Times*, June 17, 1977, in file, "Ernestine Wade," AMPAS; Hairston and Childress interviews.

105. *Variety* (daily), December 15, 1958; [Los Angeles?] *Mirror-News*, December 15, 1958; and Los Angeles *Times*, January 7 and December 21, 1958; all in file, "Tim Moore," AMPAS.

106. Ackerman, Fonda, and Gosden interviews; interviews with Alyce Correll (August 3, 1982, Los Angeles) and Richard Correll (July 16, 1982, Hollywood); and Jerry Lazarus in Richmond *Times-Dispatch*, August 20, 1981, in FFG–RPL.

107. Lonny Brooks in Los Angeles *Times*, June 17, 1977, in file, "Ernestine Wade," AMPAS; and see J. Fred MacDonald, *Blacks and White TV: Afro-Americans in Television since 1948* (Chicago: Nelson-Hall, 1983), p. 29.

108. On the proposed musical: New York *Times*, September 5, 1985, courtesy of Nancy Weiss Malkiel; clipping, Marlene Aig, source unidentified (AP item), April 26, 1987, courtesy of J. Denis Mercier; clipping, Richmond *Times-Dispatch* (AP item), n.d. [c. 1988], courtesy of Gordon K. Ely. Julian Bond, syndicated column in Gloucester County (New Jersey) *Times*, July 29, 1985, courtesy of Mercier, alleged that CBS was thinking of "reviving" *Amos 'n' Andy*.

109. Cripps, "*Amos 'n' Andy*," p. 35 (which mentions black collectors and fans of *Amos 'n' Andy* shows); and *Electronic Media*, February 16, 1987, courtesy of J. Denis Mercier.

110. Interview by telephone with Michael Avery, August 6, 1982; *Variety* (daily), May 3, 1983; and several telephone conversations with Bob Greenberg, July and August 1983.

Epilogue: A New Day?

1. See *Journal and Guide* (Peninsula Edition), June 16, 1951.

2. A concise discussion of this problem is in Gunnar Myrdal (with Richard Sterner and Arnold Rose), *An American Dilemma: The Negro Problem and Modern Democracy* (New York, Evanston, and London: Harper & Row, 1944), p. 775.

3. Myrdal, *American Dilemma*, pp. 781–783. The italics in the quotation are Myrdal's own.

4. J. Fred MacDonald, *Blacks and White TV: Afro-Americans in Television since 1948* (Chicago: Nelson-Hall, 1983), pp. 115–17. MacDonald finds Carroll's phrase quoted by Richard Warren Lewis in *TV Guide*, December 14, 1968, p. 28.

5. The following account is based on materials assembled by Claude M. Monteiro, in file, "Gosden, Freeman F.," Richmond Public Library (hereafter cited as FFG–RPL), and on an interview with Monteiro, April 17, 1984, Richmond. Besides the sources specifically noted below, the following items from FFG–RPL have been consulted: Richmond *Times-Dispatch*, August 11, 1981; and Richmond City Council, "A Resolution Designating Wednesday, August 19, 1981, as Freeman Fisher Gosden Day."

6. Richmond *News Leader*, August 11, 1981, in FFG–RPL.

7. Edward A. Leake Jr. quoted in Richmond *News Leader*, August 11, 1981, in FFG–RPL.

8. Larry Bonko in [Norfolk] *Ledger-Star*, December 22, 1982 (including quotation of Claudette Black McDaniel), in FFG–RPL.

9. Monteiro interview.

10. Richmond *Afro-American*, September 5, 1981, in FFG–RPL.

A Word About Sources

This book is based mainly on primary sources. By far the most important repository of such material is the Cinema–Television Library and Archives of Performing Arts, Doheny Library, University of Southern California. The library's Gosden–Correll Collection includes all the original scripts of *Sam 'n' Henry* (1926–1928) and of *Amos 'n' Andy* from that show's premiere until the transition to the Music Hall format in 1954. The USC collection also includes some two dozen massive scrapbooks and file boxes containing newspaper clippings on the two radio series and other mementos of Gosden and Correll's career.

The radio team's employers and their clipping services collected every reference to *Amos 'n' Andy* that they could find in the public prints. These came from newspapers and magazines of every size and type in all regions, and they include scores of items critical of *Amos 'n' Andy*. (Nearly an entire scrapbook in USC's Gosden–Correll Collection is devoted to the Pittsburgh *Courier's* protest against *Amos 'n' Andy* in 1931.) The USC collection is therefore a remarkably comprehensive and convenient aggregation of responses to *Amos 'n' Andy*—by journalists, black organizations, and listeners of both races whose letters were published on radio and editorial pages. Those responses are supplemented by a very small sampling of fan mail that has been preserved at USC, almost all of it from February 1929; the language and content of the fan letters do indicate that their authors included people of both the working and middle classes, and the letters praise *Amos 'n' Andy* from a variety of angles. USC also holds a convenient compilation made by the Columbia Broadcasting System of favorable newspaper and magazine reviews of the *Amos 'n' Andy* television series; sources for negative or ambivalent reaction to the show are discussed below.

The Theater Arts Library of the University of California, Los Angeles, holds the scripts for many of the *Amos 'n' Andy* television episodes, as well as a clipping file on the radio series containing several useful items. Pacific Pioneer Broadcasters, Inc., of Hollywood has a number of disc and tape recordings of *Amos 'n' Andy* radio shows, mostly from the 1940s and 1950s. The clipping files of the Margaret Herrick Library, Academy of Motion Picture Arts and Sciences, Los Angeles, provided biographical material on some of the actors in the TV *Amos 'n' Andy*, and on the show's director, Charles Barton; the Louis B. Mayer

Library of the American Film Institute in Los Angeles also holds some useful clippings of the same type. Mark Lipson of the Hal Roach Studios lent the author several informative files pertaining to the filming of the *Amos 'n' Andy* TV series and the deliberations about a possible successor series.

The author had the good fortune of gaining access, through the kindness of the Correll family and the special generosity of Richard Correll, to Charles Correll's personal collection of mementos. These consist largely of materials which, though from newspapers and other published sources, have never been assembled in any other single place—for example, the press clippings from Correll's years as an itinerant director for the Joe Bren Company. There are also clippings based on interviews with Correll and Gosden from the World War II era and beyond; some of these items cover the early days of *Amos 'n' Andy* more dispassionately than those generated by the press-agentry of the 1920s and 1930s. Charles Correll's autobiographical notes, though minuscule in volume, gave some insight into his childhood and his early career. The Correll family also furnished many of the photographs contained in this book.

Two divisions of the Library of Congress contain material on *Amos 'n' Andy*. By far the more important in the preparation of this book has been the Manuscript Division, which holds the papers of the National Association for the Advancement of Colored People and the National Urban League, as well as microfilms of almost all the scripts from *Amos 'n' Andy*'s first decade on the radio. The NAACP papers contain documents from the protest of 1951 which fill roughly an entire file box. (The numbering of these materials has been changed slightly since the research for this project was completed; the reader should consult the index to the collection.) The Library's Motion Picture, Broadcasting, and Recorded Sound Division holds recordings of a small number of *Amos 'n' Andy* broadcasts from various stages in the history of the series, as well as films of most of the television episodes. Long-playing records and cassette tapes of some of the radio shows are available commercially, and video outlets offer cassettes of many of the TV episodes for rental.

The Richmond Public Library kept a clipping file on Freeman Gosden spanning half a century. Though far less extensive than the Correll family's private collection, the Richmond Library's file provided the basis for several of the narrative vignettes in this book and furnished considerable detail on Gosden's early life and later connection with his home city.

Two of the research branches of the New York Public Library are important resources for any student of theater arts and Afro-American studies respectively. The Performing Arts Research Center at Lincoln Center offered recordings and press clippings of relevance to this book which, though very few in number, could be found nowhere else. The Schomburg Center for Research in Black Culture holds clipping files on microfiche concerning *Amos 'n' Andy* and related topics; the Schomburg also has some recordings of radio broadcasts of the series. The clipping files proved especially useful for studying black responses to *Amos 'n' Andy* during the later years covered in this study.

Black weekly newspapers provide a copious record of Afro-American reactions to *Amos 'n' Andy*, both from editors and readers. Clippings from a number of these papers—including many items highly critical of *Amos 'n' Andy*—are found in the scrapbooks of the Gosden–Correll Collection at USC. The author also looked directly at many issues of the *Journal and Guide*, the Baltimore *Afro-American*, the Chicago *Defender*, the *Negro World*, the Pittsburgh *Courier*, and other papers. One published work, though not always factually accurate, was useful as a primary source. This was the book compiled by the radio team's publicists early in their career, *All About Amos 'n' Andy and Their Creators Correll and Gosden* (1929).

Personal interviews conducted by the author provided a wealth of information for this study. In the following alphabetical list, the name of each person interviewed is followed not by a biographical précis, but rather by a brief description of the person's direct relationship to *Amos 'n' Andy*. Dates and places of interviews may be found in the Notes.

Harry Ackerman, director of programming (West Coast) and vice-president, Columbia Broadcasting System, during production of *Amos 'n' Andy* television series

Michael Avery, producer of television program, "*Amos 'n' Andy*: Anatomy of a Controversy," 1983 (interviewed by telephone)

Ken Carpenter, announcer, *Amos 'n' Andy* radio series

Alvin Childress, actor, *Amos 'n' Andy* TV series

Jerry Cooper, videocassette entrepreneur

Alyce Correll, wife of Charles J. Correll

Richard Correll, son of Charles Correll

James Fonda, executive in charge of casting and production, *Amos 'n' Andy* TV series (by telephone)

Herb Gelbspan, executive, Hal Roach Studios

Art Gilmore, announcer, *Amos 'n' Andy* radio series (by telephone)

Jane Gosden, wife of Freeman F. Gosden

Bob Greenberg, head of research and production for TV program, "*Amos 'n' Andy*: Anatomy of a Controversy" (by telephone)

Jester Hairston, actor, *Amos 'n' Andy* radio and TV series

Maggie Hathaway, founder, Hollywood–Beverly Hills Branch, NAACP (by telephone)

Claude Hudson, veteran leader, Los Angeles Branch, NAACP (by telephone)

Bob Jensen, engineer, *Amos 'n' Andy* radio series

Sig Mickelson, vice-president and head of news and public affairs, CBS television, during NAACP protest of 1951

Claude M. Monteiro, friend of Freeman Gosden

Elinor Harriot Nathan, actor, *Amos 'n' Andy* radio series

Ken Niles, announcer, *Amos 'n' Andy* radio series (by telephone)

Hal Roach Sr., founder, Hal Roach Studios (by telephone)
Dave Schwartz, writer, *Amos 'n' Andy* TV series
Del Sharbutt, announcer, *Amos 'n' Andy* radio series (by telephone)
Jay Sommers, writer, *Amos 'n' Andy* TV series
Olan Soulé, announcer, *Amos 'n' Andy* radio series
William Walker, actor, *Amos 'n' Andy* TV series, and Peggy Walker, his
  wife
Paul West, writer, *Amos 'n' Andy* TV series (by telephone)

···—●◉●—···

Many of the scrapbooks at the University of Southern California are not labeled in a way that allows users readily to distinguish one from another. The Notes in the present work refer to these unlabeled or ambiguously labeled scrapbooks by symbols—usually numbers—that the author has assigned arbitrarily. The following list gives a brief description of each scrapbook. Such labels as do exist are cited in original spelling and punctuation.

  C: Brown scrapbook labeled "Amos 'n' Andy—1931" (on first page: Pittsburgh *Courier* and other clippings)
 #1: Brown scrapbook, not labeled (on first page: Orange *Courier*, February 28, 1930, and others)
 #2: Brown scrapbook labeled "Pepsodent—Amos 'n Andy 1929"
 #3: Brown scrapbook, "Amos n. Andy 1929"
 #4: Brown scrapbook, lacking cover, "1929–30"
 #5: Brown scrapbook, "Pepsodent 1930" (on first page: Jersey City *Journal*, Loveland *Herald*, Los Angeles *Examiner*, and others)
 #6: Brown scrapbook, lacking cover, "1930" (on first page: Niagara Falls *Gazette*, Newark *Ledger*, Kansas City *Star*)
 #7: Brown scrapbook, with cover, "1930" (on first page: New York *Telegram* only)
 #8: Brown scrapbook, lacking cover, "1930" (on first page: Columbus *Citizen* only)
 #9: Brown scrapbook, lacking cover, "Pepsodent 1930" (on first page: Boston *Post* only)
#10: Brown scrapbook, lacking cover, "1930" (on first page, Denver *Post*, remnant only)
#11: Brown scrapbook, "Amos 'n' Andy, Sep 1930–Aug 1931"
#12: Large blue scrapbook, "1933–37"

···—●◉●—···

For the secondary literature consulted in the preparation of this book, the reader is referred to the numerous Notes, some of which include thumbnail descriptions and criticisms of those sources. Books and articles that discuss *Amos 'n' Andy* often contain erroneous information, much of it drawn from the show-business press. A few secondary works deserve mention here, however, either because they seriously analyze some aspect of the *Amos 'n' Andy* story, or because they offer opportunities for the interested reader to pursue topics touched on in this book.

Arthur Frank Wertheim's intelligent and readable *Radio Comedy* (1979) devotes one chapter to *Sam 'n' Henry* and another to *Amos 'n' Andy*. Erik Barnouw's three-volume *History of Broadcasting in the United States*, the definitive survey of radio and TV history, discusses *Amos 'n' Andy* briefly but sensitively, especially in volume I, *A Tower in Babel* (1966); Barnouw's *Tube of Plenty: The Evolution of American Television* (2nd edition, 1990), is a one-volume revised version of the original trilogy. Leonard C. Archer, *Black Images in the American Theatre: NAACP Protest Campaigns—Stage, Screen, Radio & Television* (1973), grounds its discussion of the NAACP's campaign against the *Amos 'n' Andy* television series largely on an extensive reading of the Pittsburgh *Courier*. Walter M. Brasch, *Black English and the Mass Media* (1981), has a short analysis of the dialect used in the *Amos 'n' Andy* radio series; more could be said about the sociolinguistic aspects of the show than either Brasch or the present author has room to include.

Several works of history comment perceptively on one or more facets of *Amos 'n' Andy*. Joseph Boskin, *Sambo: The Rise & Demise of an American Jester* (1986), intriguingly uses the "life story" of a popular racial image to illuminate a much broader expanse of social history. Although Boskin's discussion of *Amos 'n' Andy* is brief, the author makes some essential points and fully understands that the radio series, while keeping one foot in the past, departed in some important ways from all that preceded it. Andrew Buni, *Robert L. Vann of the Pittsburgh Courier* (1974), contains important insights into the protest against *Amos 'n' Andy* in 1931, the personality of the man who led it, and the Afro-American press as a whole. Arnold M. Shankman, "Black Pride and Protest: The Amos 'N' Andy Crusade," in *Journal of Popular Culture*, XII, 2 (1978), 236–252, focuses on Vann's protest and black responses to it.

Two other works by historians examine the television series of 1951–1953. J. Fred MacDonald, *Blacks and White TV: Afro-Americans in Television Since 1948* (1983), is a careful survey which contains a penetrating look at the content of the *Amos 'n' Andy* TV situation comedy. One of the interesting articles in John E. O'Connor (ed.), *American History, American Television: Interpreting the Video Past* (1983), is Thomas Cripps, "*Amos 'n' Andy* and the Debate over American Racial Integration," in which the author analyzes the show's content with his usual clear-sightedness and a fine sense of irony. He also presents useful information about *Amos 'n' Andy*'s years in TV syndication. While he effectively exposes the middle-class tone of the NAACP's campaign of 1951, Cripps mistakenly indicates that the intense black debate over the TV series, and serious black protest against it, burst forth before CBS put *Amos 'n' Andy* into production rather than at the time of the show's on-air debut. He therefore interprets the attitudes and behavior of the network and of *Amos 'n' Andy*'s sponsor—and, by the way, of the American Jewish Committee, the National Urban League, and the Afro-American middle and working classes—

differently than this book does. Moreover, Cripps does not examine the *Amos 'n' Andy* radio series; this allows him to conclude that the NAACP's protest of 1951, the diversity of black views that the crusade exposed, and the TV show's attempts to gloss over the racial tensions of real life were distinctive products of a new post-World War II racial atmosphere, when in fact they were largely elaborations of themes that had emerged a generation before, in the early days of radio.

An ambitious history of commercial radio which devotes much attention to the role of Afro-Americans and to black images is J. Fred MacDonald, *Don't Touch That Dial! Radio Programming in American Life, 1920–1960* (1979). Estelle Edmerson, "A Descriptive Study of the American Negro in United States Professional Radio, 1922–1953" (master's thesis, University of California, Los Angeles, 1954), a uniquely useful study, is especially informative on the point of view of black radio actors now long dead. Unfortunately, copies of Edmerson's thesis are exceedingly hard to come by. John Denis Mercier, "The Evolution of the Black Image in White Consciousness, 1876–1954: A Popular Culture Perspective" (dissertation, University of Pennsylvania, 1984), is the product of prodigious research. Mercier offers a massive, encyclopedic, historically oriented examination of black images in American popular and material culture; a book presenting his findings and analysis is planned. Of the many nonacademic histories of American television programming, one of the most intelligent and informative is Harry Castelman and Walter J. Podrazik, *Watching TV: Four Decades of American Television* (1982), which includes some thoughtful discussion of ethnic images.

Black images in film have been more widely written about than those in radio or television. Thomas Cripps, *Slow Fade to Black: The Negro in American Film, 1900–1942* (1977), is a bold, thorough, durable historical study of black images in movies, black filmmaking, and Afro-Americans' efforts to win improvements in the treatment of the race in Hollywood both behind and before the camera. Cripps's book deserves to be more readily available than its publisher has made it in recent years. Other works of interest to the general reader include Daniel J. Leab, *From Sambo to Superspade: The Black Experience in Motion Pictures* (1975); Donald Bogle, *Toms, Coons, Mulattoes, Mammies and Bucks* (1973); and Bogle, *Blacks in American Films and Television* (1989), published after the present work was completed.

Four volumes on minstrelsy are useful. Robert Toll, *Blacking Up: The Minstrel Show in Nineteenth-Century America* (1974), is by far the most ambitious attempt to place the minstrel show in its social and historical context. Hans Nathan, *Dan Emmett and the Rise of Early Negro Minstrelsy* (1962), emphasizing musicological aspects, is well researched; it includes concise descriptions of minstrel characters and shows, but gives the minstrels more credit as realistic delineators of Afro-Americans than they deserve. Carl Wittke, *Tambo and Bones: A History of the American Minstrel Stage* (1930), though dated, carries the history of minstrelsy beyond the nineteenth century. Frank Costellow Davidson,

"The Rise, Development, Decline, and Influence of the American Minstrel Show" (dissertation, New York University, 1952), contains useful details that the other three works lack.

Two lively surveys cover the history of Afro-Americans in entertainment. Robert Toll, *On with the Show! The First Century of Show Business in America* (1976), devotes generous attention to the role of blacks. Langston Hughes and Milton Meltzer, *Black Magic: A Pictorial History of the Negro in American Entertainment* (1967), though now a generation old, is both highly readable and comprehensive enough to serve as a helpful reference. Jessie Carney Smith (ed.), *Images of Blacks in American Culture: A Reference Guide to Information Sources* (1988), is indispensable to anyone who wishes to study any aspect of that field—although, as in most such volumes, the quality of the individual specialized essays varies. An exceptionally valuable introduction to American show business in all its facets, presented in the form of a critical guide to the literature, is Don B. Wilmeth, "American Popular Entertainment: A Historical Perspective Bibliography," in Myron Matlaw (ed.), *American Popular Entertainment: Papers and Proceedings of the Conference on the History of American Popular Entertainment* (1979).

On Afro-American life in Chicago in the early years of the Great Migration, see Allan H. Spear, *Black Chicago: The Making of a Negro Ghetto, 1890–1920* (1967); William M. Tuttle Jr., *Race Riot: Chicago in the Red Summer of 1919* (1970); Chicago Commission on Race Relations, *The Negro in Chicago: A Study of Race Relations and a Race Riot* (1922; reprinted 1968); and Arthur I. Waskow, *From Race Riot to Sit-In, 1919 and the 1960s* (1966), chapter 5. James R. Grossman, *Land of Hope: Chicago, Black Southerners, and the Great Migration* (1989), which appeared too late to be consulted in the preparation of this book, focuses on the Migration itself.

The essays in Alain Locke (ed.), *The New Negro: An Interpretation* (1925), introduce the reader to the concept embodied in the book's title and to the "Harlem Renaissance" as these looked to participants during the 1920s. The literature on Harlem is so extensive that any brief list must appear especially arbitrary. Early works include James Weldon Johnson, *Black Manhattan* (1930); Claude McKay, *Harlem: Negro Metropolis* (1940); and Roi Ottley, *New World A-Coming* (1943). Among the autobiographies of key figures in the Renaissance are McKay, *A Long Way from Home* (1937); Johnson, *Along This Way* (1933); and Langston Hughes, *The Big Sea* (1940). More recent historical treatments of Harlem include Nathan Irvin Huggins, *Harlem Renaissance* (1971); Gilbert Osofsky, *Harlem: The Making of a Ghetto: Negro New York, 1890–1930* (2nd edition, 1971); Jervis Anderson, *This Was Harlem: A Cultural Portrait, 1900–1950* (1981); and David Levering Lewis, *When Harlem Was in Vogue* (2nd edition, 1989). For a stimulating introduction to Afro-American political and social thought as expressed in the black press, see Theodore G. Vincent (ed.), *Voices of a Black Nation: Political Journalism in the Harlem Renaissance* (1973).

Two venerable guides to literature produced by or portraying Afro-

Americans up to the mid-1930s were written by the poet Sterling Brown: *Negro Poetry and Drama* and *The Negro in American Fiction* (both 1937, but republished in a single volume, 1969). The sweep, wit, fair-mindedness, and grace of Brown's work stand undiminished despite the passage of decades. Lawrence W. Levine, *Black Culture and Black Consciousness: Afro-American Folk Thought from Slavery to Freedom* (1977), is a wide-ranging, imaginative treatment of its general subject and of Afro-American humor in particular.

The complex challenges of Afro-American self-definition in the face of white racism are a focal point of this book. One of the most powerful, moving, clear-sighted treatments of that subject is not a work of history or social science at all, but rather Charles Fuller's *A Soldier's Play* (1981; published 1982). A fine film, *A Soldier's Story* (1984), was directed by Norman Jewison from Fuller's own screenplay.

Afro-American life in the first half of the twentieth century has been addressed in a multitude of other books, many of which examine fairly specific aspects of that history. Readers who are new to the subject may begin with two widely read surveys of Afro-American history: John Hope Franklin and Alfred A. Moss Jr., *From Slavery to Freedom: A History of Negro Americans* (6th edition, 1987); and the shorter, older August Meier and Elliott Rudwick, *From Plantation to Ghetto* (3rd edition, 1976). Both books contain bibliographical essays which can serve as guides to further reading.

Monumental studies of the Afro-American community and of American race relations in the middle of the twentieth century are Gunnar Myrdal (with others), *An American Dilemma: The Negro Problem and Modern Democracy* (1944); St. Clair Drake and Horace Cayton, *Black Metropolis* (1945), on Chicago; and E. Franklin Frazier, *The Negro in the United States* (2nd edition, 1957). An important review of Myrdal by Ralph Ellison is found in Ellison, *Shadow and Act* (1964). August Meier, Elliott Rudwick, and Francis L. Broderick (eds.), *Black Protest Thought in the Twentieth Century* (1971), provides an overview of the evolving struggle for black equality. Three other works that deal gracefully with complex, crucial subjects broached in this book are August Meier, *Negro Thought in America, 1880–1915: Racial Ideologies in the Age of Booker T. Washington* (1963); David Reimers, *White Protestantism and the Negro* (1965); and Jacqueline Jones, *Labor of Love, Labor of Sorrow: Black Women, Work, and the Family from Slavery to the Present* (1985).

The indispensable work on white racial ideology before and during the formative years of Freeman Gosden and Charles Correll remains George M. Fredrickson, *The Black Image in the White Mind: The Debate on Afro-American Character and Destiny, 1817–1914* (1971). In his *Thomas Nelson Page* (1967), Theodore L. Gross presents a compact discussion of the most important writer of plantation-nostalgia literature in the late nineteenth century. Virginius Dabney, *Richmond: The Story of a City* (1976), surveys the history of Freeman Gosden's home town. Peter J. Rachleff, *Black Labor in Richmond, 1865–1890* (1989), and Michael B. Chesson, *Richmond After the War, 1865–1890* (1981), are insightful critical treatments of life in Richmond during the time of Gosden's parents. Gaines M. Foster examines the cult of the Confederacy in his discerning and fair-minded *Ghosts of the Confederacy: Defeat, the Lost Cause and the Emergence of the New South, 1865 to 1913* (1987).

Basic works on southern politics and race during the decades after Reconstruction include C. Vann Woodward, *Origins of the New South, 1877–1913* (reprint edition, 1971); Woodward, *The Strange Career of Jim Crow* (3rd edition, 1974); J. Morgan Kousser, *The Shaping of Southern Politics: Suffrage Restriction and the Establishment of the One-Party South, 1880–1910* (1974); and Joel Williamson, *The Crucible of Race: Black-White Relations in the American South since Emancipation* (1984), which has since appeared in abridged form as *A Rage for Order* (1986). On Freeman Gosden's home state, see Charles E. Wynes, *Race Relations in Virginia, 1870–1902* (1961).

Index